Township Tidings

from Potter County
Pennsylvania

News from All of the Valleys,
Creeks and Hollows
in the County

Volume I

The Years 1880-1884

Maureen M. Lee

HERITAGE BOOKS
2007

HERITAGE BOOKS
AN IMPRINT OF HERITAGE BOOKS, INC.

Books, CDs, and more—Worldwide

For our listing of thousands of titles see our website
at
www.HeritageBooks.com

Published 2007 by
HERITAGE BOOKS, INC.
Publishing Division
65 East Main Street
Westminster, Maryland 21157-5026

Copyright © 2007 Maureen M. Lee

Other books by the author:

Potter County, Pennsylvania Potpourri: Genealogical and Historical News from The Potter Enterprise; *Volume 1, 1880-1884*

Wayne County, Nebraska Newspaper Abstracts, 1876-1899

All rights reserved. No part of this book may be reproduced or transmitted in any form or by any means, electronic or mechanical, including photocopying, recording or by any information storage and retrieval system without written permission from the author, except for the inclusion of brief quotations in a review.

International Standard Book Number: 978-0-7884-4104-2

TABLE OF CONTENTS

Introduction   v

The Potter Enterprise Abstracts   1

Index   289

INTRODUCTION

The *Township Tidings* series, totaling four volumes, was created to accompany the four *Potter County, Pennsylvania Potpourri* books. Due to the vast amount of material available in *The Potter Enterprise*, the leading newspaper of the county in the late 1800s, this series has been broken into five-year increments; 1880-1884, 1885-1889, 1890-1894 and 1895-1899.

While the *Potpourri* series covers the news stories in depth – births, marriages and divorces, deaths, court minutes, disasters such as fires and floods, crimes, politics, industry and growth, &c. – the *Tidings* series is more intimate and neighborly; who's moving in and who's moving out, who is building, local business, those taken ill, who's visiting, church activities, the harvest and the weather, &c.

Realizing that not everyone's ancestor was a murderer, bound over to court or elected to public office (some might say the latter two are one in the same!), I decided to put forth the *Tidings* manuscripts in an effort to further assist those researching in Potter County.

Potter County celebrated its bicentennial in 2004 and I am pleased to be able to record a sliver of her history by abstracting the columns of *The Potter Enterprise* for the last twenty years of the nineteenth century. This is my gift to my former home. Though I have been gone some years at this writing, my heart shall always remain in God's Country.

Maureen M. Lee
www.happeningsinthehills.com
September 2005

Township Tidings from Potter County, Pennsylvania
Volume I, 1880 - 1884

The Potter Enterprise
Thursday Evening,
May 12, 1880 –
Vol. VII, No. 1

- Mr. Brine is about ready to commence the manufacture of brick.

- W. S. Corsaw, formerly of Sweden, is now a resident of Clare county, Mich.

- A portion of the machinery for Rounsevill's handle factory has arrived.

- Joe Brown has taken the contract for getting in 200,000 feet of logs for the tannery company.

- F. M. Stevens has sold his drug store at Oswayo. Frank intends dispensing a short time at Ceres.

- D. W. Butterworth ranks high as a white-wash artist, for proof of which look at his barn and fences.

- Mr. Nye, the up-town gunsmith, is quite ill, and last week he was removed to the residence of Silas Tolls.

- Money is getting very scarce again. Dairying has not yet brought in much, and bark peeling has not commenced.

- D. F. Glassmire has a new stage wagon, or the old one repaired until it is as good as new, painted white and wine color, with black top.

- Dr. Phillips will have his dental office open to attend to the wants of his patrons next Saturday, all reports to the contrary notwithstanding.

- Last week Monday, Burt Cole of Clara was thrown from a buggy by a runaway horse, and was so severely bruised that he has been confined to the house since. The buggy was wrecked.

Oswayo.

The Lee House is open and ready for business. Lee has an opening dance the 21st of this month. The house is well finished and a credit to the place.

The Oswayo Cornet Band were out serenading Saturday evening. They rendered some fine music. The usual number of small boys followed, of course.

Fires in the woods are spreading and doing a great deal of hurt. A fine shower would do much good now.

Bingham.

Farmers are very busy doing their spring's work.

We are having very fine weather and a fine growing time.

Farmers begin to rejoice to think that their cattle can live without feeding.

Shad, or June berry trees were in blossom about a week earlier than common this year.

The most of the common schools commenced May 3d. Success to the teachers.

Fires were set in this vicinity, and will probably become troublesome if there is not rain soon.

Township Tidings from Potter County, Pennsylvania
Volume I, 1880 - 1884

Winter wheat is looking finely in this section.

The air is filled with smoke, the roads are quite dusty, large June bugs are becoming quite troublesome and everything speaks of summer.

It is said that Rufus Howe will close up his mill this week for the season, as he has cleared his mill yard of logs.

Bark peeling will soon commence.

Harrison Valley.

Business is lively.

White & Brown have about thirty cords of wood cut for the acid factory, and have contracted for about twelve hundred cords.

R. V. Pellum is working for H. Harrison, in the blacksmith shop.

J. Burtis has moved into the house owned by Mrs. Cummings.

Mrs. M. C. Erway is visiting in Groton, N.Y.

Mrs. Berry Erway fell and badly sprained her wrist on Saturday.

Still another death from diphtheria. Mr. John J. Jones lost his only daughter on Saturday last.

School has opened with Hattie Harrison as teacher.

V. Schweitzer has returned, and the J.P. is busy issuing warrants.

LeRoy Knight has just returned from the oil country.

On Sunday last, smoke was seen issuing from a manure heap near the barn of M. R. Swetland, on opening the pile, fire was discovered about six inches below the surface. Query – How did the fire get there?

Allegany.

Everything in this part of Allegany is quiet, except the excitement over the fires which are raging around us.

D. W. Rogers and Warren Gardner have been badly damaged by a fire that broke out from a fallow set by Mr. Bird. Timber and rails burned for both men, and a fine piece of winter wheat nearly spoiled, and new seeded ground burned over for Gardner. The fire is now burning on what is known as the lake lot. Yesterday a number of men stayed from Church to try and keep the fire from doing further damages, but it is almost impossible. Everything is so dry, and we have a wind every day that helps spread the fire. Fires are burning in every direction and doing great damage.

Schools nearly commenced last week. Mr. Evans is teaching again at Colesburg; Miss Graves at Judd's school house; Carrie Bishop at Andrews Settlement; Effie Benton at the red school house and Nettie Bishop at Woodville.

The Methodists will hold Quarterly Meeting at Andrews Settlement, May 22d and 23d, Rev. Stratton of Coudersport to conduct the meeting.

"Fathers provoke not your sons to anger. Sons, honor your parents that your days may be long in the land."

Ulysses.

There is a gloom cast over the people of this vicinity, Dr. Eaton's little girl as buried May 2d, after much suffering. The Doctor himself was then stricken down

Township Tidings from Potter County, Pennsylvania
Volume I, 1880 - 1884

with the same disease, diphtheria, but hopes are entertained of his recovery.

Sore throats are becoming quite prevalent in this vicinity since the warm weather. It seems to prove more fatal than it did at the first.

The 3d brought what farmers so much wished for, a fine growing time.

The roads are very dusty.

Cattle can live now without any feeding, which is a great relief to farmers.

Frank Wagoner who unfortunately got one of his legs broken, can get around with ease – with the use of a cane.

Farmers are very busily engaged in putting in grain. They say there never was a better time than the present for this purpose.

Our Graded School closed April 30.

Augustus Hopkins, who carried on a tannery on a small scale with his father a number of years in Bingham, moved to Kibbyville, Ulysses, and carried on the tannery business a few years as before, and then sold out to Mr. Plagueman all their tannery tools and left this country. After burying his wife and parents he returned to Ulysses and bought back of the Widow Plagueman all the tannery tools he and his father used in former days. A. Hopkins & Son are building a tannery near Asa Raymond's. They have already commenced tanning.

There is a young lady in this town who is learning the carpenter trade. She says she likes the business because the Carpenter comes to her home to give her lessons. Some think she will have the trade completed this fall. Now Sis if this coat don't suit you you needn't put it on.

- The tannery company have already let contracts for peeling over four thousand cords of bark on the Bingham lands. We understand the Bingham estate has contracted the logs to parties on the Allegany river, on the lines of the railroad, and the logs will be floated to their destination in the river.

- Dr. Phillips fell through one of the panes of glass in Andrew & Olmsted's store front, last week. The Doctor is a bad one on glass, and is not happy if he don't put a base ball through a window during the week, or smash one some other way.

- Mr. I. Greisel has moved his harness shop back and is putting up a new building fifty feet in depth, thirty feet of which will be two stories high. This will give him a fine sales room and a pleasant workshop.

Fishing Creek.

The farmers have mostly got through with their spring work, with the exception of planting their corn and potatoes, some have already planted potatoes.

The woods are on fire, Otis Lyman burned his fallow and the fallow burned the woods.

It is Mr. Otis Lyman that can be seen applying the persuader to those mules, and says: "Get along there for I don't care a darn, it's a girl."

Township Tidings from Potter County, Pennsylvania
Volume I, 1880 - 1884

Almeron Lyman has cut his leg very badly.

John Yentzer is improving his farm very much by building new fences along the road.

Bark peeling has commenced, and the timber is being slashed this hot weather never to grow again.

William Weimer has sold his team to Page Grocebeck for the sum of two hundred and fifty dollars.

The schools in our town have commenced. Miss Lottie Larrabee teaches the Fishing Creek school.

Orsen Corsaw has bought his farm back and intends to keep it.

Mr. Amos Morey's wife has left his bed and board.

- The Coudersport Cornet Band treated our citizens to some well rendered music last Friday evening. The band has been organized but a short time, yet few old bands can excel them in correctness and time or skill in fingering the keys.

- N. H. Goodsell has completed his new building, and now has probably the most convenient shop in the county. He has just set up a new Josiah Ross planer, patented in 1878, and manufactured at Buffalo, that will plane a stick twenty-four inches wide and five inches thick, if necessary. It is the finest working planer we have ever seen. Besides these Mr. G. has turning lathes, cut off saws, slitting saws, etc., all running by water power and all kept in good order. He may well feel proud of his shop.

- Mrs. M. Banks has rented rooms of Miss C. A. Metzger on Third street and will open a first-class dressmaking establishment on Monday, May 17.

**The Potter Enterprise
Thursday Evening,
May 19, 1880 –
Vol. VII, No. 2**

- John Carpenter, at Genesee Forks, has built and is occupying a handsome new store, 24x48 feet in size. He has it filled with new goods and is doing a lively business.

- The scene of the new tannery is a lively one. The new buildings are going up like magic, and the brick smoke stack which is to take an altitude of eighty feet is climbing skyward.

- On Friday afternoon a daughter, only sixteen months old, of C. L. Peck, Esq., of this borough, fell from a couch and badly fractured her left arm and elbow. Dr. Ellison attended her.

- Charles Tyler has purchased from J. D. Staysa a couple of acres of ground, on which stands the house recently erected at Millport, and will take possession at once. He will probably keep hotel, an institution much needed at Millport.

- By every road come tidings of disastrous forest fires. E. O. Rees informed us Monday that the Kettle Creek country was being badly scourged by fire, and that H. H. Guernsey, of Ulysses, had to fight fire for three days to save his buildings.

HOMER.

We need not grumble any more about cold weather, nor sigh for the warm breath of the tropics, for the thermometer stood over 80° in the shade yesterday. We can almost see the leaves grow, and the birds hold concerts every morning. Saw the first pair of yellow birds May 5..... Another marriage last week. Truly Hymen has not lacked votaries for the last six months, and all our young people will soon be transformed into staid and sober heads of families.....Farmers are very busy sowing and planting. Some of the oats sown first are already up. Mr. Klesa has a piece of winter wheat that looks very good. I think he has raised wheat nearly or quite nearly every year since he has been here.....Our school commenced last week with nearly the whole number of scholars in attendance – Miss Emma Adams, teacher.....We are enjoying a fair degree of health.....Mr. J. Peet and family have moved onto their new farm in Portage. They have the good wishes of their old neighbors for their peace and prosperity.....May 13. – The weather changed very suddenly on the evening of the 10th, and has continued cold ever since with very high wind. This morning men harrowing in grain and planting potatoes needed to wear coats to be comfortable.....There were several different fires running in the woods yesterday, causing serious losses in fences, timber, &c. It seems too bad that we should have so much hemlock killed just when it is becoming valuable. I think folks should take the second sober thought about putting out fire when the wind is blowing so hard. The fire blew across the fields in one place and caught within a few rods of W. C. Chesbro's barn. A sound argument in favor of insurance.

PLEASANT VALLEY.

May 14. – For the last two weeks we have had it very hot and dry. Our forests are on fire around us. If we do not get rain soon it will do a great deal of damage.....Jack Frost visited us on the 13th, doing much damage to early apples that were in blow.....Visitors are coming and going. Mr. Harl Pike and family of Bradford, McKean county, are here, guests of Simon Beckwith. Mrs. Austin Fessenden has gone to Newark, N.J., to visit her mother. Mr. Elmer Deming and family are visiting in Alfred, Allegany county, N.Y.....David Weimer has a nice lot of calves of the Holstein grade. Our farmers begin to think cows pay better than young stock. They are keeping more cows this summer than for a number of years back. What we need now is a cheese factory. There are a number of good locations for a cheese factory. I hope that some enterprising cheese man will take hold of the matter.....John McDowell sports a new dog churn.....Eldin McDowell, our boss carpenter, is on Bell's Run, at work for the Weston Bros. Eldin is a good workman, and is hard to beat.

Township Tidings from Potter County, Pennsylvania
Volume I, 1880 - 1884

KEATING.

May 12. – The fishing season has commenced with plenty of fishermen and but few fishes.....John Bundy is straightening the road, which runs through his place, and makes a great improvement in the looks of his farm.....Sabbath school commenced last Sunday, with a good attendance.....W. C. Chesbro passed through this place with his bride, on his way home from his wedding trip. Good luck to you, Warren, and may your married life be as happy as your single one has been.....Mrs. E. T. Dingee is no better and is still confined to her bed.....Mr. Henman, a minister from the State Line, preached here Saturday evening.....On Thursday of last week Mr. Joseph Dingee's family had a very narrow escape from being burned out. The fire spread from a fallow of H. A. Avery. Both the house and barn caught afire, but fortunately both were saved. Mrs. Dingee and little daughter, who were in the house, had to lie on the floor and cover their heads with blankets, in order to breathe.....Large flocks of pigeons are seen flying east nearly every day.

CLARA.

The forests seem doomed to destruction.....Mr. Sala Stevens is spending some time with his son at the old homestead.....The summer school is in charge of Miss Emma Pawson.....Mr. Jacob Cole had a logging bee Friday, getting a good job of work done.....The recent fires in the oil district are a constant theme of conversation. The loss and suffering coming home to many who have friends there. Mr. Eli Whitney, a son-in-law of F. P. Brooks, came to this place Sunday, leaving Rixford just before the fire broke out. Everything they had was burned. His family remain here while he is over there making preparations to once more begin housekeeping in that unfavorable locality.

SHINGLE HOUSE.

May 28. – The frosts of Thursday and Friday nights harvested the apple crop from the first blossoms in this section.....Jones & Dodge are fast pushing their store to completion, and when finished will present a neat front on both streets.....A tramp made his appearance in our community a few days ago, and as he was rather demonstrative (in a pugilistic way) with his soldering iron, he was taken in charge by officer Nichols for a hearing before Justice Kinner; but as the charges were insufficient to commit him, he was allowed to skip the town.....Mrs. L. C. Kinner is very ill, but hopes are entertained by her physician and her family and many warm friends, for her recovery soon.....Forests fires have damaged timber to quite an extent in this vicinity.....Luther Canfield has sold a lot of two acres at "West End" to B. Bailey, Consideration, $120.....I understand that our oil speculator is discouraged because he cannot get as much territory as he wants and will give up what he now has, and "vamoose the ranch."

HARRISON VALLEY.

Very dry. Fires are raging in the woods in different parts of the town. Considerable damage has been done to the timber, and some two hundred cords of wood which was cut for the extract works has been burned. By the assistance of neighbors the house of A. E. Holcomb was kept from being burned by the forest fires. Other houses in the vicinity had a narrow escape. We need rain very much.....Two hard frosts the past week it is feared have ruined the early fruit.....E. B. Phillips, tiring of his last enterprise at Lawrence Mills, has returned to the Valley with his goods, and taken possession of his store building again, and Hunter & Hubbard have moved their stock into the store room of N. W. Hubbard, near the church.....Miss Rawson, formerly of Ulysses, has taken possession of the millinery rooms over the store of J. W. Stevens, and received a fresh stock of goods. She has the reputation of being one of the best milliners in the county, and we trust she will do a thriving business. Martin Dodge is often seen on the street with his fine Hartland colt, and new style trotting sulkey, kicking up quite a dust.....Jacob Burtis, late of Westfield, Pa., has moved into the house of Mrs. Cummings.....David W. Knight, near White's Corners, is reported very sick.....A young man by the name of Jeffers, one of the wood choppers on the White job, was quite sick last week.

- A. Rounseville has reshingled his residence on Seventh street.

- Charles Kernan has painted his residence on East street.

- Hon. D. C. Larrabee has the cellar for his new residence under way.

- The machinery for the new tannery is being brought on to the ground.

- The peeled trunks of hemlock trees begin to deface the mountain side northeast of Coudersport.

- The Davidson house on East street is being torn down preparatory to the erection of the new bank building on its site.

**Potter Enterprise
Thursday Evening,
May 27, 1880 –
Vol. 7, No. 3**

- J. M. Bassett has a cellar dug, and stone and lumber on the ground for his new house on Water street.

HARRISON VALLEY.
May 25, '80.

The diphtheria is again raging here, and people are becoming panic stricken.

Mr. H. White lost his youngest two daughters. Mr. Leonard his youngest son, and several others are sick with the same dreadful disease.

Mrs. M. C. Erway has returned from Groton.

Donations at the Erway House this evening, for the benefit of Rev. Searles, who, 'tis said, is contemplating matrimony.

J. W. Stevens has the best stock of goods in the county. Give him a call.

Andrew Wallis thinks of locating near the Judd school house, for convenience.

Very dry. Send us that rain storm.

ELEVEN MILE.

May 22, 1880. – Gentle showers have made an agreeable change from the dry and smoky atmosphere of the past two weeks. Fires have destroyed timber and fences to quite an extent in the newer cleared places, but we feel ashamed to complain, after the news of whole towns laid in ashes, and it seems to come near home when the fiend wipes out, as it were, the business houses of our county town, at least temporarily. May more substantial buildings take the place of the old ones.....The alarm of fire was heard yesterday, about 9 a.m., from Oswayo. Bell and whistles were set going, and hastily responded to by the citizens and residents of the vicinity. The fire was discovered in the barn of the McGonegal House, and fortunately, by heroic efforts was extinguished in less than fifteen minutes after the alarm. In five minutes one hundred men were on the spot and by the time it was over some three hundred had gathered on the scene.....Planting and seeding are behind time with most of us. Many had to lay it aside to repair burnt fences and the dry state of the soil has delayed plowing but by caring more thoroughly for what we have planted will be as profitable as to spread over too much or more than we can care for properly.....Wool buyers are enquiring for the new clip. Offer 10 cents, but claim the market to be unsteady. It is suggested to those who own sheep whose fleece are "cotted" or black, not to *wash* them, as buyers will only pay price of *unwashed* wool for such fleeces, and they will pay just the same per pound as if washed.

Potter Enterprise
Thursday Evening,
June 3, 1880 –
Vol. 7, No. 4

- Dr. French has put a frame addition to the rear of his office on Main Street.

- D. F. Glassmire has his stage and express office on Second Street fit for occupancy.

- Amos Veley has added to the comfort and convenience of his dwelling by building a verandah along the front.

- P. A. Stebbins, Jr. & Bro. don't let the grass grow under their feet. They moved into their new store 20x60 feet in size, on Thursday last, and the senior partner is in New York after new goods. Before snow flies they will occupy an elegant brick store on the old corner.

- The new building to be occupied by the Bank and by the land office of John S. Ross on first floor, and on second floor by the law office of Olmsted & Larrabee, will be built of sand stone with iron cornices. Thomas McAdam, of Norristown, has the contract for its erection. The contract was signed afternoon of Friday, May 28th and Mr. McAdam was at work before night.

BINGHAM.

A little rain has been very acceptable to the people of this vicinity.

We have been having very warm weather for some time back. Pastures are becoming very dry. It is said that some farmers' sheep were starving.

Grasshoppers begin to make their appearance in great quantities.

Wire worms are destroying potatoes after being planted.

ULYSSES.

The dry weather has not disturbed business much in this place, though people begin to complain terribly fearing their meadows will not yield them much hay.

Seth Lewis' office is up and will be finished as soon as possible.

A little rain made people glad and more would please them better.

Potter Enterprise
Thursday Evening,
June 10, 1880 –
Vol. 7, No. 5

- Ansel Wood has purchased the Cross Fork stage line of A. A. Swetland.

- Mrs. Elizabeth Weltch, of Hebron, is just in receipt of back pension to the amount of $1686.40. The pension is granted for the loss of a son.

- Again we have a saw mill accident to record, though fortunately not quite as serious as the one previous. Monday afternoon, at Metzgar's mill in this borough, Henry Niles lost the two front fingers of his right hand while edging boards. The edging caught on the carrier roll, and as he put his hand under to raise the edging the saw clipped the two fingers off. Drs. Mattison and Buck completed the operation, as surgeons.

OSWAYO.

A china wedding at Leander Stillson's, the 1st inst., resulted in a goodly number of presents and a happy time, generally. Also a crystal wedding at Franklin Gales, the 28th ult. The house was filled to overflowing with people, over sixty pieces were presented. Solomon Hawley made the presentation speech; the Oswayo Cornet Band played some fine music and all were merry as you please.

Lee's dance a success; over seventy five couples attended.

Mrs. R. Ellis is here every Friday with millinery goods; stopping at the Lee House.

KEATING.

At last we have had a change, and in place of the hot dog weather, have been having some nice rainy days, which were very welcomed.

We sympathize with the people of Coudersport in their loss by fire, not only is the loss felt in the village, but by a great many out of it. We are sorry, Mr. Editor, that

Township Tidings from Potter County, Pennsylvania
Volume I, 1880 - 1884

the fire used you so badly, but we are glad that ball a paper is left to us.

The news in this place is rather scarce just now. School has not yet commenced.

Sunday School commenced about four weeks ago with a large attendance for so small a neighborhood.

All are busy finishing their planting.

Potato bugs promise to be a large crop, if any one may judge by the large number that are seen nowadays.

Herman Bridges returned home this week from McKean county, where he has been for some time. While gone he had the mumps and was exposed to the measles pretty good for one trip.

John Bundy, Jr., had a logging bee last week, and we understand that the bee did a good job for him.

Mr. Leonard Jewell, of Portville, is visiting friends in this place.

Potter Enterprise
Thursday Evening,
June 17, 1880 –
Vol. 7, No. 6

- The Second Street bridge has been newly planked.

- Z. J. Thompson is building a small wagon shop on West street.

- The tannery smoke stack has been completed. It is an imposing pile of brick.

- The bark peelers are cutting the timber east of the village, and logs being hauled to Metzgar's mill almost as fast as peeled.

- A very severe thunder storm visited this vicinity on Friday morning. The lightning was vivid and continuous, the thunder without a break, and the rain fell in torrents. In Roulet many of the telegraph poles were splintered by the lightning. Belden Burt and F. M. Windsor, of Burtville, think the lightning is altogether too familiar, as it descended the telegraph poles immediately in front of and very close to their stores and dwellings.

- Miles White has opened a grocery in the building next door to the M. E. church on Third street. We bespeak for him a fair share of patronage.

- On Friday a loop in the telegraph wire was put in from Station No. 2, Tidewater Pipe Company, (limited) to Coudersport, and the telegraph office here is now on the main line of wire, with direction communication with the other world.

ROULET.

June 15. – Mr. Jerry Coon, who has been very ill with typhoid fever, is slowly recovering. – Mrs. H. Fessenden, of Coudersport, is visiting the family of Rodney Fessenden. – L.W. Crawford returned from a trip to Bradford on Saturday evening. – Miss Sina Bristol, of Duke Centre, spent a few days last week with her friend, Nellie Boyington. – Mr. Day and Mr. and Mrs. Judd, of Wellsville, are visiting M. V. Larrabee's

people. – W. S. Brine, our census enumerator is busy run, but has failed as yet in finding any old maids who refused to tell their age.
– Mrs. P. L. Boyington is reshingling the wing of her house, although the old ones were on nearly thirty years some of them were good yet. The lightning played a number of pranks on Friday morning last, striking one end of Ben. Card's house, tearing shingles and rafters off at a great rate, but fortunately injuring none of the inmates; also the barn of Lewis Yentzer. It struck a few feet from the lightning rod, tearing rafters and injuring the inside considerably. Several telegraph poles at Burtville were badly splintered.

**Potter Enterprise
Thursday Evening,
July 1, 1880 –
Vol. 7, No. 7**

- The new fence around the Court House square has a coat of paint.

- Sheriff Covey started on Monday to convey Eugene Clark to the house of refuge at Philadelphia, to which place he was sentenced last week by Judge Wilson. Clark, with his brother George, was convicted at March term of the larceny of some ivory rings from the harness of Mr. Burt, at Burtville. George Clark was granted a new trial last week, and Eugene was sentenced as above noticed.

- At the last term of Court a view was appointed to lay a road from Seventh street in this borough to the North Hollow road in Sweden, near the house of Cyrenus S. Jones. The road will probably keep up the east bank of the river, through the farm of Dr. Ellison, then bear to the right up the Rees hollow, and so on to Sweden. It will shorten the distance between Sweden Hill and this village materially and will be the outlet for a very large quantity of hemlock bark and logs.

- George Brahmer, on First Street, is doing a good business in the black smithing line, and will continue to do good work at low prices and guarantee satisfaction.

- Considerably over one thousand cords of bark have already been peeled on the tannery company's purchase from the Bingham estate.

- On Monday last Rev. T. R. Stratton's boys with a team and wagon loaded with 1000 feet of cherry lumber met with an accident at the second street bridge. As the wagon dropped from the bridge the strain was too great for the hind axle and it broke near the wheel. Joe Stratton was thrown violently to the ground striking upon his head and shoulders, receiving severe bruises but not serious ones. The team, a spirited one, was considerably frightened, but with the end of the broken axle upon the ground could make but little headway and soon quieted down.

- We are requested to announce that the Western Union telegraph office in this village will be open on Sundays between the hours of 9 and 10 a.m., and 5 and 6 p.m. only, of which all interested will please taken notice.

Potter Enterprise
Thursday Evening,
July 1, 1880 –
Vol. 7, No. 8

- Quite a number of new street lamps have been put up in different sections of the town.

- New plank crossings have been put in across Third Street on East and across East Street on Third.

- D. F. Glassmire is putting up a barn 36x60 feet in size, on south side of Second street. It will be used for his stage line.

- Rattlesnakes are unusually plenty on the Cross Forks. Four large ones were killed in a distance of one mile last week.

- Dr. Charles S. French, of this place, has decided to locate at Millport, in this county, for the practice of his profession. He took up his residence there this week.

- Joseph Forster has rented ground of N. M. Glassmire, on "Euclid Avenue," and will put up a wagon shop. At present he has a bench up in Perkins' blacksmith shop.

- M. S. Thompson & Co. at the postoffice have added a news counter to their store room and will keep in the future a full line of periodicals, including all the weekly story and illustrated papers, the magazines and light literature.

- On Monday a large pile of lumber near Rees' planing mill, upon which a number of children were playing, tipped over. Several large plank fell upon a little daughter of Frank McNamara. One leg was badly bruised from foot to knee, but fortunately no bones were broken.

- Hebron has a population of 835, a gain of 81 since 1870. In 1870 there were many shingle mills and lumbering establishments employing many men, who helped to swell the enumeration, but who were not permanent residents of the township. Now the population is made up of farmers and citizens who are there to stay. On the whole the increase is very encouraging.

OSWAYO.

June 26. – Oswayo intends celebrating the old fashioned way, Saturday, the 3d. Judging from the advertisement it will be immense.....T. F. Bachus, looms with a nice soda fountain, which is just the thing needed these sultry days.....Look out for the new band wagon. It's nobby. Bachus did the painting.....Earl Hood's band plays for McGonigal, the 3d. Come to the celebration.

RAYMOND CORNERS.

We will not celebrate the coming Fourth of July, but we invite everybody to meet us for a picnic; on Wednesday, July 7th, on the old picnic ground south of the church. All the Sunday Schools in adjacent neighborhoods are hereby invited to attend, as we hope to have a very pleasant and profitable time. Rev. Thomas Perry, of Ulysses, is expected to be present and address the children.

WEST BRANCH.

June 24. – The oil well at Splash Dam has come to a stand still. The drill is lost in the well, and fishing tools will have to be brought from Bradford. The drill is down about 250 feet.

**Potter Enterprise
Thursday Evening,
July 8, 1880 –
Vol. 7, No. 9**

- I. A. Hollenbeck, of Hebron, was one of the graduates from the Normal School at Lock Haven on the 1st inst.

- Last Monday night the store of Wolsey Burtis, of Lewisville, was broken open and twenty dollars in money and a few goods taken. The burglars took down a portion of the cellar wall to effect an entrance. It is believed the parties reside in that section and an earnest hunt is being made for them.

OLMSTED STATION.

July 1, 1880.

The death of Susan, supposed by foul means, caused the men at the station to look gloomy. The past day or two H. looks sad, S. could not stand the sight, and B. did not swear for two hours, (he was asleep,) and Frank was so mad that he spit blue. Susan was the station cat.

Mr. and Mrs. B. Watson have had an addition to their family – a son, weight 8 pounds. All doing well.

Mr. Holly and son, of Lockport water works fame, and J. G. Benton, Superintendent of the Tidewater Pipe Line, visited this station a few days since. They give the men credit of having everything in No. 1 order, and call this the best station in the oil country. Quite complimentary to the crew employed here.

**Potter Enterprise
Thursday Evening,
July 15, 1880 –
Vol. 7, No. 10**

- The tinners are putting on the roof of C. H. Armstrong's new brick store on Second Street.

- The residence of T. Benton Brown, at Third and West streets, is being improved with a new coat of paint.

- The carpenters have commenced work on the new residence of Hon. D. C. Larrabee, at West and Water streets.

- Mrs. A. C. Havens' new house at First and West streets has assumed handsome proportions and is well under way.

- A very handsome marble shaft has been erected over the grave of Captain Arch F. Jones, in Eulalia Cemetery, in this borough.

- A. H. Pierce has purchased from Mrs. A. C. Haven a lot at the northwest corner of Main and First streets on which he will erect a boarding house.

- L. R. Bliss, the photographer, has moved into the house of Miss Eva Dyke, on East street, and Dr. E. S. Mattison occupies the rooms in Mrs. Wood's house on Main street, just vacated by Mr. Bliss.

- George H. Green has put out lately new signs for his barber shop and billiard room on "Euclid avenue" and has bought a new barber chair, keeps choice cigars and tobacco, and take it all in all has one of the cosiest business places in town.

- It is said that the rich farms around the mouth of Pine Creek begin to show signs of exhaustion from the constant cropping in tobacco. It is a hard matter to let land alone that will produce two or three hundred dollars per acre per annum.

MILLPORT.

Haying is commenced in this vicinity. Grass is thought to be a good crop in spite of the summer.....There is scarcely any fruit except the berry crop which promises to be fair.....The Fourth was duly celebrated by all who could possibly buy a fire cracker.....The excitement in regard to the murder of Mr. Ingraham is very great, as he was well known and has friends living here.....R. L. Nichols and wife are spending a few days in Hornellsville, N.Y.....Miss Della Fuller, of Manistique, is visiting friends in this place.....A. F. Witter, of Alfred,

N.Y., is spending a few days with the Sharon Band boys, as teacher.

Potter Enterprise
Thursday Evening,
July 22, 1880 –
Vol. 7, No. 11

- A severe thunder storm visited this neighborhood early on the morning of the 14th instant. A large hemlock tree south of the river in this borough was demolished by the lightning and cut into such fantastic fragments that it was visited by very many curious people during the following day and since.

- W. S. Brine, enumerator for Roulet and Keating, has kindly given us the following results of his enumeration: Roulet 649, Keating 203. This is a gain over 1870 of 124 for Roulet and 125 for Keating. The percentage of increase for Keating is probably the largest that any township in the county will show, being 260 per cent.

Potter Enterprise
Thursday Evening,
July 29, 1880 –
Vol. 7, No. 12

- Charles Reissman has reshingled his house.

- William Thomas has painted his dwelling.

- The dwelling of Mrs. A. C. Haven has been painted.

- Bendel, the tailor, has swung out a very neat and tasty sign at his shop, 2d floor of the brick store, east of the river.

- A team belonging to Leonard Davis, of East Hebron, hauled into the tannery yard at Oswayo on Saturday the largest load of bark that has gone in this season. It weighed 6,890 pounds.

- D. F. Glassmire's stage barn and appurtenances are prominent objects to the vision of this borough. It is very convenient and serves the purpose for which it was built, but it is *not* handsome.

- An eleven year old son of Charles Reuning, of Eulalia, chopped down a hemlock tree, two feet and eight inches through, the other day, and he would like to hear of some other eleven year olds like him.

- D. F. Glassmire, Jr., has moved into his new livery stable on First street, and a very convenient and well stocked establishment he has. Give him a call when you want a rig. You will always find him able to accommodate you.

- A new brick machine which turns out brick at the rate of about 10,000 per day has been set up and is at work at the brick yard on Second street, above Gordnier's mill. A new yard still above that has been opened and the prospects now are that all the brick needed by the builders this fall will be ready for them. Wm. S. and Jesse Brine are the manufacturers.

- The new house of Hon. D. C. Larrabee has been climbing skyward during the past few days and begins to develop its handsome proportions. It will be two stories in height with a mansard roof – making really another story – will have a handsome verandah along the front, and a tower entrance.

- The entrance way to the new "corner store" of P. A. Stebbins, Jr. & Bro., now in course of erection, will be composed of one stone, thirteen feet in length and four feet and one inch wide, and nearly a foot thick. It was gotten out of the common sand stone on the farm of O. T. Ellison, north of the village, was hauled to its place by the team of John M. Covey and weighs over three tons.

**The Potter Enterprise
Wednesday Evening,
August 12, 1880 –
Vol. VII, No. 13**

- Coudersport has a regular policeman.

- F. W. Knox has built a carriage house near his barn, on the south side of the river.

- Joseph Forster has built a wagon shop in the rear of the blacksmith shops on First street.

- A short time ago Orlando J. Rees and Elmer Womelsdorf killed a large rattle-snake, on the head of the Hammersley, in this county, which measured four and one-half feet in length, and was adorned with nine rattles. We have the rattles in our office.

Township Tidings from Potter County, Pennsylvania
Volume I, 1880 - 1884

- Charles Reissman has put up a bench in the second story of B. Rennells & Son's blacksmith shop, and will carry on the Cabinet making business there.

- Dr. Edgar S. Mattison has purchased a house and lot of Charles Kernan, east of the river, on Seventh street. The Dr. is repairing the house and will soon occupy it.

- Shingle House is to have a newspaper this month. Mr. Bailey, we are informed, will conduct the new venture. If the Wellsville oil field extends into Sharon, as many fully believe, Shingle House will make a large town, and Mr. Bailey will reap a harvest. We wish him success.

- Dr. S. A. Phillips, the Coudersport Dentist, has added to his office furniture a new operating chair, covered with plush and patents – all the modern improvements, a thing of beauty, and a fixture that almost entirely takes away the pain when the tooth breaks loose – so Dr. says. And then he has a bracket stand for tools, resplendent with nickel plate. He has also added to his facilities gas for the painless extraction of teeth. Phillips is up with the times.

- The lot adjoining the corner store on the north and on which recently stood the Coudersport Bank, has been purchased by F. W. Knox, who will immediately erect a two story brick building thereon, the first floor of which will be occupied by the hardware store of Norton & Doane. This fills out the block on Main between Second and Third streets, though we believe Mr. Griesel does not intend to build until next year.

**The Potter Enterprise
Wednesday Evening,
August 18, 1880 –
Vol. VII, No. 14**

- Rosco D. Weimer has purchased the Pulaski Reed farm in Roulet.

- E. O. Rees has a fine line of cigars, and smoker's articles, at his Jewelry store.

- James Turner is putting up a dwelling near Jacob Braitling's, on a lot purchased of D. C. Larrabee.

- The delivery of brick commenced on Monday morning last, and those for M. S. Thompson & Co., P. A. Stebbins, Jr., & Bro. and the Masonic Hall will be delivered at once.

- Wm. Burt has become the proprietor of the "Lewisville Hotel" formerly occupied by Seth Lewis. "Bill" is an old hand at the business and his guests are sure of being well entertained. Give him a call.

- F. W. Knox & Son are repairing their law office. A new floor has been laid in the front room, the two rooms connected by an arch instead of a door, the old windows to be replaced by larger ones and the whole structure repainted.

- Herbert S. Palmer, of Raymond, will leave about the first of

Township Tidings from Potter County, Pennsylvania
Volume I, 1880 - 1884

September, for Lyndon, Whiteside county, Ill., to engage in teaching. Herbert recently returned from the Mansfield State Normal School, which he has been attending as a student. Herb has the ability to make a first-class teacher.

- Brick laying will be commenced on the Postoffice or Union Block, Wednesday or Thursday of next week.

- A fracas occurred on Main street, Monday evening. Two carpenters working for Mr. Hall having had some difficulty with T. J. Gilbert, committed an assault upon him. For their fun the Justice exacted a fine and costs, amounting to about fifty-five dollars.

Genesee Fork.
August 16, 1880.

Died – At Genesee Fork, Pa., August 8, Ruth Fuller, aged 6 years. Daughter of Mr. and Mrs. L. Fuller of this place.

Died – At West Creek, of Diphtheria, August 8, Fred Miller aged 13. August 10, Stella Miller, aged 9. August 15, Dora Miller, aged 11. All children of Mrs. Mary Miller, widow of G. W. Miller.

They sleep now.

They wake and laugh above.

To-day, as they walked, let us walk in love,

To-morrow follow so.

Keating.
August 15, 1880.

Haying is nearly finished in this place and has been a very good crop in spite of the dry weather in the spring.

A picnic for the Sunday school of this place came off Thursday the 12th, not a very large crowd, but what were there had a very merry time.

Mrs. Emma Beebe is quite sick, also Mr. Joseph Dingee of Keating Summit is very sick with Typhoid fever.

Mr. and Mrs. James Mitcheltree left here yesterday, on a visit to Clearfield county.

Misses Elnora and Flora Quimby returned to their home in Homer last Tuesday, having been at work in Auburn, N.Y., for over a year. We were glad to see the new Enterprise out. Good luck to you.

Allegany.
Aug. 16, 1880.

We have all been thankful for the halfsheet we have been receiving since the fire, but the full-sized sheet was welcomed with gladness. Our thanks are given you, both for the paper once more, and the energy you have used in building up so soon.

A slight frost was seen this morning in some places.

Haying was finished some time ago, and harvesting is well under way.

Rev. Cole is again shedding the light of his countenance among us, he preached to us three times yesterday at the Judd school house.

Old Mrs. Gardner has been in poor health for some time.

Diphtheria has made its appearance at Andrews Settlement. A. C. Scoville's youngest son was the first victim; Fred, aged fourteen years, he was sick eight days. A daughter of R. C. Plants is dangerously sick with it now, and report says Mr. P. has it too. These are the first cases of the disease in the malignant form in this part of the town, and we hope it will be the last.

The Potter Enterprise
Wednesday Evening,
August 25, 1880 –
Vol. VII, No. 15

- In our tramp about town we notice that Albert Goodsell has recently built an addition to his house.

- We note with pleasure that the street Commissioner is having some cross walks relaid. There is need of it.

- Dr. O. T. Ellison has purchased boilers and engines, and in a few weeks will run his saw mill regardless of the stage of water in the Allegheny. The Doctor has a first-class saw mill, but its usefulness has been impaired by want of water in the river to run it, and as he cannot stand anything of that kind he makes one more improvement in his mill property that will prove of great convenience to the public, and a source of profit to himself.

- Last week A. G. Lyman received one of Blandy's portable saw mills of forty horse power, which, this week he will have set up in the woods north-west of Cherry Springs, for the purpose of cutting a large quantity of Cherry, Ash and other hard woods owned by him in that section. The engine and boiler attracted considerable attention on Friday and Saturday as it stood on Second street, where it was taken apart to facilitate its removal to the woods.

Bingham.
Aug. 23, 1880.

We are glad to hear that you are prospering and are now able to present the Enterprise in its full size, but we are willing to accept their half sheet until you saw it fit to enlarge it.

Diphtheria has broken out in E. Robbins family.

The frost on the night of the 15th did considerable damage in this vicinity.

Grain of all kinds has come in splendid in this section, though people were discouraged the fore part of the season and thought nothing would be raised. Grass was better than it was expected it would be.

Every sensible man this way is for Hancock.

Ulysses.
August 23, 1880.

Business seems rather dull here at present.

Farmers were very busy during the harvesting.

Drovers are not out among the farmers this season as they generally have been.

Seth Lewis is putting up a splendid large building. It is said he is preparing a lodge room over head for the Knights of Honor.

D. B. Jackson has sold his span of blacks that wore off the blue ribbon last fall from the Potter county fair.

Clark Crum's wife has become totally blind caused by neuralgia in the head.

Crops goods but catching time for harvesting.

Roulet.
August 23, 1880.

A number of the Roulet teachers will attend the Institute this week.

H. J. Berhands of Buffalo, spent last Saturday and Sunday with his friends in this place.

A. V. Lyman has the best garden in town.

Guy Forsyth, of Whitesville, N.Y., has been visiting his uncle M. V. Larrabee.

George Olmsted of Coudersport, was in this place Sunday last.

A gentleman whose name we will not mention has the best corn field in Roulet, also one other who has very good apples, at least they were pronounced so, last Saturday night by a party of Sioux.

A very pleasant party was given at Tauscher's hall, the 19th. Some twenty-five couples participated.

The new store conducted by Messrs. Tauscher, Larkin & Co., is doing a rushing business.

The 20th inst. the house of J. R. Fessenden, on Liniger Creek was destroyed by fire. About $25 worth of household goods were in the house at the time of the fire. No insurance.

The Potter Enterprise
Wednesday Evening,
September 1, 1880 –
Vol. VII, No. 16

- D. F. Glassmire has put up a nice new street lamp in front of his grocery.

- The first board was put through the planer at Rounsevill's mill on Saturday last.

- The first brick on the Corner Store of P. A. Stebbins, Jr. & Bro., was laid last Friday morning.

- The steam whistle at Rounseville's handle factory awoke the echoes for the first time last week.

- A. F. Raymond has been appointed post master at the new office recently established in this county, called Gold.

- Isaac Benson has purchased from Miss Kate Dent the property at the foot of Main street, occupied by Mr. Hammond. Consideration $4,000.

- The cheese factory in Eulalia at the mouth of Steer Brook made a sale last week at 12 cents per pound. The highest price yet received this season.

- Our statement last week that Mr. Lyman was to locate his portable mill at Cherry Springs was incorrect. The mill has been put up on the Cross Fork, in the old Bailey mill, and will be cutting lumber the first of the week. The lumber cut on the Cross Fork will be taken to Westport. After getting through on the Cross Fork, the mill will be removed to some point near Cherry Springs, and before spring will be located somewhere on the James Nelson branch of Dry Run. The mill is of forty horse power, the largest manufactured, and will cut from 12,000 m to 30,000 m per day. The engine boiler and fixtures weigh 9500 pounds, and was removed from the railroad to Cross Fork for less than $100.

Genesee Forks.
Aug. 30, 1880.

The news of the vicinity is sickness, sickness. Diphtheria is raging all about us, and we are almost led to cry, "come over from Macedonia and help us." At Mr. Isaac Dawley's there are four cases, one recovering; at Mr. Freeman's two cases; at Mr. George Barlow's five cases, one little boy was buried yesterday. There are no more cases at Mr. Fuller's. It has now visited nearly every house in our immediate vicinity.

Mrs. Isaac Harris is now quite sick, threatened with fever.

A little son of Mr. Orval Leach met with quite an accident last week, while playing around he jumped upon a scythe cutting one of his limbs to the bone.

A little building is now going on; Mr. John Carpenter has a new horse barn nearly completed; an L is being built to the house owned by F. Slawson.

We hear that Mr. J. Dimon is bringing in articles in the grocery line for sale.

Mrs. Lucy Schoonover of Sawyer City is now visiting friends in this vicinity.

Miss Fox from Southern Kansas is now visiting at her sister's, Mrs. Freeman.

A grove meeting is to be held at Genesee Forks, commencing Thursday, September 9th and lasting four days.

Allegany.
Aug. 30, 1880.

Harvesting is nearly finished except corn and buckwheat, and thrashing machines begin to run again.

At Andrews Settlement the cases of diphtheria proved to be light. The family of C. Ford are all sick with it now. Clara Scoville went to help take care of them, Mrs. C. being her sister, and she has taken it and is very sick.

Our Sabbath school was rather small yesterday, so many being absent, some attended the Quarterly meeting at Oswayo, and Mr. and Mrs. H. Peet and Mrs. Carrie Vellie are attending the Camp meeting.

Rev. Stratton baptised four persons yesterday, and in June last seventeen persons were baptised here, which speaks well for those converted last spring.

Visiting absent friends has been the order here with some, for two weeks past; J. Matteson and wife visited friends at Alfred, N.Y.; I. Striker and wife spent a week with friends and relatives at Greenwood and other places in N.Y. and H. Kies and sister visited friends at Whitesville.

Delmar Nelson is to attend school at Andover, this fall and

winter, and others are preparing for schools in different places.

- Last Tuesday evening Nelson Clark meet with quite a serious accident while on his way to Port Allegany with a load of cheese. At a point just below Clark's, where the wagon road crosses the railroad grade, the bank on either side is quite steep. At the time it was very dark and the team veered a little from the centre of the road, sufficient to overturn the top heavy load. Mr. Clark was thrown to the ground and the cheese was piled about and over him in such a manner that it was impossible for him to extricate himself. Mr. Greenman, who was but a short distance behind him with a load, was soon on the spot, and assisted Mr. Clark to the nearest house. Examination showed several sprains and numerous bruises. A day or two after he was removed to his home on a bed. He is now improving.

The Potter Enterprise
Wednesday Evening,
September 8, 1880 –
Vol. VII, No. 17

- Adolf Neefe, we are informed, leaves for Texas in a few days, where he intends making his future home.

- Between 1400 and 1500 feet of boards were planed at Rounseville's mill in thirty minutes, last Saturday.

Bingham.
Sept. 6, 1880.

A terrible hail storm took place in the north part of this town a few days since, which did considerable damage. Grain was completely thrashed out upon the ground. The next morning the hail was found to be three inches deep.

C. Burt has built a large farm barn this season.

No deaths caused by diphtheria in E. Robbins family. There were _____ and it is said all are recovering under the skillful treatment of Dr. Cobb.

D. B. Jackson has purchased a mated pair of hambletonians.

Miss Inez Ferris is visiting an aunt at Bradford.

Ulysses.
Sept. 6, 1880.

Business fair in this place, everything indicates a lively time this fall, especially about the day when the ballot is to tell the story.

C. Hosley has bought the John Hacket farm and intends to run a dairy next season.

There was an ice cream festival for the benefit of the M.E. Church, Sept. 1, at the hall that S. Lewis has prepared for gatherings.

Thanks to E. S. Mattison for this story thus far.

T. Burt is making his way to New York city with a drove of calves.

There is a young man in this town so economical that he is more eager for one crum than some men are for a thousand dollars.

Roulet.
Sept. 6, 1880.

J. V. Weimer is visiting friends in Canada.

W. A. Walley of Olean, N.Y., spent last Sunday in this place.

Leclare Forsyth has been visiting relatives in Whitesville, N.Y.

Miss D. E. Boyington has returned to Rixford, Pa., where she is engaged to teach the select school.

Miss Nellie Bird of Penfield, has been visiting her aunt, Mrs. R. L. White.

Major C. A. Sanbourn and daughter are attending the Seventh Day Advent Camp meeting at Hornellsville, N.Y.

Miss Lottie and Laura Larrabee are visiting in Allegany county, N.Y., near Belfast.

Will some kind friend please inform us when that donation is to take place.

Our select school opens to-day under the supervision of Mr. A. Hollenbeck.

Allegany.
Sept. 6, 1880.

We have been having some very warm days for the past week, and warm weather is needed to ripen the corn which is backward in proportion to other crops.

C. Ford's family are recovering from diphtheria.

Willie Cool was taken with diphtheria last week, but is not considered dangerous.

Walter Cool has returned from a three months trip in Mich.

Wm. Matteson is accompanying Ed. Tassell with his threshing machine.

Mrs. Sarah Peck is visiting at G. W. G. Judd's.

Mr. and Mrs. Eli Nelson and Miss Edith Haskell have been visiting friends in Andover and other places in N.Y.

Mr. John Peet and wife have started on a lengthy journey in the West.

Ira Bishop and Henry Kies have returned to the Mansfield Normal school, and Carrie Bishop has gone to the Normal at Lock Haven.

Already school directors are having numerous applications for the schools the coming winter, and not long since a man rode nearly a week to find a girl to do general housework, without finding one. Now what makes the difference.

The Potter Enterprise
Wednesday Evening,
September 15, 1880 –
Vol. VII, No. 18

- N. H. Goodsell starts up his cider mill this week.

- D. W. Butterworth sports a new side spring top buggy.

- Henry Schilderberger has rented the Brewery, and will turn it into a cigar manufactory.

- It is required by law that the supervisors in each township put up finger-boards at every cross roads. Failing to do this, they are liable to a fine of $10 for each and every act of negligence. Measures should be taken to enforce the law throughout the county.

Genesee Forks.
Sept. 3d, 1880.

A logging bee was held on John Hart's farm, in this town, on Thursday, Sept. 2d. There were 97 persons present. After supper it was proposed to take a vote for President among the sturdy sons of toil. They stood, Hancock 97, Garfield 0. This is about the way the vote will stand in Potter county in November – at least among those who work for a living and are not dependant on official pap for support.

Keating.
Sept. 9, 1880.

We are having quite a spell of weather and very wet nasty weather it is too.

Not very much news here at present.

W. H. Dingee is hauling considerable bark from this place to Keating Summit.

Mr. Charles Dingee is sick with fever.

School commenced last Monday with a good attendance, teacher William Tassel.

Politics pretty quiet, not much heard of them but the rumble of the wheels of the Electioneerers as they pass by.

A platform dance will be held at the platform near G. C. Lewis', this place, September 17. Good music and supper. All are cordially invited.

Roulet.
Sept. 13, 1880.

Mrs. R. L. White and family are visiting at Lymansville.

Miss Nellie Boyington has been very ill with diphtheria, but is slowly recovering.

C. K. C. who has been in the habit of watching the milking of certain cows in this place, is somewhat disconsolate, the milk maid having gone away to spend a few days.

J. K. Regan, telegraph operator at this place, is visiting his parents in Andover, N.Y.

J. C. French of this place, is now teaching penmanship in the Mansfield Business College.

We have a natural born imitator in this place, who desires a situation with some travelling troupe. He can be found by addressing F. H. S., Box 2044, Roulet, Pa.

Tauscher Bro's. are fitting up the upper part of their store for a residence.

Quite a serious accident occurred in this place on Friday last. Truman Willoughby Sr., while driving along Main street, neglected to put the brake on, causing the buggy to strike the heels of his horses, which started them on the run, throwing the old gentleman to the ground, with considerable force. He was somewhat bruised, but is now recovering.

- Last week, while at Alfred Cool's in Allegany, nursing persons sick with diphtheria, Mrs. Albert Goodsell of this place fell down stairs receiving injuries which necessitated her removal to her home. We are glad to know that she is improving.

- Last Thursday a little son of Fred Tauscher's, of Sweden, aged about nine years, fell upon a grain cradle, from which he received quite serious injuries. On one hip a semi-circular cut loosened the flesh and skin over a spot as large as a man's hand, which required sixteen stitches to draw together, besides a cut of three inches in length on the side. Chloroform was administered to the little sufferer. Under the care of Dr. Buck he is doing as well as can be expected and it is thought will fully recover.

- The first, and we trust the last, accident at Rounseville's mill, occurred on Saturday afternoon last. Mr. Pierce was engaged in re-sawing some boards twelve feet in length. By some means a strip three inches wide was thrown upon the saw, revolving like a flash of lightning. The board was thrown forward with great velocity, striking Mr. Pierce in the breast, knocking him to the floor. He attempted to get up but fell over unconscious. Dr. Buck was called and rendered medical aid, so that on Monday Pierce was able to be out, though very sore from the bruise.

**The Potter Enterprise
Wednesday Evening,
September 22, 1880 –
Vol. VII, No. 19**

- Bliss has built an addition to his gallery.

- T. J. Gilbert is selling sewing machines for N. M. Glassmire.

- Horace Peet, a few days since, gathered twenty-nine bushels of apples from one tree. By actual count there was 22,518 apples.

- J. M. Tyler, of Clara, has three potatoes together weighing seven pounds and eleven ounces. One of them weighs two pounds and twelve ounces.

- M. S. Thompson's & Co.'s building and P. A. Stebbins Jr. & Bro.'s buildings are about ready for the roof. The buildings are situated at opposite corners of the square, which by this time next year will be a solid block of brick.

- The second kiln of brick was cool enough to open Friday morning, and hauling was commenced at once. M. S. Thompson's building had been at a stand still for a week. Jones and Lyon were nearly out and Stebbins could only keep the men at work an hour or two. At 6:30 a.m. M. A. Fergason delivered the first load, at the Corner Store, and from that time on load followed load in quick succession.

- Sheriff Covey has leased the Baker House.

Township Tidings from Potter County, Pennsylvania
Volume I, 1880 - 1884

- Next year there will be nine brick stores and a brick harness shop on Main street. Eight of the buildings will be up this year. On Second street there is one brick store completed, and the stone bank building almost ready for the roof. It is highly probable that two brick buildings will be erected on Second street next year. If there is any other town in the State with less than seven hundred inhabitants that can make a better showing of enterprise we should like to know where it is located.

Roulet.
Sept. 20, 1880.

W. W. Eaton has bought the cheese factory of Mr. Day.

Our select school has an attendance of twenty-three pupils.

There are no new cases of diphtheria in town.

Since commencing to report for the *Journal* "Stick in the Mud" has chewed up two dozen lead pencils.

R. B. Lane is building an addition to his barn.

Mrs. D. C. Larrabee is spending the week with Mrs. M. V. Larrabee.

Born – To Mr. and Mrs. John Cavenaugh, a daughter. To Mr. and Mrs. Henry Barr, a son. To Mr. and Mrs. John Badger, a son. The mothers to these little ones are all sisters.

Germania.

A Hancock and English Club was organized at Germania, Friday evening, September 11, 1880. The meeting was largely attended and the following officers were elected: President, Henry Nieman; Vice-President, George M. Rexford; Secretary, Henry Theis; Treasurer, Charles Sandbach.

Forty-four signed the club roll.

A subscription was started to buy a Hancock and English flag, which will be raised sometime next week.

Freeman's Run.

Harvesting is about over, and crops are usually good. No frost yet.

E. O. Austin and daughter have just returned from a two weeks visit in Harrison.

The Evart school has commenced with R. W. Swetland as teacher. The Brownlee school will commence Sept. 20, with L. D. Ripple as teacher.

The Ardell Camp is rapidly filling up. They propose to take out several millions of pine the coming winter, part of which will come from Freeman's Run and part from Bailey's Run. They have constructed elaborate slides and rip-rapped Bailey's Run.

Millport.
Sept. 20, 1880.

The frosts in this vicinity have been very light so far and has not injured the corn, so it will be very likely to prove a good crop.

Our select school has commenced, with Jasper Card as teacher.

The people are beginning to wake up a little about politics since the county nominations have been made, although this community has not yet been blessed with any political speeches.

A young married lady by the name of Rodgers, who recently

came from Wales to this country, has been very sick since her arrival here, but has now nearly recovered. She was attended by Dr. C. S. French of this place.

Mr. William Ormsby has been spending a few days near Whitesville, with a brother who has been having a hard time on account of sickness in his family, several members having been taken away by death.

B. F. Greenman made our place a short visit a few days since.

Miss Laura Tyler of Clara, is attending our select school.

Allegany.
Sept. 20, 1880.

Almost the first question asked when one person meets another, is: "Are there any new cases of diphtheria?" so I will write of this first. It has only been in four families in this community thus far. Willie Cool has been dangerously ill; when he was first taken it seemed in a mild form, but it soon proved very bad, but he is now considered out of danger. Dr. Turner of Oswayo, attended him.

Political matters are creating quite an excitement with some. If a man is a voter and it is not positively known which party he will sustain, he is besieged with office seekers, and party men who are striving with all their power to sustain their party in power, and calling all that do not agree with them every thing but honest men.

Miss Eva Striker has gone to visit friends in Greenwood, N.Y.

Mr. and Mrs. Judd intend starting to-day to visit their daughters Mrs. Peck and Mrs. Benson and other relatives.

The frost has seared things here in the valleys, on the hills corn and gardens are green yet.

The weather is fine, the roads are good and the moonlight evenings splendid, and it seems the young people are enjoying them, judging by the numbers that were out riding last evening.

West Pike.
Sept. 20, 1880.

Crops in this part of the county are pretty good, though some pieces of corn have been damaged by the wire worm.

We have an abundant harvest of apples. This ought to encourage every man who has land to set out fruit trees, we sometimes fail of having apples but generally have some, and as often as every other year have a plenty. It is a good plan for those who are contemplating setting out apple trees, to consult some practical fruit grower as to what varieties do best in our latitude.

Marian Ansley has the kind of bees to keep. He had an old bee hive out in the field, to stand on and drive fence posts. One day a swarm of bees came out of his hive by the house, flew to the old hive in the field, went in and went to work and are doing well.

One of the Wellsboro and Brookland stage horses fell down and died Saturday afternoon, without as much as asking "Jim" about it. This makes two that have died within a week. Not very profitable.

Township Tidings from Potter County, Pennsylvania
Volume I, 1880 - 1884

We saw the effects of bad whiskey manifested on our streets Saturday afternoon. We wish those Brookland fellows if they must have a drunk once in a while, would go someplace else sometimes besides down in our neighborhood, and if they do come down here we wish they would get this man they are in the habit of getting drunk, a little nearer home, so he will not have to lay in the road all night.

**The Potter Enterprise
Wednesday Evening,
September 29, 1880 –
Vol. VII, No. 20**

- Many wells and springs in this section have gone dry.

- The oat crop in this county is very light and of poor quality.

- Geo. Cobb has purchased Charley Hosley's grocery at Lewisville.

- Work stopped on four buildings last week for want of timber for joice.

- The boss cabbage head we have seen this year comes from Ham White of Harrison. It will fill a bushel basket.

- W. J. Cutler of Raymond has left at this office a sunflower seventeen inches in diameter. It is of a California variety.

- Gas, from gasoline, will be used to light the Bank building, and the same thing is to be used in the Main street stores.

- George W. Sheldon, of Crandall Hill, has left at this office a blackberry cane, of this year's growth, which measures thirteen feet and ten inches in length.

- The barn on the farm owned by Leroy Lyman, opposite the Crawford Mill in Roulet, was burned Monday night. The barn was full of hay, grain, etc. We have learned none of the particulars.

- With good luck the Bank building, Stebbins Bros. store and M. S. Thompson & Co.'s store will be under roof this week. The floors have already been put down in Thompson's building.

- The Coudersport Band has secured the services of Mr. Allen of Ulysses, and the number of horns have been increased to eleven. They are prepared to furnish first-class music on short notice.

Oswayo.
Sept. 25, 1880.

We are having a good many cases of diphtheria at present. Mr. I. Stewart has a son very sick also Mr. S. Lyman of the Eleven Mile has four children and his wife sick with the same disease.

Mr. H. Brizzee hauled six tons and one hundred and ten lbs of bark to Oswayo tannery yesterday. Who can beat it.

We think the Democratic County Convention has done well in nominating such good men as they have to be elected this fall.

Ulysses.
Sept. 28, 1880.

The news from Maine caused the cannon to roar at Lewisville, Ulysses, amid hearty cheers.

Harvesting is nearly done for the season in this vicinity, a plentiful harvest it is too.

Some pieces of winter wheat are up and are looking fine.

John Smith's fine house was very much endangered a few evenings since by a lamp exploding. The oil was thrown all over the room, but they succeeded in extinguishing the flames to there was no damage done. The explosion was caused by the wick being too small for the tube. The republicans are going to sleep to awake with another new name. What will it be next, does any one know.

Bingham.
Sept. 28, 1880.

Business is quiet in this vicinity.

People generally are enjoying good health, though we hear of some cases of diphtheria. There are three more cases in E. Robbins family. The skillful treatment of Dr. Cobb could not save two of them. One died Sept. 10th, aged five years, the other Sept. 16th, aged twelve years. The other four have recovered.

In spite of the wet weather which we have had, farmers have got their harvesting nearly out of the way.

We hear every day of true and patriotic men coming over and joining that party whose motto is, Liberty. Let every true, patriotic man be at his post to sustain the Constitution our forefathers fought for.

Allegany.
Sept. 27, 1880.

We have been and are still having quite a drought, and many are bothered for water. Last night and this morning there were indications of rain, it would be gladly received by some at least.

As H. Peet was going to the factory with his milk yesterday morning, his horse shied at something by the roadside, and jumped one side so suddenly that it threw him and his little daughter both out of the wagon, and bruised them some but no serious damage was done.

M. Veeley has bought F. Tassel's share of the thresher, it is now Velley, Matteson & Co.

Miss West of Coudersport, has been visiting at E. Haskell's.

Mr. Metzgar and wife of Freetown, N.J., Mr. Chapin and wife of McGrowville, and Mr. E. Matteson and wife and Mr. Pratt Matteson from Branchport, N.Y., are visiting at Mr. Rogers' and Matteson's. Two of the ladies being sisters of Mrs. Rogers and Matteson.

Rev. Stratton preached his last regular sermon of this year yesterday, every seat was filled, which speaks well for him. He has many warm friends in this place.

Township Tidings from Potter County, Pennsylvania
Volume I, 1880 - 1884

The Potter Enterprise
Wednesday Evening,
October 6, 1880 –
Vol. VII, No. 21

- The Bank and M. S. Thompson's building are under roof.

- One of Forster's store buildings is ready for second tier of joice.

- Stebbins' Corner Store will be roofed this week and the floors down.

- Stone laying commenced on the Zimmerman lot last Saturday morning.

- Olmsted's two buildings, Farnum Lyon's and C. S. Jones' buildings, are up one story, with second story joice in place.

- J. O. Edgecomb, of the Oleona House, Kettle Creek, has rented the Baker House and will take possession this week. Sheriff Covey intended taking the house as we reported, but a statute of this State forbids Sheriff's keeping a house of entertainment.

- We have received No. 2 of the Shingle House *Palladium*, the new five column greenback paper, published by L. H. Bailey. Although the paper is not large, it is well filled with miscellaneous, political and local articles and will greatly assist in bringing Shingle House into prominence.

Oswayo.
Oct. 4, 1880.

Death has again visited our midst with that fatal disease called diphtheria. Jerome Stuart has lost one child and one grand-child, Sidney Lyman two, and Elder Miller one. Our friends have the sympathy of the entire community in their trials.

Roulet.
Oct. 4, 1880.

The woods have donned their holiday attire.

A number of the Rouleters attended the County Fair.

Hugh Burt is very low with Typhoid fever. Dr. J. S. Stearns of Port Allegany is attending him.

Reuben Card has a very neat dwelling house up and enclosed.

The pupils of the select school had a vacation on Friday last, as the teacher, Mr. Hollenbeck, took in the Fair that day.

Query: Who has the fastest horse?

"Stick in the Mud," has changed his *non de plume* and instead of sticking mud, has gone to throwing the same.

Geo. Conley has been visiting in Wyoming county, N.Y.

On the evening of the 27th ult., a large hay barn owned by Leroy Lyman was consumed by fire. About 50 ton of hay and other property was destroyed. Cause of the fire not known.

The Potter Enterprise
Wednesday Evening, October 13, 1880 –
Vol. VII, No. 22

Allegany.
Oct. 11, 1880.

We are having beautiful weather at present, and the farmers are improving it in gathering in the late crops. Weather prophets are already predicting a cold fall and hard winter, but this weather is nice enough and we ought to enjoy it without borrowing trouble about tomorrow.

Three new cases of diphtheria, one in Mr. Cool's family, and two in Geo. James'; all doing well at last accounts. One of C. Ford's little ones is very bad from the effects of diphtheria, it cannot live unless the disease takes a favorable turn soon.

Mr. Judd and his wife have returned from their visit, also Mr. and Mrs. John Peet.

Miss Edith Haskell has gone to Alleghany, N.Y., to attend school.

W. A. Gardner injured a foot slightly while logging.

Last Wednesday W. H. Matteson met with quite a serious accident, he was oiling the threshing machine, and his sleeve caught in the gearing and drew his arm in, crushing it nearly off. Dr's Ellison and Buck amputated it below the elbow. He is not able to be brought home. The accident happened in Hebron. To-morrow his neighbors are to have a bee to dig potatoes, husk corn, gather apples, etc., for him.

Fishing Creek.
Oct. 11, 1880.

Mrs. R. Church is quite sick.

Mr. F. D. Wimer and Perry Manning, of Port Allegany, went to York State to buy cows and came back with 00.

Mr. M. E. Baker has cut a fallow this fall. C. W. Maltby has cut a fallow; so the clearing is still going on.

If the people of Potter and McKean wants beef steak that is pounded before dressing, just come to Fishing Creek and they can be supplied.

- A. G. Olmsted has re-shingled his barn.

- The second kiln of brick on the Gordnier place is cooling.

- M. L. Gridley has removed into his house near the Keystone Mill.

- H. J. Olmsted has his brick building about ready for roofers.

- Owen Metzger's little girl, on Sunday last, fell into an old cellar back of the house, and at first it was feared was seriously injured. Dr. Mattison was called, who upon examination pronounced her not dangerously hurt.

- On Friday last the span of blacks belonging to Rev. Stratton indulged in a run-away. Stone was being hauled from Niles Hill and in loading a stone slipped from the wagon, falling against the heels of the horses. The team is a spirited one and in a very short time were stringing the wagon, leaving a piece here and a piece there. One horse fell down and was drawn quite a distance before the harness gave way, leaving the second horse free to go to the barn. One horse was badly cut up, the other not at all.

West Pike.
Oct. 5, 1880.

This is such an out of the way place there is not much to write.

There is some sickness on the creek. Mr. Impson has a child very sick with diphtheria, last night they thought she could not live until morning. We have escaped this dread disease pretty well so far, but fears are entertained that others will have it now.

Last night we had a lecture at our school house by one Dr. Newton, subject, "Angels and Devils." the Dr. said some very good things.

Ulysses.
Oct. 11, 1880.

Every thing moves off business like in this place.

T. Monroe, son of Charles Monroe, is on the sick list, he is threatened with consumption, his many friends wish for his recovery.

Mrs. Clark Crum is dangerously ill, there is but little hope entertained of her recovery.

Mr. Crum is enjoying good health for a man of age, with the exception of a hard cold.

T. Burt and B. Lewis started for New York with another drove of calves Oct. 8th.

Gather your apples and the remainder of your grain, for there is a heavy storm prophesied.

Keating.
Oct. 9, 1880.

Harvesting is nearly done in this place. Corn and potatoes are a very good crop, though the wire worm did what they could to make them poor, they succeeded in nearly ruining a piece of corn for A. H. Crosby, and have hurt the potatoes in some places.

G. C. Lewis is away from home digging and buying ginseng.

The wife and children of Joseph Coddington have been quite sick with sore throat.

The school taught by Wm. Tassel seems to be a decided success.

The school at the Flechutz school house commences November first, teacher, Miss Josephine Dingee of Coudersport. The one at Keating Summit which was commenced by Miss Nellie Boyington, who had to quit on account of sickness, is now being finished by her sister Miss Mary Boyington.

E. Fournes is building an addition to his house.

H. H. Beebe has moved his family to Coudersport, and his house is now occupied by Mrs. M. E. H. Everts of Homer.

Bingham.
Oct. 11, 1880.

People have been very much interested in the fair at Whitesville for a few days back. A great many attended from this section. There was a great display of all kinds of domestic animals, fowls, all kinds of produce, and every thing else you can think of. It is said there were about 5000 people present.

There was no music except the cry of the man who was calling for men to throw in their money on horse bets.

Diphtheria still lingers in the northern part of this town.

We have had two quite hard freezes of late, but the apples are not injured. People ought not to leave their apples out until the freeze, as they did last year, but gather them in at an early day.

The new church at Jones' Corner is nearly completed.

John Henry and wife have gone to Nebraska to visit their son Andrew.

Thomas Hamilton and wife are visiting relatives in the East.

Wm. Daniels has sold his farm which is a portion of G. Daniels farm to Phill. Lawrence for his uncle. We have not learned his name.

Wake up, ye democrats for Hancock and English. Let your voices echo all through the land. Put down Garfield and his fiendish band.

**The Potter Enterprise
Wednesday Evening,
October 20, 1880 –
Vol. VII, No. 23**

- Forster's second store is up one story.

- The sound of six different steam whistles are heard in Coudersport.

- M. S. Thompson and Stebbins Bros. will be in their new stores inside of our weeks.

- Goodsell is doing a rushing business in cider. Last Monday he made seven barrels.

- Mrs. H. T. Nelson has opened a millinery store at her residence, south side of the river.

Roulet.
Oct. 18, 1880.

The cheese factory closed on Friday last.

Miss Mary Bird of Lymansville is visiting her sister Mrs. R. L. White.

Miss Nellie Boyington is visiting friends in Olean, N.Y.

The Misses Larrabee have returned from their visit in Allegany county, N.Y.

A. L. Cole who succeeds Prof. Hollenbeck in our select school, has some eighteen or twenty pupils in attendance.

There were eight applicants for certificates at the teachers' examination held here the 11 inst.

A. V. Lyman of the firm of White & Lyman has returned from Buffalo, where he has been to purchase their fall stock of goods.

The young people of Roulet had a very pleasant party in Tauscher Bro's Hall on Friday night, about twenty couple participated.

Mrs. Burton lost a little son, aged about 6 years, with diphtheria, on Thursday last.

Millport.
Oct. 16, 1880.

There is a new dwelling house being built in this place by Mr. H. Stannard.

**The Potter Enterprise
Wednesday Evening,
October 27, 1880 –
Vol. VII, No. 24**

Ulysses.

Oct. 25, 1880.

We have been having a foretaste of winter for a few days past.

W. Bishop is moving on his farm in the borough of Lewisville.

Mrs. E. Hacket met with quite a serious accident. She was alone with a horse and wagon when the horse became frightened while turning the corner near Chappel's store. She was thrown out striking on her head and shoulder, and seriously injured, but is now improving.

It is said George Cobb has bought C. E. Hosley's goods and has rented his store.

S. Allen has commenced business in Seth Lewis' new building for Asa Raymond and son.

There is much husking corn, gathering apples, etc., being done while the fine weather lasts.

Mr. Bert Campbell and Miss Sarah Carpenter were united in marriage on the 13th inst. They have the good wishes of their many friends for their future happiness.

The greenback meeting was a success; the speaking was excellent, and the remarks made by Mr. Shear, impressed the people with the idea that he meant honesty, whether in office or out. The day was fine and the band gave us some good music on the occasion, they received many compliments from their hearers.

We were much pleased to see Mr. G. W. Pearsall in our place yesterday. Also our County Supt., A. F. Hollenbeck.

Mrs. Alice Munger has been visiting friends at Haymaker.

Frank Hallet has a new building nearly completed.

- Last week Dal Benson had a tip over near McNamara's. His wagon was loaded with bark, and at this point the forward tier slipped, throwing Mr. Benson to the ground. He clung to one line to stop the team, the result was team and wagon over the bank, with nobody hurt, and no damage except the time and trouble to reload.

Oswayo.

Oct. 24, 1880.

We are glad to state that the diphtheria is about played out in this place, there now being but two cases, these are the children of Sam'l Mayer.

Colman Smith's boy broke his arm while at play the other day. Dr. Turner reduced the fracture and it is doing well.

The republicans of Oswayo got out a Garfield pole some time ago and we hear that next Saturday is the time appointed to raise it.

Township Tidings from Potter County, Pennsylvania
Volume I, 1880 - 1884

Bingham.
Oct. 25, 1880.

Every thing quiet but a few days back gives us warning of an approaching winter.

Business is fair at Bingham Centre and Jones Corners.

We hear of no cases of diphtheria at present, the people seem to be enjoying good health at present.

Mr. Peck has a good assortment of goods and is selling them very reasonably. Give him a call.

Tim Monroe has gone to Arkansas to his brother, Wm. Anson, for his health.

Water is very low in this vicinity, some springs having entirely dried up. Water grist mills can do but little grinding, it is feared that winter will set in before we have heavy rains.

John Henry has written home since his arrival in Nebraska that his son Andrew has raised 1000 bushels of wheat this season and that crops were splendid in that country.

- The Eulalia cheese factory has closed for the season.

- W. W. Dunham has moved into the Will Bassett house – South Side.

- The Rev. Mr. Marshall is to move into the house lately occupied by W. W. Dunham, on Main street.

- Marion VanWegen, of Hebron, has returned from Michigan without any perceptible change in this health.

- The basement of the Graded School has been fitted up into rooms convenient for several students who may wish to board themselves the coming term.

The Potter Enterprise
Wednesday Evening,
November 3, 1880 –
Vol. VII, No. 25

- Frank Neefe is building an addition to his shop.

- We would like a correspondent in each town. To any one who will act as such, we will furnish stationery, stamps and a copy of the Enterprise.

- Last Tuesday Cyrenus Jones exhibited in our office a fine specimen of the Golden Eagle. The bird was shot on Moore's Run by Mr. Jacklin. The eagle measures a trifle over seven feet from tip to tip of wings when spread, and, when alive could have carried off a pretty large lamb without trouble. We believe Cyrenus intends stuffing the bird.

Allegany.
Oct. 29, 1880.

Cold, raw weather these days, but no heavy rains yet, consequently the roads are good for this time of year.

No new cases of sickness in this neighborhood. R. Ford's little child still continues nearly helpless, although they think it is a little better.

Mr. and Mrs. John Matteson have returned from their visit in the West. Potter county hills look high to John at present. He lost a cow by being choked, while they were gone.

Miss Mary Dwight has returned again and all are glad to welcome her home again.

Miss Louise Warner is visiting in Nelson, Tioga county.

Mrs. Neefe and her brother E. Slaughter, went to Texas a few weeks since. Mr. Neefe having gone before to have a home ready on their arrival.

W. Matteson's arm is doing well, and he is so far recovered that he was brought home to-day.

**The Potter Enterprise
Wednesday Evening,
November 10, 1880 –
Vol. VII, No. 26**

- Charles Reissman has purchased the building now occupied by M. S. Thompson, and will occupy it as a furniture store.

Oswayo.
Nov. 6, 1880.

We have a number of cases of sore throats in Oswayo.

W. M. Moyer fell from a stageing and hurt him very bad, but it is thought he will recover.

Will Smith is building a nice new house. He has it enclosed.

Charles Head is also putting up a new house.

The roads are getting very bad in this section.

We are having a very good school here, taught by Mr. Howe.

We are having a writing school taught by Mr. Wheaton, of Tioga county.

Roulet.
Nov. 8, 1880.

Politics for breakfast, dinner and supper, but since the 6th we have had a rest.

Miss Verda Pomeroy is quite sick with diphtheria.

The wind on Saturday night made sad havoc with the fences, it is said that on Sartwell Creek two barns were partially unroofed.

On Sunday morning last, Ora Nell, youngest child and only daughter of Mr. and Mrs. Dan Reed, died of diphtheria. Two other children in the same family are sick with the same disease.

Another one of those pleasant parties was given at Tauscher Brothers' Hall on Friday evening, the 5th.

The Wind.

The severest storm for many years visited this section last Saturday night. From every section we hear of roads blockaded with fallen timber.

On Fishing Creek, the dwelling house of H. Baker was blown four or five feet off the foundation, and an old log house was blown down. Wm. Tauscher's barn was unroofed and considerable other property damaged.

At Coudersport the wind was very strong, and at the Bingham Estate a large tree was broken off, another one was blown down at C. H. Armstrong's and one at the Dent property, foot of Main street. Ellison's smoke stack above town was leveled, and Rounseville's, in the village, fell to the ground and was broken twice. The telegraph wire between Coudersport and the pump station was considerably damaged by several trees falling across it. The staging in front of Stebbins' new store was scattered promiscuously, but luckily none of it struck the plate glass front.

The house at the lower end of town, owned and occupied by James Turner, was blown from its foundation. The building stood on piers, some three or four feet high, and the wind carried it four or five feet north from them. The family was in the house at the time, but escaped without any injury more serious than fright. The house was considerably shaken, but can be repaired.

The Potter Enterprise Wednesday Evening, November 17, 1880 – Vol. VII, No. 27

- Dr. Ellison is putting up a large addition to his mill.

- A. B. Mann has put down a new flag walk from his house to the street.

- Luman Andrews cut his knee with a hatchet last Thursday – just enough to make him limp gracefully.

- Henry Nelson of Coudersport last week killed a pig less than eight months old, which dressed 255 pounds.

- The Corner Store will be lighted with gas, a machine for that purpose having already been put in place.

- New crossings have been put down, on Second street opposite the Court House, and on West street at First.

- Dr. Ellison says we were misinformed as to his smoke stack falling in the heavy wind last week. It "stood the storm."

- The building owned by Farnum Lyon and C. S. Jones is up the second story, and the Masons are now adding the third story for their hall.

- F. E. Lyon, of Sweden, is preparing to remove to Penfield, Clearfield county, to engage in the butchering business. Success to him.

- The post office had a narrow escape from a lamp explosion last Saturday evening. In blowing out one of the lamps fire was forced down into the globe. Fortunately there was no explosion.

- John Burrows of West Branch raised forty-six bushels of ears of Western Dent corn on forty-two square rods of ground. The corn was sound and fully ripe, the stalks growing to the height of ten feet and over.

West Pike.
Nov. 13, 1880.

Election has passed. Every one in this neighborhood good natured.

James Ives has gone in the woods to finish his last year's job. The last of the pine on the Ansley lands.

Some one in this place gets a deer most every day. Yesterday was Robert Gibson's turn, and he got a two hundred pounder.

Amos Baker's little girl, Ruthie, cut her leg very bad the other day, by falling over an ax.

One of Mr. Glover's little girls had the misfortune to get two of her toes cut off with an ax the other day.

M. V. Prouty went to Wellsboro last week, and started for home with two new cook stoves in a lumber wagon. When he got within about two miles of home, he got out to walk and the horses got a little scared and left Mart. He said when he got home he found the horses pretty muddy, the wagon all right, but I guess they will have to sell him another stove over to Wellsboro.

We are looking for better times on Pine Creek in view of a new tannery.

Fishing Creek.
Nov. 8, 1880.

We have had one of the severest wind blows that I ever experienced on the Creek. It blew a barn on the Fred Yentzer farm, now occupied by R. Church, from the underpining, and unroofed one-third of one-half of the barn, the building is 50 by 60 feet.

It also blew a portion of the roof off Mr. Wm. Tauscher's barn, and unroofed a log house for Mr. F. D. Weimer that was filled with hay. Next it struck a log house owned by H. Baker, blowing it down to the chamber floor. The house was used as a store and granery, it also struck a log barn which was used as a shelter for wagons and farming tools, and a portion of it was used to keep hogs in, there were four hogs in it at the time and not one of them was hurt, it struck his house at the southeast corner and blew it off the foundation, moving it to the north three feet, and to the west six feet, starting the roof and doing considerable other damage to the house.

The fences all along the creek were laid low, post and board fences not excepted.

I think there will be quite a number of the young people that will be considerably smaller on account of the wind blow, and the older ones will get gray considerably quicker.

It laid the timber in all directions, laying acres in places.

Genesee Forks.
Nov. 13, 1880.

There does not seem to be much rejoicing over election at this point, which we think is an exception.

Diphtheria which has raged to a great extent here for the past two years, seems to have died out, after filling about twenty graves with its victims, and leaving many homes very lonely.

J. Dimon, our enterprising hotel keeper, with his attendants are always on hand to welcome and entertain the traveling public.

Miss Phoebe Slawson, formerly of this place, now a resident of Stannards Corners, has been visiting friends here this week, but was suddenly called home.

Miss Orissa Hurd, one of our self-made teachers, who has been a resident of this place most of the time the present year, is now attending the State Normal school at Lock Haven, in company with a Lewisville school mate, Miss Addie Douglas. Letters to friends here indicate that they are progressing finely.

D. Freeman is repairing his saw mill.

D. Hackett has bought the mill property at Perryville, and intends moving the coming week.

F. Slawson and family are among us once more. We welcome them back.

W. Whitaker, our industrious blacksmith, is giving good satisfaction. Call and see for yourself.

O. Leech, our carpenter, is building an addition to F. Slawson's house.

Mrs. I Harris has been away attending her father who is very sick.

Miss Nettie Ellis, who was attending school at Ellisburg, came home on account of diphtheria, which is said to be raging at that place.

J. Carpenter has in some new goods.

Mrs. W. Scovel, who has been sick nearly two years, is beginning to look like herself again, still she is not as well as we wish to see her.

S. C. Hurd has a very good assortment of new groceries on hand and a general supply of other goods. We are sorry to learn that the poor health he has been subject to for a long time, is not much improved.

Mrs. Mary E. Crum is engaged in teaching school on the Eleven Mile.

Elder Miller, our new minister, is very much liked.

Miss Bertie Race is attending school at Lewisville.

Miss Josephine Hickox and Miss Hattie Sherman, have returned from visiting relatives at Friendship.

Miss Libbie Arnold is attending school at Sterling Run.

The wind storm blew down a good deal of timber. Two balsam trees in R. Easton's front yard were blown down, which were set out by the mother of Mrs. S. C. Hurd, Mrs. W. Annis, who afterwards moved to the state of Wisconsin, and whose husband marked out the present site of the burying ground, and also made the first improvements on the adjoining farm.

- A mix up of L. F. Andrews' horse and Sumner Olmsted occurred on Monday. The horse reared up, fell over, and pulled Sumner over with him by the halter, and then kicked him up standing again, giving him several severe bruises.

Allegany.
Oct. 29, 1880.

The frozen ground, cold air, and the feathery flakes, that are falling, remind us that winter is approaching, and the fire wood will need replenishing, cellars banked in for the cold weather some think we are going to have by and by.

Election is passed and the farmer is no longer interrupted in his work by the candidate, with the smiling face and cordial hand shake, and I would like your support, etc., etc. If you happen to meet one you did not vote for, he passed you with a cool good morning, sir!

The schools are nearly all provided with teachers. The school at Colesburg is to be taught by Mr. Gridley; at Judd's, by E. Tassell; at Andrews' Settlement, by Miss Lettie Palmer. All to commence the first of December. At the red school house Mrs. Lettie Benton is teaching a fall term, which they have in place of winter school.

Delmar Nelson is home on a visit, through a vacation in the school at Andover.

W. P. Cool is visiting friends and relatives in Wellsboro, Pa.

Miss Ella Graves, of Shongo, is visiting friends here.

William Matteson is still improving. His arm is doing finely and he is able to walk out.

No cases of diphtheria among us at present, but several near Ellisburg.

**The Potter Enterprise
Wednesday Evening,
November 24, 1880 –
Vol. VII, No. 28**

- A. F. Hollenbeck has a new barn.

- The Meat Market will hereafter be located in the Hallauer building.

- J. O. Merrill has purchased the John Denhoff lot, on the Lymansville road, and intends erecting a dwelling and barn thereon, next spring.

- E. B. Tracey has purchased a lot in Ross' addition, and is now looking up lumber with which to put up a dwelling house for his own use.

- This week Dan VanWegen removes to North Wharton, to engage in the work of putting up a new saw mill for the Costello Tannery firm.

- Owen Metzger carries a lame hand, owing to an accident. He was splitting a stick of wood holding the block with his left hand, and as the axe descended the handle struck another stick, throwing the axe to one side, so that the bit struck the back of his hand. The axe was a dull one or he might have cut his hand off.

Oswayo.
Nov. 20, 1880.

Diphtheria still continues around this place.

Mr. Fred Costello is visiting friends in New York City.

Mr. P. C. Reynolds has his new house about ready for the masons.

We were glad to meet our old friends Ort Johnson and Sam Smock of Duke Centre, on our streets the other day. Come again boys.

Mr. J. E. Lee is to have a Thanksgiving party. Those who enjoy dancing cannot do better than to give Mr. Lee a call, for he has one of the best halls in the county.

Ulysses.
Nov. 20, 1880.

We are having very cold weather with a little snow.

We hear of a death nearly every day caused by diphtheria.

Township Tidings from Potter County, Pennsylvania
Volume I, 1880 - 1884

Clark Crum's wife died about a month ago, though he was forty years senior he is able to be around, but not as well as common.

Charles Smith, a son of John Smith, was brought home to his father's in Ulysses and buried in the Lewisville cemetery by the side of his mother who died about ten years ago. His friends and acquaintances deeply lament his untimely death.

Oscar Monroe, a son of John Monroe, whose home is in Wisconsin, is visiting friends in this county. He says his father and mother were enjoying good health when he left home.

John Henry and wife returned from the West a few days ago.

B. Howe has sold his mill property.

Mrs. C. E. Burt is dangerously ill, though there are hopes of her recovery.

There was never so heavy a crop of buckwheat in this vicinity as there is this year. Charles Henry raised 390 bushels. But other grain did not turn out as well when threshed, as people expected it would.

I would say to the democrats, be not discouraged, but try, try again. A government supported by fraud cannot stand.

Genesee Forks.
Nov. 20, 1880.

As we awoke Monday morning, and looked out on the landscape, we beheld "Mother Earth" robed in a mantle of snow. The baying of hounds on the hillside and in the valley, were among the sounds that greeted our ears. The hunters of this vicinity have gone to the "Happy hunting grounds" near Pine Creek, and other localities, among whom are D. Atherton, S. Hurd, E. Buckley and L. Hurd. Undoubtedly the additional snow made their hearts rejoice.

They are drawing in shingle bolts and logs on sleighs. Sleighs and cutters are passing quite lively.

Thursday and Friday, W. Scovel, our cheese maker the past season, carries a daily mail to Brookland. Four stages meet here daily. Two express wagons from Lewisville to Wellsville, and one from West Bingham pass through. Almost the entire load of T. Bishop's last Wednesday, was poultry to be shipped for Thanksgiving.

W. Hickox has done well in the poultry line, raising over sixty geese and turkeys.

S. C. Hurd is buying and shipping poultry.

An imposing procession passed through this place on Wednesday, with the remains of Chas. Smith, one of the victims of the Bordell fire.

Mrs. D. Smith has been very sick with Bradford fever, but is recovering. Dr. Bennitt attended her.

Mrs. F. Slawson has purchased a new Singer Sewing Machine of Agent Reeves.

I. Moses of Bradford, has his office in the store of S. C. Hurd. He repairs jewelry, clocks and watches.

S. Spencer has lost a fine three-year old colt, caused by eating too much wheat.

During the first snow, J. Dimon went out shooting pheasants, killing three but losing two on his way home. We advise him to procure a game bag. We judge he has a very fine bird dog, by the way he brings in the game generally.

P. Kane Esq., has returned to his native land, Ireland, after an absence of thirty years, on a visit, and to look after his estate.

A. Shuts has a new barn nearly completed, 32x44 feet.

The Democrats are wide awake, looking out for a justice and constable and other town officers.

The Potter Enterprise
Wednesday Evening,
December 1, 1880 –
Vol. VII, No. 29

- Nearly everybody is anxious for a fall of snow. There is a large amount of bark to haul, and a great many logs to be brought to the saw mills.

- At the blacksmith shop of B. Rennells & Son, one day last week, Charley Church set 109 horse shoes, and all of them with the exception of perhaps a dozen, were pulled off by him. A big day's work.

- C. L. Peck took his "first sleigh ride of the season" on Thanksgiving day. Near the Baptist church the cutter tipped over, and then he went into a go as you please walking match. Nobody hurt and nothing broke.

Keating.
Nov. 27, 1880.

It is a relief to open the papers once more and find something besides political items.

E. A. Whitney has taken a job of cutting logs for J. Dingee of Keating Summit, and has moved accordingly.

Mrs. E. A. Whitney who has been visiting relatives in New York state for some time past has returned.

E. Fournes has traded his yoke of oxen for a yoke of three year old steers, getting $75 to boot.

Mrs. L. S. Chesbro of Homer, is visiting her son Hale Chesbro at Olean.

The new steam saw mill at Keating had quite a smash up last week in consequence of the log not being securely fastened. The saw was broken, besides some pulleys, bands, etc., fortunately no one was hurt.

Allegany.
Nov. 18, 1880.

The farmers of our land have done something the past season besides talk politics, as witness the millions of corn and wheat now ready for export to Europe, beef and butter, likewise. And Little Potter has done something to swell the pile of butter and cheese sent away, and who makes better butter and cheese than Potter county dairymen?

Some crops in this town are good, some poor, and some variable. This is particularly the case with potatoes, some have a very fine crop and some a very light yield. F. A. Nelson dug 164 bushels from half an acre, H. and F. Hendryx about 300 bushels from one acre; Thos. Hamilton of Bingham has 310 bushels, size of ground not given; while on the farm of Truman Kibbe, were they raised 700 bushels last year, they are having hardly enough for home use; and many in Allegany are in the same condition, one man has none to sell from three acres planted.

F. A. Nelson raised as fine a piece of corn as has been harvested in many years.

Mr. Burdick of Colesburg has the brag parsnip, it measures thirty-two inches in length and is not over two inches in diameter, and over a foot of the length is not much larger than the stem of a common clay pipe. He says he "don't know where it started for."

Genesee Forks.
Nov. 27, 1880.

The first of the week ushered in the coldest days we have yet had. Every one made double quick time filling wood boxes and doing out of door work, being very careful to close the door after them. The vegetables in many of the cellars were chilled, the thermometer standing six degrees below zero.

The remains of T. Webster were interred in the burying ground of this place yesterday. A large procession followed. He was an old resident of this town.

We have secured the services of Rev. T. Perry of Lewisville, for the ensuing year. Preaching once in two weeks at 10 A.M.

The youngest son of N. Chapman is quite sick with diphtheria. Dr. Elliot is attending him.

V. Stannard was suddenly called away on Thanksgiving morning to witness the death of his niece.

Lawyer Curtis of Bradford, made a call at the hotel on the 27th inst., in passing through this place.

Our winter school commences Dec. 6, to be taught by Miss Clara Lewis of Alleghany.

Miss Bettie Race is home on a few weeks vacation.

A little girl came to stay with D. Dunbar Jr. on Thanksgiving.

Mrs. F. Sherwood of Hebron, has been visiting relatives here.

Mrs. J. Dimon has the boss baby of this place.

Thanksgiving passed off quietly in this place.

E. Hackett of Lewisville has moved, and taken possession of his mill property at Perryville.

Mrs. D. Atherton has been quite sick.

J. Smith has moved into our place.

Mrs. R. Easton has very poor health again.

The week has closed with a considerable moderation in the weather.

So far as we have learned, our democratic friends are rapidly recovering from their defeat. Most of them are so as to be about.

S. C. Hurd is still selling goods low for cash. Also J. Carpenter.

G. Caple has lost a very valuable horse.

Ulysses.
Nov. 28, 1880.

We have been having the coldest weather we ever experienced in November. The frost crept into peoples cellars, and nipped their potatoes, apples and everything that was of a freezing nature.

I am sorry to say that Tim Monroe's health has not improved, but on the contrary is worse. He has a desire to return home, and probably will if he lives to get there. 1500 miles is a great ways for an invalid to travel alone.

Mrs. Clarence E. Burt is improving.

Two children of Mr. and Mrs. Dell Crowell were taken from their embrace, by that terrible disease diphtheria. One was two years and a half old and the other but a few months. Those children were their parents joy and delight, and their all.

There are none so brutal as those who turn a cold shoulder to their brothers and sisters, parents and children.

Bingham.
Nov. 28, 1880.

Cold weather still continues, and the coldest weather that November ever brought us before.

There is not much sickness in this vicinity, except diphtheria among the children.

Mr. Thompson of Bingham Centre, buried a little boy a few days ago, and Nov. 25th his only daughter was laid by the side of her brother. She was about ten years old.

Rufus Howe has gone into his store at Bingham Centre. He has sold his saw mill property which was located in that place.

Leroy Merritt, a son-in-law of Ora Thompson, with his wife, are visiting relatives in this town after an absence of seven years. Their home is in Wisconsin, seventy miles in the wilderness, where there are lots of Indians and plenty of wild game, such as bear, wolves, etc.

- A span of colts belonging to F. B. Nelson, of Lymansville, had a lively run-away on Main street, last Monday. Just before reaching the crossing below Stebbins' the pole dropped to the ground, letting the wagon upon their heels, and then the young lad who was driving them and had managed them exceedingly well, lost control of them. In front of the Masonic Hall building the pole struck a pile of brick, throwing the wagon into the air, and turning it over. The driver was not hurt, but his little brother who was with him was hurt considerably about the back. The team and wagon were but slightly injured.

- George Brizee of Oswayo had an ankle badly bruised by a log last Sunday. Fortunately no bones were broken. Dr. Buck rendered medical aid.

- We are informed that one of Mr. Forster's buildings will be occupied by E. O. Rees, who will in addition to his jewelry business put in a stock of drugs and medicines.

Township Tidings from Potter County, Pennsylvania
Volume I, 1880 - 1884

The Potter Enterprise
Wednesday Evening, December 8, 1880 –
Vol. VII, No. 30

- Mr. August Voss has taken charge of the Germania Hotel, and is keeping one of the best hotels in the county. He has issued cards for a New Years' dance, and those who wish for a good time can not do better than to attend.

- On the 30th inst., Hon. Wm. Shear, while assisting upon the walls of the Masonic Hall, had his hand caught in the pulley by which the bricks were being raised, and sustained a severe crushing of his fingers, so badly injuring one finger that it required amputation, and tearing a nail from another.

Fishing Creek.
Dec. 6, 1880.

There is not much news on the Creek.

Otis Lyman has a little girl sick with diphtheria, she is improving.

There has been quite a quantity of logs put in the creek and there will be a larger supply of logs put in this winter than usual if there is snow.

We are having a pretty good school, conducted by Miss Lottie Larrabee, but it takes an unusual quantity of wood to supply the want of the school, not the teachers fault.

Oswayo.
Dec. 4, 1880.

This morning sleighs are flying in every direction. Lumbermen are beginning to move some logs on sleighs.

We notice that Mr. Stillman and Hoare of Yorks Corners are building a steam saw mill on F. Chapman's farm at Ellisburg. Good luck to the people of Ellisburg.

Miss Alice Hendryx of Colesburg is attending school here.

We hear that H. Lord Esq. is to move to Duke Centre.

Our new minister, Mr. North, is liked very much.

They are talking of having a Christmas tree here the 24th of this month.

Diphtheria still rages in this part of the county.

Mr. F. Backus is doing some very nice painting on cutters, this season. Those who are in need of anything of the kind cannot do better than to give him a call.

We were glad to receive a call the other day from Elder Miller of Stannards Corners, N.Y.

Roulet.
Dec. 6, 1880.

M. V. Larrabee wears the belt. Last Friday, while out hunting, he shot and killed three deer, wounding the fourth; without change of position. M. V. thinks it more than luck, all science, and no mistake. Success to him, for he always remembers his neighbors.

Born – To Mr. and Mrs. Earnest Keeler a daughter. Also, to Mr. and Mrs. Elisha Willoughby, a daughter.

D. R. Clark, late operator at this place, is now working in the T.W.P.L. Co.'s office at Williamsport.

William Willoughby lost his two children by diphtheria a few weeks ago.

Died – In Roulet, November 26, 1880, Stewart M'Dorman, aged 31 years. Mr. M'Dorman came from W. Virginia one year ago, for the purpose of working a farm for L. W. Crawford, by hard work he soon lost his health, he was taken with hemorrhage of the lungs, which ended in consumption. At the time of his death he was living in the tenant house of L. Lyman. As soon as his critical condition was known, willing hands did all that could be done to relieve the sufferer, but to no avail. He quietly passed away, leaving a wife and three small children. The town took charge of the remains which were interred in the Roulet cemetery, and on Monday, the 6th inst., sent the family to their friends in West Virginia.

Allegany.
Nov. 29, 1880.

M. A. Velley has been to Cameron, contracting beef, produce, etc.

Dec. 6. – Our sleighing has departed, but we have plenty of ice, too much for comfort.

Yesterday, a little boy, the youngest child of D. Carpenter, who lives in Sweden, was brought to the Ford cemetery and buried, after which the funeral was held at the school house. The child died with diphtheria, he was only sick a few days.

W. A. Gardner is on the sick list. A slight attack of diphtheria and inflammation of the lungs.

W. Cool is attending school at Andrews Settlement.

Girls, this is the last month of Leap year.

The Potter Enterprise
Wednesday Evening,
December 15, 1880 –
Vol. VII, No. 31

- Austin Jacklin, of East Homer, has killed 14 deer the present season.

- W. B. Rees cut the tip of one finger almost off, at his planing mill, last Saturday.

- Last Friday night was the coldest of the season. The thermometer ranging from 8 to 12 degrees below zero.

- A span of young horses belonging to John Earle, of Homer, engaged in a lively runaway on our streets last Friday. No great damage.

- Frank Welton hardly knows whether is best to carry a revolver in his coat pocket or now. A day or two since, in helping about the logway, one of the horses newly sharpened, kicked him on the hip, the calks cutting through his coat, striking the revolver, causing one chamber to explode. The ball tore quite a hole in Frank's coat and pants. Had it not been for the revolver Frank would have been crippled by the calks of the horse's shoe. So far, so good, but whether it is best to run any more risk with pistol balls is another question.

Township Tidings from Potter County, Pennsylvania
Volume I, 1880 - 1884

Allegany.
Dec. 13, 1880.

We are to have a Christmas tree at the Judd school house, every thing seems to be arranged in a systematic manner, even to appointing a committee to get the tree. A pleasant time is anticipated. All are invited.

Miss Edith Haskell has returned from attending school, and to-day commences teaching at Reynolds town.

Mr. E. Tassell does not teach at Judds', but in Roulet.

No teacher hired at this school I believe.

School commences at Colesburg to-day.

Wm. Matteson's arm is not yet well. A. Veeley is boarding there and doing chores.

West Pike.
Dec. 13, 1880.

This is an old fashioned winter so far, minus the snow.

Our roads are in an excellent condition, and have been for two or three weeks.

A little child of Mr. Martin's is very sick with scarlet fever.

Our schools have started. The Genesee Forks school is taught by Miss Evans, the West Pike by Miss Bernhour and the one at Pike Centre by Frank Brown. The teachers are encouraged to do good work by having a uniformity of text books adopted by the directors.

Our tannerymen have one building up, used as a blacksmith shop, and have part of the machinery on the ground for their mill.

Hunters are plenty, and deer too they say, but the hunter and deer seldom meet. Jimmy Foster got one yesterday, but then Jim is not a hunter, he was only out to please the other boys.

The Potter Enterprise
Wednesday Evening,
December 22, 1880 –
Vol. VII, No. 32

- M. S. Thompson has put up a new street lamp at the Postoffice corner.

- Dallas Benson, of Lymansville, killed a porker on Saturday last, that weighed 505 pounds.

Keating.
Dec. 14, 1880.

Herman Bridges of Colegrove is spending a few days a home.

Miss Laura Bridges returned home on Saturday from the Sinnemahoning where she has been teaching for the last five months.

A Christmas tree is to come off at this place in the school house, Christmas eve.

Ulysses.
Dec. 18, 1880.

People have had about all they wanted to do for a few days past to keep warm.

T. Burt's youngest daughter is dangerously ill with fever.

G. Burt stuck a jack-knife blade nearly half of the length into his thigh, while cutting bands for a thrashing machine.

Township Tidings from Potter County, Pennsylvania
Volume I, 1880 - 1884

Bingham.
Dec. 18, 1880.

Diphtheria is still among us, it is taking our little ones from among us in a terrible manner.

Charles Merrick's house was consumed by fire a few evenings since. His household goods were saved.

Fevers begin to break out among us.

Rufus Howe is doing a good business at Bingham Centre. It is said that he exchanges goods for all kinds of produce, even hemlock logs.

D. B. Jackson has fitted over three hundred pounds of poultry for market this season.

- The tinners are on hand and are now putting up the cornice on the Masonic Hall. The brick work is completed with the exception of a little more work in front. The roof is nearly all ready for the tinners. The building is an imposing one; First floor, two stores owned by C. S. Jones and Farnum Lyon, 14 feet between joice; second story, Opera House, 16 feet; third story, Masonic Hall, 14 feet.

- Last week D. F. Glassmire weighed the two heaviest loads of loose hay ever on his scales, which have been up six years. One of the loads weighed 4566 pounds net, the other 4066 pounds net. Both loads were from Emporium.

The Potter Enterprise
Thursday Evening,
January 8, 1881 –
Vol. VII, No. 33

- Morris Lent of Allegany is getting out timber for a new barn.

- Hiram Guernsey lost a valuable horse, on Cross Fork, last week.

- Frank Stevens, for several years employed at the Postoffice Drug Store, leaves for Oswayo this week, where he will open a Drug Store on his own account. Frank is a good druggist, thoroughly understanding the business, and we commend him to the people of Oswayo. Success attend you, Frank.

- A team belonging to Alf. Ayers, of Ayers Hill, ran away last Saturday, starting near Rees' planing mill and stopping on Main street. No damage except to Alf's wind, caused by following the team at a too rapid gait.

Allegany.
Jan. 5, 1881.

The most prominent theme among us is still the prevailing sickness. Many are sick with a sort of sore throat attended with some fever, who do not have diphtheria.

Yesterday the gate of the graveyard was again opened to receive the infant son of Mr. Charles Green, who died on Saturday, the 3d inst., aged two years – but I am not certain whether from diphtheria or croup as both are reported as the cause.

Charles, son of Dan Fuller, was also reported sick yesterday, with sore throat, which may end as some of the others have done.

Mr. A. G. Presho and Calvin Rogers, I learn, have both been quite sick with sore throat, and Mrs. Rodolphus Wells is now sick in a similar way.

The colored man, Rev. Mr. James, preached a very good sermon to us yesterday and is to lecture to-morrow evening on the "Exodus" from the South.

Ayers Hill.
Dec. 28, 1880.

Most of the people about here went to West Homer on Christmas Eve to attend a Christmas tree, which went ahead of anything I ever saw. There were some literary exercises that would do honor to any place, especially the poem by E. S. Tyler, and a recitation by Miss Carrie Bishop, the teacher of the West Homer school. The tree was liberally loaded to the floor, and as near as we could judge, everyone received something, and all seemed to have a first-rate time. The poor were remembered, and the little fellows were very happy; and something I never saw before was the presents all seemed to be of use. These were very few tricks played on any one, and the whole thing was over before nine o'clock. But enough for this time.

Ellisburg.
Dec. 28, 1880.

Notwithstanding the bad roads and bad weather, business is prospering a little here. We have two stores in running order. Thomas Gilliland has a fine stock of goods which he is selling to the neighboring farmers at a rapid rate; also Mr. Orson Ellis is doing a good business.

We have a very good school, taught by Mrs. S. J. Hall.

Our young friend Ed. Tucker is teaching the Raymond's Corners school. Success to you Ed.

As a general thing it is quite healthy here. Mac. Sherwood is on the sick list, Dr. Turner of Oswayo is treating him at present, and we hope he will soon recover.

Oswayo.
Jan. 2, 1881.

The exercise and Christmas tree held at the church here surpassed all expectations. The house was filled early, and quite a number could not get in. The speaking was excellent, the music ditto. The Oswayo Cornet Band rendered some fine music that was a credit to their organization, and last but not least, Santa Claus appeared upon the stage, to the amusement of the big folks and the amazement of the little ones, after a few appropriate remarks he proceeded to distribute the presents, which amounted in value to the sum of four hundred and eighty-one dollars, most all of them were procured at the stores here, which gladdened the hearts of said storekeepers.

The dance held at the Lee House on New Years eve was a success in every particular, ninety couples attended. Campbell's full Band with "Dow" Estes at the organ, and Dickinson with the cornet, opened the ball at dark and quit when the sun rose. Among those present, we noticed J. O. Johnston and wife of Duke Centre,

S. Smock and wife and C. C. Curtis of Bradford, Secretary Fish was there and Gen. Grant was expected, but being unavoidably detained at some other place, sent your correspondent in his place – we have our opinion as how Gen. Grant would be received at Oswayo now. Taken all in all, it was an enjoyable affair, and speaks well for Lee as a landlord.

S. Keller of Hebron, says he has made and sold twelve hundred pounds of butter during this last season, from the milk of eight three-year-old heifers. Who has done better than that?

Millport.
Dec. 28, 1880.

The Christmas tree at this place was a very pleasant affair and was followed by a nice dance at the Hall, with supper at Mr. Hyde's, by the way, many thanks are due to said gentleman for his efforts in preparing the Christmas tree and in making things pleasant for this holiday.

School is going off first-rate, both teacher and scholars doing their best to make our school a credit to the place.

A band dance was held at the Shingle House hotel and was a good thing for the band boys, enabling them to finish paying for their instruments, and was a success generally.

Our place is blessed with good health and is so peaceably inclined that I have no riots to record.

The Potter Enterprise
Wednesday Evening,
January 12, 1881 –
Vol. VII, No. 34

– Mr. Elias Prindle, while riding on a load of hay with "Ebb" Lunn, last Sunday, was very much injured by Mr. Lunn's endeavoring to pass a team, and resulted in the upsetting of his load near Andrew Bradford's on Sunnyside. Mr. Prindle was the only one of several on the load that was injured. He was taken to Mr. A. Bradford's, where he lay some time before he recovered under the treatment of Dr. H. A. Place. – *Shingle House Palladium.*

East Homer.
Jan. 3, 1881.

Seeing no items from this place through the columns of your paper, I thought I would give you a few such as they are.

Ira Haskins has sold out his farm to George Clark, of Wharton, and intends to move in the spring, but he don't know where he is going yet.

The late fall of snow gives the trappers a good chance to see if there is any fox or martin tracks. They are in the woods with their rifles hunting tracks most of the time.

Mr. Austin Jacklin has killed nineteen deer this fall, some of which were very large ones.

Mr. Ira Haskins killed two at one shot, shooting both through the body. They were both full grown deer, and they ran about thirty rods and both fell within four rods of each other. He says he could have killed three, he thinks, if they had been there to kill.

West Pike.
Jan. 3, 1881.

1881 is here with its pleasure for some and its sorrows for others.

Mr. Martin has had two very sick children with scarlet fever.

Ed. Wheaton's house with all its contents was burned to the ground. No insurance. This is a hard blow for Ed., and he has the sympathies of his neighbors.

James Ives has finished his job and moved out of the woods. They finished it with considerable noise for Sunday. If you don't believe it, ask Samuel Brown.

The Gale Tannery Company have their mill frame up and enclosed. They have their engine and other machinery on the ground. It will not be long before they will be making lumber for their tannery.

Weather last week twenty-five degrees below zero.

**The Potter Enterprise
Wednesday Evening,
January 19, 1881 –
Vol. VII, No. 35**

- W. Smith and Myron Rennells, of Oswayo, have each a new house partially completed, waiting for warm weather to be finished. Ed. Daggett is building them, which insures good work when completed. He never turns off a poor job.

Genesee.
Wildcat, Jan. 6, 1881.

E. J. Farnum has commenced a new mill on the site of the old one, but business has stopped until the machinery comes, which is being manufactured McKewen, Bros., Wellsville, N.Y.

C. B. Yager is doing quite a business cutting and hauling logs.

Hauling logs and bark seems to be the chief business in this section of the country.

Prayer meeting Thursday and Friday evenings in this place. On returning home from one the other evening, Mr. Tillburgh met with an accident. As he was groping his way through the woods stumbling over logs and sticks, he had reached nearly half way, when a – no it was not a bear, nor wildcat – but found himself in close contact with a huge hemlock, which demolished his chin whiskers, leaving beautiful and well formed burnsides, that looks very becoming for a man of his size.

W. T. Tracey is riding out with a fine cutter, purchased of W. L. Smith.

M. Crum and H. Hosley were out fox hunting yesterday, killed three foxes in the forenoon. Beat that if you can?

Gold.
Jan. 15, 1881.

The weather continues cold, sleighing good and people in this vicinity are improving it to the best of their ability.

On the evening of the 13th, there was a donation party at the house of Amos Raymond, at which a goodly number assembled, not alone for the purpose of being fed, but also to cheer our pastor with their presence and contribute for the support of the gospel in our midst, a cause worthy of our highest aim. The amount contributed was over one hundred dollars. A table was spread with the best attainable and all seemed to enjoy it with cheerful hearts and all seemed to have a good time.

A. E. Wright has bought a new harness; T. Carpenter a new cutter; M. H. Crumm has killed sixteen foxes, so you see that we are alive and mean to keep the wheel moving in the right direction.

- H. J. Olmsted & Sons are moving into their new hardware store, on Main street. Their new store is large and convenient, and very nicely finished in hard woods. They have a case of 200 small drawers, besides the usual ones under the shelves. A large bolt rack that will hold all sizes and lengths. The counter tops are of red oak and the balance of the counters are of hard woods, ornamented with scroll work. It is elegant enough for a dry goods store. They have a large cellar for oils, a large back room and two rooms up stairs, one of which will be used for the storage of sash doors, etc., and is lighted by a skylight, which also furnishes light for the rear of the store room. A large pulley will raise heavy goods from the rear to the Second floor. Taking it all together, it appears to be all that could be desired for a hardware store.

The Potter Enterprise Wednesday Evening, January 26, 1881 – Vol. VII, No. 36

- Bark and log hauling continue lively.

Lawrence Mills.
Jan. 16, 1881.

Diphtheria and Scarlet Fever are raging here. Miss Delia Grover has been obliged to close her school here on account of being sick with diphtheria. We hope she may soon recover.

Mr. John Ransome has two children sick with the same disease.

Wednesday morning, January 12th, Markie, oldest son of Henry S. and Clara J. Bartoo, fell asleep in Jesus. Little Markie was a sweet child, but only for a short time was he given to cheer the hearts of those who loved him best. The bereaved parents have the heart-felt sympathy of the entire community.

Fishing Creek.
Jan. 20, 1881.

We are having quite an interesting singing school conducted by Mr. Isaac Dingman.

It appears that this winter is a time for accidents and narrow escapes. Mr. Tauscher is having a pretty tough time of it.

On the 17th, H. Baker met with quite an accident. He cut a tree down for a skid to build a skidway with, as it fell it struck a leaning tree, which caused the butt to fly around, striking him on the foot and bruising it so badly that he will have to go on crutches for some time.

Mr. John Yentzer has a lamb which has only one fore leg, and that has three hoofs or toes on it. It is quite lively.

**The Potter Enterprise
Wednesday Evening,
February 2, 1881 –
Vol. VII, No. 37**

- The snow is reported about three feet deep on the hills.

- This time it is N. H. Goodsell who has been interviewing a circular saw. Last Monday he had three fingers on his right hand cut on the end; not serious, but to let the blood flow freely.

- People cannot be too careful with ashes. Last Sunday N. M. Glassmire put some ashes in a wooden tub, and a short time afterward the tub was found on fire, and yet these ashes had been taken from the stove three days previous and until put in the tub had been in a pan out in the snow.

**The Potter Enterprise
Wednesday Evening,
February 9, 1881 –
Vol. VII, No. 38**

- A Masonic lodge will soon be organized at Lewisville.

- The team of J. R. Fessenden, of Roulet, on the 5th of February, drew four separate loads of logs as follows: 1306, 1623, 1571 and 2769 feet, making 7569 feet. Come again Mr. F.

Oswayo.

We are not quite snowed under, but our roads in some places are almost impassable.

We are having a number of cases of measles here at present. The diphtheria has almost disappeared from our midst, for which we are very thankful.

Mr. F. L. Backus has gone into the lumbering business.

Mr. A. T. Smith sports a new cutter.

I understand that Mr. Frank Hendryx is about to enter into co-partnership with Mr. T. Gilliland of the Ellisburg store.

**The Potter Enterprise
Wednesday Evening,
February 16, 1881 –
Vol. VII, No. 39**

Millport.

Feb. 13, 1881.

On Saturday, a team belonging to A. J. Barnes, had been driven up to the store. A little son of Mr. Barnes' was in the buggy, and some mischievous boys chirruped at the horses, frightening them, and away they dashed with the boy, running over a mile before they were stopped. The little fellow held the lines in one hand and clung to the dashboard, making no attempt to jump from the buggy, which shows a great deal of coolness in a boy only four or five years of age.

Raymond.

The donation visit held at the house of Mr. Alanson Crowell's in Allegany, on the 10th, for the benefit of Rev. S. D. Pickett, was a success in spite of bad roads. By persevering efforts the neighbors opened a highway through and around the softened snow drifts. And it would be hard to find better spread tables or a more cheerful company than the occasion afforded.

More than $71.00 was raised and provided for, and each individual vied with the other in making the gathering extremely agreeable.

Mr. Crowell's generosity manifested by opening his house for the occasion, was the subject of much comment and congratulations.

Roulet.

Feb. 14, 1881.

Mrs. John Neother and Mrs. R. B. Lane are dangerously ill.

John Fessenden and daughter of Wis., are visiting friends and relatives in this place.

Died – In Roulet, Feb. 4th, the infant daughter of Mr. and Mrs. R. B. Lane. – On Saturday morning, Feb. 5th, Christian Fisher, aged 81 years. – On Sunday p.m. Feb. 13, Anna Louisa, youngest child of Mr. and Mrs. John Eckert.

Costelloville.

Feb. 11, 1881.

Notwithstanding the cold weather we have had, we are able to say there are none frozen yet (except a few fingers, ears, etc.) but now the rain has put in an appearance, and those who own logs would somewhat enjoy a flood.

Everything is in a flourishing condition in this section, and work is in great demand.

The tannery saw mill will be ready for operation in a few days, and they are now putting up ten or more tenant houses. What we need is a boarding house; the people are crowded in every house with workmen who have no place to board except with private families.

Wm. Burleson moved to his new farm at Roulet, last Thursday. Mr. B. was one of the first settlers here, and he will be missed very much.

M. J. Young has returned from Bailey Run, where he has been engaged in scaling logs for David Pursley.

Mr. Colgrove has moved into the house that A. G. Stewart occupied, and has opened the blacksmith shop. We all regret to lose Mr. Stewart, as we found them to be very kind and obliging people, and we hope they will be happy and successful in their new home at Sharon Centre.

Jacob Peet has recovered from his recent illness, and we see he is at work again.

The teachers' association held at this place went off smoothly, with the exception that there were quite a number absent who were on the programme, but we trust they will all be present at our next, at Nelson Run, and take an active part.

Services will be held at the M.E. Church at Wharton, on the 22d of Feb. by the Rev. W. S. Holland. All are glad to welcome W. S. Holland back from the West, and we hope he will enjoy the forests and mountains of Potter county once more.

Township Tidings from Potter County, Pennsylvania
Volume I, 1880 - 1884

Bingham.

In spite of the cold weather we have kept business moving.

Diphtheria seems to be subsiding in this vicinity.

Leroy Merrit thinks of returning soon to his wilderness home in Wisconsin.

Ulysses.

Business moves off finely in spite of the cold weather, which we have had during December and January.

Fevers are becoming quite prevalent in this vicinity.

Tim Monroe died Jan. 21st, 1881, at the residence of Perry Bingham, in Lewisville, aged twenty-one.

Mrs. William Johnson came from Michigan about four weeks ago to keep house for her father, Clark Crum, until spring.

There has been a great deal of complaining about frozen feet this winter. It makes a good market for rubber boots.

It is said there will be a trotting track made in the borough of Lewisville next summer.

Mrs. Lydia Ann Quimby, daughter of George W. Daniels, died last month aged fifty-four.

I suppose we must have winter until the middle of March, for the old bear came out and saw his shadow on candlemas day.

Result of the band supper, $100.

The Potter Enterprise
Wednesday Evening,
February 23, 1881 –
Vol. VII, No. 40

Oswayo.

Sore throats are quite prevalent in this vicinity, still it does not seem to take the form of regular diphtheria, in many cases of late.

Measles are going through the country at a rapid rate.

Thursday evening, the 17th, a Post of the G.A.R., was organized at Oswayo, to be known as the W. A. Estes Post, in honor of Lieutenant W. A. Estes, killed instantly at the battle of Gettysburg. A very interesting lecture was delivered by the installing officer, to the public generally before the organization of the order. I believe this is the Banner Post as regards the number of Charter member, and I think will eventually have more members than any other Post for miles around. "Long may it wave," is the wish of your humble servant.

I wish to say that the record of "Lieutenant Estes," mentioned above reads as follows: Lieutenant A. W. Estes, Co. H, 2d N.Y. Excelsior, buried in grave 39, Gettysburg Soldiers' National Cemetery.

Allegany.

Feb. 21, 1881.

We have had our share of the cold weather here in Allegany, and will be glad to welcome spring when it comes.

There has been no deaths in our neighborhood this winter, but a few cases of very severe sickness during the fore part of the winter,

Township Tidings from Potter County, Pennsylvania
Volume I, 1880 - 1884

but all are nearly as well as ever again.

Mr. Palmatire has bought the S. Chamberlain farm and moved on to it last week.

Rev. W. Miller has bought the farm known as the Grant farm and is not to live on it. Intends to rent it.

Mr. George Judd brought his bride home, a few weeks since, and the good wishes of all are given them. He is to take charge of his father's farm.

Eva Stryker is quite sick, and Mr. E. Nelson and several others are on the sick list.

Town meeting passed off with the usual amount of wrangling and strife. It is very easy to see a wrong in others but extremely hard to see or acknowledge it in one's own case. A few of our townsmen are great (in their own estimation) and possibly as the years pass, people will recognize the fact.

Sylvania.

P. H. Costello has his saw mill all ready to run, except the saw, and I suppose the hills of Sylvania will soon echo and re-echo with the sound of the whistle of mills and tanneries.

It is quite sickly here with the measles, but no cases fatal.

The recent thaw made the roads quite rough and bad.

West Pike.
Feb. 16, 1881.

I suppose the first thing one should write about is the weather; well, we have had a break up here as elsewhere, the ice which has so long fettered the creek, has floated down a ways and jammed up, and as a result, Pine creek runs in the road some of the way.

The Gale Tannery company have their mill running and are turning out lumber in good shape. They are now putting up their dwelling houses.

Mr. Eastman of Wellsboro, held a magic lantern entertainment at our school house on the 10th of this month. The proceeds went for a library for the West Pike Sunday school. They raised over twenty dollars which will be a great help to the school, and we are very thankful to those gentlemen for the effort they put forth for our benefit.

Our school is closed on account of the measles, Miss Bernhour, the teacher, has gone home and is now very sick with them.

B. B. Wetmore has bought the George Baker farm.

If you want a drink of cider, call on Frank Brown, for it is a girl and weighs ten pounds.

Ulysses.
Feb. 21, 1881.

There was a donation on the evening of the 16th, for the benefit of the Baptist church; their minister is from England, so the supper was after the English order, they also represented the old style of dressing, and some kinds of work, such as spinning wool, flax, washing, etc., all this seemed real besides being very amusing. Geo. Farnsworth dressed in a suit that was in the 1812 war. Indeed a splendid time was realized by all present. Results $100.

Some men are becoming considerably excited over fast horses. Charley Hosley has bought a 2:30 horse, and I suppose there will be more when the track is completed.

Our Graded School will close Feb. 22, with an exhibition in the evening.

Seth Lewis' new building more than fills the space occupied by the old one.

Some people think if the bare ground does not make an appearance soon, much sickness may be expected.

Bingham.
Feb. 21, 1881.

Nothing of importance from here this week. There is not much sickness here at present, but it is feared there will be more when spring opens.

John Henry caught three beavers during his visit to Nebraska, last fall, he brought the skins one foot and a tail home with him to show his neighbors; the tail is about four inches wide and eight or nine long, to handle it seems like handling a piece of heavy soleleather it is free from hair and nearly as black as a coal; he also brought some of the soil of that country, which looks very black and rich.

Stock looks well in this section considering the continued cold weather. There are already a number of new milk cows through the country. Rather tough beginning for dairymen.

D. B. Jackson's hens have produced between 70 and 80 dozen of eggs during the winter months so far.

Galord Crum has got the boss three-year old colts, and he knows it too.

Joshua Thompson, Clark Crum, Geo. W. Daniels and Noah Hallock, are all of the men that are left to the early settlers of Potter county in this vicinity; Mr. Hallock is the youngest, Mr. Thompson and Mr. Crum will both be eighty-five the coming spring, they are neither of them able to be about much.

The Potter Enterprise
Wednesday Evening,
March 2, 1881 –
Vol. VII, No. 41

- Eighteen degrees below zero, as usual, last week.

- C. H. Armstrong has a driven well in his store room.

- Gas was turned on in the stores of Andrews & Olmsted, Olmsted & Sons, and C. S. Jones, last Friday night.

- Charles Breisnick has returned from Keokuk, Iowa, where he has been attending Medical College for the past five months.

- Levi Harris has rented one of Mr. Forster's store rooms, and about the first of April will fill it up with a stock of clothing and Gents' furnishing goods.

The Band Dance.

The first reception of the Coudersport Cornet Band, given on Tuesday evening of last week, was a grand success in every particular.

The Opera House was not so near completion as we hoped for, but the work of the ladies of Coudersport in trimming and festoons, in a great measure, overcame these obstacles. Their work was a work of art, and they deserve great praise.

The music was good, the supper one of the best ever spread in Coudersport. Everything passed off without a jar, and so far as we know no one complained of anything.

One hundred and two tickets were sold. The next evening the Band gave an oyster supper, at 50 cents per couple, and by this means increased their profits to about $100. We trust the Band will give another ball in the near future.

Allegany.
Feb. 28, 1881.

Appointments were given yesterday, for evening meetings this week. The meetings were quite well attended last week considering that some were away, and others sick. Five were taken in full connection with the church yesterday, and two weeks ago yesterday eleven joined, which adds a little to the church here.

Eva Stryker is a little better.

H. Peet has diphtheria but is gaining now.

Several are complaining of sore throats.

Last winter people said that an open winter was so unhealthy, and this winter they say it is so very cold, no wonder so many are sick, nothing more than we may expect. The weather is always blamed for our carelessness.

The snow went very fast yesterday and last night, but this afternoon is cold again, so we may expect more ice.

Costelloville.
Feb. 24, 1881.

Measles seem to be the principle traveler in this section, and most people are quite unwilling to shelter them.

The weather is quite changeable of late, but we hope it will not turn cold again, until we have enjoyed some pleasant weather.

Our school, taught by L. D. Ripple, will close in about six weeks; and judging from the good attendance of the pupils during these six months, they will be glad of a rest.

John Brownlee and Sons, are getting in logs, and are having their mill repaired, calculating to commence business in a short time.

P. H. Costello has started his new saw mill, intending to do great business and make this valley ring with its music.

Mr. Costello has four dwelling houses commenced and intends putting up sixteen more. They have also commenced getting out stone for the store.

Rev. W. S. Holland did not get here on the 22d, as he advertised. Perhaps on the account of the railroad blockade.

Sleighing is excellent with plenty of snow, and the teamsters are improving it in drawing logs to the banking.

The Potter Enterprise
Wednesday Evening,
March 9, 1881 –
Vol. VII, No. 42

- Mr. H. B. Keihle, of Coudersport, is studying medicine with Dr. Hogarth in Port Allegany.

- Abram Jones has leased his dwelling to Mrs. McCormick and will remove to his farm in Wharton township.

- Two new houses are showing up east of the river – one owned by Enoch Tracy and the other by Wm. Yunge.

- Ed. Jeorg, of Kettle Creek, will soon remove to a point near St. Louis, to take charge of some trout ponds. We wish him success in his new home.

- Cyrenus Jones fell near the store of C. S. Jones, Monday evening, dislocating his shoulder. Dr.'s Mattison and Breisnic rendered medical and surgical assistance.

Keating.
March 7, 1881.

Our six weeks of sleighing in March has commenced in earnest, and we begin to wish that the 2d of February had been less fair.

Business has been lively, especially hauling. A large quantity of cherry logs, ties, etc., have been drawn from here to Keating Summit.

C. W. Dingee's family has the measles.

The school at Keating Summit has been closed on account of measles.

The Potter Enterprise
Wednesday Evening,
March 16, 1881 –
Vol. VII, No. 43

- James and A. Johnston have purchased the blacksmithing tools and the shop occupied by George Brehmer on Second street, and are ready to do work for all who come.

Eleven Mile.
March 12, 1881.

This most quiet of valleys seems to have gone to sleep quite. Maybe its inhabitants do not wish to disturb their common Mother's annual rest. However, a few days of warm sunshine may, while melting away the icy chains and snowy coverlet of earth, serve to quicken the dormant life of the animal kingdom.

In former years, the winter season here was of the busiest, two steam mills were kept actively at work manufacturing the choicest of pine logs into lumber, thus requiring the labor of scores of men and teams to stock them from the surrounding hills, and other scores of the same were employed in hauling the lumber to Wellsville, where the cars were laden and quickly conveyed it to the markets of the East. Now the little choice pine left, is being rapidly cut and rolled and slidden and floated away from our borders, only a few hundred acres left of what, if it was left intact, would be deemed the very cream of the soil.

But alas, it is with our noble forests as with their former owners who hunted game in their wilds. Civilization in its advance has swept them from existence, or nearly so, and perhaps a generation hence may deem it as great a curiosity to see a specimen of the graceful pine, as to interview "Lo the poor Indian."

Bingham.
March 14, 1881.

Business fair.

There is considerable sickness about Bingham Centre.

We all as one are hoping for warm weather soon.

Farmers begin to talk about tapping their sugar bushes.

The snow is about two feet deep in the woods.

E. Ludington is going to build a large barn this season.

No one can tell as yet how winter wheat will come out.

Raymond.
March 8, 1881.

Death is doing a fearful work in the south part of Allegany township. Three deaths in less than a week; and yesterday another. Diphtheria has taken two children from the family of Anson Weaver, and two more very sick.

The family of Nelson Monroe are also very sick with the same.

A lad belonging to the Raymond Sunday School has found that there are as many words in the Lord's Prayer as there are books in the Old and New Testament. How many Sunday School scholars will tell their teachers next Sunday how many words in the Prayer and how many books in the Bible?

Fishing Creek.
March 12, 1881.

Mrs. H. Maltby met with quite an accident the other day, while trying to drive a nail it flew and hit her in the eye, nearly putting out the sight. She cannot do anything in the way of work at present.

The people of the Creek made a wood bee for the widow Maltby, they cut and hauled about twenty cords of wood for her, so she will not have to freeze for want of wood.

Miss Ida Baker goes to Coudersport to attend school the spring term, commencing March 14.

Shingle House.
March 7, 1881.

Last week Mr. Burdick and his wife, aged people whose home was at East Sharon, died within a short time of each other, and were buried at the same time.

Snow till we can't rest, and the hay lots getting thin.

Lumbering done and what shall we do next?

Allegany.
March 14, 1881.

Our winter weather still goes marching on, with but little appearance of spring.

Farmers, some of them at least, are looking with long faces at their fast disappearing hay-mows.

The school at Judd's school house, taught by Mrs. Ingraham closed last week.

Mr. and Mrs. G. W. G. Judd and Miss Mary Dwight start to-day for Ill., to attend on the 17th inst., the fiftieth anniversary of a sister's marriage.

Delmar Nelson works for Wm. Matteson through sugaring, he commenced two weeks ago, and no sugar made yet.

Mr. A. Haskell is coming to live among us, he has bought Ed. Haskell's interest in the farm owned by both, and has commenced moving.

Geo. Reves is the happy man – a fine girl added to his family.

Ulysses.
March 14, 1881.

Pneumonia is quite prevalent in this vicinity, nearly every day we hear of a death from it.

Measles have broken out among us, there was a boy came down with them in the graded school the other day.

Clark Crum is about to sell out and give up business and live with his children.

Business is passing off in a prosperous way.

Winter seems loath to leave us.

Fodder holds out well in this vicinity, we hear no one complaining yet.

George Burt had a fine cow die in good flesh by getting one of her legs hung between two logs and falling into the water, chilling her legs so she had no use of them.

The other day I heard a man eighty-five years old say that last winter was the warmest winter he ever knew and this is the coldest.

Lymansville.
March 12, 1881.

Active preparations are being made this winter for early work as soon as the weather will permit.

Since the close of 1880 many improvements have been; J. M. Covey has completed a large addition to his barn on his farm here; Mortimer Benson has just finished a house 22x32, two stories high; S. F. Butler has a neat little Gothic dwelling well under way; L. A. Glace has made some improvements by adding two verandas to his house.

J. Glace with the assistance of Mr. L. Bennehof are finishing off living rooms in the cheese factory, for the use of the cheese maker's family, Mr. Glace having secured the services of Mr. Bennehof to run the factory the coming season. A liberal patronage is looked for.

Our place has been thrown into no little excitement by the arrival of a notorious female, known by the name of May Lawrence, and who is at present stopping with a resident here, and if we are obliged to have such here may her stay be short. What the end of this may be we know not, but if rumor mistakes us not, a storm is gathering in the near future.

The Potter Enterprise
Wednesday Evening,
March 23, 1881 –
Vol. VII, No. 44

- Mr. A. Keihle & Son have rented the blacksmith shop owned by W. B. Gordnier, south of the river, and solicit a share of the patronage. Give them a call.

- T. Gilliland has been appointed Postmaster at Ellisburg.

West Pike.
March 15, 1881.

Most of the lumbermen along here have got their logs on the bank.

Samuel Brown got quite badly hurt the other day by getting his foot between a couple of logs.

S. H. Martin has sold half of his farm to J. M. Kilbourne.

Bingham.
March 18, 1881.

I believe there has never before been a time when our schools were so generally and seriously interfered with by the ravages of disease as during the past winter.

Miss Grace Lewis is very sick, caused by being too studious and by the measles. She has been in attendance at Alfred University for some time.

There are a few complaining of colds, and every now and then a light case of croup, but the general health of the community is better than for some time past.

The North Bingham cheese factory is to start March 21st.

New maple sugar and syrup is beginning to tickle the children's palates in this vicinity.

Costelloville.
March 17, 1881.

Spring has again put in its appearance, and people now look forward to warm weather.

The measles are somewhat abated, but people are now contending with severe colds.

Our school having had a vacation of one week on account of the teacher having to attend court, re-commenced Tuesday.

Services was held at this place last Sabbath by the Rev. W. S. Holland. He will continue to preach every two weeks.

The new mill is doing good work now, and the carpenters are, each day, making this place look more like a village.

We hear that P. H. Costello intends to erect a telegraph line soon, reaching from this place to Keating Summit.

Allegany.
March 20, 1881.

At length Spring asserts her rights, and Winter yields a little of its power.

The fields are nearly bare, and the snow has softened so that farmers have got their sugar utensils in the woods, and a few have tapped their trees, but not much sugar made yet, they say the sap is very sweet. Last year it took a good deal of sap for a little sugar.

W. M. Slaughter had the misfortune to break one of his horse's legs last week, obliging him to kill the horse. It was one of a span of good work horses.

Another family added to our community. Mr. Beebe has moved on the Grant farm, the house has been unoccupied for the past year.

Several children are sick with sore throats.

Miss Edith Haskell commences teaching a term of school at Reynolds to-day. She commenced a term there last winter, and was obliged to leave it, owing to a very

Township Tidings from Potter County, Pennsylvania
Volume I, 1880 - 1884

severe attack of sickness. Edith is a first-class teacher, and may success attend her now.

The Potter Enterprise Wednesday Evening, March 30, 1881 – Vol. VII, No. 45

- Mrs. John Matteson, of Allegany, slipped and fell one day last week, dislocating her wrist and cracking one of the bones. Dr. E. S. Mattison rendered medical aid.

West Pike.
March 26, 1881.

Again we hear the welcome notes of the bluebird and robin.

The flood has come and the boys have gone as far as the mouth of Marsh Creek; water so low they had to stop.

Two of Wm. Smith's children were buried in this burying ground last week – one Friday night and one Saturday night, both after dark, something which never happened here before. They died with diphtheria. Others are sick in the same family with it, but hopes are entertained that they will recover.

J. M. Kilbourne has moved on the farm lately purchased of S. H. Martin.

Orm Blackman is the happy man this time – the first daughter – why shouldn't he be? Georgie says it is nicer than the twin lambs.

Frank Brown finishes up his school at Pike Centre to-day.

Lymansville.
March 26, 1881.

Genuine winter weather is the ruling element yet. March came in according to the old saying, like a roaring lion, but to all appearances now, is going out a howling menagerie.

The general health of this place has been good during this winter. We hear, by correspondents in both county papers, of much sickness, especially with diphtheria and scarlet fever among children.

The last sensation here was the arrest of the constable for making illegal returns to court, the plaintiff being the individual returned for selling intoxicating liquors. He repented of his evil ways and entered complaint against the constable for not returning him sooner. The constable, rather than languish in the gloom of the bastile, entered bail for his appearance at court. If all sellers of the vile stuff in Potter would repent likewise, intemperance will soon vanish from existence.

Ellisburg.
March 28, 1881.

Our school taught by Miss A. L. Jones, of Corning, N.Y., has just closed with an exhibition and concert in the evening. Coats Brothers and Slingerland and Westcott rendered some very fine music for the audience.

Ellisburg is still improving. We have two stores kept by T. Gilliland & Co. and O. Ellis, and both doing a fair business. We have also two blacksmith shops.

Manufacturing lumber is one of the leading industries. Two saw mills running now and another large steam mill nearly completed, with one million feet of logs to start on.

Mr. Orson Ellis is on the sick list, but is improving under the care of Dr. Turner.

Mr. R. Ellis and family have left their former place of residence to reside in Lewisville.

Mr. F. Hendryx has taken up his abode in this place.

Genesee Forks.
March 28, 1881.

A. A. Hickox takes possession of the Baker farm. George Barlow has returned from the village to his farm. George Hornsby takes possession of the Tooke lot. F. Slawson is about to move to Niles Hill in the Wellsville oil district. E. L. Fuller moves on to his farm in Bingham township. B. G. Kaple has returned and taken his old place as foreman for John Carpenter.

The Potter Enterprise Wednesday Evening, April 8, 1881 – Vol. VII, No. 46

- Joseph Lent, of Hebron, has removed to North Wharton.

Costelloville.
April 9, 1881.

The snow has nearly disappeared, making it look quite spring-like.

Columbus Rees met with a heavy loss last Thursday afternoon. His house and most of his furniture, together with all the provisions, were destroyed by fire, leaving them homeless, but we hope not friendless. Each one should do as they would like to be done by in such a case. They do not know how it took fire, but perhaps it caught around the chimney.

Sickness is again paying us a visit. James Glaspy is quite low with the fever. Mrs. Thomas Rees is quite ill. She had the measles some time ago, and they left her very poorly. Oscar Rees has been very sick with the measles.

Hugh Young is the man who steps high now – it's a boy.

Sylvania.
April 7, 1881.

Sugar makers will have to throw up the sponge and call it a bad job.

Hay is getting very scarce here in this section, folks with large stocks of cattle look kind of sober.

C. C. Rees' house was burned to the ground this afternoon. The men folks were away from home, but J. M. Rees and some others saw the fire and reached it in time to partly save the furniture. No insurance.

James Glaspy has been quite sick, and is still so, with a fever.

Moving appears to be the order of the day. John P. Havens and family and Ira Haskins and family have all moved to Costelloville to the tannery. George Clark, of Wharton, has moved on the place he bought of Ira Haskins.

Costello's steam saw-mill is doing fine business.

Some of the schools have started up again for the spring term. The Rees school is taught by Miss Wells, from Sharon; the Wykoff school by S. B. Haskins.

Raymond.
April 3, 1881.

In some towns of this county it has been, and is, the custom to pay all the teachers the same wages, irrespective of their qualifications or the amount of work they have to do. The teacher having forty scholars is paid no more than another who has but six. The teacher of the best qualifications is paid no more than one who can but just get a school. Now, for one, I would like to get a little information on this matter. Why is it so? What is the necessity for such a regulation? If this were the general custom throughout the state, what encouragement would there be, so far as pay is concerned, for one to spend time and money to become a well qualified teacher? And if this is a good plan for schools, why would it not work well in other kinds of business? Let the farmer give the same price for a poor hand as for a good one, and an unskilled mechanic – a mere beginner – let him have the same wages as the very best. But it is quite evident that such a way of rewarding labor cannot prevail in other occupations. Why, then can it work good for our schools? Perhaps some one will give some light on the matter.

Oswayo.
April 10, 1881.

The measles seem to be the order of the day in Oswayo at present, but no cases have proved fatal.

Jack Doyle has sold his house and lot to the Widow Kenyon; consideration $1,000.

Moving seems to be about as contagious as measles; quite a number have changed houses in the past week.

Charles Head has his new house about completed.

Mrs. Coleman Smith, who has been sick with rheumatism for the past few weeks, died very suddenly Monday about one o'clock. She left many friends to mourn her loss, besides her husband and two children. She was loved by all who knew her, but we feel our loss to be her gain.

Hebron.
April 9, 1881.

The people are anxiously waiting for sugaring. Some have their trees all tapped and some only part of them, but no sap yet.

Otis Lyman has purchased the mill property of William Frink and commences repairing the mill next week.

Mr. E. D. Ayers had the misfortune to lose one of his horses last week.

Russel Stillman has traded his oxen for a span of horses; so there may be some fast riding now, young ladies. See who may be first.

Joseph Lent has moved to Costelloville.

William Razy will occupy his farm the coming season.

Millport.
April 10, 1881.

The farmers of Millport say their fodder is getting a little short, and are looking a little anxiously for spring weather.

Mr. and Mrs. Jasper Card have a son, weight eight pounds. The mother is doing well as can be expected. Jasper's smile is broader than usual.

An old gentleman by the name of Potter died a few days since at the place known as the Wildcat district. He was poor and old, and ill treated by those who should have used him with respect.

Dennis Carpenter has sold his farm to a gentleman by the name of Strait.

Miss Jennie Pauson has returned to Millport, after teaching a four months' term of school.

Moses Kemp has a little son quite ill.

Mr. Daniel Dodge, of Sharon Centre, has been very sick, but is getting better slowly.

North Bingham.
April 8, 1881.

We have to record for April, 1881, a heavy fall of snow and roads drifted as bad as at any time during the past winter.

A few more cases of diphtheria in town.

Mrs. John White, of White's Corners, died last Sunday afternoon, at a very advanced age. The funeral service was on Tuesday.

Mrs. Coleman Smith was buried at Oswayo on Tuesday last. Deceased had relatives in Bingham township.

Miss Ida B. Kibbe has been quite sick, but is gaining.

Mrs. A. P. Kibbe is very feeble; cause, lung and liver difficulty.

Mrs. D. T. Hauber has been quite seriously indisposed for some time past, but is better.

Wm. Clark (recently married) appears to enjoy life and labor better than ever.

The cheese factory is doing finely, making three large cheese per day, and most of the milk is hauled on sleighs. There are nearly fifty large cheese on hand.

E. L. Fuller is moving back from Genesee Forks on the old place.

Mr. H. H. Cobb, of Spring Mills, has moved to Ulysses and is studying medicine.

Genesee Forks.
April 11, 1881.

Hall of Genesee Forks Lodge K. of H. No. 2016.

We had the pleasure of meeting at our lodge room on Saturday evening, April 9th, N. H. Roe, the father of the late Dr. L. E. Roe, in whose behalf the appeal for aid was made, and we had the pleasure of passing into his hands the sum of $216.00, which was very thankfully received by him. We have the very best of evidence that Mr. Roe is very needy and depends upon his own efforts for his support since the death of his son. Upon the receipt of the money, the old gentleman was completely broken down, but as soon as he could control himself he made a very appropriate address, which would have melted the stoutest heart. He thanked us over and over again, and as he passed out of the room his last words were, "God bless you, and my the order prosper."

Yours in O.M.A.,
Ira E. Easton, Dictator.

Dr. L. E. Roe was one of those signing the petition for the Genesee

Township Tidings from Potter County, Pennsylvania
Volume I, 1880 - 1884

Forks Lodge. The night the lodge was organized he was at the bedside of a diphtheria patient, and would not leave to take the degrees, and before another meeting the doctor was a corpse, his death resulting from diphtheria contracted at the bedside of the patient he was called to see the night the lodge was instituted. A statement of the case was recently sent to sister lodges, and the response will be learned from the above.

**The Potter Enterprise
Wednesday Evening,
April 20, 1881 –
Vol. VII, No. 48**

- R. Howland has opened a gun shop in the second story of B. Rennells & Son's blacksmith shop.

- Coudersport was dull last week. The farmers being engaged in the sugar bushes, did not leave home unless compelled to.

- Orlando Duel has returned to farming in Sweden township, after spending a year or two in the blacksmithing business at Eldred.

- The town council appointed A. G. Olmsted street commissioner, W. B. Rees fire marshal, C. S. Jones treasurer, and Harrison Koon pound master.

- Olmsted & Sons tin shop is turning out a large number of cans to be used in shipping maple syrup, many of our farmers having learned there is more money in syrup than sugar.

- Charley Neefe sold twenty-five gallons of maple syrup, at one dollar a gallon, in Coudersport last Thursday. Others probably sold as much, and it is safe to say it was a general time of sweetening up.

Pleasant Valley.
April 16, 1881.

Sugaring is the order of the day and the prospects are very promising for a good season.

Elmer Deming is preparing to build a new house the coming summer.

Hay is getting scarce here and but little will be summered over.

Allegany.
April 18, 1881.

Sugar makers have had plenty of business for the past week, some boiling night and day, and then not saving all the sap. Generally speaking sugar is of a much better quality than was made last year.

Norman Cool has gone back to Michigan to finish learning his trade, carpentering.

Mr. and Mrs. G. W. G. Judd have returned home from their visit in the west. Also, Mrs. N. Dwight.

Sore throats not all well yet.

Rather small attendance at Sabbath school yesterday, sickness and bad roads kept some at home. Wonder if that was the reason for so many being absent.

Ellisburg.
April 18, 1881.

Sugarmaking has been the order of the past week. Those who were making have been kept busy day and night.

The firm of Gilliland and Hendryx have put up an addition to their store 20x26, up and enclosed, to be used as a dwelling house.

Dr. Ashcraft of Westfield, Pa., has located at Ellisburg. We wish the Doctor success.

Stillman, Hoard & Wilson have their new mill about ready to start and soon the sound of the whistle will denote that business has commenced.

**The Potter Enterprise
Wednesday Evening,
April 27, 1881 –
Vol. VII, No. 49**

Allegany.
April 25, 1881.

Colesburg is left without a grocery. William Slocum having moved to Roulet.

H. Haskell's house came near burning last week. It caught on the roof and burned a hole through, but was discovered by a neighbor in time to save the house.

F. Mattison has returned home from the oil region.

L. Slaughter is home from his teaching at Hebron.

W. A. Gardner is preparing to build a horse barn.

Wilbur Slaughter is building an addition to his barn.

Some have gathered in their sugar utensils and are commencing Spring work. Mr. Slade has taken the lead in sowing grain here, as he put his in last week.

Genesee Forks.
April 25, 1881.

Services every Sunday by Rev. Mr. Perry or Miller, are held in the new school house, one of the best in the county.

Three vacant dwelling houses. Mr. F. Slawson has moved back to the oil region on Niles Hill. J. Smith has moved on the farm of J. Atherton. G. Hornsby has rented Leache's house; he has a good assortment of goods on hand, give him a call. J. Carpenter has in new goods, Mrs. T. D. Harris and brother have returned from Rue City; I. D. Harris came with them. Mr. E. Capple has bought the Hackett lot at Perryville at three hundred dollars and taken possession. Mr. G. Slawson has moved to Chemung, N.Y. Mr. P. Lewis has taken possession of the O. Leach lot; also Mr. A. Hickox of the W. Baker farm.

Miss Hannah Hurd closed her school last Friday, and has come to stay with us a short time.

S. C. Hurd is about to raise his new barn.

- D. F. Glassmire has put down a good sidewalk along his property on the west side of Main street.

- Joseph Forster is again back in his wagon shop and is ready to repair wagons and carriages on short notice. Good timber and good work every time. Give him a trial.

- Second Street was the scene of a lively runaway last Tuesday afternoon. A team hitched to a lumber wagon, belonging to Mr. Randall, of Hebron, started from near the mill; this side of the bridge they ran into Isaac Benson's platform wagon, bending the rear axle until the wheels nearly touched under the wagon. Neither Mr. Randall's nor Mr. Benson's team was injured.

Costelloville.
April 23, 1881.

The roads are getting dry, and farmers have commenced their work. A few have put in their oats.

Ellis Moore, who has of late been a resident of this place, was drowned at Moccason Falls, near Keating, Clinton county, the 19th. He had been employed by David Pursley since last Fall cutting logs, and went on the drive when the logs went out. He was working with the teamsters, and when the Falls were reached he with three other men were going over in a boat in which they carried their tools. As the boat touched the water below the Falls it filled with water and sank, leaving its occupants to swim ashore through the rapids. The other three men reached the shore all right, but Moore became exhausted, and his body sank. It has not yet been found, but they are searching each day, hoping they may some day find the lifeless form. It is a great bereavement for his mother to bear, he being her only child. He was drowned within four miles of where they came from. His mother starts this morning for the place where he was drowned.

Business is lively in this place now, about eighty men are in P. H. Costello's employ. This is growing to be quite a village already.

Freeman's Run.
April 21, 1881.

The snow has nearly all disappeared and the young grass looks quite fresh and green.

Warm sugar tastes pretty good just now, especially to those who do not make any.

C. A. LaMonte is helping Arch Turner make sugar this Spring. They have made about three hundred pounds.

Harry Austin is doing good work in his sugar bush.

Fishermen are not very plenty this Spring, owing to the cold weather. Haven't seen more than half a dozen trout this Spring.

E. O. Austin's health has been very poor the past winter, but we are glad to state that he is improving.

I believe that Frank Austin has adopted the little stranger who came to his house a few days since –it's a girl.

Mrs. Anna Morris is visiting her sister, Mrs. John Vannater.

L. D. Ripple's school closed on Wednesday last, with some very good compositions and declamations by the pupils.

Eleven Mile.
April 15, 1881.

The oldest inhabitant says this is the hardest winter of his remembrance, at all events, the longest.

Measles are getting more scarce. Some cases of diphtheria are reported. That name will cause a shudder when spoken in the homes of those it has bereaved.

Sugar makers have made another "taste" the past week.

Ulysses.
April 25, 1881.

Sugar-making has been discontinued for this season, nearly all the sugar tools are gathered in. There has been about nine days run and in that time A. Bice made about 600 pounds from 130 trees - $60 in nine days.

There are some snow banks in sight yet, but the warm days will soon melt them away.

John Miller is dangerously ill, and there is not much hopes of his recovery.

Diphtheria is still in the land; Alonzo Mustoe buried a little girl last week who died from this terrible disease.

Some pieces of winter wheat are not looking as well as last Spring.

Farmers begin to talk about sowing grain. Pastures being to look quite green though they have not been sprinkled with rain. The highways are dry and dusty. Fodder holds out well in this vicinity, we hear of no cattle starving to death as some prophesied.

The Potter Enterprise
Wednesday Evening,
May 4, 1881 –
Vol. VII, No. 50

- The Masonic Lodge at Lewisville will be organized May 12th, by District Deputy Grand Master Wheeler.

- D. F. Glassmire has sold his livery stable to Amos Velie, and is now debating whether the will go to Shingle House and become an oil prince, or go to Kansas and grow up with the country and negro exodusters.

Roulet.
May 2, 1881.

Charles Johnson, of Owego, N.Y., is visiting his son, A. W. Johnson, of this place.

Peter Chastain and L. B. Yentzer are having their dwelling houses painted.

A. W. Johnson has moved into his house, recently occupied by R. B. Lane, and is having it painted and plastered.

Ezra Sands and wife have moved to Hancock, N.Y.

There was a sugar party and dance at Tauscher's hall, Friday eve. Forty couples participated.

The summer schools commenced in this place to-day, with the following named teachers. Centre school, Carrie Saunders; Reed's, Sarah Cary; Card Hollow, Christia Kimm; Linegar Creek, Gertrude Boyington; Fishing Creek, Mary Brown; Smith's, Laura Larrabee, and Trout Run, Amy White.

The Potter Enterprise
Wednesday Evening,
May 11, 1881 –
Vol. VIII, No. 1

Ulysses.
May 9, 1881.

We are having very fine growing time. Farmers are improving every moment the best they can. There have been a great many bushels of grain put in the ground the past week.

Township Tidings from Potter County, Pennsylvania
Volume I, 1880 - 1884

J. Hawley is building him a house. His cellar is nearly completed.

John Miller has been dangerously ill for about three weeks. There are hopes of his recovery.

Clark Crum, though 85 years old, intends to visit his friends and relatives in Tompkins county, N.Y., next month. He has a young horse and a new buggy nearly done, which he intends to go east with, as he dislikes riding in the cars.

We have no cases of diphtheria at present.

Cobbs are becoming quite plenty in Lewisville. I don't mean corn-cobb, but four brothers, nephews of William Cobb, are residing in town at present.

The highways are dry and dusty.

Winter wheat came out better than was expected.

Business is progressing rapidly in this place; never better. People are getting the railway on the brain this way. Nothing will cure them but the sight of the engine puffing through this country.

Allegany.
May 9, 1881.

Beautiful Spring weather, and farmers are all improving it.

Two weeks from yesterday, or the 21st and 22d of May, there is a quarterly meeting to be held at the Judd school house. School commenced there last week, taught by Miss Hemple. Miss Bell Haskell commences the school at Colesburg to-day.

- Bark peelers are putting in an appearance looking for summer's work.

- E. N. Woodcock, of Lymansville, goes to Kalkaskia, Mich., where he expects to remain until Fall.

- Burt Strong had a leg badly bruised from the foot to the hip by having it caught between a log and a stump on the side hill. Dr. Buck is attending his case.

West Pike.
May 5, 1881.

Farming is the order of the day here.

George Vincent is putting in oats on S. H. Martin's land.

J. M. Kilbourne is finishing off the house he lately bought of S. H. Martin.

S. J. Acker, of Allegany, is putting up a store at the Genesee Forks.

Frank Brown bought a horse of J. Ives this week. This makes two four-year old colts Mr. Ives has sold this spring.

We expect to hear the sound of the ax soon, as there are several bark jobs let near here. No trouble for men who can peel bark to get work here this summer.

The people of this place organized a Sabbath-School here last Sunday. E. F. Turck as Superintendent.

The Gale tannery company are putting goods in their new store. They have twelve dwelling houses built, and are now at work on their tannery buildings.

Township Tidings from Potter County, Pennsylvania
Volume I, 1880 - 1884

Costelloville.
May 5, 1881.

We are having some very nice weather. The leaves have started on the trees, grass is growing rapidly, and everything seems to be in a prosperous condition.

The brick makers have commenced making brick. They made some this week for the first.

The bark peelers are making great preparations for peeling bark, and soon the forests will be dotted with their camps.

The cellar wall for P. H. Costello's store is nearly finished, and will be ready for the building in a short time.

The Rev. H. Long preaches at the Brownlee school house once in two weeks; also the Rev. W. S. Holland, affording us preaching every Sabbath. Services is held at the Burleson school house Sabbath evenings by W. S. Holland.

T. D. Mitchell who has been a resident of this place since January, starts for his home in Tioga, the 6th.

Hay, potatoes and butter are very scarce in this place.

C. A. Prouty had the misfortune to cut his foot the other day, which will perhaps detain him from work a few days.

**The Potter Enterprise
Wednesday Evening,
May 18, 1881 –
Vol. VIII, No. 2**

North Bingham.

The schools are in fine working order. That at North Bingham is taught by Minnie Ensworth, and that at the Centre by Miss Carrie M. Grover.

Mrs. Wheaton, over 80 years of age, is not expected to recover from her present illness.

Farm work is progressing finely.

The Church at North Bingham is to be dedicated on Thursday, June 2d. It is the only church building in this township, and is a union church – Baptist and Methodist. Some outside help has been thankfully received and the building is nearly finished and no debt, but the people have nothing left with which to buy an organ or bell, or to build a row of free sheds, and although I do not belong to either church organization I feel like saying, Come one come all, and cast in your mite to help those who try to help themselves.

- Charles Kernan has ceased clerking at the "Ark," and expects soon to depart toward the setting sun, finally bringing up in Colorado.

- Bendell, the tailor, is putting up a frame building on the lot purchased by him of Peter Hallauer. He will use it as a shop and dwelling.

- N. A. Pinney, of the Forest House, is now holding a position in the Bank of Coudersport. We are glad to see Mr. P. a citizen of Coudersport again.

- Last Thursday afternoon District Deputy Grand Master Charles L. Wheeler organized Lewisville Lodge, No. 556, F. & A. M. About thirty of the craft were present including a large delegation from Eulalia Lodge. The officers of the new lodge are George Marion, W.M.; H. T. Reynolds, S.W.; Frank Bronson, J.W.; Ira Carpenter, Treas.; Seth Lewis, Sec. The new lodge has a very nice room in which to hold their meetings, and starts off under favorable circumstances.

Eleven Mile.
May 7, 1881.

These are busy days for all workers, and truly so, for those who till the soil, as, if seed time is not advantageously occupied, the prospect for the future harvest is slight. To-day the remnant of a huge snow bank is yet visible, on the slope facing north, Grass is quite backward, but a warm rain and a few warm days would create abundant feed. As it has been, many flocks and herds have had little but the grass they could pick for some time.

People hereabouts are expecting to observe Decoration Day. The service is to be in charge of the G.A.R. Post of Oswayo. Three cemeteries are to be visited, and an address at 2 p.m. in the village by Major R. V. King, of Westons, N.Y., with choir singing and music by the Oswayo band.

Millport.
May 19, 1881.

A nice shower on the 16th inst., has helped the growing crops, for we were beginning to feel the need of rain.

A. J. Barnes has the timber for a new house, also the wall built for the same, which work was done by L. H. Bailey and son. Mr. Barnes will rebuild on the old homestead.

Dr. C. S. French and wife had what might have proved a serious runaway on Sunday the 15th. They were coming down the hill near the Widow Munger's, when the horse stumbled and fell, throwing him from the buggy, injuring him slightly, the reins being on the ground with the horse arose and ran with Mrs. French in the buggy, but one of the lines got entangled in the wheel, and she finally ran the horse into the fence by some means, and no damage was done except a good deal of scattering of the Doctor's bottles of medicines.

Mr. Ed. Burdic comes to the front with lamb raising this season. He has four sheep from which he has raised ten lambs. One of the sheep less than a year old, having twins. Can our farmers beat that?

The Potter Enterprise
Wednesday Evening,
May 25, 1881 –
Vol. VIII, No. 3

- Charley Welton has secured the Sinnemahoning stage line again. We are glad of it.

Eleven Mile.
May 21, 1881.

This has been a week of "wetness," for which we should be thankful, though planting is delayed thereby – as the benefit to crops already sown is great and the herds and flocks can now go "to grass" successfully.

As usual at this season the lower part of our valley has been alive with "bees," made for logging, generally, though in some cases, plowing, hauling manure, fence building, etc., are the labors performed. Dean Healy lost one of his horses by death a few days ago, and on the 20th, his neighbors with teams, thirteen in number, and plenty of men to keep them busy, gave his work a lift, encouraging to see.

The three schools on the Eleven Mile are in session. Miss Goodale in the Upper School, Miss McMullin in the Centre School and Miss Pawson in the Lower school.

Decoration service is to be opened at the cemetery near the Centre school house. The three schools are expected to attend and take part in the ceremony by providing themselves with bouquets of flowers, which they are to present to the comrades as they march between the lines of children, some of whom, purchance, may be sons or daughters of the dead soldiers, whose graves are to be strewn with those emblems of purity. By such tokens may the memories of our fallen comrades be kept bright on each succeeding memorial day.

West Branch.
May 14, 1881.

We have been passing through the scourge of diphtheria. In this settlement of about twenty-five families, we have buried six little children since the 11th of April, and on the 12th of May we buried Mr. John Burrows, under most painful circumstances. Mr. Burrows was an old man nearly 72 years old, and buried his wife last January. On Friday, the 29th of April, he had some difficulty with his son-in-law, Sidney Burrows. Mr. Burrows told Sidney he lied, whereupon Sidney struck the old man with a pitch-fork which he had in his hand at the time, the blow took effect on the side of his head, and he fell senseless to the ground, and for a short time was supposed to be dead, but he soon came to consciousness, but did not appear to be rational until the next day. Dr. Ritter, of Gaines, was sent for, who came and attended the suffering man, and hopes were strong for a few days that he would get about again, but erysipelas set in, which made him worse, but they succeeded in subduing that and then diphtheria set it, and soon it became evident that he was passing beyond the reach of medical aid, and a few minutes past 12 o'clock on the morning of the 12th of May, he breathed his last. What makes the affair seem more painful, is the fact that on the 29th of April, Sidney Burrows buried one of his children, and on the 5th of May he buried another one.

Allegany.
May 23, 1881.

The rains of the past week have brought vegetation forth finely. Fruit trees have blossomed full, and the prospects are good for a fine yield of fruits; if we escape a frost. Grass has a good start; but as usual the farmer has something to complain about, for the planting can not be done in the rain.

Mr. and Mrs. I. Stryker was called to Greenwood, N.Y., quite suddenly last week. The dangerous sickness of Mrs. Stryker's mother the cause.

Township Tidings from Potter County, Pennsylvania
Volume I, 1880 - 1884

Measles have again made their appearance at Andrews Settlement. Two or three severe cases, and runaways or runaway teams are quite frequent there, too.

Mr. Ed. Haskell's was one of the teams that ran. The buggy was overturned and the tongue broke, but no serious damage done either to the team or the occupants of the buggy.

The Potter Enterprise
Wednesday Evening,
June 1, 1881 –
Vol. VIII, No. 4

- Mrs. W. W. Dunham and Miss Sarah Ryan have opened dress making parlors in the house recently vacated by E. N. Stebbins, and are prepared to do all work in their line. Both ladies have had experience and they will give satisfaction. Special attention given to fitting.

Sartwell Creek.
May 28, 1881.

Scarlet fever is raging here. Quite a number are sick. Miss Jennie McDowell is very low with it; she is staying at John Reed's. Mrs. Pardon Jordan is having a hard time with her eyes. Mrs. Morris Manning is getting around again after a severe spell of sickness.

Sartwell Creek can boast of one large Willie, the son of J. C. Dehn. He is twelve years old and weighs one hundred and seventy-one pounds. Beat that if you can?

Mr. Elmer Demings is building a new house near his old one.

Mr. Morris Manning is building a new barn.

Potato bugs are putting in their appearance. Bad luck to you, Mr. Bug!

Crops are looking pretty good for this time of the year.

The Potter Enterprise
Wednesday Evening,
June 8, 1881 –
Vol. VIII, No. 5

Fishing Creek.
June 6, 1881.

B. A. Greene is preparing to erect a new school house right away.

Grass is looking pretty good.

The teacher in the Upper School had to close her school last week on account of being sick.

Died on Fishing Creek, in Roulet, June 3d, 1881, Mrs. Horace Maltby, aged 77 years, 9 months and 21 days. She was a devoted christian and a kind mother, and a friend to the poor and needy, both with the aid of temporal and spiritual food, and always pointing the erring ones to the Lamb of God that taketh away the sins of the world. The bereaved friends have the heart felt sympathy of the community, as we shown on the fifth by the concourse of people that attended her funeral. The Rev. T. R. Stratton, of Coudersport, preached the funeral sermon.

- Considerable saw and hammer music in Coudersport just now.

- A dozen or more buildings are under way, or will be soon, in Coudersport.

\- J. M. Bassett, of the Kettle Creek stage line, lost a horse last Thursday. It layed down in the road and gave up the ghost.

\- Candidates are looming up early. For Register and Recorder, we have been informed that F. M. Stevens, L. B. Cole, Jr., J. M. Covey, D. W. Butterworth, and Erastus Lewis, all of Coudersport, are in the field.

\- A. B. Mann has purchased half of the lot next to the Bank on the west, and intends erecting a fine brick building this season, for his law and insurance office and the *Journal* printing office. The location is a good one and we are glad that A. B. has purchased and will build. The price of this purchase was $950.

\- R. L. Dwight and family left Coudersport, on Friday last, for Broome county, N.Y., from whence Ralph starts for Leadville, Colorado. Ralph's many friends here wish him abundant success in his new home.

Sartwell Creek.
June 3, 1881.

Mr. Fred Lehman is building an addition to his barn.

Mrs. J. Jordan, of Troups Creek, Tioga county, is visiting her son, D. P. Jordan, of this place.

Mr. Frank Jordan is building a new picket fence in front of his residence, and picking up his yard, which improves its looks very much. Frank is a worker.

Bark peeling now is all the cry, But from the hills we wish to fly

And rest with those that have gone before
To sing we will peel bark no more.

West Pike.
June 1, 1881.

We are having some fine showers in this part of the country which we need very much, as the farmers began to think the hay crop would be light.

Crops are mostly in and now bark-peeling is the main business.

Last Thursday the hotel of M. J. Flynn's caught fire and burned to the ground. This makes two dwelling houses Mr. Flynn has lost by fire on that farm.

Mr. Orman Blackman's little girl is quite sick, they entertain but little hopes of its recovery.

The new store lately started by S. J. Acker is doing a thriving business.

The people of this place observed Decoration Day by fencing and otherwise improving the looks of the West Pike burying ground. They then formed an association with J. M. Kilbourne as President and F. A. Brown and Secretary and John Carriel as Treasurer. S. H. Martin, then presented the Association, with a deed of the ground on which the burying ground is situated.

Mr. Dan Crandall, our Constable, has in his custody a prisoner which is like to give him more trouble than any prisoner he ever captured before, it only weighs eight pounds but it is large enough so Dan ought to let us have cigars.

Costelloville.
June 2, 1881.

We are having very nice growing weather now. Every thing is growing rapidly, and there is a fair prospect of a good crop this year.

P. H. Costello's store is beginning to look quite "store like," and will be ready for the goods about the first of July.

Two Sunday Schools were organized last Sabbath near by. One at the Burleson school house, and one at the Brownlee school house.

The Burleson school house will be taught by W. S. Holland. It opens next Monday.

Mrs. Thomas Wrench, of Rixford, McKean county, Pa., is spending a few weeks at her father's – Mr. Jacob Peet.

Miss Lilly Rees returned home from Emporium on the morning of the 29th, where she has been very low with the fever.

The pests of the season – fishermen, potato bugs and sewing machine agents.

Millport.

Having been upon the road for the last few days, perhaps you would like to know what I saw. We left Friendship in the forenoon and proceeded towards the spouters of Richburg. On the road we met numerous oil operators that were returning to the railroad; one man asked us if we had seen a "hoss thief" on the road, we told him we hadn't seem him, but had met an editor, he said it was about the same, and drove on. On arriving at the well we were surprised to find everything quiet but soon found the reason, it being Saturday, most every one keeps that day in that vicinity. We saw a number of rigs in process of building, one already up, another nearly built and lumber on the ground for others, but did not learn who was putting them up or on whose farms. At Richburg village, workmen were engaged upon a new building which they said was being put up for Chas. Day, formerly of Oswayo, to be used for a store.

On Horse Run we found them unloading a boiler and engine for a new well about a mile above the old Horse Run well. At the lower well the drill was going down slowly. Excitement runs high in some parts of Sharon township, although not enough to cause any neglect of crops. Most of the farmers have their crops about all in.

R. L. Nichols is fitting Liberty Hall into dwelling rooms to rent.

Frank Hallett is building upon his lot near the school house, and Wm. Hornsby has a cellar dug on his lot above Barnes' store.

Allegany.

We are just closing up one of the most beautiful spring seasons the farmers of Potter ever had to do work.

Our people since the last case of diphtheria (in the family of A. G. Presho) are enjoying very good health; every body is busy and every one can find plenty to do. Even strangers passing, and in the night time "find some mischief still for their idle hands to do." Week before last some specimen of animal creation, in passing along the road near A. G. Presho's, found a saw log 16 feet long on the skids which they very carefully rolled off and swung around across the road and left, they also found a two horse wagon by the side of the highway, this they very quietly backed into the field and down a hill with the evident intention of running it to destruction in a deep gulley, but it refused to go quite far enough to be ruined; they then carried the neck yoke to parts unknown. Will you ask Sheriff Monroe if he has any light jobs to let around the jail, (inside I mean) such as looking through the grates, or scouring stone floor! If those dear fellows come along again and bring the neck yoke, perhaps we will have it made over a little and give it to them to wear for an ornament.

A. G. Presho's boy, Charlie, made quick time going to the house for some seed corn a few days ago. Being sent for a horse to work and corn to plant, he put the corn in a rickety old tin pail and mounted his horse with only a halter. Nellie did not like the sound of the old pail, and Charlie's whoa! whoa! did not amount to much, so the little trip of 60 or 70 rods was made in double quick time. Charlie held to the corn and Alton stopped the horse when they arrived, so no harm was done.

Ulysses.

Everything looks very prosperous in this vicinity, though winter wheat does not look as fine as last spring at this time.

Clark Crum says the last logging he ever done he logged off 1 ½ acres with a yoke of three year old steers, the year before he was eighty-one years old.

Farm hands are very scarce about here, they all seem to like bark-peeling better.

Eggs fell from 17 cents to ten last Tuesday. Quite a fall.

Diphtheria and fevers seem to be wearing away, we hear of no new cases at present.

Some thinks it has been the warmest weather they ever experienced in May before.

They don't mean to give up building a track. They are raising money with a subscription paper to pay for the land to built it on, which is $600 for ten acres in the Borough of Lewisville, but a few rods from the village.

Three millinery shops in town. I should think ladies might be accommodated in the bonnet line.

I think farmers would be willing to throw in the land the railroad would occupy for the sake of having cars run through this country.

Eleven Mile.
June 4, 1881.

The growth of vegetation is so rapid, that in case Mr. Vennor predicted frosts come as advertised, within the next few days, great damage would result, but no need to borrow trouble. The professor may be mistaken.

The crops are now about planted or sown, and farmers will get time to "take breath," and prepare ground for buckwheat, hoe corn, potatoes, etc., also work out the highway tax, and then – the work of harvest will begin. So the busy round of labor goes upon the farm, and in the office or work shop, it is much the same.

Decoration day exercises in Oswayo were reversed in order somewhat by reason of the rain, but there was a fair attendance and the services were interesting. The children of the day schools and Sabbath Schools were in procession with bouquets of fair flowers. These boys and girls whose memories hold no pictures of men marching with waving banners to strains of martial music, for the defence of our country's flag, may learn lessons of loyalty and patriotism from wreaths and immortelles as they fall upon soldier's graves. As in the round, the spring time brings the flowers, so each return will find less surviving of those mustered in a score of years ago, to scatter them over dead comrades graves, and soon the last straggler will have joined the great vivouac of the Grand Army gone before. Major King gave a very interesting address at the M.E. church, and Mrs. Wells read an appropriate poem. Short addresses were made at the cemetery by Major King and Rev. Miller. Decorating services were made by the comrades of the G.A.R.

Roulet.

Miss Evalyn Cunningham who has been visiting her uncle, L. W. Crawford, since December last, started for West Va., her home, this a.m. Miss C. has made many friends while here.

Wm. Burleson is painting his dwelling house.

Mrs. Horace Maltby, the aged lady who fell down stairs two weeks ago died from the effects Thursday morning last.

A. W. Johnson has built an addition to his house.

The Potter Enterprise
Wednesday Evening,
June 15, 1881 –
Vol. VIII, No. 6

- Frank Butler killed a large bear on Denton Hill Monday evening.

- J. O. Merrill is building a new barn near his new house, on Lymansville street.

- The heaviest man in Coudersport, George Baker, weighs 250 pounds. We have several who *think* they weigh more.

- D. W. Butterworth says he is not a candidate for Register and Recorder. We take it back, Will. We were misinformed.

- The new Catholic church at the Irish Settlement, Genesee township, will be dedicated on Sunday, June 19th. Services will begin at 10 o'clock a.m.

- The Grabe brothers, last week, purchased of D. F. Glassmire a lot just below where the old stage barn was located, on Main street, 25 feet front, for $800, upon which they will soon erect a two-story frame building to be used as a furniture store.

- Efforts are being made with fair prospects of success, towards forming a stock company at Lewisville, for the purpose of engaging in publishing a weekly newspaper. Over $350 have already been subscribed by the citizens, and there is every prospect of raising the balance. George Budd, of Michigan, now a compositor in the Enterprise office, and A. H. Owens, a *Journal* typo, are to be the publishers. We know by experience that both the boys are good typos and industrious young men, who will make a success of the paper if any body can. The Enterprise wishes them good luck in their new undertaking. We are always glad to see practical printers go in business for themselves.

Pleasant Valley.
June 10, 1881.

We are having quite a wet spell. It has rained for three days pretty steady, which will give the ground a good soaking.

Crops look well here. Winter wheat is excellent and the out look is for a good crop. Potatoes look well, and so do the bugs.

Scarlet fever is raging here. John Reed's family have had it, but are better now. N. C. Hammond has had two children sick with it. Elmer Deming has a child very sick with it.

Millport.
June 12, 1881.

The oil excitement in this locality is nowhere compared with that of the railroad. Some doubt its being built, others are confident of it.

Mrs. James Dickinson has trained a couple of lambs to follow her about and perform several tricks as handy as dogs would.

Jeff Burdick and Mrs. Matilda Hill were married by E. A. Graves, J.P., the 4th inst. Also the week before, at Elllisburg, Mr. Selden Sloat and Miss Stella Kempt, all of Millport. Good wishes for all parties concerned.

Sartwell Creek.
June 10, 1881.

The farmers are so engaged in plowing their buckwheat ground that they do not stop for rainy weather.

Mr. Reuben Card is preparing a piece of ground for wheat, and we hope he will have a good crop. He is a hard working young man and generally succeeds where other fail. Last fall he built a new house, and this spring he has been leveling off his yard picking up the rubbish that is always laying around after building. He intends to build an addition to his house this summer. In speaking of cellars we think that his cellar is the nicest one on the Creek. We wish you abundant success.

Bark peelers a few days ago were complaining of the dry weather. But for the past ten days the trees have stood pointing their lofty heads towards the sky. Plenty of rain.

Mr. A. J. Lewis has gone to Covington, Tioga county, to see about getting his pension.

The scarlet fever is spreading very rapidly. But we have not learned the names of those that are sick.

Oswayo.
June 11, 1881.

We are very glad to see the sun shine once more. It rained so long that people who has much work to do are very impatient for good weather, especially the bark peelers, who are obliged to have their board, but they have to let it rain.

We were in hopes that diphtheria had taken its departure forever from our midst, but there are some new cases.

Eugene Colgrove's youngest child is quite sick, but we hope ere long she will be well again.

Many of the good people met last evening at the church to make arrangement for a festival for the Fourth, and we expect to have a grand old celebration the coming Fourth. We hope to welcome many friends and also many strangers, and we hope to have a good time and enjoy ourselves, and help others to do the same.

The Potter Enterprise
Wednesday Evening,
June 22, 1881 –
Vol. VIII, No. 7

- Work has commenced on George Ross' new house.

- Martin & Stevens have sold their meat market to Mr. Tassell.

- Elvin Wormelsdorff has rented B. Rennells' house, vacated by James Johnston.

- Mr. R. Howland, the gunsmith, is manufacturing a nice article of birch beer – a very pleasant, non-intoxicating drink.

- M. L. Gridley has his Bowling Alley in running order. His rooms are not complete yet, but they alley part is completed, and we now hear the music of the spheres and the pins.

- Perry Brigham has again taken charge of the Lyman House, at Lewisville, and we have printed for him invitations for a Fourth of July Dance. Bill $1.50. If you want a pleasant time, patronize Brighman's dance.

- P. A. Stebbins has returned from a visit to Michigan, where he, with three other brothers, held a reunion. The average age of the brothers is 74 years and if the others are as spry at P. A., they make quite a team of boys even yet.

North Bingham.
June 17, '81.

The dedication of the church at this place was well attended, considering the storm then prevailing. The subscription and collection amounted to four hundred and six dollars.

A Sunday School was organized last Sunday with Mr. N. Lewis as Superintendent.

The cheese factory at this place is doing a larger business then ever before. They are making nineteen cheeses per day. Nearly five tons of our cheese has just been sold at 8 ½ cents per pound.

Eleven Mile.
June 18, 1881.

Healthy weather for grass, and young ducks, has prevailed the past two weeks. Hoeing and road work are behind hand, by that same token. But as an offset, Jack Frost has failed to nip vegetation for us, so far, and the man who sowed other grain, the last of April, on last year's buckwheat ground, depending on Jack to kill the young buckwheat, now views with sadness, the wheat struggling, all in vain, for the mastery, and cries alas! it never failed me before – "hardly ever."

Our quiet little valley is as yet, undisturbed by the din of railroads, or gush of oil, only as in dreams or fancy, the denizens may think they hear, from Millport glens and hillsides, the echo of locomotives' shrieks, or that the derricks lofty frames supplants the stately pines, thus dethroning monarchs that have swayed for centuries over the lesser works of nature. Whether dreams and fancies are ever realized or not in this case, in all probability, a few months time will suffice to decide, or at least, to indicate more plainly.

The Potter Enterprise
Wednesday Evening,
June 29, 1881 –
Vol. VIII, No. 8

Ulysses.

Rather discouraging to farmers to think they are obliged to wear their coats to keep warm the last of June. We have had two quite hard frosts, one on the morning of the 22nd, and one the 25th, doing considerable damage.

Mrs. Minna Brown, daughter of John Smith, went to Michigan last spring to join her husband who had been there some time, was brought home to be laid by the side of her brother, Charles Smith, who was burned to death in the oil country.

John Miller is at Wellsville in care of Dr. Trumans. We hear that he is improving.

Week before last there were five funerals in Lewisville.

Old Mrs. Hallock, mother of Noah Hallock is confined to her bed, caused by a fall.

Dr. Stout returned on the 23d from a visit in several of the Western States extending as far as Nebraska.

John Rooks, one of the early settlers of Potter county, and whose home is in the far West, is visiting in this county, calling on all of his old acquaintances.

Geo. W. Daniels is very low, there is no hopes of his recovery.

Crops look very well considering the unfavorable weather we have had of late.

Farmers will soon commence haying.

The court of common pleas granted O. D. Jackson a divorce.

West Bingham.

Last Thursday, June 23d, a stranger traveling through the country, broke open the house of Joseph Coulston while his family and himself were at Wellsville, and took his watch, revolver, a box of cartridges, two gold rings and some money. The next day, Friday forenoon, Coulston got track of the stranger, followed him to Genesee Forks, from there to Whitesville, thence to Ricksville, where he found his watch and chain and soon learned the thief was in the neighborhood stopping at his brothers. Saturday morning his brother brought the watch to Ricksville for repairs, which was recognized from the description given by Coulston. A warrant was issued and the man was arrested. He said his name was Charles Hannas. Coulston told him that he would have to go back to Potter county with him, which he consented to do, giving up the rings and revolver; Coulston getting back to West Bingham with him at one o'clock Sunday morning. As soon as day-break V. M. Stannard issued a warrant for him and soon the Constable of Genesee took him in charge. He appeared unconcerned, said he had broke jail at Bath and let out some prisoners. Later. – A Deputy Sheriff from York State has come after the prisoner, and says there is sixty dollars reward offered for him, so he started for Addison, N.Y., this morning.

Willard Bacon sheared sixty fine sheep for T. Coulston in one day and did the work good. Hard to beat we think.

Allegany.
June 27, 1881.

The frost put in a tardy appearance, but has done enough damage to suit us all. Gardens and crops in the village are badly damaged in places; on the hills nothing hurt to speak of.

On account of so much rainy weather crops are not as good as many thought they would be. Corn rotted in the ground in places and had to be planted the second time, which makes it late. New seeded grass looks well.

W. A. Gardner has his horse barn up and nearly finished out side.

Sartwell Creek.
June 27, 1881.

Quarterly meeting last Saturday and Sunday of the United Brethren in Christ, at this place. Closing sermon Sunday evening by Rev. D. C. Starkey, presiding Elder. Quite a number were present from a distance. After the sermon Brother Starkey thanked the people for their kind attention and for the collection which was received Sunday morning, amounting to $13.47. We love to meet with those who love the Lord, and we are sure that he will reap his reward in Heaven after death. "Christ died to save sinners."

Rev. Albert Jordan attended quarterly meetings at this place, and to visit his numerous friends and parents, Mr. and Mrs. D. C. Jordan. He returns to labor next Wednesday, and our prayers will follow him, and our best wishes.

The corn crop is very poor and some are putting on the drag and preparing the ground for buckwheat. We hope the crop will prove more successful than the corn has.

Scarlet fever is abating some, Miss Minnie Wright we hear, is sick with it. She is attended by Mrs. Brooks, who is having excellent luck here.

– Dr. French's new house on Water street is looming up in fine shape.

Rees & Dunham are doing the work.

- Aleck Johnston's new house on Water street is up and pretty well enclosed. Lew Glace is shoving it along.

- Several frosts last week clipped corn and potatoes in different sections of Potter county, doing considerable damage.

- Last Saturday while Wall. Benson was attending a barn raising at George Yentzer's, in Sweden, his little boy, while at play, fell from an elevated plank, sustaining a fracture of his left arm below the elbow and wrist. Dr. Buck reduced the fracture.

Millport.
June 26, 1881.

The drill has started at the Sharon Centre well, on the site where a derrick was erected two years ago. All are anxiously awaiting developments.

Hornsby's dwelling is enclosed and is being rapidly pushed toward completion.

James Dickinson has received a new supply of buggies and platform wagons.

There is a report that D. C. Chase is lying dangerously ill at the residence of his daughter, in Tioga county.

Roulet.
June 27, 1881.

Leroy Lyman and Villa Lyman have each had their tenant houses painted, and Mr. Burleson's barn shines forth with a coat of brown paint.

J. R. Fessenden and Clista Kimm are both invalids with rheumatism.

Miss D. E. Boyington, who has been teaching for some time in Rixford, is home on a vacation.

The Potter Enterprise
Wednesday Evening,
July 13, 1881 –
Vol. VIII, No. 9

- When completed, A. G. Lyman, at the Bird place, will have the finest saw mill in Potter county.

- Mr. Greisel is cutting cap stones, etc., for his brick harness shop. This building makes the Main street block solid.

- Our youngest attorneys, Messrs. Newton, Cole and Gear, start for Kansas next week, with a view of locating for the practice of the law.

- The Fourth of July at Germania was a success. Three dances had all that could be accommodated. Mr. Voss, of the German Hotel, was compelled to turn away over thirty couple for want of room. There was no fighting and everything passed off pleasantly.

Keating.
July 7, 1881.

Crops look well in this place. The frost on the 21st and 25th of last month did but little harm. the fruit crop promises to be very large.

C. W. Dingee has moved his old house and is preparing to build a new one this fall.

The school in this part of the town is kept by Mr. Lydia Ingraham, and as far as we know, is in a flourishing condition.

A camp meeting will be held in the grove at the school house in this place, commencing August 19th and lasting over Sunday.

Millport.
July 8, 1881.

The drill is down between eight and nine hundred feet at the Sharon Center well.

A number of our citizens went to Oswayo the Fourth to see the celebration. It was pronounced by all to be the boss fizzle of the day. No speaking, no fantasies, no nothing, but a large crowd of people. Four hundred eat dinner at the Lee House, and one hundred and sixty couples for the dance. Two hundred and thirty eat at McGonigal's, and ninety-two couples at the dance. The dance music at both houses was excellent. The Ulysses Cornet Band was present during the day. They are first-class in every respect, and without their presence the Oswayo celebration would have been non est.

Charles Tyler has sold his farm to Horace Clear, of Allentown. Possession given this fall. Consideration, $3,500.

Ellisburg.
July 4, 1881.

Died at Ellisburg, Pa., June 30th, 1881, of consumption, Inez, wife of Orson Ellis, aged 36 years. How little yet how much is comprehended in these few lines, dead, yet living. Mrs. Ellis was taken ill January 2d, and during her long illness felt fully confident of the tender mercies of an all wise Providence. Expressing her willingness to die if it was her Heavenly Father's will. If spoken to of her sufferings, she would say it is nothing in comparison to what our Saviour suffered. Mrs. Ellis was universally respected and will be very much missed in the neighborhood, and it is a heart rending loss for her husband and friends. She was a loving wife, kind and obliging neighbor, combined with her cheerful manner, won many friends. We truly sympathize with husband and friends in their bereavement. I can point them only to one great Physician, who can heal the broken-hearted, and that is Jesus.

Costelloville.
July 8, 1881.

We have been favored with some very hot weather of late, but yesterday afternoon we had a very hard shower with wind combined. The wind blew off a portion of the rafters of the large barn the Young boys raised the other day. It also did other slight damages.

P. H. Costello's new store is ready for the good. It is said to be the largest in the county. Coudersport will, no doubt, lose some of its "pink calico customers" now.

They are progressing finely with the tannery.

Crops are looking favorable. There is a fair prospect of a good crop of apples this fall, if the "rose bug" does not destroy them. It is a new kind of a bug here, and we hope this may be the first and last visit.

Allegany.
July 11, 1881.

The relatives of Mr. and Mrs. Henry Haskell made them a surprise, it being the tenth anniversary of their marriage, or tin wedding. They were the recipients of numerous presents, and a good time was enjoyed by all.

Haying is the order of the day now with farmers, and if this warm weather continues, no one can complain that hay will not cure.

Allegany can boast of four graduates this spring. Miss Carrie Bishop from the Normal School at Lock Haven. J. P. Collins and H. H. Kies from Mansfield, and W. Collins from a commercial school in New York.

Raymond.

I am very sorry to be obliged to tell you that the dreadful diphtheria still lingers among us, but we hope this time no fatal results may follow, for as yet all the cases are light. The two children of Mr. Burdick and Mrs. E. E. Kelley all have it, but the children are recovering, and Mrs. Kelley, we hope, not worse. The two children of F. A. Nelson also had very strong symptoms last week, but the Doctor decided it not diphtheria.

They have quite a full Sunday School on Sweden Hill; also a small one at the new school house above Colesburg. Last Sunday the two met together at the latter place, and enjoyed a very pleasant time. The little school house was filled so that all could not find seats. We hope that both schools my be profited by the meeting, and that all the Sunday Schools in the county may be well and profitably attended through the entire season.

Eleven Mile.
July 9, 1881.

This hot weather is favorable to most crops. Corn seemed too far gone to be revived, but a few hot days will cause it to push forward again. Hay harvest is now the farm work at hand. Old meadows, as usual, are light, but those newly seeded will yield fair crops. Oats look fairly, at present, and potatoes are doing well.

Sartwell Creek.
July 7, 1881.

Quite a wind storm visited our place one week ago last Tuesday night, which done considerable damage to the fruit trees. Four apple trees in the orchard of D. P. Jordan were destroyed by being blown over and broken off; also a cherry tree belonging to J. E. Dehn was broken down. Some fences were turned topsy turvy. The damage has not been estimated. Yum, yum.

The haying season is now on hand, and the young men and maidens have nearly all returned from the Fourth to go to work, and make up for lost time. Go ahead, boys, now is the time to have your fun while you are young, but be careful that the kisses you received don't make you sick. Oh, the candy we meant.

Bark drawing seems to be the news of the day.

Mr. Dorman Card and his sister Rosy, are going to Clarksville to visit their sister in that place.

Mr. George Beckwith who has been sick for some time is getting better. He has had a pretty sick time of it.

**The Potter Enterprise
Wednesday Evening,
July 20, 1881 –
Vol. VIII, No. 10**

- Main street bridge is being replanked.

- Our farmers are busy in the hay field, and the yield in most sections is reported good.

- D. F. Glassmire has purchased the black team owned by A. G. Olmsted. They go on the new stage line.

Roulet.
July 18, 1881.

Leroy Lyman is improving the looks of his residence by building a porch.

Born – July 3rd, to Mr. and Mrs. Don Manning, a daughter. Also to Mr. and Mrs. Clarence Green, three daughters, all of which died. Their weight was two pounds a piece.

Died in this place, July 13th, Mrs. Ann Hazen. Also July 9th, Martin, youngest son of Lyman and Mary Burt.

Ulysses.

Everything seems to be in a flourishing condition in this place.

People seem to be quite healthy at present. The most complaining we hear is about such awful warm weather, the thermometer ran up to 90° in the shade the 10th.

Crops look well except corn. Apples are not as plenty in this section as they were last year.

Haying will be the order of the day now for a while, but we hope it will be cooler weather for the workmen's sake.

Fred Baker is driving daily a splendid pair of creams.

A fine shower on the morning of the 11th was greatly appreciated.

There are a number of new houses being built in Lewisville which makes quite an improvement.

The late comet has not excited much curiosity in this vicinity.

**The Potter Enterprise
Wednesday Evening,
July 27, 1881 –
Vol. VIII, No. 11**

- Z. J. Thompson has opened a grocery in the building east of the Enterprise office.

- The first crop of potato bugs are emigrating. For a few days past they have been leaving M. L. Gridley's potato patch, headed for some planted later, across the road. The fence is covered with the bugs, and the walk presents evidence of hundreds of them which have been trampled by pedestrians.

Freeman's Run.

Is this weather warm enough for you?

Everybody is haying this week.

Georgie Turner cut his foot quite badly a few days since.

Our Sabbath School is progressing finely with D. A. Everett as Superintendent.

The new store at Costelloville is being rapidly filled with goods.

I have heard that black raspberries are infested with a poisonous insect this year, which cannot be seen without the aid of a microscope. Will some of your readers please tell me whether this is so.

Burtville.

Haying seems to be the order of the day. Mr. J. K. Burt has his nearly finished.

Mr. J. H. Larkin's health is very poor and seems to be on the decline.

Mrs. C. H. Barr has been quite seriously ill, but we are glad to say is improving now.

Mrs. Edwin Grimes has been somewhat indisposed, but is convalescent again.

Died July 9th, Martin, youngest child of Mary and Lyman Burt, aged 4 years and 7 days.

Little Martin was a very bright and lovely child. None knew him but to love him. May God console the parents in their affliction.

Martin we shall ever miss you,
Friends can never fill the space
That is vacant by your absence,
Who can fill our darling's place.

Little Martin thou hast left us,
Here thy loss we deeply feel;
But 'tis God who hath bereft us;
He can all our sorrow heal.

Oswayo.
July 24, 1881.

The Fourth of July with its amusements are among the things of the past, and the people are all very busy haying, and thanks to Providence for the good weather, they are getting along nicely.

We are very sorry to hear that Mr. A. S. Lyman, of the Eleven Mile, received quite a serious hurt while engaged in loading hay scales at the depot at Wellsville, but he is getting along well.

Rev. Mr. North, of our place, is about to organize a temperance meeting on Tuesday evenings, at the M.E. church. We hope he will succeed, and that the people will assist him and with the help of the Lord drive the demon of intemperance from our land.

Ulysses.

The Seventh Day Advents have been holding tent meetings in Lewisville for some time past.

Mrs. T. Burt fell down stairs a few days since injuring one of her arms quite badly.

George W. Daniels is a little more comfortable. I understand he is under the care of Dr. Post.

It is thought by some that the potato crop will be a failure on account of drought and potato beetle.

Streams are becoming very low and rain is needed.

People have been lively the past two weeks putting in hay, which is a very good crop in this section.

Winter wheat harvest has commenced.

Township Tidings from Potter County, Pennsylvania
Volume I, 1880 - 1884

Allegany.
July 25, 1881.

The showery weather of to-day makes slow work in getting in hay. We have had two weeks of good hay weather, and farmers have improved it in this neighborhood. Some have finished and others are very nearly through.

I. Stryker had the misfortune of getting his shoulder broke one day last week. It makes it bad for him as his haying is not finished.

The relatives and friends of Mrs. Alice Neefe, sister of M. W. Slaughter, were pained to hear of her death in the faraway land of Texas. The disease was measels.

Does any one know what causes the unusual action of some of the pear trees this year? I have seen several that have blossomed the second time, and while the trees had fruit on. The blossoms come on the growth of this year; some of them have pears growing from the second crop of blossoms, making two sizes of pears on one tree.

Measles still linger in the vicinity of Andrews Settlement.

The Potter Enterprise
Wednesday Evening,
August 3, 1881 –
Vol. VIII, No. 12

- Work has commenced on the new tannery at Harrison Valley.

- A. H. Owens removes to Ulysses this week, where he will publish a newspaper.

- Grabe Brothers have commenced work on their new furniture store, on Main street.

- The Masonic Hall, in this place, will be dedicated with appropriate ceremonies about the first of September.

- B. S. Wakely, of Clara, last week cut a blackberry cane of this year's growth, which measured 13 feet 2 inches in length.

The Potter Enterprise
Wednesday Evening,
August 10, 1881 –
Vol. VIII, No. 13

- "School ma'am" next week.

- Ripe apples are plenty.

- The postoffice has been neatly lettered.

- The frame of George Ross' new house is up.

Pleasant Valley.
Aug. 5, 1881.

Haying is nearly done in this town, and oat harvest is upon us.

Elmer Demming has the frame up for his new house.

Asher Burt was kicked by a horse one day last week, but is so as to be out now.

N. C. Hammond has bought the Austin farm in the east part of this town.

The wife of Niles Fessenden is very sick with brain fever.

There is to be a picnic in the woods near Robert McDowell's, on the 12th of August. Come one, come all, and have a good time.

Ansil Joseph is happy – it's a boy. Weight, 8 ¾ pounds.

Costelloville.
Aug. 5, 1881.

We are having some very warm weather of late. The thermometer stood 90 degrees below zero, today, in the shade.

O. J. Rees and George Brahmer, of Coudersport, are surveying for Costello this week.

Farmers are getting their haying and harvesting done, notwithstanding the weather we have been having.

Bark peeling is nearly done away with for this year.

Our Sunday School conducted by L. D. Ripple, is progressing finely. Good attendance, good order and good lessons, are our aim.

Eleven Mile.
Aug. 4, 1881.

The past few days have been very busily occupied by hay makers, and as is usually the case, the work is at various stages of progress. While a few have finished, others are in the midst, and still others have scarcely begun. The yield is fair and quality good. The bad weather last week and this, caused much extra labor and some damage to hay that was exposed, and to the wheat not secured. But a few days of dry weather will suffice to get all secure. The scarcity of help has been felt by most farmers all the season, but by the aid of machinery, and in some cases, of the girls of the household, the work has made fair progress, when the weather would permit. Farmers are selling their produce at good prices. Two-year olds bring $20 to $25 each; lambs from $2.75 to $3.50; wool, so far as sold, brought 36 to 38 cents per pound; butter 18 to 20 cents. The prospect is bright for the future for all workers, to expect busy times, and fair remuneration for their labors.

The Potter Enterprise
Wednesday Evening,
August 17, 1881 –
Vol. VIII, No. 14

- K. Zimmerman has rented the house next to the blacksmith shop, owned by B. Rennells.

- John Ryan is building a new house on the lot where he now lives – South side of the river.

- Prothonotary Crosby has received the Medical Register, and physicians should now step up to his office and comply with the law.

- Mr. Greisel has a portion of the brick on the ground for his harness shop and the front iron work is in position. His building will be a two-story one.

- On Thursday last O. L. Hall, of Homer, was thrown from a load of hay, one of the wheels passing over his head and neck. His face was badly cut and he received numerous other severe bruises. It was a close call.

- J. O. Merrill has moved to his new house on the Lymansville road, and now sits under his own vine and fig tree. In a few months Mr. Merrill has transferred a vacant sidehill lot into a comfortable home. He has a very pretty house, good barn, and has set out trees, and ha reason to be proud of his possessions.

Fishing Creek.
Aug. 12, 1881.

Haying is over.

Oat harvest is the order of the day.

Mr. James Church cut three of his fingers nearly off with an ax. They are doing finely.

David Yentzer cut his foot pretty bad so that he will have to walk with crutches.

Mrs. Otis Lyman is very sick.

We are going to have an oil well on the Creek near Michael Dehn's. We all expect to be rich when we get oil, and then you will see some swelling about here.

North Bingham.
Aug. 12, 1881.

Most of our farmers are through with their haying and harvesting is about ready.

Many people from this vicinity have been to Pine Creek after huckleberries, and some of them have had excellent luck.

The yield of hay is much larger than last season.

J. L. Rooks, of Burlingame, Kansas, has been making his numerous friends and old acquaintances a call, and has just started on his return home.

Mrs. M. Perry, of Girard, Mich., is visiting her daughter, Mrs. A. Kibbe, and intends to remain all winter.

For this season of the year our climate is very healthy.

Millport.
Aug. 12, 1881.

H. D. Blanchard died suddenly at his home, near Sharon Centre, this morning. The deceased was advanced in years, and had been failing in health for some time.

Chauncy Staysa's platform dance was well attended. Dickinson and Bailey furnished the music, which was excellent.

I see that McGonigal has been repairing his hotel at Oswayo, which improves the look of things very much.

Moyer Brothers and Reynolds have opened a first-class furniture store, and keep everything in the undertaker line cheap.

Van Kuren and Henyon has opened a meat market at Millport, and no oil found east of Shingle House.

Gold and Raymond.
August 12, 1881.

Farmers are busy and locals are few.

Picnics are crowding in between the busy days of finishing haying and cutting oats and wheat.

Hay has been put in good order.

Some heavy winds has come with the thunder storms of late, and hail also in places.

Mr. Ryon had one of his cattle killed last week by lightning, and a good many trees have been struck, but no buildings or persons in this vicinity that I know of.

What might have been, but was not a serious accident occurred at the store at Raymond some weeks ago. A lamp was knocked off the dry-goods counter, broken, and the oil took fire, among papers and rags, and but for the presence of mind displayed by two or three persons in throwing on several pieces of cloth, smoking ruins would soon have been in place of the store.

A daughter of D. W. Green also had a narrow escape a few days ago from being burned to death by the explosion of a small oil can by which she was trying to kindle a fire in the stove. The very small quantity of oil in the can was all that saved her or the house. Don't kindle fires in stoves with kerosene oil.

Lymansville.

The busy season here (with farmers) is almost over. Hay was a light crop. But what there was, was got in good shape.

Oats are gleaming golden, and the heavy cradle swung by sinewy arms are laying them low on the lap of mother earth.

The cheese factory is still in motion, propelled by the skillful hand of Mr. Bennehoff, who deserves the sincere thanks of all the patrons for his sterling endeavors to keep "the ball rolling." His cheese takes the highest price in market, and it is hoped that those who have withheld their dairy this season, will by another, give the patronage which this enterprising branch of industry so well deserves.

The Andrews Brothers still occupy the store vacated by J. M. Spafford. They have a good assortment, and are ever ready to attend to the wants of their customers. Come and all, and give them a call.

Mrs. George Yentzer occupies the house vacated by T. Monroe.

Genesse Forks.
Aug. 15, 1881.

We again venture to jot down a few of the passing events here, for the benefit of those interested.

Everybody is busy. Harvesting of grain and fruit seems to command the chief attention of the farmers.

The drawing of hemlock bark to Wellsville, and of merchandise from there, including other business, causes the air to resound with the music of jolting wagons and voices of teamsters, day and night.

One of the novelties here is a nice swing up, in the grove across the bridge from Main street, also tables erected for those who would like to have a picnic excursion on the banks of the beautiful Genesee.

Our summer school, taught by Miss Clara Lewis, closed with a picnic that was very much enjoyed by scholars and patrons.

We gladly welcome Miss Orisa Hurd home again, after a year profitably and pleasantly spent at Lock Haven State Normal School.

The Oregon fever still clings to J. Dimon. It is thought his only remedy is to sell and move thitherward.

**The Potter Enterprise
Wednesday Evening,
August 24, 1881 –
Vol. VIII, No. 15**

Allegany.
Aug. 22, 1881.

No frosts in this part of Allegany yet, Vennor's prediction to the contrary notwithstanding, but last week, the first of it was cold enough for fires to be necessary for comfort.

The dry weather ripens grain fast. Wheat and oats nearly all secured, and already the hum of the threshing machine is heard.

Veley and Matteson have bought a seperator to their machine and intend to do a rushing business this fall.

Mrs. F. Lent still continues very sick. The Dr. pronounces her a little better.

Old Mrs. Wildman has gone to Cortland County, N.Y., to live with her daughter.

Mr. E. Nelson commences his job of drawing bark this week.

Sartwell Creek.
Aug. 20, 1881.

The people in this vicinity have got all through with their harvesting and are preparing to haul bark, of which there is a large quantity to be drawn.

There is to be a donation held at the parsonage next Wednesday evening for the benefit of Rev. Brooks, to which all are invited.

Yesterday the people of Sartwell Creek and vicinity attended a picnic held in Mr. Robert McDowell's woods. The exercises commenced with a speech from Rev. Brooks, after which there was speaking by the scholars, which we think was well done. After the children were done with their exercises, Mr. Clinton McDowell, a graduate of the school at Alfred Centre, entertained the public with some select reading, after which there was a bounteous feast spread out before us that all partook of, we hope with grateful hearts, grateful to our Heavenly Father for the blessings that we are enjoying every day of our lives. After dinner there was a swing put up and the young people enjoyed themselves very much, as well as the older ones. After we had got through with swinging, we all returned to our several homes to wait for another picnic. The picnic was a grand success, and we hope the teacher, Miss Read, will be benefited by it as well as the scholars.

We expect that in a short time our roads will be lined with new buggies. Messrs. Lehman, Card and Read, we hear are going to buy them each a new one.

Apple trees are laden with fruit here, and consequently there will be lots of cider made.

- Dr. Edgar S. Mattison has moved into the house owned by R. L. Nichols, recently vacated by J. O. Merrill.

- We understand that D. W. Butterworth, who has published the *Journal* for the past six years, has accepted the management of a daily paper some where in New Jersey, and will quit the *Journal* about November 1st, next.

- Carl Zimmerman has purchased a lot of thirty-three feet front on Main street, just north and adjoining the meat market of Begell & Tassell, for $800. He will at once put up a building to be used for a boot and shoe store and cigar store.

**The Potter Enterprise
Wednesday Evening,
August 31, 1881 –
Vol. VIII, No. 16**

- Sheriff Monroe now has nine prisoners in his care.

- The first oysters of the season were brought in by Miles White last week.

- Thermometer ranging among the nineties every day, is getting monotonous.

- Butter is selling at twenty-four cents per pound, and most of the dairymen holding on for a rise.

- Wednesday morning of last week there was quite a frost in some sections of this county, cutting the vines.

- Major Kilbourne, of Pike, was in town last Saturday. He reports the water in Pine Creek lower than ever before known by him, and he is one of the old settlers.

- R. L. Nichols has had a well drilled at his house, 30 feet in depth, with 25 feet of 3 inch casing to shut off surface water. O. H. Crosby also had a well drilled 28 feet in depth.

- The great complaint is dry weather. Springs and streams are failing; many farmers are compelled to drive their stock miles to water. Late buckwheat will be a failure, owing to want of rain, to which may be added the hot, broiling sun, which causes it to blast.

- Messrs. Cole, Newton and Gear, admitted to the bar of Potter county, June court, and who immediately afterward started for the west, with a view of locations for the practice of their profession, have returned to old Potter, satisfied that the west is very much overrated.

Eleven Mile.
Aug. 25, 1881.

Nice time this to clear off the fallows, as well as to secure the harvest of grain.

Threshermen are on the "war path," with new machines and old. Yesterday Messrs. Cole and Martin threshed 77 bushels of oats for B. F. Lyman, the yield from one and one-fourth acres of ground. Also two acres of land yielded for him about 50 bushels of white rye.

We were glad to see our old neighbor, William Dalrymple, able to visit the neighborhood again. He is crippled yet, however, from the effects of a vicious horse last June.

J. H. Leach had his leg fractured last Monday, while getting bark out from his slashing. The grabs came loose from a log he was moving with his team and it swung around so as to catch his leg and break a bone near the ankle.

Mrs. Virgil Spencer on Saturday last, threw herself on the protection of the Poor Masters of Oswayo, claiming that she was that day thrust from the house by his sisters, and by his consent, with her babe, some two months old, was kicked out. The authorities intend to see that her case is justly met.

William A. Crosby, Esq., has been recently engaged in fixing the sites of some of the township corners on the State line, preparatory to setting of permanent monuments thereon by the Commission of Survey for New York and Pennsylvania.

The Potter Enterprise
Wednesday Evening,
September 7, 1881 –
Vol. VIII, No. 17

Roulet.
Sept. 5, 1881.

Don Manning has his blacksmith shop up and enclosed.

Mrs. John Abbott was burned quite severely on her face and hands while attempting to light her fire with kerosene oil, the other day.

Miss Maud Westcott, who has been ill with diphtheria is recovering.

The farmers are complaining of a very poor corn crop this fall, but nevertheless the young people do not think so, as every Saturday or Sunday night finds them visiting corn fields, orchards and melon patches.

Allegany.
Sept. 5, 1881.

September 1st brought us the much needed rain; but it was no gentle shower. It began between five and sick o'clock p.m. and it was so dark lamps had to be lit. In this place the storm was not as severe as at Andrews Settlement or Ellisburg; there it was accompanied by hail and lightning. The hail injured some of the crops and gardens and the lightning struck in several places, but one house, that of J. C. Bishop, was injured. Fortunately the family escaped unharmed with the exception of slight shocks.

Several of the young people are preparing to attend a select school at Andrews Settlement. Mr. Heysham, of Nelson, Tioga county, is to be the teacher. He is a graduate of Mansfield, and experienced teacher and a first class school is anticipated.

Mrs. F. Lent breathed her last Sept. 3d. She has finished her life's work in less than 20 years; leaves a little one of seven months, a husband and parents, sister and many friends to mourn her early death. She was prepared to do the will of her heavenly father without a murmur. May we all be prepared to meet her.

Millport.
Sept. 3, 1881.

A party of young men living at Shingle House, having heard that arnica and alcohol was given by many surgeons, sometimes, concluded to try the remedy for "drouth of the stomach," one day last week, having procured a goodly supply of the article, betook themselves to a secluded nook and proceeded to test the quality of the medicine. The result did not prove satisfactory as expected. It is found that arnica liniment will bring the drunk on, but it is rather rough on the stomach.

Jeff. Burdic has moved into the unoccupied half of Liberty Hall.

Will Hornsby's house is finished, and it is a beauty.

There is a scarcity of stone masons in this section, and more are needed very much.

There will be a dance Friday night, Sept. 9th, at Liberty Hall, for the benefit of Leroy Witter.

A bear has lately been seen prowling around in Clara township.

Ulysses.

Business is moving off very briskly about here.

Men are leasing all the land they can get in this vicinity, for oil.

The new printing office in town is quite a curiosity.

The tannery at Harrison Valley is a fine thing for the bark haulers in this locality.

A fine shower was gladly received last Thursday evening. A great many springs and wells had yielded to the hot rays of the sun.

John Miller has sold his mill property to John P. Russel and moved to Wellsville. The mill will be carried on by Russell.

Diphtheria is among us again. A little girl died at Bingham Centre with this terrible disease a few days since.

Harvesting is over except the buckwheat, which is badly injured by the drouth. Potatoes and corn are almost a failure in this section.

In the recent shower we hear of considerable damage done by lightning. It is said to have been the heaviest storm ever known in this section. T. Coulston lost a cow and we hear of a number of buildings being burned about the country.

There is a great call for calves in this section. Drove after drove have been driven out of the county.

A. Worden will soon commence picking his hops.

- George Ross and Andrew Stevens have started a new livery stable. At present they occupy Sheriff Monroe's barns.

- Dan. Monroe is anxious for Court week. This piling in from two to five prisoners every Tuesday will soon crowd our jail to its utmost capacity, and they will be slopping out over the walls or creeping out through the keyhole – if they are too lazy to dig out.

- On Thursday this section was visited by a refreshing shower, lasting nearly five hours. During the entire day the air was filled with smoke, which obscured the sun. At five o'clock it was necessary to light the lamps. From the south-west heavy clouds and smoke rolled up, making anything but a pleasant picture. But soon the rain came down steadily, being unaccompanied by heavy wind, and everybody was pleased. North of there the storm was much more severe.

Eleven Mile.
Sept. 3, 1881.

All things have cause to rejoice, in that the monotony of heat and dust has been relieved. The report of the "artillery of the heavens" was tremendous to hear. The heavier part of the storm was east of this locality. We hear that the barn of McDermott in Genesee, was struck by lightning, and with its contents, was burned. Also a house in the same township was struck and damaged. The only wonder seems to be that more damage was not done, or some person killed.

On Wednesday the Sunday School picnic came off, with a large attendance and good time, as could be with the heat and dust, to encounter, going and coming. The exercises consisted of singing by the children, addresses by Deacons Jones and Toreey, and the usual manipulations with the mouth of hungry bodies upon the good things freely furnished, not omitting candies and lemonade. Several of our Eleven Milers were kept from attending in consequence of their presence being required at Oswayo that day, as witnesses, etc., on the suit of Oswayo Overseers of the Poor vs. Virgil Spencer. The defendant was that day arrested and brought for hearing before Squire Estes and A. S. Lyman, justices, which resulted in his being bound over to court of Quarter Sessions, to answer the charge of deserting his wife, Mrs. Ida Spencer and their child, two months old. D. C. Larrabee for the plaintiff, and C. L. Peck and Samuel Beebe for the defence.

The Potter Enterprise
Wednesday Evening, September 14, 1881 – Vol. VIII, No. 18

- Miss Matilda Doerner has opened a school for small children in the building on West street, recently occupied by Z. J. Thompson as a wagon shop.

Genesee Forks.
Sept. 5, 1881.

It has been very dry here. The dust averaging about six inches on the road between this place and Wellsville, for some weeks past.

All were wishing for rain, which came September 1st, commencing at five o'clock in the evening, and lasting until midnight. For some time it was a continuous peal of lightning and flash of lightning.

A water-spout came to earth on J. Ryan's farm, tearing the earth to some considerable depth and breadth. The water in the West Branch of the Genesee overflowed its banks, reaching nearly to S. C. Hurd's store, tearing the gardens in its course, carrying away that bridge and eight others on the Ellisburg road. Damage estimated at about eight hundred dollars.

Miss Bettie Race is recovering from diphtheria.

Mr. G. W. Hackett had two ribs broken and his shoulder dislocated by his team running away.

Miss Orisa and Hannah Hurd have gone to begin their fall terms of school.

North Bingham.

The rain, welcome rain, is falling for the first time in nearly four weeks. Seldom has there been so much rejoicing, and so general to hear the thunder roar and see the lightning flash, as at the present time.

Ever since Sunday afternoon of Aug. 21st, 1881, we have been able to boast of having three Pecks of humanity at the Corners, formerly only two Pecks. Of our additional Peck I would respectfully say she weighs 7-6, which means seventy-six, and as that is a patriotic number, it is evidently a good sign and may be an indication of something about to happen. I sincerely hope and humbly trust that we may yet be able to boast of the possession of at least a bushel of that very acceptable commodity.

Harvesting is well advanced and the threshing machines are at work. As far as heard from, the yield of grains is excellent.

Potatoes are few in a hill and small at that. I hear that offers of seventy-five cents per bushel for potatoes in the field are refused.

The Sunday School at North Bingham is well attended. The average attendance of teachers and scholars being about one hundred, besides visitors.

The Potter Enterprise
Wednesday Evening, September 21, 1881 – Vol. VIII, No. 19

- Basset brothers have opened a meat market on East street.

- Mrs. Patrick Shannon, of Hebron, has left at this office, a hen's egg measuring 7 ¼ by 6 ¼ inches in circumference. The egg was laid by a small dominic hen.

- A grand stand is being built on the fair ground 26 x 96 feet in size, calculated to seat five hundred people, with refreshment stand underneath. L. A. Glase does the work for the society, agreeing to wait for his pay until the receipts from the stand itself will pay the bill. Under the circumstances the people should be liberal in patronizing the stand, and thus help themselves (to see the races in comfort), the society and Mr. Glase.

Eleven Mile.
Sept. 17, 1881.

Rozell Bros. have cleared off five acres of nice fallow and sowed it to wheat.

Dean Healy has put in three acres.

The young child of Mr. and Mrs. Virgil Spencer died on Tuesday morning, of cholera infantum.

Among the good yields of grain, may be mentioned that of A. Walker, of twenty-two bushels of Clawson wheat, from one bushel of seed on about one-half acre of ground.

Buckwheat yields 40 bushels per acre, so far, as an average.

North Bingham.
Sept. 16, 1881.

Last Tuesday evening an enormous meteor was seen by some of the people in this vicinity. There was no noticeable atmospheric disturbance at the time of its passing, which indicates that it had not yet entered our atmosphere. It is described by one who saw it as being as large, in appearance, as a small load of hay. It was so brilliant as to light up the earth in its pathway. Its course was south of east and it probably fell in Africa or the Indian ocean. Before it passed from sight an explosion seemed to occur and large pieces were detached from the meteor and seemed to accompany it on its journey, and the pieces had the appearance of large balls of fire. Was it a fragment of one of the comets? There was only optical evidence of any explosion.

Mrs. J. B. Robbins, of Spring Mills, died at 4 p.m., last Tuesday. Her maiden name was Minerva Raymond, sister of J. L. Raymond, of this place. The flower of the Raymond family has fallen. So beautifully even tempered in her ways that not one in ten thousand could successfully compete with her in that respect. She was born in Feb. A.D. 1818, and was in the sixty-fourth year of her age. She had been for many years a member of the Baptist Church.

As a rule, the summer has been a healthy one, with very few cases of diphtheria and but little of summer complaint.

- Dr. C. H. Sharpe removes from Millport to Oswayo this week and will open an office in the J. L. Moyer House.

- J. L. Moyer, of Oswayo, will take charge of the Wilcox Mill, on the South Branch, this week.

- Henry Lamberton's new house, at the mouth of the South Branch, is up and enclosed. It will be a very handsome and commodious dwelling.

- August and Theodore Grabe have opened a new Furniture Store on Main Street, invite the attention of the public. Their stock is all new, and they propose to sell at reasonable prices. They pay special attention to repairing and both of the boys are good workmen.

The Potter Enterprise
Wednesday Evening,
September 29, 1881 –
Vol. VIII, No. 20

- Amos Velley has sold his livery stock to James and Aleck. Johnston.

Freeman's Run.

Born, Sept. 18th, to Mr. and Mrs. H. H. Beebe, a daughter. Weight, nine pounds.

C. W. Dingee has his new house up.

Miss Laurie Bridges and Miss Eva Lewis are attending school at Coudersport.

Coudersport jail ought to have a few more inmates. Last week E. F. Whitney had $30 stolen, from his house and just before the hired man of C. W. Dingee had his watch stolen.

Henry Harris is digging a well.

Raymond.

Whatever else the Potter county farmer complains of this fall, he has no cause to grumble because there is so much rain he cannot secure his crops. – Never perhaps in our history, as a county, were the hay, oats and late crops, all secured in such excellent condition. Buckwheat, although predicted an entire failure, in some cases proves to yield well for the amount of straw and is of fine quality.

What corn is grown is beautifully ripe and most of it in the shock.

Potatoes, although a light yield, are excellent in quality.

Living in the county for almost forty years, I think I never saw the streams and springs lower than now. Many have been drawing water for some weeks; but the health of our people is very good. Few cases of severe sickness have occurred during the summer and we try to feel grateful that the dread Diphtheria has not been among us for some months.

Roulet.

Select school commenced last Monday.

Born, Sept. 6th, to Mr. Jno. Tenbrook and wife, a daughter.

Miss Gertrude Boyington has gone to Olean to attend school.

Mr. Alonzo Greenman and wife have been attending Camp-meeting at Hornellsville.

The Potter Enterprise
Wednesday Evening,
October 12, 1881 –
Vol. VIII, No. 22

- The first ice of the season formed last Tuesday night. It was not very thick, but its cold qualities was equal to that of the January product.

- W. H. Tassell, who has been reading medicine with Dr. C. S. French, of Millport, is attending lectures at the College of Physicians and Surgery, Baltimore, Md.

- Charley Breisnick has gone to Keokuk to finish his Medical Course and will return with the Sheepskin in the Spring. Breisnick is bound to succeed. He has always paid his own way. Last Spring he came from Keokuk broke, and since that time by hard work and economy has earned and saved a sufficient sum to pay his expenses the coming winter. Any young man who can do that has the material in him to make a success in any profession he may undertake.

The Potter Enterprise
Wednesday Evening,
October 19, 1881 –
Vol. VIII, No. 23

- L. R. Bliss has purchased of Mr. F. W. Knox the building lot directly west of the Baptist church. Consideration, $400. Mr. Bliss will put up a dwelling house on his new purchase.

Township Tidings from Potter County, Pennsylvania
Volume I, 1880 - 1884

- Chris. Schautenberger is not likely to suffer for a lack of potatoes for the use of his family this season, and by practicing a little economy in their use will have a few left for seed in the Spring. Last week he finished digging the tubers and upon measuring them up found that he had nine hundred and twenty bushels. He received an offer of 85 cents per bushel for part of them, in the field. Mr. Schautenberger will market his crop in McKean and Cameron counties.

Eleven Mile.
Oct. 15, 1881.

A real surprise party was gathered at the house of Mr. and Mrs. A. S. Lyman, on the 10th inst., but very pleasant nevertheless. The occasion was their twentieth wedding anniversary. They had no thought of celebrating the event, and consequently, were caught in the usual wash-day exercise, by the first arrivals, but an early adjournment of those exercises were effected, and soon the arrivals increased; then with the abundance of eatables, with which they came equipped, upon an extension table (which they left on departing) a right royal feast was spread. As evening came, the younger people appeared and soon their lively games were in progress while their elders enjoyed a social chat. Refreshments were partaken of again and, with kindly salutations, the party retired at a seasonable hour, leaving highly cherished memories of usefulness and value to host and hostess. The families present were those of Wm. Dalrymple, of Bolivar; D. Kelly, J. T. Rathbun, Mrs. C. Healy, G. F. Rowlee, B. F. Lyman and A. V. Butterfield, Eleven Mile; Walter Wells, W. W. Crittenden and Mrs. Hunt, Oswayo; Mrs. H. O. Yale, Willing, N.Y., and A. D. Colcord, Coudersport. Other friends sent lines of regret that they could not attend. Those from Mr. and Mrs. W. A. Crosby, accompanied by a sett of flat-irons, closed with hoping "you will be able to keep your pathway smooth through life." Mr. and Mrs. G. K. Smith were kept home by sickness of family. They sent presents which are highly cherished by the recipients thereof, who, though sad by reason of the broken home circle, yet feel that they have cause for joy and thankfulness after twenty years of life together.

Raymond.

Drought is over, but springs and well fill up slowly.

Pastures, a few weeks ago, so dry, are now looking green like Spring.

Some severe cases of sickness on either side of us.

Mrs. G. W. G. Judd is quite low with rheumatism and inflamation. Dr. Post is attending her. Her daughter, Mrs. Peck, is with her.

Walter Guernsey is also sick with the typhoid fever.

James Smith, for some time past visiting his parents at Raymond, starts for Michigan this morning.

Last Monday a party of seven persons viz: Mrs. Heggie, Mr. and Mrs. Amos Raymond, Mr. and Mrs. D. L. Raymond and daughter and Daniel Raymond, started on a visit to Michigan.

Miss Jane Swain, for some time past living in the family of her brother, Rev. J. L. Swain, is about to return to her home in New Jersey.

Robert Allison and wife just made a flying visit from Spring Mills, to this place to see Mrs. Allison's sister, Mrs. Lenora Presho.

Oswayo.

Mr. Mike Kline and Miss Mary Barr were married, at Sharon Center, on the evening of the 8th inst.

Mr. and Mrs. Wm. Moyer rejoices in the birth of a fourteen pound boy, which occurred on the 10th inst.

Chas. Head has a contract to deliver seventy thousand feet of pine lumber at Richburg. Consequently the road is lined with teams hauling it to its destination.

Ed Crittenden has got the "boss" span of horses in the county. He refused two hundred and fifty dollars for one of them a short time ago.

Our church members are divided into two parties at present, and Eugene Colgrove is tickled all over at the way the gospel is taught in Oswayo.

The Potter Enterprise
Wednesday Evening,
October 26, 1881 –
Vol. VIII, No. 24

Allegany.

Beautiful fall weather just now, crops nearly all secured and some farmers have commenced fall plowing.

Mrs. G. W. G. Judd is very low about down to death's door. Her children are all with her at present, also a sister and husband, Mr. and Mrs. Wilmot of Ill.

Old Mr. Bird's hand, that was crushed in the cider mill, is doing well, under the treatment of Dr. Ashcraft of Ellisburg. The people of that place ought to be thankful, that they have a physician, that does not refuse to visit a patient after dark, in case of an accident, and that can ride two nights in succession, if called to do so.

- Andrew Berger, of Summit, cut his left wrist with a chisel last Saturday, barely missing the artery. Dr. Mattison dressed the injured wrist.

- Rock Andrews already has a large gang of men at work on his Dingman Run lumber job. Geo. Boyer has also commenced cutting logs on his job.

- T. Benton Brown, Elvin Womelsdorff, Julius Doerner and Emmerson Miles, for the last few months forming part of the Engineer Corps of one of the Allegany narrow gauge lines, returned home last week.

Fishing Creek.

Jefferson Sweeves, formerly of Jefferson county, has moved into M. E. Baker's house.

B. A. Green has the new school house inclosed and has commenced painting it.

Township Tidings from Potter County, Pennsylvania
Volume I, 1880 - 1884

David Calkins has his new house completed and ready to move into.

The oil well is down 1000 feet. When at 500 feet a large vein of salt water was found. The derrick was boarded up last Saturday and no one is allowed to go into it.

Raymond.

Warmer.

Not much wet.

E. E. Kelley has a bonanza. 'Tis not a boy. 'Tis not a girl, but Ed is, or ought to be, a happy man. The drillers have struck oil. That is they have found water and we hope Kelley will no longer be obliged to haul water for a mile on a stoneboat, as he has been obliged to do during all this long drought. The drillers began work last Monday morning in the bottom of his well, and after going some over 30 feet through solid rock struck a good vein of water. We hope others of our neighbors, having "balky" wells, will try this new remedy with equal success, for 'tis no easy or pleasant matter to be obliged to haul water a mile or more for weeks together.

James Pierce and wife, of Allegan Co., Mich., old time residents and pioneers of Allegany, are visiting friends in Allegany and Bingham.

The new store at Gold draws near completion and Frank Raymond's house is also nearly finished.

The Potter Enterprise
Wednesday Evening,
November 2, 1881 –
Vol. VIII, No. 25

- A. A. Swetland has moved to Westfield.

- Will Absom has removed to Bolivar, N.Y.

- Mrs. R. L. Nichols has a new Phaeton, from the Sardinia carriage works.

- Eldred Wood found a fine two-year old bear in his trap, on the West Branch, last Sunday morning.

Costelloville.

Not hearing from this part of the county in some time, we think it time to inform you of what is going on here at Costelloville.

Business is as lively as ever. The men are working from six a.m. until six p.m.

The telephone line is now being put up by Thos. Wrench, of Rixford, Pa.

We have had a number of heavy frosts this Fall.

There are an abundance of apples this year, and cider making seems to be the order of the day.

It is very sickly around here now.

J. V. Flynn is very low with typhoid fever. He is being attended by Dr. Ellison, of Coudersport.

Geo. Quimby has the typhoid fever.

Eldred Clark has been very sick with billious fever, but is recovering slowly. Dr. Stephens, of Port Allegany, attended him.

Mrs. Edward Glaspy, daughter of Miller Rees, died on the 25th inst., of fever, after an illness of about three weeks.

Our school is progressing finely, under the management of Miss Sylvia Quimby, of Homer.

The Brownlee school, taught by L. D. Ripple, is also progressing.

Mr. and Mrs. Jacob Peet returned home, last week, from visiting their daughter, Mrs. Thos. Wrench, at Rixford.

You may ask, "why Mr. Whitcome is so proud of late." Surely he has a right to be. It's a girl.

Eleven Mile.

Fall plowing and getting in readiness for Winter are now among the varied employments of farmers. Getting apples, potatoes and other products to market, furnishes an agreeable change of labor, especially that part which pertains to receiving and disbursing again the proceeds thereof. Everything edible, for man or beast, finds ready sale, at fair, if not high prices, and the prospects are that such will continue to be the situation for future years.

Benj. Thomas has leased some 200 acres of land in the vicinity of the State line, near the Crandall lot, and has a rig up and expects to start his drill next week and is expected to make a genuine effort to find oil. At any rate there is no doubt but that within a year this territory will be tested to quite an extent.

A dozen members of G.A.R. visited the Post at Sharon Centre the 22nd inst., and were right royally entertained with refreshments, soft tack and good rations by the hand of comrade Burdick and household, and no less agreeably so, socially, by the boys, especially so, by comrade Hitchcock's sabre drill and the discussion of comrades on the relative merits of sabre and bayonet, as weapons.

J. T. Rathbun jumped from his haymow and seriously lamed his leg.

The Potter Enterprise
Wednesday Evening,
November 9, 1881 –
Vol. VIII, No. 26

Genesee Forks.

We are yet reveling in the delicious breeze of balmy autumn weather. But like the decline of life, winter is slowly but surely approaching. How little we realize when engaged and occupied in the bustle and activity of life, that

Time, the destroyer

Will desolate all.

And with the rest of the world, time brings a few changes to our little place. I notice that J. Carpenter has made quite an improvement to his neat looking store, by a nicely painted front, and a large addition being built on back.

P. Lewis has his shop completed and is now engaged in business as a blacksmith.

Stephen Hurd's store now presents a neat appearance, with a nicely built wall underneath.

The school, at this place, is progressing finely under the management of Miss Addie Douglas.

J. Carpenter had the misfortune to loose a nice horse not long since.

Raymond.

Fair.
Rain.
Frosts.
Ploughing.
Husking.
Wild geese.
Woods bare.
Evenings lengthen.
Fresh apple juice.
Looking for School Marms.

H. F. Weaver, who has been, for some weeks, laid by with a lame foot is getting around again.

While Eber Bebee was ploughing this week, on the Hendrix farm, he found quite a patch of strawberries in full bloom.

Mrs. Rodolphus Wells is very sick and Walter Guernsey has a very severe attack of throat disease. I don't know whether it is diphtheria or quinzy.

Wm. Clark, so badly hurt some weeks ago, by being thrown from a buggy, is slowly gaining.

Alva Carpenter is still very sick.

Drillers were going towards the house of Zalmon Moore yesterday; and that means another well of water.

Frank Conable sends a lot of cattle to Emporium this week.

Every body busy and plenty of work for all.

If any one goes without bread 'twill not be for lack of opportunity to earn it.

Forest House.

In addition to the dwellings built during the spring and summer, other structures have been added, and new numbers have been added to the population of this place.

The new depot is rapidly nearing completion and the grading around it has been greatly improved.

It is a well known fact that we have no dram-shops in our immediate vicinity, yet the evil effect of a too free indulgence in the ardent can occasionally be seen, even in this place.

Frequent visits to our neighboring village, Port Allegany, seems to have a demoralizing effect on some of our resident young men.

We will not, of course, positively assert whether it is the change of air, or the quantity or quality of water? with which they satiate their thirst that causes them to act more like maniacs than men on their return.

We have a resident shoemaker in the person of A. J. Larkin, and as he is a skillful workman, the lack of employment is a thing unknown to him, since locating here.

"Whom the Gods love, die young." Had the "Gods" manifested any affinity for boys of the stamp of Allie Glover, (a pupil in our school) our teacher, Mrs. S. J. Hall, would have escaped shameful treatment, at his hands, at the close of school on Friday last.

Judging from the extent to which Glassmire's "narrow gauge" is patronized, we conclude it is the popular route for parties who are desirous of reaching a rail road.

Hand to hand encounters seem to be in order in this place of late. Several fights have came under our notice of late, and both, the assailants and assailed, have come out of the attack in an unsound condition. Our eyes and head are all right so far, but if this state of affairs exist much longer, we expect to share a proportionate portion of the bruises or else get over a large tract of land in a small space of time.

All of the "boys" have smoked of late, and Joseph Klein (our blacksmith) was the individual who "set em up," he having taken unto himself a partner to share his joys and sorrows. We wish him all the joy and happiness attainable in this life, and trust he may not lack for help to "strike when the iron is hot."

Jacob Frantz has given up running the Briggs' mill.

A. J. Allen also, has "petered out" on a log job let to him by H. A. Avery.

The telephone line, connecting this place with North Wharton, is about completed.

Any number of teams, laden with farm produce, pass through our village daily, enroute for Emporium and points beyond.

- Mr. Henry Schilderberger now occupies the south half of the Zimmerman building and is engaged in the wholesale and retail cigar trade, manufacturing his own cigars. His cigars are made of pure tobacco – no cabbage leaf filling.

- The Grand Army of the Republic and the Equitable Aid Union now occupy their new quarters over Z. J. Thompson's grocery, where they have very pleasant and comfortable rooms. Both organizations are in a prosperous condition.

- Mr. D. W. Butterworth, for several years publisher of the *Journal*, leaves this morning for a New Jersey city where he fills an engagement as foreman of a daily paper. Mr. Butterworth is a practical printer and every way competent to fill the position. He leaves many warm friends who wish him success in his new field.

Millport.

The splendid fall weather has given the farmers ample time to gather crops and do their fall ploughing. To-day, there is a change, and we are having quite a snow fall and the air is very keen.

A. J. Barnes has his house completed and his family have removed thither.

Mr. H. J. Elliott, of Wellsboro, has rented the Colwell house and will soon become a resident of this place.

Dr. Sharpe has moved to Oswayo.

Mr. J. L. Warner has his house newly painted.

Allegany.

Muddy roads and cold disagreeable weather is what November usually brings us, and this year is no exception to the rule.

Whooping cough is making its appearance among us.

Mrs. G. W. G. Judd died last Thursday, (Nov. 3,) and was carried to her last resting place yesterday in the cemetery at Coudersport. The funeral services was also held at the M. C. Church there. She has gone down to her grave fully prepared, after a long life of usefulness, both in her own family and in the community around them. In her sickness, she was a great sufferer, yet could praise God while passing under the rod. Rev. Dillenbeck, the new preacher in charge, delivered the funeral discourse. Waldo Judd and mother was in attendance at the funeral. Other relatives from Oswayo also.

**The Potter Enterprise
Wednesday Evening,
November 16, 1881 –
Vol. VIII, No. 27**

- Snow on the hilltops Monday morning.

- A telephone line from Westfield to Coudersport via Ulysses and Brookland is talked of.

- The new road connecting Cherry Springs with the East Fork is completed. The length of the road is five or six miles. A petition is being circulated asking for a mail route from Wharton, up the East Fork to Cherry Springs, with a post office at Hull's.

Keating.

Rainy weather is what we are getting just now and that is just what we need, the creeks and springs being very low.

A. H. Crosby is building a porch on his house.

John Miller moved his family to the oil country last week.

The new road which is being built from this place to Portage township, is getting along slow but, we think, sure. At the first letting of the jobs, James Reese took 478 rods which he did not work and it was let again yesterday, H. Bridges bidding off 78 rods and Alvin Rennels the remaining 400.

**The Potter Enterprise
Wednesday Evening,
November 23, 1881 –
Vol. VIII, No. 28**

Ellisburg.

People, about this place, are generally well.

Mr. G. Moody, our blacksmith, is very sick, but hopes are entertained of his recovery.

Mr. Orson Ellis has his store and dwelling finished and painted, and is now doing a lively trade.

Mr. S. Stillman, will soon have a large stock of logs at his mill.

Mr. T. Gilliland & Co., have their store well filled, and are doing a thriving business.

Our fall school, taught by Miss Anna L. Jones, of Corning, N.Y., closed on Saturday last.

It is rumored that a test well is soon to be put down, at or near, this place, and it is hoped that oil may be found.

Millport.

Since our last writing, death has been in our midst and claimed for its own a son of Lewis Carpenter, a young man just beginning life for himself. William will be sadly missed by his sisters and brother. His parents have the sympathy of the neighbors in their affliction. His disease was fever.

Mr. Chas. Taylor is also very sick with the fever. He is attended by Dr. Booth of Ceres.

Mr. Wallace Sloat has a new hired girl, a few days old, which he intends to keep until some young man carries her off.

There has been a marked improvement in this place, this season, in the way of building, stumping land, etc.

Eleven Mile.

The length, breadth and thickness of the *mud* is unmeasureable here and a few miles north-west towards Bolivar traveling is feasible only by balloon or across lots. It is a first rate time to stay at home, kill the hogs, grind sausage and in other ways while away the time until Vennor gets the mud frozen solid.

Lumbermen are wishing for a good winter of snow, to move the millions of logs now being prepared for hauling.

A Mr. Johnson has moved a saw mill onto a lot, near the State Line, where the Wellsville and Coudersport road crosses it, which is expected to prove a great convenience to people in this vicinity.

The oil well (Ben Thomas') is in progress, but operations are slow, as his leases only require him to have it completed next April.

Luther Brizzee who, for several years past, has been a town charge, has lately been granted a pension for disability incurred in the United States service. For eight years he has been unable to walk from paralysis caused by sunstroke, originally. His back pay was six thousand five hundred dollars and he draws fifty dollars per month. This is the largest payment made to any claimant for pension near here. But no one should be envious of his good fortune, for who would take the disability for the pension?

**The Potter Enterprise
Wednesday Evening,
December 7, 1881 –
Vol. VIII, No. 30**

Allegany.

Last week dandelion blossoms were found quite plenty, as fresh and bright as they are in May.

Colds are a plenty as they usually are at this season of the year.

Mrs. Cal. Ford is very sick with erysipelas, and has been for the past week. Friday of last week Mr. Ford was taken down with the same disease. Mrs. Will Ford is sick with throat disease.

M. A. Veeley is the proudest man among us, all on account of that fine girl baby.

Miss Edith Haskell is home from school at Lock Haven, until after the holidays, and reports the school in a flourishing condition.

W. A. Gardner is the man that will find plenty of work for himself and boys, as he is going to work Wm. Matteson's farm for the next four years, together with his own. Matteson goes to Genesee Forks to live, commences moving this week.

H. Beeby has moved to Coudersport is going to drive stage through the winter.

The men that have lumbering to do are impatient for sleighing while the farmers that have not yet finished plowing are in no hurry for it to freeze up.

- Last year ice houses were filled before this time.

- The trade in sleigh bells and buffalo robes is very light.

- A very poor winter for lumbering and other business thus far.

- Our farmers are doing considerable plowing for spring crops.

- Ball playing on the Square Dec. 3d does not happen every year.

North Bingham.

Keep close watch over the little ones, for there is much sickness among them.

Mrs. Hamilton Warner, of Harrison township, died recently.

The North Bingham Cheese Factory has closed operations for this season. The amount of milk received the last day was a little over a thousand pounds.

Mr. and Mrs. B. J. Baker have an addition to their family – it's a girl.

Sartwell Creek.

Skidding logs and preparing for winter is the order of the day.

Our winter school commenced last Monday under the management of Miss Sarah Carey.

Mr. Andrew Oleson, of Wisconsin, is a guest of Mr. Ole Hanson. Mr. Oleson is a nephew of Mrs. Hanson.

An infant child of Joel Fessenden's was buried on the 28th inst. About three weeks ago Mr. Fessenden's wife died; he has the sympathy of his many friends.

Roulet.

The store of White & Lyman has been repainted and a new stock of goods added.

Mrs. Laroy Lyman, who has been visiting her daughter, in Michigan, returned a few days ago.

Lewis Lyman and family, of Sartwell Creek, have moved to Newark, N.J.

Miss Annie Aylesworth is building a dwelling house.

L. W. Crawford is remodeling and otherwise improving his dwelling house.

On Thursday last the many friends of Mr. and Mrs. L. B. Pomeroy gathered at their residence to celebrate their China Wedding. They were the recipients of a number of useful as well as ornamental presents, of which, they were well deserving.

Forest House.

It certainly is December. Yet the weather we have had so far, is not, generally speaking, in keeping with the month. No snow to mention. No sound of sleigh bells, no sleigh rides yet this winter. Will it always be thus? We hope not, and trust that a fall of the "beautiful" sufficient to enable all to observe the coming Holidays appropriately, is still in store for us.

The small break in the boiler at Brigg's mill has been repaired and again the buzz of the saw is heard from dawn till after dusk.

Tie making is getting to be one of the foremost industries in this place – of high altitude and pure air. They are sold to various railroad companies and command a fair price.

The store, near Avery's Hotel, has been recently renovated and fitted up to accommodate a stock of goods which B. S. Colwell, of Portville, N.Y., has put in it. It will be remembered that White & Lyman, of Roulet, run the above store for nearly two years and retired from business, in this part of Potter. Made too much money (?) in such a short time. Mr. C. is a man of means and even if he should retire from business here, with additional experience and less means, he will have the satisfaction of knowing that humanity has been benefitted.

The old depot, which was used since the building of the road, is no more – torn down and destroyed.

The Potter Enterprise Wednesday Evening, December 14, 1881 – Vol. VIII, No. 31

Allegany.
E. D. Carr, and wife from Kansas have moved on the G. W. Presho farm.

Anson Weaver began his school at the corner's last Monday and Miss Lettie Palmer at Gold.

Will Clark of Gold recovers very slowly from his hurt by being thrown from a buggy in the Fall.

The little tannery at that place is turning out some very nice looking upper leather.

A. C. Wright has made a nice improvement on his farm by clearing off and ploughing an old fallow of 7 or 8 acres.

Alva Carpenter is gaining very slowly.

One of the traveling agents inquired at the Corners a few weeks ago, "if every body whose name is Raymond is n the mercantile business?" "Every place I come to I find a Raymond or some connection, in the store" – This remark led us to count up, and here is the result.

F. A. Raymond & Co., at Gold; A. F. Raymond, Son & Co., Ulysses; Fred Raymond, Ceres, N.Y.; A. A. & D. L. Raymond, Lymansville; J. L. Raymond & Peck, North Bingham; Lovina Raymond, Millinery Goods, Coudersport; Frank Conable, son in law of Amos Raymond, Raymond; F. D. Leet, son in law of Amos Raymond, Emporium, and Thos. Gilliland, son in law of Daniel Raymond, Ellisburg. So we will call this the mercantile family of Potter county.

- N. H. Goodsell has made over 4,000 bushels of apples into cider this season.

- Johnston Brothers have sold their blacksmith shop and tools to Lyman Baker.

- Robt. Smith has moved to Oswayo village and will open a meat market in that thriving place. We trust his venture will yield him rich returns.

- Zimmerman has opened his boot and shoe store. He keeps all kinds of boots, shoes and findings. Sole leather, upper leather, morocco, needles, thread pegs, and everything that a shoemaker needs. Boots made to order and repairing promptly attended to.

A Narrow Escape.

On Sunday evening, as W. Bassett and Rev. A. Cone were returning from a funeral in Sweden, and when just east of the mill, on Second street, the fastenings of the tongue to the carriage gave way and Rev. Cone was thrown out upon the frozen ground striking upon his head. W. Bassett was thrown over him and fell upon his hands. Except some bruises both escaped without injury. The horses were caught at the river near Mr. Benson's.

Millport.

Mr. Charles Tyler, who had been ill, for a long time, of typhoid fever, died on the 6th of Dec. He was a kind neighbor and many sorrowing friends attended his funeral, which took place at his home. His bereaved wife has the sympathy of all.

Nobody visits, for it is so muddy that nothing but business cause people to pass over the bad roads.

Oswayo.

The people of this quiet village are enjoying very good health at present.

Mr. Amos Cole, of Corning, N.Y., and Miss Ella Cone, of this place, were joined in the holy bonds of matrimony last week. We wish them peace and prosperity.

Mr. G. K. Smith has opened a blacksmith shop, next door to Snath's wagon shop, where he will attend to all business in his line.

We are sorry to record the death of George Moody, of Ellisburg. The Spiritualist M.D. failed to save him.

The Potter Enterprise
Wednesday Evening,
January 4, 1882 –
Vol. VIII, No. 33

North Bingham.

Our district school is being well taught by Miss Grace Lewis of this place.

One day last week Mr. Dewit Chase of this place caught a beautiful Robbin-s at Spring Mills, N.Y. Success to the happy couple.

On Christmas eve there was a beautiful and well loaded tree at the church in this place. Six hundred and thirty five dollars and twenty seven cents together with twenty eight closed packages were distributed among the people. The total value of the presents is estimated at seven hundred dollars.

J. L. Raymond of this place says that he has nothing to do with the store here except that he buys about as many goods there as any one. N. J. Peck is the sole proprietor, and his sales for the month of Oct. A.D. 1881 were three thousand nine hundred and eighty six dollars and eighty cents.

- Dan Olmsted is teaching school in Homer.

- James Rounsville is teaching school in Sweden.

- Rounsvill's mill had to shut down last week, too much water in the Allegheny.

- No mails from the South Saturday on account of high water in the Susquehanna.

- D. W. Butterworth has purchased the Pierce property, south side of the river, for $900.

- D. W. Butterworth has taken charge of the *Journal* printing office, and will be found at his post as smiling as ever.

- Isaac Benson has purchased the vacant square north of Joseph Mann's residence, paying therefor the sum of two thousand dollars.

- R. W. Swetland is attending the State Normal School at Lock Haven. Potter County now has twelve students attending this institution of learning.

- E. C. Franke, of Sweden, has returned from Binghampton, where for some time he has been attending Lowell's Business College. Mr. Franke has received his diploma.

- With the opening of the new year the Wellsville, via Oswayo, stage line passes under the control of D. F. Glassmire, Jr. Dan has experience and will run a good line, and we hope will accumulate much wealth thereby.

Pleasant Valley.

A green Christmas for 1881.

Muddy roads and plenty of rain is the general complaint.

Elmer Demmings has moved into his new house.

Judge N. C. Hammond has moved to Coudersport.

Times are dull but an occasional dance or oyster supper breaks the monotony of the long evenings.

The United Brethren will hold quarterly meeting January 7th and 8th, 1882, at the Reed school house.

Mrs. Fred Lehman is quite sick.

Mr. and Mrs. Arthur Witter spent Christmas at Turtle Point.

Mr. and Mrs. Rosco Weimer spent Christmas with Mrs. Weimer's parents at Friendship.

Married – At the residence of the bride's parents, December 24th, 1881, by John Davison, Esq., Mr. Alva A. Thompson and Miss Julia Hanson, both of this place. A long and happy life to the couple is the wish of their many friends.

Born – To Mr. and Mrs. John Reed, a daughter.

Eleven Mile.

After a month of very unseasonable weather, this last day of the year is not quite so, and it is to be hoped the future of the winter weather may consist of snow sufficient for log drawing and other team work. Lumbermen have stopped cutting with only half the desired quantity skidded.

An epidemic cold has hold of many subjects, and whooping-cough contributes its agreeable convulsions to the younger persons of the community.

At the annual election of A. W. Estes Post G.A.R. the following were elected, J. D. Lee, C.; A. S. Lyman, S.C.V.; Wm. Moyer, J.V.C.; G. F. Rowlee, Q.; John Davis, O.D.; G. R. Wilber, Sur.; Wm. Fessenden, Chaplain; Levi Robbins, O.C. A. S. Lyman Representative to Department Encampment. J. B. Stewart Alternate. J. C. Wilkinson was appointed Adjutant. W. L. Shattuck Q.S. The officers elect are to be publicly installed on the evening of Jan. 14th, after which a soldier's supper of hardtack, bean-soup, coffee, etc., is to be given for the benefit of the Post funds. Rations 20 cts. each. Commander John M. Covey of A. F. Jones Post, acts as Mustering Officer for Installation.

**The Potter Enterprise
Wednesday Evening,
January 11, 1882 –
Vol. VIII, No. 34**

Millport.

The funeral of Mr. Isaac Barnes, who died suddenly on the 2d inst., took place on the fourth of January. The sermon was preached by the Baptist minister of Coudersport. There was a large attendance, and the discourse was good and will long be remembered by the people here.

Ross and Alonzo Nichols had quite a runaway on Tuesday last. Just between Barnes' store and the Millport bridge the strap on the neck yoke broke and let the tongue fall which frightened the horses. One of the men jumped out and got them by the bits but failed to check them. The driver ran them into the fence of R. L. Nichols, where they broke loose from the buggy and ran a short distance before they were stopped. Injured one of the horses slightly and broke the buggy and all the fence.

Oswayo.

Much sickness about there at present.

Adelbert Smith is very sick with fever.

Dr. H. H. Munson is failing rapidly, and others are complaining of various ailments.

Fifty-seven couple attended the dance at the Lee House last night. A good attendance considering the roads.

John Barr has a matched span of grey horses, big fellows and good ones.

- D. W. Butterworth has purchased the *Potter Journal* and assumed entire control. Since coming under the charge of Mrs. M. W. Mann the paper has been creditably conducted, and shown evidence of more earnest, conscientious work than most county papers can boast of. Mr. Butterworth has experience and will make a success of his venture.

**The Potter Enterprise
Wednesday Evening,
January 18, 1882 –
Vol. VIII, No. 35**

- First sleighing of the season on Wednesday last.

- Albert Lyman is sending large quantities of cherry lumber to the railroad.

- Edward Forster has rented a lot of D. F. Glassmire, next to Grabe Brother's furniture store, and will at once erect a building, to be occupied by himself as a harness shop. Ed is a good workman, steady and industrious, and will give satisfaction every time.

East Hebron.

Mr. and Mrs. H. G. Booth recently celebrated the anniversary of their Wedding, twenty-five years ago. A large number of friends and relatives were present and everybody had a pleasant time. Our friends, who thus celebrated their silver wedding, received a number of presents, not all of silver, but very nice nevertheless, and as tokens of esteem and friendship, of more than money value.

Mrs. Margaret McDowell, and two sons, from Wisconsin, are visiting Mrs. H. G. Booth, sister of Mrs. McDowell.

At a Christmas dinner at Patrick Shannon's, four generations were seated at the same table.

Our school is progressing finely under the efforts of Adelbert Hollenbeck, teacher.

Eleven Mile.

The heaviest snow-fall, so far this winter, came Tuesday night, and not enough for sleighing at that.

Business outlook for lumbermen is not encouraging except to those who may be independent of the aid of snow, to get stock in upon, or those who have a stock on hand.

"Times" are extremely dull in this vicinity. The whooping cough causes more stir than all other agencies together, and that is on the decline, it is hoped.

Lorenzo Snow and family, who removed some years ago to Nebraska, have been here on a visit. He is a blacksmith and runs a large wagon factory there, and is well suited with his Western home.

The friends of M. H. Johnson, who removed two years ago to the Black Hill country, Dakota, may be pleased to learn of the health and prosperity of himself and family in their far away home. He occupied a homestead of 160 acres and is encouraged in cultivating crops for the maintenance of the family, and finds ready sale, at good prices, for the surplus, to the numerous mining camps nearby. In short, notwithstanding the want of schools, as yet, and the inevitable privations of new settlers life, they are well pleased and quite contented with their Dakota Ranch "away beyond the West," and live in hopes of a speedy competence in that rapidly growing section of our land.

The Potter Enterprise Wednesday Evening, January 25, 1882 – Vol. VIII, No. 36

- J. B. Benson sports a new Portland cutter.

- Gales Tannery, at the mouth of the West Branch, is receiving 110 cords of bark per day.

- L. C. King has rented M. L. Gridley's building on Main Street and intends making alterations, so that he can accommodate travelers.

- Albert Lyman, of Sweden Valley, has shipped about 200,000 feet of cherry lumber since the freeze up. All this has been hauled, by teams, to Port Allegany, and he still has a large amount to ship.

Allegany.

Young lambs in Allegany.

Mr. Beebe's horse broke its leg recently, on the road, and had to be killed.

Daniel Raymond is getting better and so is E. B. Morley and his child.

A. A. Presho is sick with billious fever.

Our sleighing is light as yet. Maybe more will follow.

Oswayo.

Delos Hawley has rented the Lee House and took possession last Monday. The former proprietor, J. E. Lee, is going to make his home in York State during the interval afforded by the Lease.

Parties are leasing land in this vicinity preparatory to putting down an oil well. Said well to be commenced in thirty days after the land (300 acres) is secured. Two hundred and twenty-five acres have been leased already.

Saw and shingle mills are running night and day here to supply the demand that Richburg makes on us for building material.

The Potter Enterprise
Wednesday Evening,
February 1, 1882 –
Vol. VIII, No. 37

- Mr. VanWinkle, the tailor, has rented rooms over Greisel's harness shop.

- The high wind, of last Thursday night, blew the smokestack of Metzger's mill to the ground.

- A number of our citizens filled their ice houses last week. The ice was from five to eight inches thick.

- Rev. Leavenworth has purchased the Wm. Pinney property, this side of the Braitling stone quarry.

- Charles Reissman has sold his horse to Charley Welton, to replace one that recently dropped dead in the road.

- According to borough ordinance, cattle are not allowed to run in the street during the winter, but they run just the same.

Keating.

Business is lively here.

The new road between here and Portage township is nearly done.

Our school is progressing finely, under the control of Miss Amy White, of Coudersport.

Lyceum every Tuesday night and preaching every two weeks by Rev. W. Holland.

Our mail route which we advertised as lost a short time ago has been found, it will go through this place twice a day, from Coudersport to Keating Summit then back to Coudersport, thus bringing the mail to us from both ways.

E. Fourness has been appointed P.M. and the office named Vine.

Forest House.

On Saturday last, Mr. Briggs' mill caught fire, but was extinguished with but little damage.

Potatoes sell at $1.05 per bushel. What are we Irishmen coming to?

J. W. Dingee has seven teams hauling logs to Briggs' mill.

This cold spell has made us all sigh for the violet and sunflower, two or three more and we shall take to Wilde poetry ourselves.

Allegany.

Erysipelas has again made its appearance among us. Mrs. M. A. Veeley is the victim and very sick. I believe she is attended by Dr. Ashcraft of Ellisburg.

H. Veeley has bought the boss span of horses.

F. Kies has sold his team.

M. A. Veeley is still buying supplies for the lumber camp.

A. Cool and son are still cutting shingle bolts. W. M. Slaughter is working for them.

The sleighing is gone again, and it looks dubious for log and bark drawing.

There are so many sick, that the attendance at church was small yesterday.

The Potter Enterprise
Wednesday Evening, February 8, 1882 – Vol. VIII, No. 38

- Dr. C. S. French, of Millport, is making arrangements to remove to Coudersport, to practice medicine.

- Dr. Ashcraft, of Ellisburg, has rented rooms over C. S. Jones' store and will move to Coudersport, for the practice of his profession, soon.

Forest House.

Snow in abundance assists lumbering that is carried on here to a great extent.

About twenty teams are busy hauling logs to the mills located here.

Pinkeye has reached the Summit. A. E. Williams has one valuable horse afflicted with this new disease. This is the first and only case in this section that has come under our notice.

Frank Farnam, an operator in Briggs mill, met with a serious accident one day last week while helping switch a car.

R. L. White is shipping lumber from this point to Buffalo.

W. G. Clark has taken possession of VanVorhees' mill and will put it in operation soon.

Pusher No. 12, an engine belonging on the railroad passing our village, was burned up, together with the round house at Shippen, last Friday.

Township Tidings from Potter County, Pennsylvania
Volume I, 1880 - 1884

Raymond.

Sleighing at last.

Yesterday, Feb. 5th, was the birthday of Ole Bull.

Mrs. E. B. Morley badly sprained her ankle, last week.

The donation at Gold, for Rev. Kelley, resulted in a help to the Elder of about $60.

Rumor says we have lost another Potter county boy, James Smith; gone to Michigan and got a wife.

Lester Vanderburg is visiting at D. L. Raymond's and looking toward his Nebraska home. Will leave, for the west, in March.

Roulet.

The young people of this place tripped the light fantastic toe at Tauschers Hall last Saturday night.

The people of Roulet have awakened at last to the necessity of having a church and are pushing the idea right along. J. V. Weimer comes to the front by donating a lot on Main St.

Goodall & Barr have opened a furniture and repairing shop in Mrs. Abbott's building. There were ten rocking chairs brought in for repairs in one day, this shows there isn't so much swinging on the gate.

Eleven Mile.

But little snow here, and therefore, the teams are idle and logs lie piled where skidded, nine-tenths of them. A snow flurry now and then gives encouragement for a day, and then as quickly vanishes.

The Potter Enterprise
Wednesday Evening,
February 15, 1882 –
Vol. VIII, No. 39

- Lumbermen are not happy.

- W. B. Gordnier is getting in a good stock of logs.

- Geo. Adams has leased the sawmill at Lymansville.

- Pipe for the Coudersport water company is being delivered today.

- A move is being made for the erection of a Methodist church at Harrison Valley.

The Potter Enterprise
Wednesday Evening,
February 22, 1882 –
Vol. VIII, No. 40

- An Iron or Stone bridge across the River at Second street is talked of.

- A Mr. Stevens, of Alfred, has purchased the Genesee Forks cheese factory paying therefor $1,200.

- D. F. Glassmire, Sr., is putting up a small dwelling house on Main street, between First and Second, for the use of his stage driver.

- Mrs. D. W. Butterworth has sold the Pierce property to Mrs. McCormick, and has purchased the Merrill property, on Lymansville street.

Allegany.

W. Peet has sold his farm to H. Veeley. Do not know the price paid.

I. Stryker takes the lead here, in making sugar.

Mrs. M. Veeley has recovered from ercysipelas, but has been suffering from a very bad throat.

Peter Green has another horse that has pink eye. There has been several cases of it near here, but none fatal so far.

East Homer.

The Terwilliger Mill is now cutting out some fine lumber.

Leonard Davis has received his new saw and we think the shingle bolt piles will soon be cut out.

We hear that O. W. Sikes wold be glad to rent his mill.

Our Singing School, under the care of Mr. Whitford, of Alfred, is meeting with success.

The Potter Enterprise Wednesday Evening, March 8, 1882 – Vol. VIII, No. 42

- Considerable Maple sugar has already been made and considerable more old sugar has been made over and sold as new.

- The log drive passed Coudersport last week. A week of sleighing, which we are not likely to get, would make another drive.

- R. Howland has removed his shop to the rooms formerly occupied by Greisel, as a harness shop, on East street. Mr. Howland has a fine stock of tools and will repair any part of your broken gun, or for that matter make you a gun entire. Now that the pigeon season is about to open, examine your guns and remember that you will want them in good shape when the birds begin to fly.

Oswayo.

The Reynolds Bros. have sold their planing mill to George and Horace Brizzee. Consideration, $1,700. Possession given immediately.

One of Erin's fair daughters lately arrived at Oswayo from the mother country and became the bride of Mr. Michael Maher. Miss Lettica Rigney was the bride's name. Good wishes follow them.

D. M. Wheeler steps high. It's a girl. Weight six pounds.

At the regular meeting of the A.W. Estes Post No. 125, G.A.R., on Saturday Evening, Feb. 25th, a large delegation from G.H. Barnes Post, Sharon and some comrades of --- Wessells Post, Portville, were present and a goodly number of members of A.W. Estes Post. After the regular order of business, which included the muster-in of four recruits, a social greeting about the Post was highly enjoyed, until nine o'clock when, supper being announced, the "boys" readily fell into line and marched to the McGonigal House where were nicely served up abundant rations of oysters, in styles to suit the taste of each. About forty guests and the same number of their hosts, comrades of the visited Post, partook of the viands and after a "smoke" all around, at eleven o'clock the comrades wended homeward retreating in good order. It is hoped they safely reach their camp and having the countersign were soon snugly stowed in their bunks, their slumbers guarded by household angels, and no fear of rattling drum with its "long roll" or shrill bugle's "boots and saddles" to disturb them. The feeble and ailing ones were provided with quinine at Surgeon's call, and were thus braced up for the assault upon rations and the homeward retreat.

A.W. Estes Post Ladies Society have held two sociables or campfires from which they realized about $20. A portion of this they used to purchase a Bible and other furniture of the Post Centre table. The gifts are heartily appreciated by the Post and will be gratefully accepted. The Society propose to continue the course in the future, devoting the proceeds to the benefit of the Post.

**The Potter Enterprise
Wednesday Evening,
March 15, 1882 –
Vol. VIII, No. 43**

- E. O. Rees has rented a store in Olean, and in a few days will remove his stock of jewelry to that place. Mr. Rees is a good workman and we are sorry to see him leave Coudersport. We wish him success in his new field of labor.

Forest House.
A new shoemaker presented himself to Mr. and Mrs. Larkins on the 24th ult., and was received into partnership. His weight is ten pounds.

Mr. Morgan, boarding at Mr. Allard's (formerly from Emporium,) was badly cut in the right arm, through the culpable carelessness of the man hewing ties with him. The cut was nearly six inches long, and Mr. H. was obliged to go to Port Allegany for surgical aid. He is suffering greatly from loss of blood. Mr. M. is by trade a carpenter and millwright, and is well known in Harrison Valley and other places in this county, where his acquaintances will be sorry to learn of his misfortune.

Eleven Mile.
Weather for March so far, seems in more seasonable order than for previous month.

Considerable sickness has prevailed, none fatal of late, until yesterday, when the infant child of Moses D. Kibbe, died of an affection of the lungs.

Wm. M. Rowlee, formerly of this place, who has resided for the past four years at Duke Centre, died last week at that borough. He had been in the army toward the close of the war, having been drafted.

Some excitement is raging in the vicinity of the headwaters of the Honeoye Creek in relation to oil. A few weeks will serve to ebb or flow its wave. At present one can only surmise that something is expected of it, by the activity in real estate thereabouts.

Don Lyman, who has been in the Black Hills country since Oct. 1879, has returned to his home here again.

Messrs. Chas. Day and G. H. Lyman have sold out their oil well supply store at Bolivar, and will likely engage in some other business soon. It is supposed they made a handsome investment there, as they were having a good trade, but Charley was always ready to sell anything he owned (except his wife and boy) provided he had a fair price offered.

Chris. Walker who bought a farm near Bolivar within two years for about $3000, has now sold the same for $17,406. The tide of fortune seems to flow to him readily, while perhaps to others she is the most fickle of dames, ebbing away their coffers.

Bingham.

Robbins and blue birds, those harbingers of Spring, have put in an appearance in Bingham and therefore "Winter has flown." If that is really the case, Winter must have dodged us this time only giving us an occasional puff from one of his wings as he flew past.

Business is lively, plenty of work and wages good.

Much complaints of colds, mumps and such like but not much serious illness.

Rev. A. H. Briggs likes to live here better than at Westfield and so he has just moved back on his farm.

The Singing School at North Bingham is progressing finely.

The Common Schools are generally closed and have proved very successful.

The sugar makers, or some of them, have had a fine run of sap.

The birds sing by day and the weather is so fine that the cats squall a night.

Allegany.

Three of J. Mattesons young children have had scarlet fever.

Mr. O. Dwight is no better and no hopes are entertained of his recovery.

On Wednesday of last week the neighbors and friends of I. Stryker cut wood for him, and the following Friday a wood bee was made for Mrs. O. Dwight.

- Charley Earle, a little son of John Earle, of Eulalia, met with a severe accident on Sunday last. Charley, with a little brother, was in the yard tapping a maple tree, and Charley came up behind his brother just as he was drawing back a double bitted axe to score the tree, the blade of the axe struck Charley on the side of the face just above his mouth, making a wound an inch and a half long. Dr. Buck was called and rendered surgical assistance. The lad will not be seriously inconvenienced by the wound, but will probably carry a reminder, in the shape of a scar, for many a day, perhaps for life.

**The Potter Enterprise
Wednesday Evening,
March 22, 1882 –
Vol. VIII, No. 44**

- Chris Mehring is building a new house, up McNamra Hollow.

- Mr. S. VanWinkle has moved into the rooms over Greisel's Harness Shop, where he now has very convenient quarters for carrying on the tailoring business. Mr. VanWinkle is a first class workman, and we are glad to learn, is driven with orders. One day last week he received orders for four suits, from Lewisville, where he formerly resided.

Roulet.

A. W. Johnson and Mrs. F. D. Weimer are in Oswego, N.Y. where they were called by the death of their mother, Mrs. C. W. Johnson.

There will be a singing school organized here next Thursday night, by Isaac Dingman of Hebron.

On Monday the 13th quite a serious accident occurred in this place, by which Volna Weidrich had an arm broken while playing on a scaffold in the barn. He fell a distance of fifteen feet, striking on his left arm, breaking the wrist.

Forest House.

Every resident of Potter county knows that the past winter has not been the best that ever was for lumbering and the interests connected therewith. Yet the people here, have done remarkably well in getting in logs; and what little sleighing we have been favored with has been improved to the best advantage.

The two mills, located here, have been turning out lumber at the rate of six hundred thousand feet per month, for the past two months.

There has been a small army of men engaged in tie making in this vicinity the past winter. Charles Glover has been the most successful of any; he having made ten thousand ties.

The Potter Enterprise
Wednesday Evening,
March 29, 1882 –
Vol. VIII, No. 45

- Fred Wimmer has opened a barber shop, in Kline's building.

- James Johnston is now sole proprietor of the Coudersport livery.

- Lant Crowell has purchased the E. O. Rees property on Main street.

- Dr. Frank Buck and W. B. Rees have entered into partnership in the Drug Business. The Doctor will continue the practice of medicine.

- Hammond's Tannery is to be enlarged.

- Mrs. John Pearsall was accidentally struck, with a knife, by her little daughter one day last week, cutting into one corner of her eye. Had the knife struck half an inch to one side it would have destroyed the sight.

Eleven Mile.

Roads have not been delightful here, all Winter, but the present month they have been exceptionally bad.

On the 19th the children and grandchildren of Mrs. M. E. Lyman met with her on the occasion of the seventy-eighth anniversary of her birth, and the 21st the family and friends of B. F. Lyman assisted him to celebrate his sixtieth anniversary of birth.

Preparations for farm work are being made on all sides, but the laborers are few and work needing to be done is manifold.

Oswayo.

Thos. Robbins has moved to Hornellsville.

George Brizzee has moved into the house formerly occupied by the Reynolds Bros.

The Reynolds Bros. have purchased Thos. Gilliland's store and stock of goods, at Ellisburg, and have gone into business there.

"Lin" Porter, having concluded that boarding out was rather expensive, sought the acquaintance of Miss Nettie Brockway, secured the services of Rev. Wm. North, rented a house in the Tannery row, and has commenced housekeeping in good style.

The first of April is approaching and several changes in residences are expected, which will be duly noted in our next budget of news.

Millport.

A few of the lumbermen are hauling on trucks, and a hard enough time of it they are having for the roads are awful.

There is great consolation in a shiny day now and then as it makes business for the sugar makers.

It has been a pleasant sight to see two little boys, sons of Mr. Isaac Lewis come through town with a pair of young steers which they have broken to drive very nicely, and to the boys credit be it said, they do not drive them, by yelling and whipping, but use better judgment than some men do in breaking steers.

Our summer school is to commence on the 17th inst., taught by Mr. Jasper Card, who it is expected will give satisfaction, he having taught several terms of school at Millport.

J. D. Staysa is renovating the old hotel.

No serious sickness in this place.

Allegany.

Mr. Peter Green has taken the Colesburg farm and hotel, that has been occupied by Ed. Haskel. He takes possession the first of April.

Mr. Haskell moves to Coudersport.

Mr. Bardon works Mr. Green's farm.

Warren Gardner has a tenant in his house on the hill, Mr. Dingman.

Dull sugar weather thus far, and plenty of mud as every one finds that has occasion to travel.

The Potter Enterprise
Wednesday Evening,
April 5, 1882 –
Vol. VIII, No. 46

- Wallace Abson has purchased a lot of John S. Ross, South side of the river, and has the stone on the ground for the foundation of his new house.

- Byron Ives dropped the blade of a sharp axe into his foot last Saturday while acting as axeman in the Survey of the McKean lands. Not serious as yet.

Whites Corners.

The farmers are making sugar and the season bids fair to be a good sugar season.

The company of the Excelsior Cheese Factory have organized with Frank Zimmer as cheese maker, and W. B. Jennings, salesman for the coming season.

N. M. Brooks is intending to go into the mercantile business again soon. May he be successful is the wish of the community.

Roulet.

Eber Card, who is attending school at Lock Haven, is home on vacation.

The friends of Mr. and Mrs. Isaac Lyman assembled at their home, on the evening of the 25th ult., to celebrate their 30th anniversary of wedded life.

Lon Fessenden has the material on the ground for building a dwelling house on Main Street.

George Conley was the fortunate fisherman on the 1st inst., he succeeded in hooking 38 of the speckled beauties.

Bingham.

Death has again invaded our vicinity. Fayette McCarn, a man of sterling worth died recently, after a severe illness, with Bright's Disease. He was a depot master and had served in that capacity for several years. He was the eldest son of L. E. McCarn, Esq., of this place and died at his father's. He leaves a wife and children who with loving parents, brothers, other relatives, and numerous friends mourn his loss.

A daughter of Wm. and Samantha Ensworth, also died of Diphtheria, March 23d, at 6 p.m., in the fifth year of her age.

Also a child of Seldan Carpenter, aged about seven months, died of congestion of the stomach and lungs.

Mr. Carpenter left home leaving his family in usual health, almost immediately thereafter the child fell sick and died in about twenty-four hours, so that when the father returned, his little darling had gone to be numbered with the angels.

Our sugar makers are reaping a rich harvest, that is, those of them who have plenty of storage.

The Potter Enterprise
Wednesday Evening,
April 12, 1882 –
Vol. VIII, No. 47

- Mrs. Miles White was quite seriously hurt one evening last week, by being run over by a couple of young men, running a foot race on the sidewalk.

- In surveying west of Colesburg April 7th, O. J. Rees discovered a line (running north on a variation of 40 deg. 25 sec.), 162 years old, said line is supposed to be a line run when the Connecticut Purchase was located. This is supposed to be the oldest line in Potter county. Mr. Rees blocked two trees and brought one of the blocks to John Ross, Esq., who had it as a curiosity in his office.

- One of the stage horses belonging to D. F. Glassmire, Jr., met with an accident, near Stone Dam, that will keep the horse in the barn for a long time, if not ruin him entirely. The horse stepped on a stick in the road with his front foot, the other end of the stick caught the hind foot just at the top of the hoof, and was forced between the outer shell and the lining of the hoof, breaking off. The horse suffered intensely and it was found necessary to cut open the hoof to remove the piece which was about one and three-fourth inches long by half an inch thick.

Eleven Mile.

The entertainment given by the Oswayo Dramatic Association was the great event of the past week in this vicinity, on Friday evening April 7, at the M.E. Church.

The Drama was entitled "The Social Glass, or victims of the bottle," in five acts.

Dramatic Personae.

Charles Thornley – S. B. Hawley; Doctor Slater – Will Smith; Harold Hadley – Eugene Ames; John Farley – F. E. Drake; Bob Brittle – Ernest Rice; James Hollis – C. J. Tubbs; Eva Thornley – Mrs. Emma Smith; Nettie Nettleby – Hattie Brown; Mrs. Farley – Mrs. Levin Robbins.

The house was well filled and by an appreciative audience, and to say that the Drama was a success, is but weak praise. Without detracting from the merits of others however, we may be allowed to say that Miss Brown as Nettie Nettleby and Mr. Rice as Bob Brittle succeeded very much in their efforts "to make people happy" while Mr. Drake as the landlord and drunkard was very perfect. The music was choicely rendered for the occasion, by Prof. Wheeler and Miss Este assisted by the choir and added greatly to the effect of the play. The receipts of the evening netting some twenty-five dollars, were for the benefit of G.A.R. Post at Oswayo.

The drama will be repeated next Tuesday eve, April 11th for the benefit of the Oswayo sabbath school.

Bingham.

At North Bingham they have had a term of thirteen lessons, singing schools and now have a choir nearly as good as that at Spring Mills. They are to have several more lessons, so Spring Mills had better look well to its laurels.

No case of Diphtheria, nor any fever, except pigeon fever.

The cheese factory has not started yet on account of the high price of butter.

Allegany.

Mr. J. C. Bishop, of Allegany township, had a shock of apoplexy recently. He has regained the faculties of his mind and the use of his limbs. But fears are entertained of his entire recovery.

Keating.

John Bundy, jr., who has been sick for some time, is gaining slowly.

D. D. Everett's has sold his house at Keating Summit and moved to this neighborhood.

Meredith Fournes cut his foot quite badly recently while splitting wood.

H. Bridges has repaired his saw mill and is now sawing.

Forest House.

Spring having made its appearance, the song of the blue bird and robin can now be heard daily, together with sounds of industry in our locality.

Fifty or more persons have visited this place lately in quest of pigeons.

Two new houses are being built already and more will be erected at an early day. Our city does not grow up in a single night like they report in the oil country, but the prospect is favorable for a city in a few years.

Thomas James, of Larrabee, has opened meat market here. The people in this place will appreciate this departure on the part of Mr. James, and no doubt will sustain him in his branch of business.

The Potter Enterprise
Wednesday Evening,
April 19, 1882 –
Vol. VIII, No. 48

Whites Corners.

Spring has advanced slowly for a few days, but is getting warmer now.

They are receiving about 3000 pounds of milk per day, at the cheese factory and the quantity is still increasing.

Mrs. Stevens, mother of S. K. Stevens is very sick and not expected to recover.

The Potter Enterprise
Wednesday Evening,
April 26, 1882 –
Vol. VIII, No. 49

- Wm. M. Smith, formerly of Wharton, has built a new hotel at Harrison Valley, and opened it to the public. Mr. Smith knows how to keep a hotel, and will keep things in ship shape. William's many friends will find him as jovial as ever. When you go to Harrison Valley stop in and see Mr. Smith.

- Several months ago Mr. Sherwood was arrested for trespassing on the Gale lands. Last week he was again arrested for stealing pine timber from the Gale lands. He is now out on bail. He will doubtless be prosecuted to the full extent of the law, as Tommy Gale is getting tired of having his timber appropriated by others.

Roulet.

Teachers examination to-day.

R. L. White has improved the looks of his property on Main St., by building a neat fence around it.

Eddie Yentzer caught a trout on Wednesday last, which weighed one pound.

Misses Laura Larrabee and Sarah Carey have commenced their summer schools.

W. L. Nichols formerly of Port Allegany, is telegraph operator at this place.

Genesee Forks.

Some changes at this place, although it may occupy so small a space.

J. Dimon our former landlord has gone to Virginia. Mr. Childs now owns the hotel. As far as we learn is doing a thriving business.

Mr. Stephen's now owns the Norman Dwight property, consisting of house, lot and cheese factory. He contemplates making cheese the coming season.

Philo Lewis has moved on to the Stephen Hurd farm.

We expect ere long that the clang of the car wheel and the scream of the whistle will be reverberating through our valley, as railroad is the talk of the day; surveyed through here last week.

B. F. Sherman is now at Allentown, running a meat market.

Methodist quarterly meeting is to be held here next Saturday and Sunday, commencing Saturday at 2 o'clock. Rev. Stevens, officiating as Presiding Elder.

Forest House.

If we understand the beginning, rightly, of Spring, it commenced the first day of the present month. Spring may have began then, but the weather which makes Spring so enjoyable has not been felt as yet by any of us mortals who reside on the mountains. In place of warm sunny days we have had for the most part, cloudy, cold days forcibly reminding one that Winter still held its sway.

One fight and one dance on Wednesday, and another dance minus the fight, on Friday, sums up the amusements for the past week, in this place.

D. C. Riman, of Tonawanda, N.Y., has completed a house and recently began living in it.

If some one wold come here and build a boarding house it would be a blessing to many of the laboring class.

W. G. Clark has let the job of hauling and loading his lumber to J. W. Dingee. Mr. Clark will build a plank road and the work will be commenced soon.

Owing to the cold weather prevailing, so far this month, fishermen have been scarce. This fact in turn cannot be said of pigeon hunters.

The Potter Enterprise
Wednesday Evening,
May 3, 1882 –
Vol. VIII, No. 50

- Twenty-one lock boxes are to be added to the Coudersport Postoffice outfit, soon.

- The plank walk on the north side of the Court House square has been taken up and will be replaced with a gravel walk. The trees in the square keep the walk so damp that plank lasts but a year or two, and the Commissioners, on this account, have decided to make the change.

- Willard Easton was quite severely hurt by the kick of a horse, at Wellsville, one day last week. J. V. Freeman, of Genesee Forks, handles the reins on the Wellsville stage and mail route until Willard's recovery.

Bingham.

Since I last wrote we have had one case of Diphtheria, and that one very light. Several cases of

Pinkeye are reported among our people and some of them very severe cases.

Thanks to the favorable weather and their industry our farmers have their Spring work well in hand and everything seems to indicate a busy and prosperous season.

West Branch.

The pigeons are nesting here. They commenced with a small nesting but have been adding to it until there is a large nesting. The commenced flying down the valley a little Thursday morning; there is a very large crowd of pigeoners here.

Lon Louge caught a young squab last Saturday morning. It weighed 9 ¾ pounds, when dressed. It is a hen squab, and they are going to try and raise it.

The Potter Enterprise
Wednesday Evening,
May 10, 1882 –
Vol. IX, No. 1

- D. F. Glassmire has the frame of his new house up, on Main street.

- John Omerod has purchased the Ingraham property, on Fifth street.

- Miles White has received his Commission as Justice of the Peace, and is ready for business, in his line.

- We have it from reliable information that the grading on the Wellsville and Ulysses railroad will begin next week. This is cheering news, indeed. On with pick and shovel!

- The County Commissioners have put down a plank walk on the North side of the Square. After making all the arrangements to put down a gravel walk they discovered that a borough ordinance required plank or stone, hence the change.

Oswayo.

George Gillmore got his hand caught on a circular saw at the planing mill, last Tuesday, his thumb was nearly cut off. On Wednesday a Polander got caught in a chain belt at the tannery, and was seriously squeezed, but not seriously injured.

There has been an epidemic of babies in this section, this spring the last one on record belongs to Mr. and Mrs. Frank Gee, it's a boy – nine pounds.

The tannery mule closed its earthly career to-day. He always was a contrary mule, and finally refused to draw his breath. Rest his kick in peace.

A. M. Thompson from Bingham Centre has moved into part of A. T. Smith's house, and is working for Smith in the blacksmith shop.

Herman Granes, son of E. A. Granes of Sharon Centre, was thrown from his wagon, and injured so that he died, Thursday night.

West Branch.

George Burrows died last Wednesday morning of consumption, he leaves a wife and one child. George was not quite 22 years old.

Township Tidings from Potter County, Pennsylvania
Volume I, 1880 - 1884

Mr. Wm. S. Moore is slowly but surely approaching his end by that terrible malady, cancer.

Whites Corners.

Farmers are looking blue at the prospect of a light crop of grass.

School commenced May first, with Miss Emma White as teacher.

The cheese factory is running very successfully under the management of Mr. Zimmer. Has made one sale at twelve cents per pound this season.

Allegany.

The Hotel, at Colesburg, is undergoing repairs. It is reported that there is soon to be a grocery and postoffice at Colesburg again.

A new boy baby at Cal Ford's.

The school directors met at C. Ford's to decide in regard to building a school house near there. School houses are more plenty now in Allegany than money to support schools.

Schools nearly all commenced last week. Miss Bell Haskel teaches at Colesburg; Miss Lottie Webster at Woodville; a lady, from near Millport, at the Settlement. No teacher for the Judd school last week. I hear that Miss Clancy commences the school to-day. Miss Nettie Bishop teaches at Raymond.

Forest House.

Our farmers are making slow progress with spring work and if the fitful weather of the past week continues the season must necessarily be late or backward.

Preparations are being made for the coming bark peeling season. Several jobs have been let and prices for peeling and delivering on cars, range from $2.75 to $3.50 per cord according to location of timber.

Eleven thousand ties were inspected by an official of our railroad recently. About twenty per cent were classed as culls. As culls bring but half price much dissatisfaction has arisen with makers on account of so many being classed as culls.

Saw mill hands are a scarcity, we infer from the fact that one of our mills has been running short handed lately.

Fourteen of our young men had their hair clipped on Sunday, and now they resemble a lot of prison convicts.

School opens Monday with Miss Dora Boyington as teacher.

Abraham Fairbanks has built a house and become a resident and will be employed by J. W. Dingee.

The Potter Enterprise
Wednesday Evening,
May 17, 1882 –
Vol. IX, No. 2

- It is expected that the cellar wall for the new dwelling house of H. A. Gridley, on Main street in this village, will be completed this week. The cellar is one of the largest and finest in this village. The house is to be 28 x 30 feet, with a wing 26 x 28 feet. When completed it will be a very fine building and will add much to the beauty of our village. – *Ulysses Sentinel.*

Eleven Mile.

The backwardness of the season forms a principal topic for conversation now, and speculating on the future prospect. Some are waiting for Spring weather to warm up, while others have cast their seed upon the soil having faith in the resurrection thereof – in due time.

The G.A.R. Post, at Oswayo, will observe the services of Decoration Day on June 2d this year. This arrangement was made so as to take part in the service at Coudersport, May 30th. The citizens of the vicinity will join with the Post, and a satisfactory order of exercises will no doubt be arranged and carried out. Will give it next week as particulars are not now all fixed. The Post will meet each Saturday evening until Decoration Day.

Roulet.

Work on the church has commenced.

A flood in the river for the past few days was a picnic for the lumbermen.

Work on the R.R. is being pushed rapidly, by the gentlemanly contractor, Mr. H. C. Blakeslee.

Miss Perkins of Ulysses is teaching music in the place.

There will be a donation for Rev. Brooks, at Michael Dehn's May 18th.

The cheese factory opened May 8th, with a good patronage.

Raymond.

Oats nearly all sown – ground soaked so much that 'tis now unfit to work.

Grass has grown as much in three or four days as all the spring before, and if the balance of this month is as wet as thus far hay will be plenty.

Sugaring held on late and the last runs of sap were let go to waste.

Extensive repairs are being put on the Colesburg mills buildings. As one of the workmen on the roof was carrying a bunch of shingles, he slipped and went from the roof to the ground followed by the shingles, which struck him on the back hurting him badly, but not fatally.

F. A. Nelson has rented the J. H. Heggie farm. Mrs. Nelson is still quite sick.

Our cheese factory is running.

The Baker farm is occupied by Manly Perkins.

The Potter Enterprise
Wednesday Evening,
May 24, 1882 –
Vol. IX, No. 3

- Bark peelers are plenty and busy.

- Considerable drunkenness on our streets lately.

- There are nearly two thousand laborers to work on the Pine Creek railroad.

- Amos Veelie has purchased the livery of James Johnston. Johnston proposes to start another livery.

- Edson Hyde, of Coudersport, has purchased the George Ward house and lot on Main street, Ulysses.

Keating.

Lots of new board fence being built.

C. W. Dingee has moved back from Keating Summit.

Our day school is taught by Miss Amy White, of Coudersport. This is the second term taught here by Miss White, she is liked well by all.

The Sabbath school is well attended. Elder Holland preaches once in two weeks.

G. C. Lewis is hauling potatoes to Emporium.

Miss Hattie Whitney is quite sick with fever.

Yesterday afternoon as Mr. Bridges was working in his saw mill one of the sleepers broke, letting him down about ten or twelve feet. Mr. Bridges' head, face and right arm was very badly bruised. No broken bones.

Whites Corners.

The weather has been more pleasant for a few days and we hope it will remain so.

Nearly all the farmers are through sowing in this section.

S. J. Stetson has had a valuable team sick with pinkeye. His family has all been ill, Miss Edith dangerously so. On Thursday afternoon a fine yearling belonging to him fell breaking its leg, and having to be killed immediately.

Mrs. Hunter, mother of Stephen Edwards of this place, died on Thursday last. The funeral services were held at Jasper, N.Y., the following Sunday.

Allegany.

Farmers are getting long faces over the late spring, but little planting done. Many gardens not made. Vegetation comes on very slow.

The pinkeye still rages with some horses; some are having it very hard; and a similar disease is afflicting the people.

Another Alleganian married. I. P. Collins has taken one of Mansfield's fair daughters, to share with him life's joys and sorrows. May they find all of the first, and few of the last.

The Potter Enterprise
Wednesday Evening,
May 31, 1882 –
Vol. IX, No. 4

Raymond.

Rains.
Oats sowed.
Corn planting.
Potato planting.
Making garden.
Apple blossoms.
Good prospect for fruit.

J. L. Collins and wife have an addition to their family – a daughter-in-law. Don't know whether Allegany has gained one and Mansfield lost one; or whether Isaac is to leave us.

Frank Woodcock is the boss farmer on raising oats. He is sowing about one hundred and ten bushels of seed this spring.

The boss fisher boy, of Allegany, is Ray. Nelson, a little fellow seven years old. One day last week he caught fourteen fine speckled trout and brought them home for his sick mother. Little four year old brother Harry went along and carried the string. Mrs. Nelson does not gain very fast – has not sat up any in eight weeks.

The Sunday school at the new school house near Elder Carr's starts out well under Elder Carr as Superintendent. Also Sunday school at Gold, A. E. Wright, Sup't. One at North Hollow, Sweden, Daniel Carpenter, Sup't. One at Harmontown (alias Wildcat) Elder Hotchkiss, Sup't. Should be one in every school district in the county, especially when districts are too far apart to combine.

- Twelve thousand live pigeons have been shipped from Coudersport in the last two weeks.

- Ed. Forster has quit the harness business, on account of poor health.

Oswayo.

Friday, Morris son of James Stillman was severely injured by a log rolling over him, while playing near them; he is in a fair way to recover.

Saturday the personal property of the late James McDougal is sold at administrators sale.

Ellisburg.

Ellisburg is still improving.

The new saw mill built by Mr. Armstrong, of Corning, N.Y., is being completed as fast as possible. The old mill was torn down and the new one stands in its place.

Other changes has also been made. Mr. John Pye, our former landlord, has moved out of the hotel, and Mr. Frank Hendryx has taken his place.

Mr. Josiah Webster is building a new house, 25 x 50 ft.

Mrs. J. H. North, of Goshen, Conn., a former resident of this place, has returned to the home of her childhood. We were glad to see her looking so well, and to welcome her back again, and, should think the dear old state of Connecticut must be very agreeable.

Our school taught by Mrs. Ida Wilson is prospering finely.

Eleven Mile.

The usual quiet of our little valley is undisturbed by sad accident or funny incident, but a young man of the vale who some two years since wedded a wife has, we understand, been entertaining the people at Oswayo village, with a free show, no hats passed even, of that, to him, burdensome attachment. Last summer, after arrest by complaint of poor masters, for his non-support etc., this poor lad concluded to in future provide for his family. He soon hired her out, and occasionally hired her board at some place. In this charming fashion the time has passed, until last Tuesday, he went to Oswayo to move his lady to another boarding place, but when once in the buggy, the wife was strongly determined to stick to her husband, and for half a day she "held the fort" or buggy seat, driving up and down the street; as her Virg moved, so she followed, and the pair held converse and argument pro and con her proposal to keep house, and cease to be the laughing stock for the community. To this was added advice of citizens, and one lady gave the contemptible husband (?) a very good ten dollar lecture, but he was obtuse and persevering. Finally the sun went down and becoming desperate, the fellow unhitched "Jim" from the buggy and pulling from her the reins, mounted and made off as if he was going home that way – his strategy succeeded, the poor wife sadly dismounted from the horseless vehicle, and the brainless apology for a man, slipped back and putting the horse quickly to the buggy, put him to his speed and run the gauntlet of sticks and stones, and imprecations of the deserted wife. If this affair was to happen in some localities there would be a bucket of tar and some feathers wasted, but, as it is much indignation is manifest, and may lead to something more tangible.

The Potter Enterprise
Wednesday Evening,
June 7, 1882 –
Vol. IX, No. 5

- Good log flood in the Allegany, Sunday and Monday.

- David White, of Sweden, fell in a fainting fit caused by vertigo, in front of the Nichols' House, one day last week. The attack was not serious and in a short time he was about, as usual.

- Three thousand live pigeons were shipped from this point Monday morning, for the great shoot at Niagara Falls. This 3,000 shipment completes the contract for 20,000 live birds, which has now been filled from the West Branch nesting.

Millport.

A very pleasant time in this place on Decoration day.

At eight o'clock in the morning the Post (G.H. Barnes Post) met at Sharon Centre, and accompanied by the Sharon band they proceeded to the cemetery of Clara. Many people were present and a short address was delivered by L. H. Kinney. The procession then returned to the Sharon Centre cemetery and Capt. Kinney delivered a stirring address, in which he spoke tenderly of our dead boys, and gave noble words of encouragement to our living soldiers. His kind words will be treasurer in the hearts of those who mourn their dead heroes. After the services at Sharon Centre, the Post proceeded to East Sharon cemetery, followed by a large procession. Mr. L. H. Bailey delivered the speech at this place which was a very creditable one. Our Decoration Day has been a very pleasant one this year for which we are thankful.

Oats in this place are almost a failure on account of the wire worms. In fact no crop is forward but grass.

The dwelling of W. J. Brown caught fire on the roof, and made quite a blaze as there was a strong wind at the time. The crowd that quickly gathered worked lively for a short time and soon extinguished the fire.

Township Tidings from Potter County, Pennsylvania
Volume I, 1880 - 1884

The Potter Enterprise
Wednesday Evening,
June 14, 1882 –
Vol. IX, No. 6

- Mr. Edward Forster, on Saturday last, sold his property on the Lymansville Road, consisting of twenty-five acres of land, a good house and barn, and all well improved, to R. L. Nichols, for $2,500 cash. This is the cheapest piece of property we have heard of changing hands in this section for a long time. Mr. Wentworth will occupy the place.

- Pine Creek lands are worth treble what they were one year ago.

- Mr. E. Peltz, of Carter Camp, this week commences the erection of a saw mill at that point. Mr. Peltz has a good location and a mill there will prove of great convenience to the surrounding section.

- Having sold his twenty-five acre farm, Mr. E. Forster will again remove to Coudersport. He has rented the building so long occupied by A. S. Armstrong as a shoe shop, and will stock it up with groceries, etc.

- Albert Lyman, of Sweden Valley, has purchased a large new steam saw mill to put in his mill at Sweden. The one now in use there he intends removing to the Cross Fork, where he has a large quantity of cherry lumber to cut. Mr. Lyman is now shipping large amounts of very fine cherry lumber from his Sweden Valley mill.

Eleven Mile.
This is June 10th, and the apple trees are only about in full bloom.

The exceeding wet weather has given grass quite a start.

Winter grain looks fairly good.

Oats are badly used by the wire worms and wetness.

On the night of the 3d inst. a water spout must have broken in the vicinity, as the following morning our land upon side hills, recently plowed, was badly turrowed by the water, and the corn, potatoes, &c., washed out to a great extent. So taking the situation all around the farmer may not be blamed for feeling somewhat discouraged at the outlook.

- Dr. Freeman, assisted by Nye and others, last week removed a tumor from the jaw of Chas. O'Harra, of Genesee. O'Harra had visited Buffalo and other places, and surgeons had declined to operate on him, believing it would kill him. He withstood the operation finely and bids fair to recover entirely.

Whites Corners.
The weather continues cool and crops are backward with the exception of grass and fruit, but the prospect for these is excellent.

We understand they are receiving 13,000 pounds of milk daily at the cheese factory.

H. O. Chapin's eldest daughter, Clemmie, has been quite sick with diphtheria but is now recovering.

Mr. R. H. Taggart is building a new blacksmith shop.

Township Tidings from Potter County, Pennsylvania
Volume I, 1880 - 1884

The Potter Enterprise
Wednesday Evening,
June 21, 1882 –
Vol. IX, No. 7

- Lewis A. Glace is now putting up the derrick for the Germania Oil Co.'s No. 8, between Oleona and Carter Camp on Kettle Creek. Seven wells have been drilled, all reported dry.

- Charley Reuning's little child, of Homer, was severely scalded last week. The family were at the supper table, and the child pulled over the teapot full of boiling tea, which spilled upon its neck, left shoulder, arm and feet. Dr. Buck rendered medical assistance.

Ulysses.

Not seeing any thing from this place lately, I thought perhaps a few items would be of interest.

The farmers of this place are making some improvements this summer.

Mrs. Kibbie is painting her house.

R. H. Young is repairing his barn.

H. Hosley is building a large dairy house.

D. W. Smith lost a fine carriage horse on Saturday of last week, the cause of death is unknown.

Whites Corners.

The long looked for summer weather has at last made its appearance.

Crops look well, with the exception of corn which is very backward.

The prospect for all kinds of fruit is excellent.

A number of the farmers are setting tobacco plants, which is a new experiment with some of them.

Eggs and cheese bring a good price, which makes the farmers feel very happy as that is the source from which they get most of their money.

Miss Zelica Taggart is instructing a class, at Troupsburg, in vocal and instrumental music.

The Potter Enterprise
Wednesday Evening,
June 28, 1882 –
Vol. IX, No. 8

- Bark peeling is rushing, and accidents are very numerous this season.

- Water mains are being put down on the north and east side of the square.

- Dr. Edgar S. Mattison has put up a telephone between the Postoffice and his residence.

- Charles Reissman is making arrangements to erect a two-story cabinet shop and warerooms, and also a barn, on the hitherto fire limits.

- Mr. John R. Groves, I. P. Collins and Miss Annie Jones will have charge of the various grades in the Coudersport school for the coming year.

- John Krusen last Thursday, while at work peeling bark near Mark Harvey's, was struck on the head by a falling limb, which cut his scalp badly and rendered him unconscious, as he fell to the ground he struck his leg near the knee upon the sharp edge of an axe making a very painful wound. Dr. Buck rendered medical aid. We understand he is doing well.

Roulet.

Eber and Orson Card, who have been attending school at Lock Haven, are home, on vacation.

Lewis Yentzer has improved the looks of his dwelling house by building a porch.

Henry Kimm is preparing to build a house on the grounds where the old one stood.

Allegany.

Fine growing time. Winter grain looks well, but oats and corn now bid fair to be a light crop. The prospect now is an abundance of fruit of all kinds.

The donation, for Rev. Dillenbeck, was not as largely attended as it would have been if it had not been held in so busy a time of year, but a fine social visit was enjoyed, besides the benefit received by the elder.

D. W. Rogers has a flock of sheep that has averaged over nine pounds of wool per head.

Norman Cool has returned home from Michigan, owing to poor health.

And now H. Veeley is expected to bring on the cigars, owing to that fine boy baby.

Costelloville.

June 23d, 1882.

Yes, we are still alive, working hard and doing as well as could be expected.

Although we have had such a late spring, the crops are looking splendid. There is not going to be many apples this year, but we hope the farmers will put, what few there are, to a better use, than they did last season; no doubt they have seen the effect of their *cider* ere this.

P. H. Costello & Co. have purchased twenty-six large horse teams and have sixteen in their employ besides.

Bark peelers are putting in good time now, working from five a.m. until seven p.m.

There is estimated to be about 250 men in the bark woods this summer.

There has not been many fishermen in here this spring, though trout seem quite plenty. M. J. Colcord caught one the other day that weighed one pound and one ounce.

On returning home from the tannery store, last Saturday morning, Jacob Peet had the misfortune to lose a horse with the blind staggers.

Last Saturday a young man entered Dr. Breisnick's office, noseless. He had had the luck to fall on a spud cutting his nose off; but with needle and thread and a skillful hand, the doctor replaced the nose making the young man feel quite happy again.

Will and Charley Basset, of Coudersport, intend laying the

cellar wall for Mr. Costello's new house.

Joe Codington is laying up the cellar wall for Jacob Peet's new house.

Columbus Reese's house is nearly finished.

The meat market is kept here, this summer, by Mr. Chaplain.

G. W. Berfield has left the boarding house, and returned to his farm in Homer. A gentleman by the name of Williams has taken his place. Mr. B. was much liked in the boarding house, and the boys regreted his leaving.

Mr. Crittenden has been among us again, and has organized a Sunday School which will be held Sabbath after noon. There is also one organized at the Brownlee school house which will be in the morning; both have good attendance and we hope they will be a success.

The Rev. Kiester preaches at the Brownlee school house once in two weeks, sabbath morning, and the Rev. W. S. Holland preaches here every Sabbath evening.

We are not going to have any school here this summer, for some reason. It would do in some places, where there are larger scholars to attend, but in this place two-thirds of the scholars are small, and can not go in the winter, therefore they will be deprived of school all together.

The Potter Enterprise Wednesday Evening, July 5, 1882 – Vol. IX, No. 9

Eleven Mile.

A few weeks ago it was a common event, of nearly each day, to hear the terrific explosions of glycerine and cans from the adjoining towns of Alma and Bolivar. But since the excitement at Cherry Grove, there has been such an exodus of oil operators from the Allegany county field and a consequent decrease of drilling and shooting wells there, that the familiar salute is almost entirely missed, and if the panic is kept in force it will result in the ruin of many men, of moderate means, who have it tied up in that vicinity.

Our valley is, as usual, quiet. Crops are now coming forward rapidly, and hopes are entertained that the harvest will be abundant, for all of the backwardness of the spring.

Road mending is now in vogue, and soon will follow the hay and grain harvest and before we are hardly aware, the fruit of Autumn will claim our care, and the sharp frosts will herald the approach of winter, from whose varying reign we have but just been relieved. So the rapidly revolving seasons swirl along, and bear us onward whether we will or not.

Help for farm work is now quite unattainable and farmers get on the best they can, trusting that there will be help let loose from the bark woods by haying time.

The Potter Enterprise
Wednesday Evening,
July 19, 1882 –
Vol. IX, No. 10

- Benj. Rennells has purchased the Keating hemlock on the flat south of the river and is peeling bark.

- Z. J. Thompson has moved his wagon ship to the rear of his grocery, giving him a very convenient back room for storage.

- August Voss, the proprietor of the Germania Hotel, received a ball in his right hip while handling a revolver recently. The wound is painful but not a dangerous one.

Freeman Run.

We have endured the hope long deferred that maketh the heart sick.

Thirty-three years ago, when P. Harris moved in, bringing a wife, reared in the haunts of civilization, to bury her alive in the wilderness, with true pioneer grit he prophesied, "there will be a postoffice and store this side of Coudersport, in fifteen or twenty years, my dear."

But, there isn't.

They promised us an office, and said it's name should be Vine. It was a squash vine. The striped mauraders probably served it as they did my Hubbard's, not a plant left from over two hundred. No wonder the Latin's said *"Sic transit"* etc. I'm *sic* myself.

Potatoes are an uncertain crop.

Corns looks rather well.

Apples better than in most parts of the county.

Hoeing is nearly done.

E. Fourness brings on a new mower.

Haying will soon be the order of the day.

Grass is abundant, far ahead of any recent year.

Keating.

Alvin Rennells is finishing up his job on the road between here and Portage.

E. A. Whitney is very sick.

W. H. Dingee is afflicted with a boil, on the back of his neck.

As. Mr. H. H. Beebe was coming from Portage township the other day, he had the luck to see a large black bear; unfortunately for Mr. B. he is not in the habit of always carrying his gun, or even a revolver in his pocket, so Mr. Bear merely run his tongue out at him and left.

Crops look tip top, especially the grass, which will be a large crop.

Roulet.

George Conly has fitted up a barber shop in the room over White & Lyman's store.

Born – to Mr. and Mrs. Lewis Yentzer, a son. Weight twelve and three-fourth pounds.

The work of laying iron on the railroad is progressing slowly but surely. Last accounts they were at Coleman's mill. Some trouble is anticipated at Coleman's "dugroad," on account of the railroad monopolizing the wagon road at that place. We understand the engine is to be put on the road this morning for the first time.

Township Tidings from Potter County, Pennsylvania
Volume I, 1880 - 1884

Sartwell Creek.

The rain – still it comes. It has been so wet all summer that crops are all poor excepting grass which looks very nice.

Strawberry shortcake and strawberries and cream are among the luxuries now seen on our tables.

The Fourth was very dull here. Some of our young folks went to Oswayo and Port Allegany and seemed to have a good time, in spite of the rain.

Mr. Larkin died, at the residence of his son-in-law, W. H. Slocum, on the 9th inst., at an advanced age.

Our school, under the care of Miss Emma Austin, will close in about five weeks.

The U. B. Quarterly Meeting, of the 8th and 9th inst., was very largely attended.

We expect soon to hear the scream of the engine and to see the oil derricks looming up all around us.

There is already one derrick erected on Morris Manning's place and the men are ready to go to drilling as soon as they get some wood cut. David Fisher is engaged in cutting it. They will need about one hundred cords.

Eleven Mile.

Haying is at hand, and an abundant crop will be harvested if "hay weather" is provided.

The work of hoeing has been delayed by the frequent rains.

Corn is past help, it would seem, yet it grows fast and with suitable weather may ripen.

Potatoes are, generally, quite promising. But it is early yet to predict their yield.

Apples, of most varieties, are to be a light crop, in most orchards – but hope there will be enough for home consumption.

Blackberries are to be the mainstay for fruit, as they are plenty, in a green state.

The papers report a rainy Fourth in many localities, and it may look singular for us to say that a more beautiful and bright Independence Day never dawned than that of 1882 in this vicinity. So we will say no such thing. Fact is, it rained too much to work in a barn, all day, and the celebrating was very limited indeed.

Whites Corners.

The weather is fine, and farmers are busy with their haying. There is a large crop of hay this season. Most other crops are looking well and by the acres of potatoes they will not be selling for $1.00 per bushel next year.

The cheese factory is running very prosperously under the management of Mr. Zimmer. They are making upwards of 20 cheeses of 60 lbs. each per day. Cheese sells at a good price this season which keeps the farmers happy.

The general health of this community is good.

Our Sabbath school has gone where the woodbine twineth.

Those who have put out tobacco plants are having a lively fight with the worms.

The festive potato bug has put in his appearance as usual, but they are easily controlled.

**The Potter Enterprise
Wednesday Evening,
July 26, 1882 –
Vol. IX, No. 11**

- James Turner has the frame of his hotel up.

- W. B. Gordnier has sold 35 mowing machines and 25 sulky rakes this season.

- B. F. Greenman, a former resident of Hebron township, has opened a music store at Eldred.

- Harry Glassmire stepped on a broken bottle, one day last week, cutting a gash an inch by an inch and a half in his foot. Dr. Mattison rendered medical assistance. Harry is doing well.

Oswayo.

A Mr. Fessenden from Roulet has opened a wagon shop in Smith's building.

Misses Elsie Sharpe and Nettie Tubbs have gone to Pike, to spend the fall and winter at Pike Seminary.

**The Potter Enterprise
Wednesday Evening,
August 2, 1882 –
Vol. IX, No. 12**

- Farmers are busy putting in a No. 1 hay crop.

- Huckleberries are ripening. The crop promises to be immense.

- The first huckleberries of the season last Friday, at a shilling a quart.

- James Turner's Hotel is assuming an imposing appearance. It will have a French roof and is three stories in height.

- N. M. Glassmire, on Sunday last, went to his hen house, to gather in the eggs. Natty thrust his hand into a barrel where the hens had made a nest, and as his hand was approaching the bottom, he looked for the eggs he was to pick up. One look was sufficient. The barrel contained a full grown skunk in the prime of life. The animal was not disturbed, but Natty imagined all sorts of things, principally strong smells. The way he backed out was a caution, and his nose has hardly got down to its usual place yet. Natty calls it a hair-breadth escape. The skunk was finally dumped into the river where it met with grim death, and death, as usual, won the game.

Roulet.

John Yentzer has painted his house and built a very neat porch.

The depot for the C. & P. A. R. R. in this place has been located on the land of A. V. Lyman. A new road will be opened through by White & Lyman's store, and will be built by some of our most influential citizens, who have already commenced the building of the road and bridge.

Township Tidings from Potter County, Pennsylvania
Volume I, 1880 - 1884

The Potter Enterprise
Wednesday Evening,
August 9, 1882 –
Vol. IX, No. 13

- O. A. Lewis Post G. A. R., Ulysses, will be mustered in, by A. S. Lyman, of Eleven Mile, on Saturday, August 19th.

- Charles Reissman is painting his barn.

Whites Corners.

Farmers, in general, are through haying and report a heavy crop.

Our school closed on the 4th inst., with an afternoon entertainment.

Mr. Wm. White, who has been suffering from an attack of apoplexy, is now recovering.

The Potter Enterprise
Wednesday Evening,
August 16, 1882 –
Vol. IX, No. 14

- Beechnuts and Butternuts will be a big crop.

- Isaac Benson has gone to Michigan in search of health.

- T. Benton Brown's family have removed to Jersey Shore.

- The last victim of glass – Arthur Ormerod, who stepped on a piece last Saturday, cutting his foot quite severely.

- James Johnston has purchased the Bassett barn, east of Joseph Mann's residence, and removed it to a lot just south and east of the Main St. bridge. Jim will have his livery in it in a few days.

- Bullis Brothers are making arrangements to get in a large amount of hemlock this coming winter. Ed. Cornell will build a camp the head of Rees' Hollow, with stable room for twelve teams. With a good fall of snow the Allegany will be filled up with logs.

- A select school will be opened at Andrews Settlement, Sept. 4, by Miss Carrie Bishop. Terms, $1.00 per month.

- The plug in the cross pipe, at the intersection of Fourth and Main street, was forced out yesterday, causing a small flood on Main street. For some time the Patrons of the Coudersport Water Works were deprived of their favorite beverage – Cold water.

- A few years ago D. C. Larrabee purchased a strip of rough swamp land along the river from Main St. to the dugway. He spent some money draining it and filling in. Now every one of these lots except one has a house upon it. Neefe's new one is just up, completing the list and the place, which was formerly anything but interesting, is now an ornament to the town and furnishes homes for eight or ten families. It has been a good investment in the improved appearance of that section, besides paying well for the money invested.

Millport.

The late rains have made haying pretty dully, and it is feared will also cause oats to rust. Potatoes will probably be a good crop, and corn looks fair. There is every prospect now of a larger crop of blackberries than we usually have.

The farmers have been much annoyed by sheep killing dogs in this place.

Mr. and Mrs. Geo. Varney have a little son.

Dr. Haight has located in Millport, and will be welcomed by the people here, who felt the need of a good physician in this place.

Oswayo.

Oswayo was treated to a free circus on the streets, last Tuesday, two members of the church [only the church is divided] got to discussing in a benign way the merits of their business, and as both are engaged in the same kind of work, the discussion assumed the Wilson and Sullivan style of argument; the one we will call Wilson allowed that the "Sullivan" was a son of a female canine. Sullivan denied the soft impeachment, and attempted to forcibly impress it upon the cranium of Wilson. The referee climb the fence to get out of danger, the seconds slid out of sight, and the two combatants finding themselves deserted by their allies. Each took refuge behind their respective shop doors and could only be induced to come out under promises of protection, and that dinner was spoiling while waiting for them.

Mrs. D. C. Miller, of Wisconsin, is visiting her old home in Oswayo, after an absence of twenty years.

Fire was discovered in G. K. Smith's shop this morning about four o'clock. When first seen the flame had gained such headway that they were beyond control. A top buggy, two set of sleighs, one set carpenter's tools and blacksmith tools were lost. Cause of fire unknown. No insurance, loss $250.

The Potter Enterprise
Wednesday Evening,
August 23, 1882 –
Vol. IX, No. 15

- Water in the springs and streams is very low.

- Benjamin Rennells is making 2000 railroad ties.

- Blackberries are selling from 8 to 10 cents per quart.

- Frost on the hills last Saturday morning, damage slight.

- D. F. Glassmire has received several new buggies for his livery.

- Hemlock sufficient to peel 240 cords of bark has been slashed on the Eulalia Farm.

- Capt. L. C. Kinney has received a back pension of over $3,000. Cap. deserves it, and we are glad to record the fact that it has been granted him.

- Second St. has been surveyed by order of the town council. By this survey the Keystone mill is found in the street; Grom's house, ditto, and the mill race also. The borough line is found to be about forty feet east of supposed location.

West Branch.

The 11th inst., the West Branch Sunday school, and the two schools taught by Miss Rosa Crane and Mrs. Mary Aylsworth, with the citizens of West Branch, held a picnic in the grove back of Mr. Logue's. Swings were rigged up, and the fore part of the day was spent in swinging, chatting and in social meeting with friends and neighbors. About one o'clock a bountiful repast was spread and all partook of it, with a relish born of a good appetite and a good supply of good things. After dinner a well timed and very instructive address was delivered by Rev. Sanford Dickinson, which was followed by Rev. Sidney Stocum, giving a history of the rise, progress and usefulness of Sunday schools. After this the sports of the day were resumed and continued until about five o'clock in the evening. This is the first picnic ever held in West Branch, and the people are so well pleased with it that they want me to tell the people about it.

Keating.

The crops look well, especially the potato-bug crop.

The pleasant rain on Tuesday last was very much appreciated as it was very dry.

Mrs. Beebe's baby is badly afflicted with the crysipelas.

J. W. Dingee, of Keating Summit, is doing his haying on his farm in this place.

Cyrus Lewis, who has been visiting his brother G. C. Lewis returns to his home in Nebraska in a few days.

George Mulhollon has gone to Missouri, his domestic trouble was too much for him.

Sartwell Creek.

Haying is the order of the day, and every farmer is working early and late, to get this abundant crop into their barns.

Hired helps seems to be very scarce around here. Where are all of our young men and women, are they all married, or do they think it a disgrace to work?

It has been, and is now, very sickly around here.

Our school closed with an afternoon entertainment.

Berries are quite plenty this year; black rasp-berries are nearly gone, but blackberries take their place.

Mrs. Coon Dehn has canned nearly two bushels of black rasp-berries.

Miss Mina Lehman had a little girls' birthday party recently. They reported a good time.

The donation at the parsonage was largely attended. The result was a good time for the young folks, and twenty-two dollars for the minister.

Allegany.

Haying, that has been delayed so much by the rainy weather, is nearly all finished, and harvesting well underway, winter grain cut and some threshed. W. Ford and C. Palmetier have their threshed and report a good yield. Apples and plums will not be as plenty as we expected earlier in the season.

Last Saturday morning a slight frost in the valleys.

Schools have nearly all closed, except the one at Colesburg.

There is to be a union Sabbath school picnic, of Judd's, Andrews Settlement and Ellisburg schools, Aug. 30, to be held in J. C. Bishop's grove. All are invited.

The Potter Enterprise Wednesday Evening, August 30, 1882 – Vol. IX, No. 16

Whites Corners.

Farmers are busy with their harvesting. Grain proves better than some expected.

Blackberries are plenty in this section.

Buyers are seen nearly every day in this locality offering high prices for all kinds of farm produce which keep the farmers good natured.

Mr. H. Hurlburt is building a barn. He will have to hurry as he wishes to finish it in time to store his tobacco of which he has the finest piece in the place.

Mr. Dewitt White sold a span of horses, aged somewhere in the teens, for $375, and a few days after bought a team just as good and only 4 years old, for $300.

R. H. Taggart has nearly finished his new shop.

Born – On the 20th inst., to Mr. and Mrs. A. A. Ross, a daughter.

Roulet.

Born to Mr. and Mrs. J. V. Weimer, a son.

W. W. Eaton and brother have opened a boarding house in the cheese factory.

H. H. Kies, of Andrews Settlement, commences a select school in this place, the 11th of September.

Niles Fessenden, of Pleasant Valley, supplies the people here with fresh meat.

Died, in Roulet, Aug. 4th, 1882, Orvalla, wife of J. K. Burt, aged 63 years, 7 months and 9 days. Death has come into one of our families, and in a few days wrought a work which months and years cannot repair; made heart wounds which no lapse of time can heal. Unstayed by prayers and tears, he has performed his task, and hurried a kind sister, an affectionate wife and devoted mother down into the long, unbroken silence of the tomb. Of all the losses which we are called to sustain, few are more sad than the decease of the mother of a large family. When such departs, the tenderest feelings are stirred, and the deepest emotions of sorrow overflow the soul.

"Yet again we hope to meet thee,
When the day of life is fled,
Then in heaven with joy to greet thee,
Where no farewell tear is shed."

- Albert Lyman is shipping large amounts of cherry lumber.

- The Coudersport Graded School, fall term, commenced on Monday.

- The C. C. & A. R. R. is likely to be extended to Harrison Valley, this county, as soon as money and men, consistent with economy in the construction, can build it.

- A new side walk has been put down on the east side of Main street from the bridge to Jones'. Those south side people are getting very tony, since the erection of the depot.

- Farmers are claiming that potatoes are not turning out near as well as expected. Joe Carey, of Roulet, has, we are informed, twenty-five acres of the tubers, which will not yield him as many bushels as ten acres did last year.

- The Boro Council are awakening to the fact that several nuisances exist. At their last meeting they ordered R. L. Nichols, owner of the Nichols House, to remove or improve hotel privy. John Grom was ordered to remove obstructions which he had placed in the street, above the Keystone mill. Norman Dwight agreed to wall and cover mill race, above the Keystone mill, before spring. Several other places need looking after.

West Branch.

A little frost Saturday, Sunday and Monday mornings, the 19th, 20th and 21st, but not enough to do much, if any, damage.

Haying is pretty much through with. The crop is unusually large.

Oats are not a very large crop in this valley.

Our summer terms of school are about closing. Miss Rosa Crane and Mrs. Mary Aylesworth, our teachers, are attending the Teachers' Institute at Lewisville, this week.

Miss Rosa Crane goes home from the Institute to attend the fall and winter terms of school at Coudersport. She has been very successful here as a teacher. She will have the good opinion and well wishes of all her acquaintances here.

Costelloville.

Business seems to be as lively as ever with us.

Alfred Costello & Co.'s house is progressing finely. It will be a great improvement to Costelloville when it is completed.

We notice another neat little dwelling house going up, south of the Co.'s store, on Head and Quimby street.

A Swede, who has been employed at the tannery for some time past, died on Tuesday last. There is another one who is not expected to recover.

The Potter Enterprise
Wednesday Evening,
September 6, 1882 –
Vol. IX, No. 17

- Squirrel shooting is now legal.

- Orange Strong has been granted a back pension of $1,850.

- A. Disbrow, of Lewisville, has received a back pension of $1850.

- Gale, of the Pike Mills tannery, has about 16,000 cords of bark peeled this season.

- There is talk of building a large tannery at the mouth of Moore's Run, Sylvania township.

- Amos Colcord, of Eulalia, has a hen turkey which layed 102 eggs the past summer. Amos thinks she will do for a Christmas turkey, but has no hopes of getting the bird fat in time for Thanksgiving.

- Shingle House is nearly large enough to apply for a borough charter.

- Frederick and Wm. Cowburn have opened a new meat market, in the Denhoff building, south side of the river.

- Wm. Boyer will soon open a vegetable and meat market in the Glassmire's building, formerly the Express office.

- L. C. Kinner & Co., of Shingle House, have raised the front of their store and put in a new floor in one department. Arrangements are being made to erect an addition forty feet in length. The firm reports business good.

- Sharon Township is putting up the best bridge in the county, at Shingle House. The stone abutements are nearly in and are composed of large stand stones set in mortar. The span will be of iron and the total cost will be about $2,500. Sharon keeps up ten bridges within the limits of the township.

- Jones & Dodge, of Shingle House, have their new store up and shingled. It is 24 feet wide by 80 feet in length, with an elegant cellar. It will be the best store building in Sharon township and very convenient. The firm will make it headquarters for everything in their line. They understand their business.

Oswayo.

Everything moves quietly in this vicinity.

Mrs. Haskins is improving her property on Main street.

Lincoln Porter has moved into the Harry Lord house.

Eugene Colegrove is fixing his house over, making additions to it.

**The Potter Enterprise
Wednesday Evening,
September 13, 1882 –
Vol. IX, No. 18**

- There is a call for dwelling houses in Coudersport.

- F. W. Knox sports a very fine new double phaeton.

- S. A. Phillips has sold his black horse to J. W. Allen. Consideration $175.

- L. F. Andrews is making preparations for a heavy job of lumbering, on Dingman Run.

- Obadiah Merrill is running the stage from Wellsville to Ulysses. Obe takes to a stage as naturally as a duck to water.

- C. M. Herrington, of Sweden, has recently built a new store, and now has very comfortable quarters. By fair dealing he has built up a good trade.

- Mrs. P. L. Boyington and Miss Gertrude Boyington, of Roulet, visited Coudersport last Thursday afternoon, coming up on the construction train. Miss Gertrude had the pleasure of being the first lady to ride the *entire* length of the C. & P. A. railroad, having previously made the trip from Roulet to Port Allegany.

Roulet.

Select school opens to-day with a good attendance.

Fon Fessenden and Henry Kimm are building new dwelling houses.

J. Sullivan has the foundation built for a new house.

O. R. Webb has bought the Pat Carey farm on Trout Run.

A very pleasant party, to those who attended, was held in Tauscher's hall Friday night.

Allegany.

Harvesting is nearly finished. Oats are quite good, but potato vines are struck with blight, and some pieces are rotting quite bad.

Corn will be good if frost holds off a week or so longer.

Ettie Stryker and Frank Palmeter are attending school at the Settlement, others preparing to attend soon.

W. P. Cool's new house is raised and partially enclosed.

The Potter Enterprise
Wednesday Evening, September 20, 1882 – Vol. IX, No. 19

- Potatoes are selling for 50 cents per bushel.

- James Johnston has put up an addition to his livery barn.

- F. W. Knox is building an addition to his tenant house, occupied by Will Abson.

- Ole Hanson, of Burtville, has shipped over $200 worth of blackberries to a canning establishment in New York.

West Branch.

Wm. S. Moore passed way, at three o'clock, on the morning of the 14th inst. His death cannot be anything but a relief. No possible view of the future can place him in a worse situation than he has been in for the last year or two. He died of a cancer, which commenced on the lip and eat his face away in a horrid manner, until death put an end to his sufferings. He was about sixty-three years of age.

Fishing Creek.

Threshing has commenced.

Bark hauling seems to be the order of the day.

The youngsters of Roulet met at Tauscher's Hall, last Friday evening, for the purposes of "tripping the light fantastic toe," which they did in a most becoming style until about three o'clock when they departed to their homes, well satisfied with their little party.

The Dehn school, taught by Miss Sara Carey, will join the Fishing Creek Sabbath school in the Union Picnic, Sept. 22nd, which will be held above Mr. Dehn's, on the Crandall Hill road. Come one and all and bring your baskets well filled.

Whites Corners.

The patrons of the cheese factory seem to be well pleased with the management and Mr. Zimmer is making thirteen cheese per day, at present.

Farmers are nearly through harvesting in this vicinity, and threshing machines are busy.

Buckwheat is an excellent crop.

Oats prove better than was expected in the first part of the season, although they were hurt some by wire worms and wet weather.

Corn will be a good drop, if the frost does not come for a few days, to prevent ripening.

Fruit is not very plenty and what there is, especially apples, is very small.

Mr. Homer Hurlburt, by hurrying some, will have his barn finished in time to store his tobacco.

Bingham.

Two great sensations in one week are rather unusual in this vicinity, but we have them this time.

First and foremost, is that D. T. Hauber had to be hooped to keep him from bursting with joy, and all because it was a bouncing boy.

Last, but not least, the Baptist Association held its session at the Union Church, at North Bingham, on Wednesday and Thursday of this week. The sermons were elaborate and interesting, the attendance was very large, the attention good, the weather fine, the hospitality of the people was fully equal to the emergency and all the circumstances combined to make a most enjoyable occasion.

The crops, as far as harvested, are good. There are but few apples in this section. Pears are not plenty. Plums are worth two dollars per bushel.

The corn husks are very thick and indicate heavy snows next winter.

Chips from Costelloville.

Sept. 16th and no frost yet.

Corn and buckwheat promises a good crop, this year, if the frost holds off; but potatoes are small and not very plenty.

Alfred Costello & Co. sent several loads of leather to Keating Summit on Tuesday for the first.

Jacob Peet's new house is improving fast.

C. G. Judd started on the nigh inst., for the Pennsylvania coal mines. He has come to the conclusion that it is *his* lot to "earn his bread by the sweat of his brow." Good luck to him.

Will Brownlee left on the 13th inst., for Poughkeepsie, N.Y., where he enters a commercial college. Will is an enterprising young man and we wish him grand success.

E. O. Austin did not hoist his sign for the "Freeman Run House" in vain. There was a traveler stopped there the other day, and engaged board until twenty-one years of age. – It's a boy.

Oswayo.

So you have the railroad through. Well, now we can heartily congratulate our county-seat in that its citizens can now so readily get out of the woods.

The Oswayo valley is, it seems, likely to be the scene of railroad operations in the near future. So called "oil men" have been here recently and it is rumored that several test wells will be drilled in the valley soon. Our citizens are trying to deport themselves in a manner becoming to their prospective future, and will no doubt each be in readiness for their part of its labor.

The Potter Enterprise Wednesday Evening, September 27, 1882 – Vol. IX, No. 20

- Dr. E. S. Mattison has put up a lamp on his dwelling to light the street in front.

- Cowburn's meat market has been removed to the Armstrong building, Third street.

- Francis Hammond has erected a bridge across the river, in front of his tannery. He will have a switch, and next year will put down rails to the tannery.

Oswayo.

As Wm. Jones was returning from meeting, on the Eleven Mile last Sunday, coming by way of what is known as the "turkey path," he discovered a good sized bear in the roadway, after viewing each other a few moments, his bearship moved off into the bushes, and Mr. Jones concluded that his business, at home, needed his especial attention and departed for the same forthwith.

Bears seems to be plenty in this section, for a lady, living on the Eleven Mile, reports seeing two bears on Pineo Hill, some two weeks ago while blackberrying. They were not considered dangerous however as they appeared quite tame.

Jack Martin is trying to rival Wellsville teamsters, in drawing heavy loads of bark. He has drawn seven loads from the McDougal farm, the lightest netting 7,220 pounds, the heaviest 8,490.

The picnic of Post 125 G.A.R. was a success in every feature. It lasted two days.

Keating.

Harvesting is the work which nearly all are engaged in at present.

Crops are all pretty good, though the potatoes are rotting some.

Our school, taught by Miss Amy White, of Coudersport, commenced last Monday.

E. A. Whitney and family have moved to Keating Summit, to keep lumber shanty for J. W. Dingee.

Mr. Dingee has moved his family back to their home in this neighborhood.

Clarence Reed cut his foot while slashing the road between here and Portage, but we understand that it was not a serious wound.

Mrs. M. E. H. Everett intends moving to Alfred Center the first of October.

Chips from Costelloville.
Sept. 22, 1882.

Quite a number of accidents have occurred here of late. Little Johnny Boyle fell into a liquor vat and was seriously scalded.

There is a great deal of sickness in this place. Several have died already. Mrs. David Jones departed this life on the 16th inst. She was an exemplary christian woman and will be deeply mourned for by her affectionate husband and children. They have the sympathy of all their friends.

Mr. Woolfinger buried his youngest daughter, Lena, aged 11 months, this afternoon, disease, whooping cough – which is very prevalent in Costelloville.

Mr. Thome is also on the sick list. Mrs. Westfall is very low – doubts are entertained of her recovery. Six cases of fever are reported in the Tannery buildings.

The Potter Enterprise
Wednesday Evening,
October 4, 1882 –
Vol. IX, No. 21

Bingham.

The frost has not been very severe this season, and the corn crop is very good.

The threshing machines are beginning to work.

Mrs. A. P. Kibbe and master Archie have gone to Michigan, to visit a sick relative.

Wm. Clark has his new house well under way so that the plasterers are at work.

John Raymond has sold his farm and stock and become a partner with Peck in the store at North Bingham.

Allegany.

How many rise early enough to see the comet? All ought to.

W. Stryker has a good potato crop, and a fine lot of squashes.

Will Matteson has grown tired of Potter county hills, and gone to Michigan.

Our Sabbath school is of the past. We ought to remember "that in union, is strength."

The most enjoyable picnic of the season, for the little ones at least, was held at Colesburg a few weeks since. It was for the children exclusively, and they had a happy time.

By the death of J. C. Bishop a gloom is cast over the community, and a loss is felt by all in the many ways he was of use among us, both as a friend and neighbor. He and A. G. Presho were both Justices of the Peace, and both have been removed by death, leaving that office vacant in Allegany township.

Whites Corners.

Jack Frost has kept away remarkably well. Farmers have got their corn and tobacco harvested and out of his reach.

Mr. Leonard Snyder lost a very valuable horse last week, and what is worse, its death broke up one of the finest matched teams in this vicinity.

W. S. Reed is intending to teach a class in penmanship in this place. A meeting being called for Friday evening to organize the school.

- Wm. Dent has the frame up, and the roof partially on his new saw mill just below Brookland. The mill is a very large one and bids fair to be one of the best in the county.

- Belden Burt is rebuilding his saw mill at Burtville. He will soon have a first class lumber producer. Morris Manning is in charge of the new structure which is a guarantee that it will be No. 1.

West Branch.

No frost here yet to do any damage.

Corn is mostly out of the way of frost, some pieces are already cut up, it is said to be a fair crop.

Opinions differ in regards to potatoes, some say that it is a good crop, and some say that the crop is very poor.

Henry Baker, of Tioga county, is here with a gang of men opening up the coal veins on the Knox lands for inspection, if found satisfactory they will be bought by the Addison & Northern Pa. R.R. Company.

Millport.

Crops are nearly all harvested, and in spite of the cold summer we have had will be pretty good.

Potatoes are not so poor as was feared at one time.

Corn will be fair, and buckwheat is good as far as I have noticed.

Echoes From West Homer.

The turning of the leaves remind us, if the frosty nights and morning do not, that winter is fast approaching, and we are soon to be once more walled up in the snow drifts.

Farmers are busily engaged in threshing buckwheat, which seems to yield well this year.

Potatoes are poor, that is so many are rotten. One farmer had three men digging, one day, and the result at night was, he had three *bushels* of sound potatoes.

Mr. Dennis Hall and family have gone to Keating Summit, where they intend making their future home.

The Potter Enterprise
Wednesday Evening,
October 11, 1882 –
Vol. IX, No. 22

- T. J. Gilbert is again a resident of Coudersport.

- Dr. Eaton, of Lewisville, sports a new pair of Mustang ponies.

- George Brehmer and family started for South Carolina last Monday where they will spend the winter at least. A host of acquaintances wish them good luck.

- L. H. Cobb has purchased the American Hotel. Consideration $1,800. Workmen are now putting in a foundation and the house will be finished at once, in good style. The house will be newly furnished and thrown open to the public at an early day.

West Branch.

Messrs. James White and O. G. Metzger, of Coudersport, are here at work at their cherry timber. They have rented the saw mill of Mr. George Mitchell for a term of three years; they are putting in a circular saw. Elmer Aylsworth, of Coudersport, and Wm. Trask, of this place, are doing the mill wright work for Messrs. White and Metzger. They have two teams at work trucking in logs.

Our fall and winter term of school commenced last Tuesday, Mrs. Mary Aylesworth, of Coudersport, is the teacher.

There are some lumber jobs starting but I will tell you more about them next time.

Roulet.

Miss D. E. Boyington is teaching at the Forest House.

Leroy Lyman and S. B. Pomeroy left on Friday for the northern part of Mich., for the purpose of hunting, they expect to be gone some time.

American Express and ticket office of the C & P A R R at this place is at the store of White & Lyman.

Sartwell Creek.

Summer is gone once more and Fall has made its appearance, bringing a few slight frosts and many are suffering with severe colds.

Delbert Witter started the 18th of last month on a pleasure trip west.

Dorman Card is attending the school at Roulet.

Bark drawing, in this part of the county, will soon be a thing of the past for this year; and, indeed, the time has been well filled.

The first United Brethren Quarterly Meeting, for this conference year, was held at this place last Saturday and Sunday, with very good attendance.

Potato crop is reported as very good, except a rotten one now and then.

Very few apples in our orchards this fall.

Eleven Mile.

This delightful October weather is very nice for potato harvest and all kinds of work indeed – Farmers have abundant cause for thankfulness for the results of their labor for the past season; for though the spring was so backward, that at one time it seemed nothing would be likely to amount to much, the crops have nearly all yielded good returns, and bring fair prices, with ready market. And it may be well for us when again we feel inclined to croak at the faulty weather of seed time, to call to mind the season of 1882.

Threshing is mostly done and a few days more of this fine weather will see the crop of potatoes and the few apples secured.

The thirty-fifth wedding anniversary of Mr. and Mrs. B. F. Lyman was made the occasion last Saturday of a surprise visit from many of their friends and neighbors. The company came prepared with the where-with-all for supper, and after pledging anew the old time vows, the happy pair sat down to the table well loaded with the usual feast of such occasion, and as the guests departed it was discovered they had left a lot of nice presents and money, in remembrance of the occasion. The original marriage notice reads:

MARRIED.

By Rev. O. Hopson, Sept. 29th, 1847, B. F. Lyman and Miss Sophia Wood, at Fairhaven, Vermont.

**The Potter Enterprise
Wednesday Evening,
October 18, 1882 –
Vol. IX, No. 23**

- Mr. Chaffee has built a carpenter shop on main street, just south of the bridge.

- Will H. Tassel has gone to Baltimore where he will attend the college of Physicians and Surgeons the coming winter. Will expects to graduate this term.

- Mr. H. B. Keihle, a medical student with Dr. Hogarth, Port Allegany, has gone to Buffalo, N.Y., for the purpose of finishing up a course of lectures at the Buffalo medical college.

- Stovewood is selling at $1.50 per cord and seems to be plenty.

- J. M. Covey has opened a coal yard and will supply all who need hard or soft coal, at reasonable prices. Call at the Nichols House.

- Mrs. Charlotte Niles has purchased of Benson & Olmsted the house, for some time past occupied by Geo. Green, south side of the river. Green moves into the Rennells house on West street.

- J. M. Covey has rented the Nichols House, and is repairing and refitting the same. The Colonel makes a good landlord, and will make it pleasant for all who stop with him. His many friends will be glad to give him a call.

**The Potter Enterprise
Wednesday Evening,
October 25, 1882 –
Vol. IX, No. 24**

West Homer.

Nothing of importance has occurred in this vicinity recently to relieve the monotony and quietude for which our neighborhood is noted.

One can well imagine to-day that the "melancholy days" of autumn are upon us, but who can complain, after so long a season of delightful weather.

The farmers are busily engaged in preparing for winter.

O. L. Hall has lately moved into the house so long occupied by his father. We understand he has the entire farm under control.

H. H. Chesbro, formerly of Olean, is at present visiting his old home here. Mr. Chesbro goes to Virginia soon, where he intends making his future home.

West Branch.

Last Sunday Mrs. M. V. Prouty, of Pike, was up here with five of her children, on a visit at her father's, S. M. Conable. While going home in the afternoon, one of the clevis pins worked out and let the whiffletree drop down against the legs of one of the horses, which caused the team to become unmanageable. Mrs. Prouty and the children were thrown from the wagon and all of them were more or less injured, except one of the little girls. One of the little boys, Jesse, was so badly injured that he died the following Tuesday, and was buried here Wednesday, in the West Branch Cemetery.

Clara.

Our school has been in session three weeks in charge of A. J. Evans, who is an intelligent and efficient educational worker, he was enquiring the other day "if school directors ever so far forget themselves, in Clara, as to visit the schools?"

T. Brooks and family, of Michigan, are visiting at his father-in-law's, A. P. Hay; they intend to spend the winter here.

Bark hauling is in order yet.

Lester Burton and wife have been having a terrible run of typhoid fever. Lester is a trifle better, but she is having a relapse, they are attended by Dr. Chas. French, of Coudersport.

James Reed has moved into a part of Mr. Herring's house for the winter.

Ellisburg and Vicinity.

Our neighborhood has been enlivened during the past two weeks by the welcome presence of former residents Mr. and Mrs. Joseph Winegar, now of Cass City, Mich. On the evening of the 16th inst., their friends to the number of sixty or over congregated at the residence of B. F. Bishop, to celebrate Mr. Winegar's fortieth birthday. All enjoyed the privilege of meeting and conversing with these western friends who we hope will not absent themselves so long again. After supper music and a few games, "Some wee short hour ayount the twall," each "took aff his several way," and silence reigned supreme throughout the little hamlet of Andrews Settlement.

We understand that Wm. Eaton has sold his lot on Main street to a Mr. Dennis, who is putting up a house thereon.

The residences of James Currier and B. F. Bishop are undergoing repairs and the former is digging a well preparatory to moving on his new farm, when the house is ready for occupancy.

The new residences of Josiah Webster and H. G. Hurd are approaching completion.

W. W. Collins is teaching the public school on Cobb Hill; Miss Lettie Palmer that in the Presho district.

The select school at the Settlement has twenty-five pupils at present, five having left, among them Nettie Bishop, to teach on Yochum Hill, in Abbott twp., and Libbie Reynolds, to attend the select school taught by Miss Alice Hendryx at Ellisburg, while her parents are absent on a trip to Iowa.

The carpenter work on the Ford school house is completed. Allegany now boasts nine school houses, and, as she found it impossible to pay wages that would insure first class teachers when she kept but eight schools open, many anxious parents feel that a millennium, in school matters, is close at hand.

About a week since a gentleman came through here looking up chestnut poles for a new telegraph line through by Genesee Fork and the Honeoye. As telegraphs are the forerunners or railroads, if we get the one we shall feel encouraged in regard to the others.

Allegany.

The fifteenth marriage anniversary of Mr. and Mrs. M. A. Veeley occurred on Oct. 13th. It was remembered by their friends and neighbors, in a joyous social gathering of fifty or more in number. They were the recipients of numerous presents.

Apples are selling for sixty cents per bushel and packages found.

If any one wants to know how long a chase a young pig will give before being caught, ask M. Veeley and his boys.

Now comes the season of husking bees and pumpkin pie.

The Potter Enterprise
Wednesday Evening,
November 1, 1882 –
Vol. IX, No. 25

Whites Corners.

The weather is better than it usually is this time of the year.

Mr. Leroy Smith is digging a well – guess he finds hard digging by the noise he makes blasting.

S. J. Stetson purchased an organ a few days ago. His daughter is now receiving instructions of Mrs. A. P. Elder.

The writing school is progressing finely. Those who cannot write can fight.

Mr. A. P. Elder is now working in his new shop which is connected with R. H. Taggart's wagon shop. They are now ready to supply the public with work as they are first class workmen at wagon making and blacksmithing, people will do well to patronize them.

Geo. C. White, one of our old bachelors, came to the conclusion that it was not good for man to be alone and one day last week saw him a happy bridegroom.

Mrs. Colston, living near this place, was buried on the 25th inst.

- Apples selling at 50 to 60 cents per bushel.

- The Chestnut crop in Potter county is not large this year.

- A new billiard room has been started in the John Denhoff building.

- D. F. Glassmire, Jr., has sold his Wellsville stage line to Mr. Lane, of East Hebron.

West Branch.

Another accident last Thursday, Mr. George Mitchell has a saw log roll over him while working on the Hemlock lumber job of his son Lon. A long knot carried the log over his head, so that his head was not injured, but his body seemed to get more of the heft of the log. There were no bones broken, and at the present time he is able to be out around.

Business is quite brisk here, from 15 to 20 teams make daily trips with bark to Gales tannery.

There will be 6 or 7 million feet of hemlock put into the West Branch creek this winter, if the jobs are all completed that are under way.

Chips from Costelloville.

Mr. George Folmer, the boss tanner, and family became occupants of their new house on Head and Quimby street, this week.

Mr. George Colegrove has left this place and has now become a farmer of Sylvania.

C. C. Rees moved into his new house last week. Mr. Rees has a nice house well finished and we hope scores of comfort awaits them.

Jacob Peet's house is nearing completion.

Alfred Costello's house is nearly finished.

Messrs. Hugh and Matt Youngs have left farming for the present, and gone to doing carpenter work. They are now putting up a handsome dwelling for Henry Halock & Co., on Grove street.

The Potter Enterprise Wednesday Evening, November 8, 1882 – Vol. IX, No. 26

- The depot at Roulet is enclosed and roofed.

- Fred Davenport, of Wharton, has rented the American House, and will soon open it to the public.

- Albert Lyman is making arrangements to cut out a large quantity of Cherry and Ash on the Prouty.

- Benjamin Rennells is limping around, the cause thereof being a rusty nail, point up, which he incautiously stepped on a few days since.

- Jacob Braitling is cutting a very nice monument from sand stone, to be erected on the grave of L. Bird, late of Sweden township.

Keating.

Beautiful autumn weather.

H. Bridges is building a new wood shed out of an old one.

Lyceum every Tuesday evening.

Born, Oct. 26th, to Mr. and Mrs. James Micheltree, a son.

Nov. 2nd, to Mr. and Mrs. Josiah Hackett, a son.

James Micheltree is building a new house.

E. Fournes and A. H. Crosby are drawing bark to Hammond's tannery.

West Homer.

Frank Klesa has been doing the fall threshing in this neighborhood. Each farmer reports a fine yield of grain. Who says Homer is not progressive, when her inhabitants raise their own bread?

Mr. Curtis Baker is the happy possessor of a new team, with which he intends putting several thousand feet of lumber into the mill this winter.

J. P. Gates sports a new platform buggy.

The Potter Enterprise Wednesday Evening, November 15, 1882 – Vol. IX, No. 27

- Nelson H. Goodsell is running his cider mill.

- F. B. Nelson & Son have purchased the Main Street meat market of Ed. Greisel, and propose running the best market Coudersport has ever had. They have the means and energy to do it. Give them a trial and see how you like them.

- Frank Monroe, Guy Woodard and Mr. Carsten had a bear hunt on the hill north of town recently. They kept watch of bruin, who was up a tree several hours during the night, occasionally sending a ball into him and wondering why he did not come down. Seventeen shots were fired and finally the bear came down. It proved to be a monster hedghog, which would weigh about forty pounds and which in the darkness they had taken for a small bear.

West Homer.

Election has passed by very quietly with us. One of the chief features of the day was the disposing of the school yard fence, which has proven to be more effectual in keeping cattle within the enclosure than outside.

A. J. Quimby and family have moved from Costelloville to this neighborhood.

Costelloville.

O. J. Rees and Watson Dike, of Coudersport, are surveying a railroad from Costelloville to Shippen, which will be used for the Tannery Co.

T. U. Thompson, of Williamsport, who has commenced lumbering here some time will soon have his slide, of three and a half miles, completed from the head of Darian run to the bank of the river.

Had some accidents as follows: Ole Benson, who had a hot bath in a vat of liquor and was more scared than hurt. Philip Wall, who was hurt by a run away team, will soon be able to work again. Both of the Tannery row. Also, a man at John Brisboides camp cut the main branch of the anterior libral artery off while on his way to the camp.

Roulet.

R. L. White is building an addition to his house.

Wm. Boyington has built a good side walk from his house to the store of White & Lyman.

The depot, at this place, is nearly completed. When finished it will be a neat little building of two rooms. The waiting room is sixteen by sixteen and the freight room twelve by sixteen.

Orson Card is teaching at Hebron.

H. H. Kies closed a very successful term of school last week. The directors have engaged him to teach the Winter term at this place.

**The Potter Enterprise
Wednesday Evening,
November 22, 1882 –
Vol. IX, No. 28**

- The river at this point was frozen over last Sunday morning.

- Ed. Greisel has purchased the Billiard Saloon, South side of the river.

- The New Model Furniture Store will henceforth be conducted by G. H. Grabe. Theodore Grabe having retired from the firm.

- Abram Jones is putting up a large two story frame building on his lot nearly opposite the depot. We have not learned what it is intended for.

- J. O. Potter has sold his house and lot on Main street, known as the R. H. Baker lot, to W. T. Hosley and G. W. Merrill for $800. Hosley will put a meat market on his part, and Merrill will erect a tenement house on his. – *Sentinel.*

- It is reported that the Catholics of Coudersport contemplate erecting a church building at an early day. They have a fine square of land south of the river, the gift of the Keating Estate, and their church members number enough to warrant the move. We hope they will push this matter.

West Homer.

The social event of the season was an oyster supper at O. L. Hall's last Saturday evening. All enjoyed themselves immensely.

Teams, bound for the lumber camps, are passing here daily. Lumbering seems to be brisk below us.

L. L. Quimby raised a barn last Friday.

Chips from Costelloville.

We are having beautiful autumn weather of late, giving every one a change to prepare for the winter.

Mrs. John Brownlee returned from the Park House, Rome, N.Y., last week. She has been there for the past seven weeks being treated for cancer. We think she has returned entirely cured.

Miss Edith Haskell, who is conducting our school, spent last Saturday and Sunday at her home in Coudersport.

M. J. Young returned last week from the hunting grounds of Elk county. He reports seeing a number of chipmunks. No other game mentioned.

Genesee Forks.

News items from this place of late have been rather scarce. But with the rest of the world our little place improves. Time as it hurries along improved by busy hands produces changes, noted not perhaps by the rest of the hurrying world, but of importance to the little nook which each may occupy.

The new railroad does not seem to produce much excitement, yet they steadily keep at work. The last grading done on the Pierce flats near the West Branch.

Soon we leek diggers expect to hear the forest reverberating with the clang of the car wheel instead of the clink of the leek hook.

One new store at this place, George Leech now occupies the store below J. Carpenter's.

Mr. Chiles, our hotel keeper, seems to be quite successful in his business.

Miss Ellen Clancy occupies the house owned by Mr. Williams, and is engaged in dress making.

F. Slawson has renovated his house with a new coat of paint, which now presents a neat appearance. Also Mr. Dewit Atherton has improved the appearance of his house by the painter's brush.

Miss McDonald closed her school the 10th with an exhibition which was said to be a success.

Allegany.

Cold and dry, therefore no deep mud as yet. Some people are troubled for water. So many wells and springs being dry. Some families in the northern part of the town drawing water two and three miles.

Daniel Wells has rented Wm. Matteson's farm and moved on to it.

W. Cool is moving into his new house.

Miss Witter is to teach the Judd school this winter.

Adrian Gardner in the Ford district. The schools are not all supplied with teachers yet. There seems to be a scarcity of experienced teachers, most of them preferring to go where better wages are given. Our town is well supplied with school houses, but not with school money, or pupils.

Students attending the select school at Andrews Settlement report a good school, also a Lyceum, not so good.

The Potter Enterprise Wednesday Evening, November 29, 1882 – Vol. IX, No. 29

- Nearly six inches of snow fell last Sunday, giving the boys a chance to brighten up the cutter shoes.

- Mark Harvey, of Hebron, while trimming a fallen tree last Wednesday, cut his left foot very badly. He fainted away from loss of blood. Dr. Buck dressed the cut and Marcus is improving rapidly.

- H. H. Hall, of Allegany, has been working on the Cornell's lumber job for a short time. Last Thursday, while taking care of his cattle, he stepped upon the rope one of them was tied with. This frightened the steer, and throwing up its head and pulling back threw Horace upon his left arm and side, dislocating the left shoulder. Horace fixed it up himself and then called on Dr. Ashcraft for medical assistance. Hall is doing well.

- M. L. Gridley is making arrangements to open a flour and feed store, in the building owned by him on Main St., for some time past known as the King Hotel.

West Branch.

Lon. Lougee carries his mouth in a sling. He fell a tree across a log and the butt of the tree bounded up and struck him in the mouth. So he is on the retired list at present.

John Persing has husked two hundred bushels of ears of corn this fall. He was ninety-three years old the fourth day of last October.

The log jobs are progressing steadily and as well as could be expected considering the lack of men.

Mr. Tomkle has sold out his log job up the Beach Flat Brook. Bill Putt is running it now.

Roulet.

Miss Mary Boyington is teaching in Olean.

Dr. Fisher, of Cortland, N.Y., has located in this place.

Tauscher's Hall is being finished off into dwelling rooms.

Belden Burt has built a blacksmith shop and has it in working order.

Keating.

The yearly coming of the Scranton hunters is over. They have come and gone again and joy go with them. One party put at G. C. Lewis, the other at the mouth of the Freeman, at Monroe Hackett's, they had the luck to go home as empty handed as they came, and we presume a little lighter pockets. The party at Lewis' killed five deer.

C. W. Dingee is building a horse barn.

After drilling through eight feet of solid rock H. Harris has found water in the well he has been digging.

The church going people are getting very tired of appointments and disappointments, they would much rather have a little preaching.

H. H. Beebe is very busy building a cellar under his house. Mr. John Bundy is laying the wall.

Miss Laura Bridges, who has been teaching school on the turnpike, has closed her school for a few weeks on account of whooping cough in the school.

The Potter Enterprise
Wednesday Evening,
December 6, 1882 –
Vol. IX, No. 30

Allegany.

Good sleighing, and lively times for team work, but a scarcity of water.

Warren Gardner is drawing his produce to the Forest House.

Schools nearly all commence to-day, except those that had fall terms and do not have winter school. Miss Miller, of Sweden, teaches at Colesburg; Miss Reynolds at the Settlement, and C. L. Slaughter again at Woodville. It denotes a good teacher when they are hired successively.

Whites Corners.

It is generally healthy here, but very dry.

People are glad to see the sleighing, but would rather see some water first.

Our school opened Nov. 20 with Mr. Adams of Troupsburg teacher. Mr. Adams taught our school last winter and was well liked by all.

Mr. D. White has sold his farm to H. O. Chapin. I understand Mr. White has bought a farm near Lymansville.

Township Tidings from Potter County, Pennsylvania
Volume I, 1880 - 1884

The cheese factory has closed for the season. The patrons seem to be well pleased with Mr. Zimmer's management.

Some excitement was occasioned in this place last week by the sudden death of Miss Ella Cummings living near Harrison Valley. She was well to all appearance till Friday evening, when she was taken ill and died immediately.

- Telephone line a sure thing.

- S. P. Olmsted sports a new cutter.

- Blacksmiths are the busiest men in town.

- Belden Burt, of Burtville, has his mill about completed. It is the best water mill in the county.

- Lumbermen have been improving the late fall of snow, and many logs have been put in at the mills and into the streams.

- Ole Snyder has rented rooms over the Corner Store and will soon open a law office. Ole has built up a good practice in Port Allegany, and will do well here.

- L. F. Andrews has two million feet of Hemlock on the skids, on Dingman Run. He commenced trailing to the river on Thanksgiving day. About twenty-five men are now employed on his job.

- Fred Davenport has opened the American House to the public. The house is a new one, large and commodious, and the furniture is new from top to bottom. Fred invites his friends and the traveling public to give him a call, believing that one call will result in a second.

- While on his way to the Dingman Run lumber camp last Thursday afternoon, L. F. Andrews, accompanied by Ben. Dennis, had the pleasure of a dump into the snow and a walk part way to camp. The cutter struck a root and tipped over and the horse left the boys at this point. The dash and crossbar of the cutter was broken, and the horse received a few scratches. The boys were not hurt, simply scared and mad.

- B. Rennells & Son commenced Monday afternoon, cutting poles for ten miles of the telephone line from Coudersport East.

- Wm. F. Yunge is clearing up the pine shingle timber on the Seward lands, about Cherry Springs. The tract embraces about 7000 acres, and there yet remains considerable first-class shingle timber. The timber will be worked up at Gordnier's mill in Coudersport.

Millport.

Our place cannot boast of many changes since our last writing, yet A. J. Barnes has remodeled his store, making it look better outside, also making it more roomy and more convenient inside. He also has it well filled with winter goods.

People generally think that W. J. Brown done a big thing in raising one thousand pounds of pork from two hogs.

School will commence the first Monday in Dec., kept by Miss Lillie Doyle, who is an experienced teacher.

West Homer.

Snow, sleighbells, and lots of hunters, who seem to regard "Southwoods" as their "Mecca," although none of them seem to leave the woods at night with more than what they came in, in the morning, unless it is the *tracks* they fill their pockets with, but which, alas, they find melted ere they reach home.

O. L. Hall is one of the most enterprising of citizens, with the help of his hired man he gave the school house a much needed scrubbing, thereby saving the town a small bill.

W. M. Quimby is buying a large quantity of cherry lumber, which he intends having drawn to the mill as soon as good sleighing comes.

Costelloville Items.

I've heard that wood sells for $1.50 per cord in this place.

The sleighing commenced Nov. 27th and continues good.

Twenty deer and four bear were killed by the hunters, of this place, last week.

Buckwheat pancakes are the prevailing luxury of the day.

Thanksgiving was observed in the usual roast goose and turkey style.

The Potter Enterprise Wednesday Evening, December 13, 1882 – Vol. IX, No. 31

- The lumbermen are shoving in a large amount of logs. Cornell has sixteen teams hauling on sleds.

- Dan Baker has removed from Ulysses to Coudersport, occupying a part of Dr. French's house, East street.

- I. C. Staysa, of Port Allegany, has removed to Coudersport, occupying the house recently vacated by Wm. Thomas.

- D. C. White, of Whites Corners, has purchased the Jacob Peet farm in Homer, and will soon remove to his new purchase.

- On Friday last Miss Edith F. Doerner, of Coudersport, closed a two months term of school at Olmsted Station, and on Monday of this week commenced a three months term at Fishing Creek. The term just closed, gave good satisfaction to all parties.

- M. L. Gridley has his feed and flour store in operation, keeping on hand the best brands of flour, feed, coarse and fine meal, and in the spring he will put in lime, plaster, cement, &c. Mat is selling very reasonable, and will be glad to see all his friends. Grain of all kinds taken in exchange for goods.

Township Tidings from Potter County, Pennsylvania
Volume I, 1880 - 1884

Hebron.

Richard Mitchell has had the bad luck to lose a good horse; it broke its leg in the stable one night, in some unknown way.

Log hauling is the principal business here now, and the sleighing is splendid for that. An accident occurred Saturday on the road, Mr. Bradley's team getting over the bank the load upsetting hurting one of his horses badly. A son of Mr. Bradley's who was driving narrowly escaped by jumping from the load.

Henry Rogers moved Sunday from Millport, into a part of Frank Swimmer's house.

Herm Baker is to move for the winter into a house of J. S. Barnes.

School at the mouth of the Branch commenced Monday in charge of Miss Rose Clancy.

Chips from Costelloville.

Frosty whiskers, icy nose.

Chattering teeth and frozen toes are the complaints of to-day.

Christmas is coming and our cold weather *has* come; some of our citizens are complaining already of the long winter, hay being scarce, they have been obliged to commence feeding the straw from their bed.

Hunters are swarming the woods from all parts of the country, in hopes of finding some kind of game on which they may level their guns; but many return to their respective wigwams disappointed, notwithstanding several attempts were made the other day to kill bruin, who had climbed a giant hemlock tree on the hill side back of the tannery; some time was taken in discussing as to whom should be the owner of bruin, as "Slim Jim" was the first to see him ascend the hill – Dick saw him take refuge in the tree and Will was *sure* his would be the fatal shot. But alas – soon the carpenters, book-keeper, beam-hands, teamsters, clerks, etc., returned to their work somewhat *tamer* than when they left it, for the said *bruin* turned out to be a piece of hemlock bark lodged in the limbs of the tree. The boys say nothing more of bear hunts.

Johnnie Boyle broke his leg last Monday on returning from school; he was trying to jump on a bob-sled when his foot caught, dragging him some distance and breaking his leg. Dr. Briesnick was called upon to officiate and he is now doing well. It is not long since Johnnie was prostrated from the effects of falling into a hot vat.

A pleasant little wedding took place at the house of C. C. Reese on Thanksgiving Day, uniting Miss Lillie Reese of this place and Mr. Monte Edwards, of Emporium, in the bonds of Holy matrimony, by the Rev. Holland. May all their clouds have silver lining.

Whites Corners.

We have snow enough for sleighing and the people are improving it to the best advantage hauling logs, &c.

Blacksmiths and sleigh-makers are having plenty of work at present.

On Thursday night last some miscreant broke one of the panes of glass out of the front of Chapin & Kane's store and scattered Paris Green over a large gin of dried apples. Any one who will stoop to such low business is not fit to live among civilized people.

Roulet.

S. B. Pomeroy and Leroy Lyman have returned from their hunting trip in Michigan.

Benjamin Card, who has been sick for some time, is gradually failing.

Rev. Bennet holds services in the school house once in two weeks.

Born to Mr. and Mrs. John Tenbrook, a little daughter.

Freeman Run.

Hunting is the excitement just now in this part of the world, just what the average is we don't know, but guess about three hunters to one deer. Big stories are told of seeing fourteen in a drove, but not very many have been killed yet.

J. W. Dingee has moved his family back to Keating Summit.

On Thanksgiving day the remains of Joseph Crane, of Coudersport, were brought here for burial. This is the third one of Mr. Crane's family that has been buried here within a few years. The family have the sympathy of the entire neighborhood.

On Monday evening Mr. Harris' family went to supper, leaving a lighted candle standing on a large centre table in the sitting room. Shortly after the table was discovered to be in flames, a large quantity of papers and magazines were burnt up, several nice books were ruined, also a large table spread was burned. It is supposed that a paper was thrown down near enough to the candle to set it on fire, as the candle was not tipped over.

Sabbath school has adjourned until May next.

Genesee Fork.

As time advances toward New Year, Old winter holds full sway, and the stinging blasts of winter causes lagging steps to hurry into a quicker pace. The snow gradually falling keeps sleighing in good repair, which is improved by the busy teamster. The hauling of telegraph poles forms a large portion of the teaming.

There are a number of workmen boarding at the hotel. More men are expected this week. The poles as far as West Bingham (we learn) are set. The snow is also improved and enjoyed by the many little ones, coasting is the sport of the day. No stern teacher mars their enjoyment, as Mr. Race has not succeeded in finding a teacher. Where oh where! have all the teachers gone? They have gone after better wages.

Miss Hannah and Orsie Hurd commenced their schools to-day, both teach in the town of Ulysses.

J. Carpenter is still building an addition to his store, also a carriage house.

The Potter Enterprise Wednesday Evening, December 20, 1882 – Vol. IX, No. 32

- Thermometers in Coudersport registered from twelve to fourteen degrees below zero, Monday morning.

West Homer.

School has commenced once more in this neighborhood, under the management of Charlie Stillman, who has the reputation of being a first class teacher, we hope our school may receive the much needed improvement this winter.

O. L. Hall is drawing hemlock logs to the mill, while W. C. Chesbro is putting in W. M. Quimby's cherry, at the same place.

Will Lathrop has bilious fever.

Raymond.

If it is colder in Greenland than it is here I would prefer not to go that way. But it is a fine healthy winter, and good for business, but not so good for cattle, they have to live on half water rations and walk quite a distance for that.

Mr. Henry Rogers met with a bad accident Saturday evening. He and Mr. Whipple were running a wood saw when in some way it slipped and tore his hand badly near the thumb. They took him home and called Dr. Presho to do up the wound. He will probably get along all right, but it will stop his preparations for going in the lumber woods.

- B. Rennells & Son have already delivered the poles for six or seven miles of the Telephone line, from Coudersport east. The line will run via Lyman's mill, Sweden and Brookland.

The Potter Enterprise
Wednesday Evening,
December 27, 1882 –
Vol. IX, No. 33

- Ed. Cornell has about two million feet of hemlock banked along the Allegheny above town.

Chips from Costelloville.

We are having some excellent sleighing now and those who have not already engaged a sleighride are waiting very anxiously for their turn to come.

Miss Edith Haskell closed her school, this week, until after the holidays.

Mr. and Mrs. Henry Hallock intend giving a New Years ball to the young people of Costelloville. A grand time is anticipated.

A new boot and shoe shop has been opened by Chas. Howe, on Pine street, next door north of the St. Hallock House.

Mr. Sam Haskins did nothing last week but receive congratulations on his girl.

Freeman Run.

The water, which has been very low, has been somewhat improved by the thaw of a few days back.

Mrs. A. E. Williams, of Keating Summit, died last week, leaving a babe but two weeks old. The remains were taken to New York state for burial.

Eleven Mile.

The water famine has been seriously felt in this locality, and the thaw now in progress is very welcome.

Township Tidings from Potter County, Pennsylvania
Volume I, 1880 - 1884

Miss Gallagher, who began teaching in School No. 5, near Rathbun's, has gone home, and as yet no successor has been appointed.

Lumbermen have been very busy hauling logs to the mill and river bank, and have got those nearly all hauled that were skidded.

Hay and other fodder has disappeared quite fast. Sheep have consumed it rapidly. Last winter at New Years, many had not fed sheep anything only as they picked grass while roaming the fields.

**The Potter Enterprise
Wednesday Evening,
January 10, 1883 –
Vol. IX, No. 34**

- Mrs. Wm. Shear, while feeding a cow last week, fell from the stable loft, severely bruising her left shoulder.

- Ed. Cornell commences banking logs below town to-day, Monday. He has 2,500,000 feet banked near Ellisburg.

- The law firm of Benson & Peck has been dissolved. Mr. Peck, we understand, has rented rooms over the Corner Store and will open an office there this week. Mr. Peck has practiced law here for several years, and with good success. His knowledge of the law and careful preparations will command a good practice.

Whites Corners.
Fine winter weather. The people are improving the sleighing to the best advantage.

Elder Schoville has been holding revival meetings at North Fork for some weeks past, assisted by Elder Howland. Good success has attended them in this work.

Messrs. Warner & Zimmer are building a new store near the cheese factory. They are working busily, expecting soon to have it filled with goods. Success to the boys.

The paris green mystery is not yet cleared up. Some parties were arrested for the crime but were discharged for want of proof.

Oswayo.
The excellent state of the sleighing is worthy of notice, as it enables the log-hauling to go on so rapidly that a few more days of such will suffice to get them to their floating places on the streams – while getting the peeled hemlock trunks to these various market places is of quite doubtful profit to their owner, yet it affords employment to all who wish to so employ their time, and in the aggregate many thousand dollars are put in circulation thereby.

The family of Walter Wells who were in attendance at Alfred University during the Fall term are now at home again, also Miss May Delemater who was there with them. Our citizens not excepting Mr. Wells, are glad to see his family at home again.

Hebron.
Such beautiful sleighing never before was seen! (at least not for two years.)

About two million feet of logs have been put into the Oswayo, or upon its banks, between the mouth of the South Branch and the Topeka bridge.

Mrs. Emma Moyer is not expected to live. She has been attended by Dr. Turner, of Oswayo, Dr. Remington, of Shingle House, and Dr. Clark, of Wellsville. They do not, I believe, give any hope of her recovery. The family are very destitute, there are five small children, nearly all of whom have frozen their feet terribly. Something should be done at once for them. The father, besides being a cripple, has cultivated an appetite for whiskey, which article is of course, more necessary than bread for his starving children. Oh, would that no drop of this "devil's broth" might ever again be manufactured, to tempt our poor weak humanity from the ways of peace and health and consequent happiness!

Millport.

The past week has been unusually eventful for this place. On Saturday afternoon and evening (Dec. 23) the teachers met in an Association here. The attendance was good, especially in the evening when the house was filled to overflowing. Much interest was manifested by all, outsiders as well as members, especially was this noticeable during the discussion of the question, Resolved: "That Normal training is necessary to successful teaching." Of course the word necessary gave the question away to the negative, if it had been *desirable* for instance, the affirmative would have stood a sure chance of success, but as it was both sides were very ably discussed, especially by Mr. Evans on the negative. He is one of our best teachers, and has become so almost entirely by his own efforts, and under many difficulties, he therefore thinks with reason that Normal training has not been necessary for him, but where there is one who will have the perseverance and ability to train themselves, there is at least ten who, without the encouragement and help of our Normal Schools, will do nothing to materially advance their standing as teachers. But let us all do what we can to encourage these local Institutes. They certainly do more effective work in proportion to the effort, than our County Institutes.

Christmas night was duly celebrated by two Christmas trees, one at the Hall and one at the residence of A. J. Barnes. After the Christmas tree at the Hall, a dance was given. A large company participating therein.

- John C. Cavanaugh has been appointed Mercantile appraiser for this year, by the County Commissioners.

Roulet.

J. L. Smith and Wm. Harvey, of Traverse City, Mich., with their families are visiting their former homes in Roulet.

The teachers association, which was held here one week ago, was well attended.

L. S. Marsh, a former resident of Roulet, but now of Olivet, Mich., is visiting his son, Miles, in this place.

Luther Neother, who was taken to the State Insane Asylum at Warren, is no better.

Benj. Card was taken to Smethport one day last week, to be operated on for tumor in the side, by Dr. Freeman.

Keating.

Several of our young people attended the Teachers Association at Roulet last week, and reported a first rate time.

The School had a vacation last week.

The young people enjoyed a candy party at C. W. Dingee's, on News Years night.

G. C. Lewis has a new teamster, Mr. Lord, of Homer.

E. Z. Dingee has traded his span of horses for a yoke of oxen getting twenty-five dollars to boot.

West Branch.

This Wednesday forenoon, Dec. 27th, Lon. Litchell had the misfortune to break one bone of his left leg. They were loading logs and Lon was holding a log to keep it from rolling over the sleighs, when the cant-hook gave way and let the log roll off, and at the same time his feet slipped which prevented him from getting out of the way and the log fell across both legs bruising them badly and breaking one bone of the left leg below the knee. Dr. Meine, of Germania, set the broken bone.

Last Sunday a party of men from Gale's tannery and one of the lumber camps went to Germania and when returning in the evening got into a row among themselves and during the melee several pistol shots were fired and one man was shot in the arm. I am unable to learn how bad he was hurt.

The people of West Branch had a Christmas tree at the Crippen Run school house on Sunday evening. The tree was more than full of presents and it would have been a good time but for the whiskey that was sloshing around.

On Tuesday, Moses Hirch, of Pike, went off the dugway just below Gale's tannery, with a load of leather and broke a leg badly.

Chips From Costelloville.

The holidays are passed – Santa Claus has come and gone again; and we have nothing to do now but return to the work designed us for the year '83. Several homes were made happy by a Christmas tree – others enjoyed their presents without the tree, while some, we are sorry to hear, had the tree, minus the presents.

Some of the young people of this place spent New Year's night at Mr. A. Burleson's, keeping time with music furnished by the Costelloville band until the wee hours.

West Homer.

Two of Homer's young people have commenced 1883 with happy hearts and bright anticipations of the future. Mr. John Quimby was united to Miss Lydia Crosby, by Rev. W. S. Holland, on Jan. 1st.

A. W. Lathrop received a severe cut on his hand, by the glancing of an axe, which his son as using. Mr. Lathrop also has a daughter very sick, dangerously so we hear.

The Potter Enterprise
Wednesday Evening, January 17, 1883 – Vol. IX, No. 35

- B. S. Colwell has recently built a new store, 25 x 70, at Keating Summit.

- The Potter County Telephone Co., (limited) is to have a "limited" existence. The Telephone Monopoly have decided to rent no more instruments but offer to buy old lines and build new ones. The Potter county company, at a meeting last week, decided to sell out at once. The poles are nearly all delivered along the line, and over half of them set. The monopoly agree to complete the line and operate it.

- We want a correspondent in Lewisville, Harrison Valley, Sunderlinville and Shingle House. Who will fill the bill?

Keating.

Sleighing is fine and business is lively.

The genius of the neighborhood commences to develop; we have a magic lantern show in our midst.

A large amount of bark and logs are being hauled from this place.

West Branch.

Last Monday morning, the 8th inst., a man by the name of Isaac West was killed while working on the slide, on the Charlie Brown lumber job at Pike Mills. A small log jumped out of the slide and struck him on the side of the face and broke his neck, he was about 20 feet from the slide on the upper side. Mr. West had a wife but no children; she left their home that morning on a visit to friends in Delmar, Tioga Co., Pa. Mr. West was taken to Wellsboro for burial.

The sleighing is very good here and business is very lively. The log jobbers are running in their logs at a lively rate. White & Metzger are getting in a very nice stock of Cherry logs, their mill is ready for work but there is no water to run it.

Homer White, of Coudersport, is teaching the school at the Forks of the West Branch.

Willis Conable has started a grocery here.

The Addison & Northern Pa. R.R. Co.'s Engineer Corps were here last Saturday running their first line. They have gone back to Gaines, and are running their locating line from Gaines up this way.

West Homer.

Jack Frost is busy sketching landscapes on the window panes.

Beautiful sleighing and people are improving it hauling hay, bark, wood, &c.

Rev. W. Holland preached a good sermon to the people of this place on Sunday, the 7th inst. He will preach here once in two weeks and we do hope that his labors will be appreciated.

Mr. Charlie Stillman is teacher of our school this winter. He, with the energetic ones of our neighborhood, have organized a lyceum. We hope all will take an active part, as we need something of the kind to "drive dull care away."

Township Tidings from Potter County, Pennsylvania
Volume I, 1880 - 1884

Miss Hattie Chesbro was very abruptly snatched from our midst by a gentleman from Scranton. We have no idea how long he has had her in view, but this is certain he was not long getting away with her when he once got possession. We are sorry to lose Hattie for she was one of our best. May her days of married life be long, with just enough shadow to temper the glare of the sun.

Also on New Year's day Mr. John Quimby and Miss Lydia Crosby were married by Rev. W. Holland. Wilbur are you asleep and dreaming? Are you now aware that you are like

"The last rose of summer, left blooming alone,

It's lovely companions faded and gone."

Why what would you do, suppose some one

Should come and take Libbie from you?

Hold down your head and blush with shame,

And die with old age, without wife or fame.

- A. A. Swetland has moved to Harrison Valley, that being the terminus of the stage route hereafter, as Mr. W. M. Smith has made arrangements to carry the mail from Harrison Valley to Westfield and back. By this means the Westfield stage proprietors, Swetland & Tracey, expect to make better time and make connections with the trains at both ends of the route.

The Potter Enterprise Wednesday Evening, January 24, 1883 – Vol. IX, No. 36

- A. E. Hollenbeck has removed his law office to the building so long occupied as a law office by Isaac Benson.

- R. L. Nichols had a wagon shed crushed in by the snow last Saturday, doing some damage to wagons beneath.

- More logs are now in the Allegheny river than ever before.

Oswayo.

Winter is fleeting away, so far in a manner delightful for the lumbermen and teamsters, who prefer activity to idleness.

The school at the Centre (near Rathbun's) is vacant yet. Mrs. Benton, who is teaching the lower one, is engaged to teach a spring term at the Centre school, to begin about the middle of February. Miss Maggie Doyle teaches the upper school. J. C. Wilkinson the one near V. R. Kenyon's. Miss Bishop and Mr. Hall teach the village schools.

Roulet.

Of what good is the depot this cold weather without a stove?

Three of J. Kimm's children have the diphtheria, they are attended by Dr. Fisher.

Benj. Card died at Smethport, last Monday; his remains were brought home and interred in Card Creek cemetery Friday.

An oyster supper was held at the residence of J. V. Weimer last Saturday evening.

Chips From Costelloville.

The weather seems to have taken a turn, and since the 13th it has been quite unfavorable for out door work.

Mr. Ephram Reed, aged sixty-nine, died of typhoid fever on the evening of the 17th, after an illness of six weeks.

The Hone & Beers boot and shoe establishment on Pine St. came very near being destroyed by fire, one night last week; but fortunately the flames were extinguished before much damage was done.

The Potter Enterprise
Wednesday Evening,
January 31, 1883 –
Vol. IX, No. 37

- W. I. Lewis has purchased the house recently erected by Dan Neefe, on Water St. He takes possession next spring.

Whites Corners.

We have had a fine run of sleighing for some time, but it is thawing to-day. People are in hopes it will thaw more as water has been very scarce all winter.

The school is progressing finely under management of Mr. Adams.

Donations are the order of the day. There has been three on this charge within two weeks. Well it makes a place for people to go and the money helps so much toward paying the preacher.

There was an oyster supper at the residence of N. M. Brooks on Friday evening last. All who attended enjoyed themselves very much.

- Last week Cyrenus Rennells drove into Johnson's livery barn and while unhitching, a plank tipped up letting the horse through the floor. From the floor to the ground it is several feet and the horse found a very uncomfortable place for a short time. No serious damage.

Keating.

Fine sleighing continues as also does our winter weather only a little more so on Tuesday morning the 23d, the thermometer stood at 24 degrees below zero.

We are so glad to learn that Costelloville is a temperance town, we never should have mistrusted it if they had not published it in the paper.

Hebron.

Our good sleighing has enabled our lumbermen to finish their work much earlier than usual.

Wm. Woodard has returned from his job on the Honeoye and will begin skidding again on Whitney Creek next week.

Mort Kenyon has a job of putting in the Gale logs.

An oyster supper for the purpose of raising funds to buy an organ for church purposes was given at Leroy Burdick's last Saturday evening, but I have not learned the amount received.

Mrs. Emma Adams Lane is teaching at Hebron Center, having

given up her school at Wilkesbarre for one nearer home. Miss Hettie Lane, of Honeoye, goes to complete her school at Willkesbarre.

The Potter Enterprise
Wednesday Evening,
February 7, 1883 –
Vol. IX, No. 38

- Last Friday evening about nine o'clock the woodshed on the Ross Farm at Lymansville, occupied by F. B. Nelson, was burned. The building stood by itself about twenty feet from the house and was well filled with seasoned wood, making a very hot fire. The rear of the dwelling was badly scorched, but a free use of water saved it from burning down. Ashes kept in the woodhouse caused the fire. Mr. and Mrs. Nelson and one of the children were sick in bed at the time.

West Homer.

Jacob Peet has bought G. W. Berfield's farm produce, hay, oats, &c., and is hauling it to Costelloville, his familiar face is always welcomed by his friends, among whom he has passed thirty-five of his life, though John Gordnier and Warren Chesbro seem to be the favored ones.

Matie Johnson has been teaching the school on South Hill the past week for J. B. Colcord, he being obliged to give it up on account of sickness, was confined to his bed a few days, but is around again, though not looking very rugged, was attended by Dr. Ellison.

Ed. Greisel, of South Hill, was married to Miss Dell Dingman, of Coudersport, last Wednesday evening. Yes, boys, it is true, Ed has really got the matrimonial halter slipped over his neck now he has to begin to think up excuses why he was out late, you know, do not envy him.

A part of the roof of the old log house, once the home of Jacob Peet, has fallen in under the heavy weight of the snow this winter, it could but bring feeling of sadness when we think of the *many* that have found rest and comfort under its mossy roof. It has withstood the storms of thirty-five winters, but Time has done its work with this as well all things, its mission is filled, and it must sink to earth and rot in oblivion.

Why can not our school house be filled on Sunday mornings, as well as Thursday evening? Come and hear Brother Holland preach one of his good sermons, and you will *all* go to your homes feeling better than when you came.

The Potter Enterprise
Wednesday Evening,
February 14, 1883 –
Vol. IX, No. 39

- Roll butter sold for 25 cents per pound, last week in Coudersport.

- M. L. Gridley has purchased the coal yard of J. M. Covey, and will supply customers.

Keating.

People have been wishing for water and a thaw all winter and now they have got it, more than they wished for some of them.

Parties are numerous, a molasses candy party at H. Bridges last Friday evening, and a coasting party Monday evening on the hillside near Mr. Harris'.

A. H. Crosby had the misfortune to jam one of his oxen's feet quite badly last week while skidding logs.

One of E. Fournes' horses has a bad shoulder, supposed to be caused by a bad fitting collar.

Ethel Beebe got a severe bump while coasting last Monday.

On Tuesday three tramps, two men and a woman, came into this place begging their way along, said they came from the Catskill mountains and were going to Ohio.

G. C. Lewis is drawing some very fine cherry logs to Keating Summit.

Sartwell Creek.

This is the week for valentines.

Cold weather is with us yet, and bids fair to be for a while.

School taught by Dorman Card, has had a vacation of four weeks on account of his illness. He is slowly recovering.

Very many in this vicinity have been, and are still, counted on the sick list.

Mr. D. P. Jordan, while engaged in hauling out wood, last Thursday, caught his foot under the moving log and before he could remove it bruised it very badly.

Log drawing has nearly disappeared from this place and times are dull, except occasionally a wedding or two.

Mr. Eldin McDowell, formerly of this place, and Miss Mary Coleman, of Port Allegany, also Mr. William McIntosh, of Erie Co., Pa., and Miss Jennie McDowell, were united in the bonds of matrimony, Feb. 6th.

Death has again entered our community and taken one from our midst. Mr. Reuben Card, after an illness of about four days, suffering untold agonies, with that dreaded disease erysipelas, passed from this earth of sickness and sorrows. He has left a vacant place in this neighborhood which none can fill.

The Potter Enterprise Wednesday Evening, February 21, 1883 – Vol. IX, No. 40

- Charles Reissman is getting lumber on the ground for his new Furniture Store and Cabinet Shop, on Second street, where his old stand was located.

Allegany.

What they say of this vicinity.

That one man in Allegany raised so large a crop of corn that it is not all husked yet.

That there is water plenty now for man and beast.

That C. L. Slaughter and N. Cool each are the owners of fine cutters.

That the Velley brothers have taken the lead in hauling large loads this winter.

That Mr. Metzger is to run the saw mill on the Colesburg farm.

That the oyster supper at the Colesburg house was a success.

That our schools are generally running in good order.

That there is a petition in circulation for the road to be opened up from Mr. Burdick's to A. Wells.

That Daniel Wells had the misfortune to get one of his horses badly cut on the ankle with the sharp crust.

Correspondence.

There does not seem to be any interesting news from this neighborhood just now. I might tell about the weather, the thaw, the rain, the breakup, but the weather at Coudersport is about the same I suppose, except you have more water, more of a freshet than we have. We are more secure on these hills; the sources of the Alleghany being mostly below us, we never fear a flood. We need no Babel. Castles in the air may sometimes be built; they perhaps, are as common on one locality as another.

The death of Wm. E. Dodge is announced. Many in all parts of the country will feel his loss. His benefactions have been very numerous and widespread. Forty years ago he took an active part in helping on agencies and enterprises designed for the public good. If I am not greatly mistaken he formed a plan, or resolution, when first entering upon business of giving a certain percentage of his gains to religious and philanthropic causes. I rather think he kept that resolution all his life. And his business increased amazingly. For some years I was accustomed to see him very often. He made no parade of his good deeds. It seemed to give him pleasure to help others. He spoke of his gifts as investments. Very few know better by experience than he, the words, "It is better to give than to receive." He sent $200 to help build the church at this place. He seemed to have a blessing for everybody. It was pleasant to be in his company, and to hear him talk. He was a great business man, very exact in all business transactions. Seldom does a man obey the Scripture injunction better than he "Diligent in business, fervent in Spirit, serving the Lord." The great success was not due to any extra education, if I remember right he had only a limited common school education. His extensive knowledge was due to his great diligence in picking up knowledge and information after his school days ended. If the young men of the country would have the like success, and leave such a name, let them do likewise.

RAYMOND.

Bingham.

We have had plenty of snow with very good roads most of the time and an immense amount of business has been done thus far this winter.

The saw mills have heavy stock of work on hand.

A larger amount of building is in prospect than ever before. Everything seems to indicate a state of unusual prosperity.

Several deaths have occurred, notably among others were those of Mr. Peter Chase, of Whitesville, N.Y., Mr. James Statham, North Fork, Pa., Mrs. A. P. Kibbe, N.

Bingham, Pa., and Mrs. Brown of Bingham Centre, Pa.

Millport.

It has been quite sickly in the place for some time past. I make mention of Mrs. J. Henley, who was taken suddenly insane, and of the infant son of H. Brown, also the little son of S. Sloat, who are quite sick.

A. J. Barnes had the misfortune to lose his pocketbook with about $300 in it, but was lucky enough to find it after it had been lost a couple of weeks or so.

The water in the creek is rising fast, and log runners are getting their boots spiked ready for business.

Hebron.

Ad. Stevens had the bad luck to lose a good horse last week. The team were hauling logs for Dr. Ellison, and in coming down a steep hill, the logs got the start of the horses much to the detriment of the horses – and Mr. Stevens.

Mr. Culiver, while drawing a load of hay down the Eleven Mile on Sunday last, had the misfortune to have one of his horses slip and break a leg.

Mrs. Culiver is among the missing. She leaves two little boys to mourn her loss.

There is to be an Oyster Supper at Henry Lamberton's Wednesday evening, Feb. 21st, for the purpose of raising funds to get an organ for the church on Crandall Hill.

Don Lyman, of Eleven Mile, while unloading a load of logs, slipped and fell through a hole in the bridge near the Rathbone place, breaking one bone of his leg, below the knee and dislocating his ankle. Dr. Ellison, who had come over to see Jay Shattuck, was called in and the limb is doing as well as could be expected. He is being cared for by his sister, Mrs. Day, at her home on the Rathbone place.

To-day it is raining, and if it does not turn cold before to-morrow there will be a flood of log-running.

The Potter Enterprise
Wednesday Evening,
February 28, 1883 –
Vol. IX, No. 41

- Clara township comes to the front. Last Tuesday that township elected two lady School directors.

- Charley Crawford, of Roulet, has gone to St. Louis where he has secured a situation in a real estate office.

- We understand that F. W. Knox contemplates erecting three small houses on his property, south of the river, to rent.

- Mrs. D. W. Butterworth has purchased of C. H. Armstrong the property south of the river, so long occupied as a parsonage. Consideration, $1,500.

- The ladies of the M. E. Church are making an effort to build a parsonage. The building will be erected back of the church facing on Fourth street. Estimated cost, $1,000.

Township Tidings from Potter County, Pennsylvania
Volume I, 1880 - 1884

Millport.

The fellow who has no *creek* in his back, or a broken nose, or a sore shin from slipping on the ice is nowhere!

Letters from Sedgwick City, Kansas, report the death by diphtheria, of Nellie, oldest daughter of Charles Barnes, formerly of this place.

The little son of Nettie and Herbert Brown has been very sick for some time, they have little hope of his recovery.

Mrs. Ella Henley is thought to be hopelessly insane. This afflicted family have the sympathy of all.

Hebron.

Two weeks ago yesterday A. J. Barnes had the misfortune to lose his pocketbook while rolling logs on the banking ground near Mrs. Cone's; last Friday he was looking for it, almost hopelessly however, as he did not know anything within two miles of where he had lost it, when lo! lying between two logs the lost was found. The money and papers had partly fallen out and were hanging on some willow twigs, there was $260 in cash and as much more in papers. It is plain that if A. J. Does not "hang his harp on a willow tree" he does his money.

Those who attended the Teachers Association at Oswayo, Saturday evening, from this place, pronounce it a decided success. The people of that place evidently know how to entertain the teachers and make them welcome. This occasion stood out in striking contract to the *melee* of New Year's night, 1883.

Mr. Chauncey Lewis and family are moving this week to Allentown, Pa. Mr. Lewis will, I believe, start a livery in that place.

Whites Corners.

There are many on the sick list at present.

Mr. James Statham died very suddenly a few days ago.

Mr. T. Farnum and family moved from this place to Harrison Valley, on Wednesday last.

The town election passed off very quietly this year.

The people failed to convict Mr. Brooks of poisoning dried apples and so they did the next best thing – elected him Supervisor. Surely "straws show which way the wind blows."

We have lost one of our old citizens, D. C. White moved to Coudersport last week.

The Potter Enterprise
Wednesday Evening,
March 7, 1883 –
Vol. IX, No. 42

- Lewisville is encouraged over her railroad prospects, and is also talking water works.

- Mrs. Laura Newton has donated to the Methodist Society of Sharon a parsonage lot.

- S. A. Phillips has bought of Amos Vellie the James Turner property, on Water street.

- Between twenty and thirty buildings will be put up in Coudersport before next Fall.

- Mose Hirsch, of Pike, who had his leg broken in three places, about Christmas time, is able to be out again.

West Branch.

Mrs. Main Stowell is very sick, there is but little hopes of her recovery. She is over 81 years old – Mr. Lemuel Hammand is still confined to the house.

Sleighing is not very good since the break-up.

White and Metzger are starting up their mill.

Hebron.

Warren Ellis and family have moved to the mill, near the Stone Dam.

Alphonso Harris occupies the house vacated by Ellis.

Ben. Lamberton met with a serious accident on Monday last. He and his brother were getting out drags of wood, he cutting and Charles drawing. While Charles was gone with a drag, Ben. fell one tree upon another, the falling tree splitting and falling upon him with such force as to crush him to the earth where Charles found him insensible, and, as we feared, nearly dead; but a knoll of ground had partially broken the force of the falling tree, and Dr. Turner being called found no broken bones, and it is hoped there are no other injuries that will prove fatal, although he is pretty badly bruised and hurt.

Mr. Soloman Lamberton has his mill nearly ready for running, but has been bothered with the machinery, as the boys say, "his fragments don't match."

Will and Ed Crittenden have bought the Shattuck mill and taken possession.

Clara.

Marion Manly has begun getting in logs from the Hollenbeck lot.

Juna Stevens and family have moved to this place, they reside for the present with their daughter, Mrs. Glines, and are welcomed to their old home by lots of old friends.

The most exciting election news is the election, by a large majority, of Mrs. E. A. Glines and Miss Helen D. Brooks to the office of school directors. I am happy to say that the ladies can read and write which has been something that can not always be said of the numbers of that honorable body in this town.

Next Friday closes a five months term of school taught here by Mr. Evans of Ulysses. Mr. Evans has given universal satisfaction in this neighborhood, he is not only an excellent teacher, but a gentleman of culture and refinement, and destined to be a "Potter County boy" of whom we shall all be proud some day.

An exhibition will be given by the school Saturday evening next, one of the many attractions will be a spelling match.

Township Tidings from Potter County, Pennsylvania
Volume I, 1880 - 1884

The Potter Enterprise
Wednesday Evening,
March 14, 1883 –
Vol. IX, No. 43

- H. T. Nelson's dray horse enjoyed a runaway Monday morning. Damage, nothing.

- We have heard of hay selling as low as seven dollars per ton, at the barn recently.

- Herman Kiehle has returned from Buffalo Medical College where he has been attending lectures the past winter.

- W. H. Tassel has returned from Baltimore where he has just graduated from the College of Physicians and Surgeons. We understand he intends locating at Oswayo.

West Pike.
Mrs. E. O. Bennette has been quite sick with typhoid fever, but is recovering.
Mr. S. J. Acker's little boy, Virgil, has been quite sick for some time.
O. L. Blackman is drawing lumber from Brookland, with which to build a new barn.
C. C. Flynn has just moved on the place which he recently purchased of C. F. Turck.
Neighborhood dances are the rage at present. Two this week.
Mr. Sinette is a happy man. It is a little daughter that gladdens his home.

Oswayo.
Nearly all the able-bodied of our citizens are in attendance at court this week and no doubt the balance will be there next week.
March 27th the G.A.R. Post hold memorial and anniversary exercises. In the p.m. memorial service with address by Rev. W. Miller in honor of Andrew W. Estes for whom the Post was named will be held, and in the evening the other exercises, addresses, poems, songs, comprising a "camp fire," as known among the "boys."

Roulette.
A little son of Dr. Fisher has the scarlet fever.
George Helwigg, of Turtle Point, has rented Mrs. Abbott's building and will start a drug store.
Miss Rose Card, of Sartwell Creek, died of scarlet fever, the 28th ult.

Genesee Forks.
Notwithstanding the inclemency of the weather, a company of 51 or 52 friends from this place and Ellisburg, relatives from York's Corners assembled at Norman Chapman's March 10th to celebrate their fifteenth anniversary of their wedding day. It proved a complete surprise to them, but was none the less enjoyable. Some presents were given, a bounteous repast was served, which with meeting old acquaintances, and pleasant conversation, the afternoon passed only too quickly. We wish Mr. and Mrs. Chapman many happy returns of the day.

Township Tidings from Potter County, Pennsylvania
Volume I, 1880 - 1884

We hear that Mr. Perkins' horses became frightened when nearing the Forks and ran a short distance, running against the sign post and demolishing the sign at the Chile Hotel, at which place they were caught, no one hurt.

Miss Hannah and Orsie Hurd are now at home. School closed Friday.

Chips From Costelloville.

Miss Edith Haskell has been obliged to discontinue her school on account of poor health, and has left L. D. Ripple to conduct the last month; we regret losing her as a teacher, for she was of the first class, and are sorry to know her cheery presence will join us no more. Miss Haskell was well liked by all and we would welcome her return at any time.

Several persons are sick and are now under the skillful care of Dr. Breisnick.

Death visited us again last week and claimed the only child of Mr. and Mrs. S. B. Haskins, also an infant child of Mr. and Mrs. Sol Dale.

Allegany.

The funeral services of Mrs. Calvin Ford was held at the Judd school house last Saturday, five children are left motherless, a home without a wife and mother, and a vacant place in the neighborhood not easily filled.

The donation was not well attended, owing to so many's being sick. Almost every family has one or more members sick, mostly with colds and distemper that is so prevalant this winter.

Keating.

Many are busy getting ready for sugaring as a good sugar season is expected.

Our winter school of five months' duration closed on the 23d.

Rev. W. S. Holland preached an excellent sermon here on Sunday evening last.

Genesee Forks.

Business seems to be in a good condition for so small a place.

J. B. Robbins, who is now engaged in the boot and shoe business, has purchased a lot of Pierce, and is about to erect a new house.

George Leach is now making preparation to build a store 80 x 26, 20 ft. high from wall; cellar under the entire building.

O. D. Stephens is making preparations to run his cheese factory the coming season. The prospect is that it will be a success. People will do well to patronize him as he is an efficient cheesemaker.

Our enterprising landlord has built an ice house, and has it well filled.

Religious services at this place every two weeks, Rev. Miller, Pastor, who is well liked.

The Potter Enterprise
Wednesday Evening,
March 21, 1883 –
Vol. IX, No. 44

- Eggs 20 cents per dozen.

- Two bird dogs, belong to W. I. Lewis and S. P. Olmsted, on Friday last, killed ten white leghorn hens for D. F. Glassmire, Jr.

- John R. West, of Sharon township, registered the first dog in the book kept for that purpose in the Prothonotary's office, last week.

- Alvin Rennells, one day last week, had his foot caught between a stump and a moving log. A team broke to stop at the word, saved him from a serious injury.

- Last week Maggie Ryan had some teeth drawn. The hemorhage resulting required the attendance of a physician, and it was several hours before it was stopped. Dr. Mattison stopped the flow of blood.

- Moses Hirsch has sued Pike township, claiming damages to the amount of ten thousand dollars, for injuries which he received last December, when his load slipped over a dug way and his leg was broken in three places.

- One day last week the team of Horace Nelson had a runaway on Main St., starting near J. M. Hamilton's and coming to a halt at Second street; at Miles White's the team took the sidewalk, passing so near Stebbins' plate glass window that it seemed a mystery how the glass escaped contact with the whiffletrees.

South Eulalia.

Spring is coming.

March is doing its work, blowing winter away.

If you want to see snow drifts, take a ride over South Hill, any time between now and the Fourth of July.

Apples are selling here for one dollar per bushel at the door, rutabagas would like to, but can't.

Lawrence Whitman has moved his family to Pump Station, where they will take charge of the boarding house. Lawrence will provide, and Mrs. Whitman and her sister Matie (who accompanied them) as cooks can not be beat, therefore we know their boarders will fare "sumptuously."

Mr. and Mrs. Oscar Rees, of Sylvania, made our place a visit on Thursday last, they expect soon to start for Neb. Mrs. Rees will visit her brother, Uriah Hackett, who left here a number of years ago, he writes he has a good farm with everything comfortable around him.

Hops, taffy pulls, and oyster stews keep monotony at a distance.

John Klesa is going to build a neat little house on his farm this summer, how is this boys? I thought it took all the dimes and dollars a young man could raise to pay for cigars and livery rigs, didn't you?

Whites Corners.

Farmers are getting impatient waiting for sugaring.

There is a great deal of sickness in this place. We hope when the weather gets warmer the general health will be better.

Rev. Schoville is trying to collect money enough to finish paying for the parsonage. If the church members would try and practice what they preach it would be a great help to him.

Our young merchant Willie Warner has gone to the city to purchase goods to fill up their new store.

Freeman Run.

The house of E. Fournes came very near burning last week, fire caught from the chimney under the plaster, but fortunately was discovered before much damage was done.

James Micheltree has moved into his new house.

Married March 6th, at the residence of C. W. Dingee, by the Rev. W. S. Holland, Mr. Newell Pangburn and Miss Rena Bennet. Much joy and happiness is the wish of their many friends.

Many are sick with sore throats in this neighborhood.

Allegany.

The school at Colesburg closed last week, and gave an exhibition Saturday evening which did credit to both teacher and pupils.

Higley Green is to work three months for Mr. Bishop, at the settlement.

There is talk of having a dry goods at Colesburg.

B. Hillegas has had the misfortune to get badly hurt, while working on N. Dwight's log job in Bingham. He was brought home yesterday.

Farmers are preparing for sugar making. In some bushes, on the hills, the snow is still very deep, so that it will be very hard work to get in with teams.

Sartwell Creek.

Mrs. Reuben Card was called to Clarksville, N.Y., Saturday, by the illness of her daughter, Mrs. Wm. Hill, who is very sick with erysipelas.

Delbert Witter returned from Michigan last Thursday, after an absence of nearly six months.

The U.B. Quarterly Meeting will be held at Card Creek, the 24th and 25th of March. A good attendance is expected.

Messrs. Thomas and Henry McDowell and their mother, who have been visiting friends and relatives in this place, have returned to their home in Wisconsin.

The Potter Enterprise
Wednesday Evening,
March 28, 1883 –
Vol. IX, No. 45

- M. V. Larrabee, of Roulet, has a house cat 23 years of age, still able to masticate beef, but not much use as a mouser.

- The prospect for a saw mill at Roulet, near the Station, is reported good. A. V. and Leroy Lyman have offered inducements in the way of land and privileges that ought to secure a mill, and it is believed that one will be erected this coming summer. The Lymans have shown public spirit that is decidely rare. We wish Coudersport had a dozen such men.

- James Johnston has removed the barn from the O. J. Rees lot, to his own lot, on Water Street. Eight horses drew it down West Street at a good pace.

Raymond.

Joseph Phillips died at Gold on Thursday.

The donation party here Friday night was largely attended, $100 was the result.

Germania.

The theatre, concert and dance recently held here for the benefit of the sufferers by floods in Germany realized $152.50 clear of all expenses.

An noon on Wednesday, March 21st, the house of Philip Hoffman was destroyed by fire – ashes kept in an out house the cause of the fire. Two men half a mile from the house saw the fire and ran there. They succeeded in saving the contents of one room only. The man of the house was absent, and his family were in Ridgway. His loss is considerable as the house was well furnished. After the fire sixty dollars in gold was found in the ruins.

Hebron.

Mrs. Frank Gale died Friday, the 16th inst., after an illness of one week only. She leaves a husband and three children to mourn her loss.

Charles Day has sold his timber tract to Wallace Dwight.

Mr. Day will remove his family soon to Wellsville, where he contemplates making a permanent home.

Lots of wintergreen berries on Lamberton's Hill!

One more warm day and the log-runners will make it lively along the banks of the Oswayo, as there is about three million of logs lying between the mouth of the Branch and the Topeka Bridge.

Millport.

We are sorry to announce the death of Champion Munger of this place, who was buried on the 20th inst. He leaves many mourning friends, and his widowed mother has the sympathy of all in her affliction.

Mrs. Kemp of Eleven Mile was also buried on the 23rd. Her death caused a great shock in the neighborhood, and much sympathy is felt for the husband, who is left with four small children, the youngest being but a few days old.

There is much sickness throughout the neighborhood.

Clara.

To-day Champ. Munger of Millport was buried here. He leaves a wife, and many relatives and friends to mourn his loss. He was attended in his sickness by Dr. Remington of Shingle House, he had an attack of Erysipelas, but died, I understand, from some lung disorder.

Mr. L. Brooks and family have returned to Michigan.

Mr. and Mrs. Sala Stevens returned from Cincinnati and occupy the farm lately sold by John L. Brooks to Wm. Cobb.

The last meeting of the Liberal League was interesting and well attended in spite of the bad weather. Mrs. Ella A. Glines is librarian for the League and has many valuable books not often met with in a circulating library of that size.

The school here at its closed presented Mr. Evans, the teacher, with a copy of Spencer on Education.

Mr. Julius Moffit is getting in logs to new mill (which by the way has a whistle that regulates the solar system). Mr. Moffit expects to build a cozy little house this summer.

Eleven Mile.

Nearly four months of sleighing and no apparent decrease of snow in many places. The snow storm of yesterday was mild enough, had it been on a western prairie to have passed for a blizzard.

Death, whose harvest is reaped at all seasons, and consists of people of all ages and classes, has been active. Yesterday Mrs. Kemp, wife of Welcome Kemp, was buried at the cemetery here. Four motherless babes are left without her brooding care. At the same hour at Oswayo Mrs. Franklin Gale, Sr., was laid in the place appointed for all to lie, and one week ago to-day her son's wife was buried, she too left four children of tender years to the care of her bereaved husband.

On the 9th inst., Philemon C. Lovell was buried from the church at Oswayo. His obsequeies were attended by Gardner Post G.A.R. of Bolivar, N.Y., Estes Post of Oswayo and Barnes Post of Sharon. Rev. N. North preached a beautiful sermon on the occasion, and the body was buried with the use of burial service of the G.A.R. So we see that no exemption is made from the stroke of the Destroyer. Much illness exists from a distemper or cold that prevails very extensively hereabouts.

Cutting wood, getting logs to mill, splitting rails and getting ready for making sugar are some of the various kinds of work now in progress.

The winter being so prolonged indicates a short Spring, but in this climate April is a month of uncertainties, as to the weather, and it may require all its sunshine and showers to melt off the snow and ice enough to bare the fields for the plow and harrow.

The Potter Enterprise Wednesday Evening, April 4, 1883 – Vol. IX, No. 46

Allegany.

The first spring month has past, with no sugar made. It looks like Spring to-day. A few have a part of their bushes tapped, while others are waiting for sugar weather.

The roads in places are very bad, as those that travel them find, without being told.

Sabbath school is to be organized next Sunday, at the Judd school house.

Mr. Scoville has moved his house hold goods to Colesburg.

The store has to be moved and repaired before the goods are put in.

Mr. Wm. Matteson has moved back on his farm. Mr. Wells moving to Coudersport.

Orson Dwight's family are to move on N. Dwight's home farm.

Rev. Miller's son is expected to take his farm, now occupied by L. Dingman.

Mr. Smith has rented and taken possession of H. C. James' farm.

M. W. Slaughter's hand, that was hurt in the winter, is still very bad.

Miss Marcia Stryker is to go to Lewisville, to engage in dressmaking.

C. L. Slaughter is engaged in the book business at present.

N. Cool is at Coudersport engaged at carpenter work.

Mrs. Wm. Matteson is in very poor health. It seems to be very unhealthy at present. Nearly every family having one or more members indesposed. Mr. G. W. G. Judd is improving.

Another couple have joined the matrimonial number, Geo. Collins and Miss Monroe. May peace and prosperity attend them.

- W. T. Dike will open his bakery about the middle of this month.

- The borough council have authorized the construction of a foot walk to be attached to the east side of the Main street bridge.

- We understand Luther Seibert is preparing to erect a building, at the corner of Main and Second Street, to be used for a law office.

Cross Fork.

Mr. Norman Chapman has rented his farm to a Mr. Thompson who has moved on the place. Mr. Amasa Robins has sold his farm to David Peet who moved on the place last week, his son George Peet is to remain on the homestead.

Lyman Hackett has bought the goods and rented the store belonging to Stephen Hurd and is now also a merchant in our place.

We notice that Bruce Robbins has his new building enclosed.

Cheese factory to commence operation the first day of May.

North Wharton.

Notwithstanding our wintery weather and bad roads, we are working from 6 a.m. until 6 p.m. The teams are doing their usual amount of work and the gong is sounded three times a day at the Gem Dining Hall, reminding us of the many tables which are spread thereat with eatables prepared for the inner man.

Our school conducted by Miss Sally Morley is progressing nicely; I believe there are some fifty pupils in attendance.

Mr. Clark LaMonte and wife left on Monday last for Rome, N.Y., where Mrs. LaMonte is to remain to be treated for a cancer.

Mr. Seymour Sweet, who has been in A. Costello & Co.'s employ for two years, and in the store for the past year, left on Wednesday last for Little Falls, N.Y., - may fortune smile on him, is the wish of his many friends.

On the evening of the 26th inst., the young people of our town took an active part in the reeling, waltzing, dancing, gliding at the Gem Dining Hall, to the music of the Coudersport string band; refreshments were enjoyed at 12 m., and all went to their many homes convinced that no such an enjoyable time had been anticipated or participated as this – all return their thanks to the host and hostess for their kind hospitality and hope ere long it may be repeated.

The Potter Enterprise
Wednesday Evening,
April 11, 1883 –
Vol. IX, No. 47

- VanWegen's mill is cutting out lumber at a rapid rate.

- Charles Reissman's building will be enclosed and under roof in a day or two.

- Abram Jones has re-commenced work on his building, nearly opposite the depot.

- Patrick Carey has part of the lumber on the ground for a business place, just south of the Denhoff building.

- High water and logs are cutting the flats on the John Taggart farm, very badly, doing a vast amount of injury.

- The Tannery bridge, at Fourth street, has been the scene of an almost continuous log jam for several days. Four or five drivers have been dunked there and seven canthooks lost in the water.

West Branch.

Lewis Campbell has bought the Flora Stocum farm on Crippen Run, and Flora and her family have gone West to Nebraska.

Mrs. Stowel is very sick yet.

Mr. L. Hammond is able to be out again and the trout have to suffer in consequence thereof.

Homer.

The folks are all talking about making sugar, but that is about all they have done yet.

Mrs. Oscar Reese of Sylvania is visiting her sister, Mrs. G. C. Lewis. Mr. and Mrs. Reese intend to start for Nebraska next week, accompanied by Mr. Monroe Hackett and family of Portage. We wish them a safe journey and a pleasant future in the far west, where they intend to make their home.

John Bundy, jr., had the misfortune to lose his pocket book on Saturday last, somewhere between here and Brownlee's mill in Portage, twelve dollars in money and some papers were lost. It has not been found at present writing.

Mr. Josiah Hackett is seriously ill with the western fever, hopes are entertained of his recovery.

The roads are in a terrible condition, making it almost impossible to travel, except on foot.

The Potter Enterprise
Wednesday Evening,
April 18, 1883 –
Vol. IX, No. 48

Whites Corners.

Some of the farmers have been raising tobacco, and we have a cigar manufactory here now. Have not yet learned the name of the manufacturer, but those who are judges say he makes a very fine cigar. Cannot say myself having had not experience in the matter.

There has been some changes in real estate here. A. A. Ross has sold one of his farms to Mr. Waters, of Mills, and the other to Mrs. N. M. Brooks.

- The Lehman bridge was carried away during the flood last week.

- Mrs. Henry Taubert has lumber on the ground for a new house, south of Mrs. Fickler's.

- James Turner has purchased a lot south side of the river, and is preparing to erect a dwelling house.

Whites Corners.

Farmers are trying to make sugar but have not had much success as yet.

There is considerable sickness around here.

Mrs. John Snyder was buried at this place a few days ago.

The Cheese Factory started on the 2d of April under the management of Mr. Zimmer. The society elected the same officers as last year.

Quarterly meeting services will be held here on Sunday next.

Warner & Zimmer have established themselves in their new store and are ready to accommodate the people with first class goods.

Hebron.

This week has been a busy one along the banks of the Oswayo, floating out the logs; about thirty men were employed and a group of the "froggers" at a distance would remind one of a "Phantom Party."

At last the logs are out of sight – were below Millport Wednesday.

Mr. and Mrs. Dunbar have a fine baby boy.

Charles Day and family have removed to Wellsville. Mr. Day thinks of visiting West Virginia this summer in pursuit of fine timber land.

J. S. Barnes lost a fine yearling on Wednesday of bloody murrain. Have heard of no other cases as yet.

Mrs. Cone has leased her farm to James Stilson, of Oswayo, for the coming year.

Millport.

Teachers' examination to-day, out of a class of eight, seven received certificates, although the examination was considered much harder than last year. Miss Buckbee is doing her work conscientiously and well, and ought to be appreciated.

The log-runners had a picnic on the bank near Topeka to-day. A. J. Barnes had dinner sent at 10 o'clock a.m. and 3 o'clock p.m., and a general basket picnic was the result. Table cloths were spread on the ground and a warm dinner with coffee served.

Query. Who sells the alcohol which a select few drink on the "drive" this spring?

The friends of Mrs. Henly entertain hopes of her final recovery from her attack of insanity.

Chips from Costelloville.

The recent flood has taken all the logs and peace and happiness now reigns in and around Costelloville once more.

Farmers are commencing their work.

We notice the pride that is taken in cleaning up the yards, they are being graded, shade trees and shrubbery planted, making our town look much better.

A Sabbath school has been organized here, which receives good attendance.

Our school conducted by Miss Morley closes on Monday next.

We now have a daily passenger stage from Costelloville to Keating Summit, of which Putt and Chapell are proprietors, besides the mail which is driven by C. C. Rees.

Mr. and Mrs. John Brownlee went to Rome, N.Y., one day last week for the third time, entertaining fears of another cancer, but returned in a day or two much encouraged. She is very feeble, but we trust she will wholly recover in time.

Mrs. Clark LaMonte returned home from Rome where she has been for the past month, being treated for a cancer – we hope she will not be obliged to make a second trip there.

A sociable hop was enjoyed at the Moran House, on the evening of the 14th inst., where our young people tripped the light fantastic to their heart's content. The party passed off very pleasantly, and we hope to be invited there again soon.

West Branch.

We are having a little too much water just now; the road below here is impassable in places. Some of the small bridges are afloat, and the Crippen dug-road is sliding into the creek in places.

Supervisor Burrows is at work with a gang of men at the dug-way blasting the rocks to make a roadway; he will soon have the road passable if the water does not rise too high. If we should get much of a rain there is no telling what it would do.

The Coudersport and Germania mail route is all right yet.

The Potter Enterprise Wednesday Evening, April 25, 1883 – Vol. IX, No. 49

- In a few days Coudersport will have four millinery stores in full blast.

- A. B. Mann expects to build two or more dwelling houses on the hill west of West street.

- James Johnston has sold his livery barn to Wm. Cott. The building is to be remodeled into a grocery.

- Iron has been purchased by the Water Company for extending mains from Second street north up West street.

- Amasa Carmer, of Oswayo, has purchased a lot of F. W. Knox, nearly opposite the American Hotel, on which he intends to erect a shoe shop.

- Chris. Schaudenberger, of Eulalia, has commenced the erection of a building, north of Grabe's Furniture Store. It will be used as a millinery store.

Township Tidings from Potter County, Pennsylvania
Volume I, 1880 - 1884

- Dr. S. A. Phillips, Dentist, has associated with himself Dr. R. S. Wrean, formerly of Bath, N.Y. Dr. Wrean will come here about the 1st of May.

- The Catholic church is canvassing to see how much can be raised for church building purposes. If the circumstances will warrant, a church will be erected nearly opposite John Ryan's residence.

- The South side of the river has the building boom this spring. At least sixteen buildings will be completed this Summer, and the number bids fair to reach twenty. Most of them will be dwelling houses.

Allegany.

The sugar makers can take new courage, as the ground froze quite hard last night, and those that will take the trouble to cut the trees over will be likely to get a good run of sap. But a small amount of sugar has been made this spring. The first sugar party of the season was held at W. A. Gardner's, a good visit and plenty of sweet was reported, can't say from participation, as I was not one of the invited ones.

The Sabbath school was organized on week ago Sunday, with a good attendance, most of the old officers were re-elected, Wm. Peck superintendent, and Mr. Carpenter assistant, and a few other officers changed.

The goods are being brought in to fill the store at Colesburg, and there is talk that the P.O. will be re-established. It will be a great convenience to the inhabitants, should this be so.

The young gent that demanded board at M. A. Veeley's a few weeks since is well pleased with the place and seems determined to stay.

Old Mrs. Ford is cutting her third set of teeth; she has worn artificial teeth for years.

C. Ford has Mrs. Morrison and daughter working for him and caring for his little ones.

Sartwell Creek.

The music of the birds proclaim to us the glad tidings that Spring has come once more with its cheering presence.

But very little sugar has been made at this place this spring.

Our school term closed the 9th inst.

Burt Thompson moved to Crandall Hill Tuesday.

Ray Grimes and his wife of Card Creek started for Dakota the 9th of April, where they intend to make their home.

Moses Washburn has rented his farm to Niles Fessenden and Mr. Washburn is going to work out for a living.

A smart runaway was experienced here last Friday afternoon. Mr. C. Dehn was driving his colts along the road when the bridle of one of the horses broke, which frightened it and they ran nearly half a mile before they could be stopped. No other damage was done.

Arthur Witter can hold his head as high as any one now. It is a boy.

Genesee Forks.

Maple Sugar making is not a success. We heard of one man

taking a bush for two-thirds of the sugar and made twelve pounds. I am sure they will have maple sugar for sale.

With Spring comes moving and cleaning (which every man likes, we know, especially setting up stoves).

The cheese factory is receiving a thorough renovating preparatory for cheese making.

Mr. Elimus Hackett, who rented Mr. Hurd's store, has moved.

Stephen Hurd has rented the house owned by Mrs. Williams and has also moved.

Mr. Bruce Robbins has his new building nearly completed, and has moved into it.

A. C. Race has sold his farm to Will Atherton, who is soon to take possession.

Silas Hurd has exchanged his western land with Theodore Hurd for a timber lot.

Mrs. Atherton, an old lady residing in this place, is very sick, not expected to live. Her two daughters from Canisteo, N.Y., are now with her.

Our Sabbath school is now organized, we hope to see all take an interest.

Eleven Mile.

April skies are beaming brightly this morning over the frosted earth and seem to give promise of a warmer time soon, though the seed time is late.

The snow is in places only just gone, in fact it may be seen in remnants of large snow banks here and there yet.

Repairing fences is one of the heaviest taxes that a farmer pays, to say nothing of the first cost of building them. That work with plowing now occupies the farmers here. Last fall it was so dry that but little plowing was done and in consequence there is heavier work for man and team now.

The long steady winter has at length yielded its sway, though with great reluctance, and the modest Spring with becoming grace appears to be slow to assume control of the weather. One thing is almost always true however that when the Spring-time is backward and seed-time late in consequence the season of growth is nearly always favorable for good crops generally. So we must take courage and busy ourselves getting work along, so that when the seed-time does come the sowing and planting can be done with dispatch.

There seems to be nothing done in the way of selling and buying real estate hereabouts. The nearness to developed oil territory perhaps induces land owners to hang on to their property, or place it at such figures that it would be dear for farming purposes alone, and so we are waiting with all patience that we are capable of, for something to happen to break the "spell," meantime we have to raise potatoes, buckwheat, &c., and land owners pay their taxes cheerfully?

The Potter Enterprise
Wednesday Evening,
May 2, 1883 –
Vol. IX, No. 50

- One by one city airs and city luxuries are creeping in. Watson Dyke has put into his bakery a

Township Tidings from Potter County, Pennsylvania
Volume I, 1880 - 1884

peanut roaster. Fresh roasted peanuts on tap all the time.

Keating.

What has become of our sugaring? Of one thing we are certain, we have not had any to amount to anything. The buds are starting and the sugar makers are drawing in their tubs and fixing for farming.

D. D. Everette moved his family from this place to his farm in Homer township on Thursday last.

J. R. Dingee is the owner of a miniature printing press. It does very nice work, such as printing names on cards, envelopes, etc.

Someway our last letter from this place was headed "Homer." Whose fault it was we do not know. [It was the devil's. – Ed.]

North Bingham.

There has been about the usual amount of coughs, colds and other sorts of complaints called rheumatism which has been giving our people a little extra attention.

The Temperance lecture from Charts by Mrs. S. A. H. Lindsey was very interesting and instructive.

Teachers examination was splendid and as far as I have heard gave excellent satisfaction.

Mr. John Raymond, the new merchant at North Bingham, seems to be giving satisfaction.

Preparations for building are going on at a rapid rate. Four new houses are to go up in sight of the corners this season. One cellar is already well under way toward completion.

Business is lively with the exception of sugaring. There has been but little maple sap and what little there was, was of poor quality. Sugar makers grumble, and consumers also find fault.

The annual cry of the plow-boy is being extensively heard through this part of the land.

The Potter Enterprise
Wednesday Evening,
May 9, 1883 –
Vol. X, No. 1

Sartwell Creek.

Farmers have begun spring's work in earnest, by turning the surface of the earth, and placing the seed therein.

Sabbath school was organized last Sunday, and all is favorable for an interesting school.

James Phenix started for Delaware last Thursday, where he may remain for some time.

School commenced at the Reed school house the 31st of April, under the management of Miss Laura Larrabee.

The centre school is taught by Clistia Kimm, and the upper school by Minnie Wright.

Miss Mary McDowell is preparing to erect a fine dwelling this summer. She has the old one moved away, and will soon have a new one in its place.

Allegany.

The past two weeks have been noted for wedding anniversaries. April 27th, a surprise party of about thirty young people gathered at the residence of W. P. Cool, in remembrance of their first year of wedded life. A pleasant evening of enjoyment, with nothing to mar but the darkness in returning home.

Saturday afternoon and evening, May 5th, the 20th anniversary of Mr. and Mrs. Peter Green was celebrated by the gathering together of nearly a hundred friends from this town and other places. The presents were of various kinds and nice, dress goods, linens, laces, china, glass, majolica, &c. The tables were spread with a bounteous supply of good things to eat, which was partaken of by all. Everything passed gayly till the late hours, when the friends took their departure, wishing Peter and Mary many happy returns, &c.

In some sugar bushes more sugar was made after the freeze of the last week in April, than any time before this spring, but it was of an inferior quality.

Whites Corners.

Leroy Smith intends moving into his house next week.

L. D. Mack has the frame of his new barn up.

Mr. Waters has moved on his place.

I understand there has been one sale of cheese made at 14 cts.

W. Rutherford sold some common dairy cows a few days ago for $50 per head.

S. Edwards has moved into the house formerly occupied by F. Farnum.

- Ham. White, of Harrison Valley, called on us Friday. He gives the encouraging news that the Valley will have a broad gauge railroad running within six weeks.

- New sidewalks should be the order of the day.

West Homer and North Eulalia.

The event of the season – house cleaning and cross men.

Sugar making is among the things of the past, and not much of that, consequently, pie-plant pies without sugar, how delicious!

Don't you know what Joe Coddington is smiling about? Why, his last *boy* is a girl, about a week old, *that's why*.

C. Breunle is about to raise a large barn on his farm.

John Taubert and Truman Quimby are hauling some of their lumber home from the new mill.

Our Sabbath school was organized on Sunday last, Mr. White elected sup't, Miss Rose Quimby, sec'y; and Mrs. Emma Gordnier, librarian.

Our district schools are both in session.

Mr. Andy Holt, of Homer, and Miss Mary Gifford, of Eulalia, were married April 29th, by O. L. Hall, Esq. Now girls as *Andy* is no more in the market, you will be obliged to turn your tearful eyes in another direction. *You surely have our deepest sympathy.*

The ladies of our place were invited at the house of our new neighbor, Mr. Cameron, to celebrate the seventeenth birthday of his daughter, Miss Dell, the afternoon was passed away very pleasantly, and amid the gossip and laughter, that is usual with a company of ladies (especially if

Miss Libbie is among them) a quilt was taken from the frame and BOUND, and after partaking of a *delicious* supper the more *sedate* ladies returned to their respective homes, leaving the young and hopeful to trip the light fantastic toe till – they ought to have been home.

- The ground has been staked out for the M. E. parsonage, on Fourth street.

- James Turner's house is rapidly approaching completion. Mr. Keihle's on the same square is not quite so far along; J. M. Covey and Sheriff Monroe are clearing off their lots. The Sheriff expects to build soon. Zimmerman's houses are nearly completed and both are rented. John Denhoff has recently purchased a lot on the square east of Gillon's, and is preparing to erect a new house. John Abson and Joe Griesel have bought lots of the Ross Estate; both are preparing to build.

Keating.

Born April 24 to Mr. and Mrs. Joseph Codington, a daughter.

A deer ran through the fields of H. Bridges and C. Fourness crossing the road between their houses, which stand but a few rods apart. Several stood and watched the graceful animal till out of sight but none tried to harm it.

Sunday School was organized on Sunday last. Mrs. Mary Fournes Sup't, Mrs. Emma Beebe assistant, Mrs. James Bundy sec'y and treasurer, James Bundy Bible Class teacher.

Our day school will soon commence which will be taught by Miss Laura Bridges.

On Tuesday evening Elder Cone from Coudersport preached here, we understand that Mr. Cone intends preaching here once in two weeks in the future. The people will be well pleased with this arrangement as we have had but very little preaching here for the past year.

- H. C. Rukgaber has bought the old George Brehmer blacksmith shop on First street and is now prepared to do work in the general blacksmithing line. Mr. Rukgaber is a good blacksmith and thoroughly understands his business.

The Potter Enterprise
Wednesday Evening,
May 16, 1883 –
Vol. X, No. 2

- The telephone line works like a charm.

- Patrick Carey has the frame of his store building up.

- A team at work on Isaac Benson's side hill, in this village, went down over the bank some twenty feet, horses, harness and wagon in one heap. No damages worth mentioning.

- The Railroad is putting in a switch to VanWegen's mill.

- Lon Crosby has completed the survey of the land whereon Harrison Valley's railroad station is to be built. It is opposite Erway's hotel, between the road and the stream. Grading has been commenced on the road.

Roulet.

School commenced to-day under the supervision of Miss Bell Baird, of Renova, Pa.

Leroy and A. V. Lyman, and Sam Angood, spent last week fishing on the Cross Fork.

C. J. Burt and wife started this morning for Arkansas on their wedding tour. They have the best wishes of their many friends.

John Eimer and Don Manning are each building a new barn.

Mrs. L. A. Brooks has moved her house out on Main Street, and is now pleasantly located.

Joe Knowlton has built a porch and otherwise improved the looks of his house.

Frank Morey had the misfortune last week to fall on his axe and cut a severe gash in his side. Dr. Sterns of Port Allegany, and Dr. Fisher of this place, dressed the wound.

Orchard Street has been graded and is now one of the neatest streets in Roulet.

The Potter Enterprise
Wednesday Evening,
May 23, 1883 –
Vol. X, No. 3

- N. Fleshutz has opened a shoe shop in N. M. Glassmire's building, East street.

- There are now 150 men at work on the N. Y. & N. P. R. R., between Gaines and Pike Mills. We understand they propose to run an excursion train from Pike Mills on the Ever Glorious.

- Hall Nelson's dray horse had another of its regular Monday runaways this week, starting from M. L. Gridley's it took the sidewalk and kept it until it reached the Post Office – as usual no one hurt.

Genesee Forks.

Although being cold and backward, farmers have their work pretty well caught up. We are promised a seed time and harvest. Therefore they sow expecting to reap. How cheering the thought that the promises of God are sure.

Death again has entered our midst. This time the reaper's sickle has cut down an aged one, who has withstood the blasts of many winters. Mrs. Catharine Billings, aged about 75 years, died May 15th. She was one of the early settlers of this place, endured many hardships and trials, but now the cares of life for her are o'er. She peacefully rests, these words come forcibly to my mind as one after another passes away. "Are you ready, are you ready, should the Lord call to-day?"

Will Atherton and family are now cozily installed in their new home.

A. C. Race now resides at Shongo, N.Y.

The cheese factory is in operation. We hear is doing nicely.

Millinery goods are kept by Mrs. Baker, at the store of Limas Hackett. A. J. Carpenter also has some millinery goods.

Schools are all now in session in this town. The Ellisburg school is taught by Miss Clancy; Chapman school by Miss Webster; Genesee Fork school by Miss Stillman; Hurd's Valley school by Mrs. Crum.

Whites Corners.

The weather has been very good for farmers lately and they have improved it putting in their crops. Nearly all the spring seeding is done.

H. O. Chapin has sold the D. C. White place to Rev. Walter Statham.

Mrs. H. Stebbins died very suddenly on Monday last with apoplexy. Her daughter Mrs. Hurlburt intends to keep house for her father and brother in the future.

We have a cigar manufactory here. Why the Government should legalize the making and selling of tobacco and cigars when the statistics who that there is as many young men ruined by tobacco as by liquor, is one of the things that I cannot comprehend.

Hebron.

Mr. Sol Lamberton has at last got his new saw and is making business lively about there.

S. Keller and Theb. Swift are each to build a new house this summer.

Frank Swimmer has built a new chimney, and is getting out stone for a cellar.

Mrs. Freeman Blanchard and sons, formerly of this county, have returned and located on Whitney Creek, purchasing a piece of land of A. J. Barnes. They commenced with the true pioneer pluck, putting up a shelter tent and living camp style until their house was enclosed. They have built a snug house 16 x 24 feet, and intend to hew out a home out of this rough place. I wish them success.

A restaurant is reported on Whitney Creek, kept by a woman (?).

Abe Solomon is the boy to clear land and he struck his forte I guess when he located on South Branch. Mr. and Mrs. Amos Coe have removed to Corning, or near there. Mrs. Cone who accompanied them has returned.

A fine boy baby has found a home with Mr. and Mrs. J. S. Barnes.

Some one at Oswayo must fine it profitable selling whiskey, as parties returned from there Saturday evening intoxicated. It is a glorious thing to live in a "Temperance County!"

The Potter Enterprise
Wednesday Evening,
May 30, 1883 –
Vol. X, No. 4

- J. W. Allen has a horse badly cut up in a wire fence, last Thursday.

- Charles Reissman's furniture store is about ready for occupancy.

Freeman Run.

The hard frost we have been having has hurt the grass considerably.

T. R. Reed has bought him a fine yoke of cattle, giving $160 for them.

John Bundy, Jr., is building a new barn.

Our school is having a vacation on account of the sickness of the teacher, Miss Laura Bridges. Dr. French, who is attending her, pronounced it a very severe case of inflammatory rheumatism.

The Potter Enterprise
Wednesday Evening,
June 6, 1883 –
Vol. X, No. 5

Bingham.

Farmers have their work well in hand and the crops look well, although the season is somewhat backward.

Fruit of all kinds, so far, promises an abundant harvest.

Mr. J. L. Raymond has sold twenty acres off the north end of his farm at North Bingham, where Mr. J. H. Chase, the purchaser, will build his new mansion instead of building it on the site of the old one up on the farm as he had intended. The cellar is already well under way.

Business seems to be prospering finely.

The physical health of our people appears to be unusually good. Their moral condition is without any noticeable improvement. There is about the usual amount of effort at matchmaking and upon this subject, it is very proper that I should say a few words. Love, deep and genuine, should be the only incentive to marriage. Undue influence and often times deception have much effect in producing unhappy marriages and in crowding our courts with divorce cases. That such business is often engaged in even by professed christians is a disgrace to the civilization of the nineteenth century. I know a community where many professing christians, engaged in serving satan and worked so hard at serving the devil, that they got sweaty; took cold, and became so chilly that three weeks of "protracted effort" failed to warm them. It is to be hoped that they will soon return to serving the Good Master who would not over work them and endanger their eternal welfare.

Roulet.

Henry Chasten is building an addition to his house.

Rev. Brooks has built a neat little barn on Main street.

Jack Goodall has built a new fence around and otherwise improved the looks of his lot.

The remains of Mrs. Julia Thompson, who died in Hebron, was interred in the Sartwell Creek Cemetery, on Tuesday last.

Leroy Lyman is building an addition to his house, for the express purpose of having a room to arrange his mineral and geological specimens and stuffed animals in. When finished Mr. Lyman will have a collection he may well feel proud of.

Allegany.

We used to say years ago plant corn when apple trees are in full bloom. If that rule holds good now, then it is not too late yet for apple trees are now in full bloom on the hills. Fruit trees of all kinds are loaded with blossoms and bid fair for an abundant crop.

Grass comes on slowly, while many pieces of winter wheat are an entire failure, others medium, with now and then a piece that looks well.

Daniel Wells has sold his farm to a Mr. Byam.

No preaching yesterday owing to funeral services on another part of the charge.

Sabbath School here and at the Settlement moves along finely.

We hear no complaints about school marms, so conclude all are suited with the teachers.

- Stone is being hauled for the foundation of the addition to the Postoffice building.

- The first strawberries of the season, for this place, sold for 25 cents per box last Thursday.

- Nelson Brothers last week sold their meat market to Mr. Scott, the gentleman who recently purchased the James Johnston property.

- The borough ordinance prohibiting calves, horses, &c., running at large in the day time and cows after nine o'clock at night seems to be a dead letter. It certainly is not enforced.

Eleven Mile.

It is all very quiet in our little pleasant village.

Fallow burning was quite extensive until the 30th inst., when the rains put a stop to that industry. Several logging bees and other methods have served to add to the area of cultivated lands – many acres, and fencing and other improvements has added much to the looks of some farms.

The district schools are now in session for the summer term. Miss Alice Hall teaches at the Central school, Miss McGinnis the lower one and Miss Maggie Doyle the upper school.

Planting seems to go slowly, and there is not a large amount of it in progress.

From this place only a very few went to attend Memorial service at Oswayo yesterday. It is understood that it was quite successful at the village. They had addresses by L. D. Estes and Rev. W. Miller and N. North of the M.C. Church. Three cemeteries were visited and appropriately decorated with flowers and the stars and stripes of our land were planted on some ten graves, one more than last year. P. C. Lovell was the last one laid to rest, of the number, but no doubt they will soon be multiplied more rapidly as the years pass on.

Dean Healy is superintendent of the Sabbath school at the Kemp district, and A. S. Lyman of the one at the Centre district, with a good corps of teachers, and some 25 scholars each.

Dalrymple & Johnston have sold some of their wild land in Oswayo to the Crittendens, S. E. and W.W., and they intend to manufacture the timber at their mill, which they bought last fall of Wm. Shattuck in Hebron.

Fruit trees are blossomed quite generally, but these East winds may blast the blows. Some think of them as effectual for this purpose as a frost.

Freeman Run.

Some of the farmers are complaining that their corn has rotted in the hill.

G. C. Lewis and E. J. Dingee have each purchased a new Ithica organ.

Sheep shearing has commenced.

Almost every day parties of fishermen may be seen passing; but the boss ones that have been over this way come from Port Allegany with a kerosene oil can strapped upon ones back filled with, well we can't swear to just what it was filled with – but one thing we do know it had to be reduced. Queer oil they have down in Port.

Temperance society organized here on Saturday last. The society meets every two weeks on Saturday afternoon at two o'clock.

H. H. Beebe has bought himself a fine accordian.

The logging bee of Frank Klien last week was well attended and Mr. Klien got a good job done.

John Bundy is building an addition to his house.

The Potter Enterprise
Wednesday Evening,
June 13, 1883 –
Vol. X, No. 6

West Branch.

Mrs. May Campbell died yesterday afternoon, June 7, at the residence of her parents. She was the daughter of Erastus Crippen, she leaves a babe not yet three months old. May was not quite sixteen years old, but was a large, robust looking person; she attended the Decoration ceremony at Wellsboro, on the 30th of May, and took a cold that soon terminated her short life. She was attended by Dr. Reynolds of Sunderlinville and Dr. Meine of Germania. They called the disease rheumatism.

Elder Stocum has two children down with measles. We expect a general run of the measles through this place.

There are some Indians up the creek peeling bark for the Gale tannery. There was a death of a child among them, last week, the body was taken to Germania for burial. According to report, the burial party had quite a "wake."

We are unable to report anything from the coal prospectors as yet, except that they are still at work.

- The rainstorm Saturday night drowned five black leghorn chickens for W. I. Lewis. Mrs. Fickler had eleven go the same way. Several potpies spoiled.

- Last week as a thunder storm was coming up, C. L. Peck attempted to "cut out" the Telephone instrument at the Nichols House. He succeeded, but the wire was so charged that he received a shock that he felt in one arm for nearly a day. He won't do it again.

- The registry list of Coudersport Borough contains, up to date, 240 names, the largest number of voters ever registered in the borough.

- The Overseers of the Poor, of Coudersport, last week levied a tax of ten mills, appointed A. B. Mann clerk and Frank Stevens collector for the ensuing year.

Sartwell Creek.

We have had very wet weather for the last three weeks.

Farming is somewhat backward on account of the excessive rains which has kept the ground too wet to work a good share of the time. Much planting is yet to be done. Some planted their corn about the middle of May but owing to the inclemency of the weather it rotted in the ground, then they planted it again but with the same result, and now they are about to give up in despair.

Grass is growing finely and promises a good crop if nothing begalls it after now.

Winter wheat, in some places, is almost a failure.

Fruit promises well, with the exception of the grape, as many of the vines were winter killed.

Bark peeling is not carried on as extensively as usual this season.

Our school is progressing finely under the management of Miss Laura Larrabee.

The U.B. Quarterly Meeting will be held on Saturday and Sunday, June 16 and 17, at the school house near the parsonage. To which all are cordially invited. Able speakers will be present and a good time is anticipated.

We have a depot near the mouth of the creek on the C. & P. A. Railroad. It is small, but good enough what there is of it and enough of it such as it is.

Sartwell Creek.

Peeling bark has commenced, but on a rather small scale, as yet, which is in part on account of the cold, wet weather we have had this Spring. Spring's work is also very backward.

W. Witter is preparing to build a new house this summer.

Mr. Calvin Burt and wife have bought them a home in Arkansas where they intend to make their home for a while. May fortune attend them.

Maurice Manning moved to Port Allegany last week. Mr. Rice has purchased his farm.

Millport.

Crops begin to look well in spite of the backward Spring, and it is thought the frosts did not injure the fruit blossoms as was feared at first.

There is quite an improvement in this place in the way of new fences, building, etc.

I noticed a new piece of ground cleared by John Henly, which makes his farm look much better.

Decoration Day passed off with the usual ceremonies, by the Barnes Post, and was largely attended by our citizens. Capt. L. H. Kinney delivered a fine speech at Sharon Centre, also, Rev. Rheinhault made appropriate remarks which were listened to with interest by the large audience who heard the speakers. The Sharon Band was present and done well.

Colesburg.

Farmers have their planting done and now contemplate buckwheat seeding.

We are now to have a postoffice, a want long felt by this community as the inhabitants from this vicinity were obliged to go or send to Coudersport for all mail matter.

Mr. Scovill, our enterprising merchant, is doing a good business. I should judge, by the amount of goods he is receiving; he is a live Yankee and thinks a quick sixpence better than a slow shilling.

On the 4th inst., Barney Palmer received a back pension of $1300. It comes very acceptable to Mr. Palmer as he has a large family to support and an invalid wife. This amount judiciously expended will make them comfortable.

Our saw mill is doing a good business. Mr. M. is obliged to saw night and day to keep pace with the demand.

Our school is as good as the best. The scholars all speak well of their teacher.

Miss Josie Smith, of Raymond, teaches the Presho School.

West Homer. – South Eulalia.

The general health is quite good in this place at present.

We have been visited by heavy storms the past week.

Planting is done.

Grass looks well.

Bark peeling is the order of the day.

Mr. Cameron attended the funeral of his mother, Mrs. Raymond, June 2d, she was buried in the Coudersport cemetery.

Born – To the wife of Wm. Dennis, a son, June 4th. What is remarkable about this child is, it has ten grandparents.

Mr. and Mrs. George White and Mr. and Mrs. Ben Cook were the guests of Wm. White one day last week, suppose they came to see the new baby, as that is where it is stopping for a short time.

Joe Colcord and Miss Mary Jackson partook of the marriage feast at Pump Station, last week Monday.

Albert and Betsy laid the bark job aside, greased the harness and buggy, and took a ride over Crandall Hill to see Robert Peet's new baby, last Saturday. We hope they did not get caught in a thunder storm.

Ed. Tyler and his mother have moved back on their farm. Ed. is now turning his attention to raising pumpkins.

Our Sabbath school is superintended by Mr. James Bundy, of Kating, there being no one in our town willing to act, we were under the necessity of calling on another neighborhood to furnish us one. Mr. Bundy superintends two schools each Sunday.

Our schools are progressing finely; the one in West Homer being taught by Miss Close of Westfield, and the South Hill by Miss May Nelson of Coudersport. We think Miss Nelson is working hard for the interest of her pupils.

- Strawberries sold for 16 cents per basket, last week.

- Houses for rent are still at a premium in Coudersport.

**The Potter Enterprise
Wednesday Evening,
June 20, 1883 –
Vol. X, No. 7**

- New cross walks are numerous in Coudersport, and growing more so.

- Karl Zimmerman is connecting his tenant houses with a spring on the hill back of them.

- Hill street, or High street, or Glassmire Miles street, the street on the side hill west of West street, is being graded and made passable.

- Will Abson has the frame of his new house up, South of Gillon's.

Freeman Run.

The quarterly meeting of the United Brethren, which was held here the 9th and 10th, was well attended.

G. C. Lewis lost his best cow last week, and John Bundy had an ox drop dead in the road last Wednesday. What was the trouble with the cattle is not known.

Clarence Reed had the misfortune to cut his right knee quite seriously on Tuesday. Mr. Reed was peeling bark for his brother, G. R. Reed.

Grass is going to be a large crop, and there promises to be an abundance of fruit.

Victor Beebe stepped upon a potato hook, running one of the tines into his foot, hurting him severely.

Roulet.

Work on the Union Church is progressing finely.

Mrs. Minerva Lyman, Mrs. P. A. Webb, Mrs. P. L. Boyington, Mrs. S. B. Pomeroy and Edith Pomeroy attended the Taggart reunion, at Almeron Nelson's in Lymansville, Thursday last.

Leroy Lyman had a valuable horse kicked so badly, a few days since, he was obliged to kill it.

Whites Corners.

Mr. Levi Elliot arrived here from Millport a few days ago. He intends moving on the place owned by Mrs. Brooks and managing Mr. Brooks' store.

R. H. Taggart has his new house nearly finished.

A. A. Ross has moved on the place owned by Homer Hurlburt.

A gentleman who, I understand, is a good judge of cigars, passed through this place the other day and pronounced our home made cigars rather green.

Clara.

The heaviest rain of the season came on the evening of the 10th.

Burt Campbell and wife rejoice over a bran new baby boy.

James Tyler has the misfortune to lose a horse this week.

Sala Stevens has moved into the house recently occupied by Florentine Stevens. Florentine and family have "vamoosed the ranch" for parts unknown. He is still under bonds to appear at Court this week.

Wedding cards were received by many friends here from Mr. and Mrs. T. A. McMahon, of Martinez, Cal. Mrs. McMahon, *nee* Martha R. Chase, was a Potter county girl and has the congratulations of many warm friends from here.

Township Tidings from Potter County, Pennsylvania
Volume I, 1880 - 1884

Hebron.

Grass bids fair to be splendid this year. But those who are just planting potatoes can not expect a rich harvest.

Theb. Swift is building the cellar for his new house.

Mrs. Stillson was prostrated by the lightening which struck near Mrs. Cone's, Saturday evening.

Our school is in session, in charge of Miss Witter.

Sala Stevens and family came near having a serious runaway on Sunday last. They were driving near Henry Lamberton's when they struck the horses with the whip, and as they started a bit broke, and they ran for some distance, throwing every one out of the buggy and breaking it considerably, but no one was injured I believe.

The Potter Enterprise
Wednesday Evening,
June 27, 1883 –
Vol. X, No. 8

- Charley Neefe and family are about removing to his farm in Sweden.

- Work was commenced on Monday clearing off the square for the Catholic church.

- Wm. Sherwood has settled with the authorities for damage to his horse, received a year or more ago by falling into the trench of the water company at Second and Main street. He receives seventy-five dollars in full.

- Walt Abson has commenced the carpenter work for the M. E. Parsonage.

- Nelson Brothers have repurchased the meat market and will take possession to-day, Tuesday.

- The excavation for the new building corner of Main and Second street is nearly completed. O. J. and W. B. Rees have made a bargain (papers not yet signed) for the lot; consideration $1,600. It is their intention to build of brick 38 x 60 two stories, to be divided into two store rooms below, cellar full size of building. It will be an ornament to the town. Now give us a good brick hotel and Coudersport can then wait patiently for Magee and the N. Y. & N. P. R. R.

West Pike.

We are having very warm weather, at present, but plenty of rain.

Farmers are busy hoeing their crops.

Bark peeling is carried on quite extensively.

Our school opened June 4th. Miss Addie Douglass, of Ulysses, teaches.

Our Sunday school is well attended and seems quite interesting.

Alonzo Haxton has purchased Mrs. Rogers' house and lot and will soon take possession.

Wm. Turck is improving the appearance of his house very much.

West Branch.

W. E. Womelsdorf and his men have broken camp and gone to

Addison. The coal investigation is not completed, but they had to leave to run some railroad lines that could not be delayed. Before leaving here they examined a route through a notch in the mountain to run a railroad to Kettle Creek. They found the grade much better than they expected, and make the summit, at the notch, two hundred and seventy-five feet lower than the Hog Back. Mr. Womelsdorf thinks that the prospects for a railroad through here to Kettle Creek are quite flattering. There is an extensive coal bed on Kettle Creek that the road would reach.

Wm. Trask has sheared seventy-six and one-half pounds of wool from ten sheep, the biggest fleece weighing twelve and three-fourths pounds, washed wood, from a two year old ewe that has raised a lamb this season.

Colesburg.

Good weather for web-footed fowls.

On the 16th inst., Mr. and Mrs. Eli Nelson celebrated their eighteenth anniversary with a variety wedding. There were about ninety guests and they presented Mr. and Mrs. Nelson with many very beautiful presents as a token of their kind regards.

Magee's surveyors, who are surveying a route through from Westfield to Olean, stopped over Sunday with Peter Green. They report the grade from Colesburg to the summit, near Raymond's, about sixty feet to the mile. I have been informed that after reaching Olean they will survey the route through via Genesee Forks.

Almeron Nelson is laying the foundation for a horse barn on his farm occupied by Willet Barnes.

Miss Nettie Kohler has been quite sick but is now able to resume her duties as teacher in the Harris district, Sweden township.

Bingham.

W. G. Raymond and G. W. Colvin are at work on a ceallar at North Bingham and we expect soon to see a large and commodious residence rise above the large and well finished cellar.

Five nice new residences in one little village and all in one season will make the people stare and wonder as to what is coming next.

Our Sunday school is in a very flourishing condition.

Preaching every Sunday with good attendance and excellent attention.

The Potter Enterprise
Wednesday Evening,
July 4, 1883 –
Vol. X, No. 9

- East street has been cleared of logs.

- The frame of the M. E. Parsonage is up.

- The berry crop promises to be a large one, as usual.

- It is again reported that the Episcopal church is to be built at once.

- A. H. Haxton, of Pike, has recently received $2,060 arrears of pension, and will hereafter draw $30 per month.

- The N. Y. & N. P. R. R. is organizing a corps for running a line from the West Branch down Kettle creek.

- A. C. Millard has leased the Rounsevill planing mill.

Sartwell Creek.

It has rained almost incessantly for nearly four weeks, but looks favorable for good weather once more, which makes us all smile.

Lewis Lyman had the misfortune last week to lose one of his horses.

The people of Sartwell Creek had the honor of a series of lectures, last week, which they pronounced very good. If he had told them the moon was made of green cheese perhaps they would have believed it to be so.

Quite a wind storm passed over this place last week uprooting trees and unroofing barns and sheds.

Ole Hanson raised a barn frame last Friday.

Another lucky runaway occurred here last Saturday afternoon. The team of Mr. Maynard, of Port Allegany, had been tied to a post and left for some time, and growing uneasy they broke the post off and then started for pastures new. They ran nearly a mile before stopping, bruising the buggy some but doing no further damage.

If there were less visiting on Sunday and more attending church it would be more honor to Sartwell Creek.

The Potter Enterprise
Wednesday Evening,
July 18, 1883 –
Vol. X, No. 10

- D. F. Glassmire sports a Bradley cart.

- Harrison Valley people expect trains to be running in about ten days.

- Nelson Brothers have enlarged their meat market by erecting an addition.

- Some fields of potatoes are showing signs of rust. Caused by wet weather.

- Too much water is interfering with the laying the abutments for the Second street bridge.

- The Episcopal Church Society, of Coudersport, has let the contract for the erection of a stone church.

- Joseph S. Hull is erecting a fine house on the East Fork. It will be large enough to accommodate fishing parties and hunters and give them first class quarters.

- Mr. S. VanWinkle has removed to Caniseto, N.Y. For more than a year he has successfully carried on the tailoring business here, giving good satisfaction. His work is first class in every particular.

- James McNulty and John O'Donald had a chopping match recently. The match was in cutting down a tree and cutting off a log. McNulty's tree was a trifle the largest and O'Donald's came to the ground first, but before he could cut off his log, McNulty was ahead, coming in winner by seventeen seconds.

Freeman Run.

At last, after a good deal of trouble and almost a law suit, we have a new fence around our school house lot.

Elmer Bundy had the misfortune to cut his foot quite bad recently, while peeling bark.

Sartwell Creek.

Bark peeling is nearly over for this season.

Haying has commenced, but as yet it is not carried on very extensively on account of the rainy weather. It rains so much we think it a good hay day if it does not rain three times during the day. They say a wise man makes hay when the sun shines; this being the case, I do not see how a wise man would make hay when it rains all the time.

G. W. Witter had the misfortune to lose one of his horses a few days ago. Mr. Witter begins to think it no trick to lose a horse. He says it is not half the trouble for him to lose a horse as it is for him to get one to lose.

Mary McDowell has the frame of a new house raised, and it is being rapidly inclosed.

North Wharton.

One evening recently while Thomas Conroy was examining a cartridge he held it over a lighted lamp, when it instantly exploded, tearing off a portion of the thumb and two fingers of the right hand. He was taken to Coudersport where Dr. Ellison dressed the wound. When will some people learn that fire and powder do not harmonize.

Willie Moore, a boy fifteen years old, met with a serious accident recently, while at work in the bark woods. He was fitting for the spudder when the tree he was working on commenced to slide and before he could get out of the way, the limbs caught and dragged him down the hill, tearing his flesh in a horrible manner.

Bingham.

Two of the five new houses for this place are up, so that our visitors can have an opportunity to note their general appearance.

Mrs. T. Kibbe, of North Bingham, is in failing health.

The Railroad will probably stop at Harrison Valley for the present. Most of the teams and some of the workmen were discharged last Saturday. The civil engineers, including chief engineer Ford, were also discharged; excepting one assistant who, with two hands, will be engaged for a few days in finishing up the civil engineer work at the Valley. So no Railroad for Bingham nor even a survey for Whitesville at present.

Millport.

The ever glorious Fourth has come and gone, that is I suppose it has by the number of carriages that passed this place Wednesday on their way to Oswayo, and the limpsy, lackadaisical look of their occupants as they returned on Thursday.

Township Tidings from Potter County, Pennsylvania
Volume I, 1880 - 1884

James Dickinson is building a fine residence 36x32 feet on his place just below town, in the suburbs as it were; he has one of the finest cellars in the country. The house is enclosed and work progressing rapidly under the supervision of Mr. Christman.

Mr. and Mrs. T. J. Macmurray, of Juneau, Wisc., are expected on Thursday to visit their mother, Mrs. Salina Staysa.

It seems to me if Mr. R. L. Nichols, who owns Liberty Hall, were a bit public spirited he would fix up the upper story for a good hall; as it is it is not fit to use, although for want of a better place people go there to hold their Christmas Trees, Donations, Concerts and various entertainments altho it is so open that music is mostly "wasted on the desert air," and one is in danger of "catching their death o' cold" in attending.

Colesburg.

Hay is quite poor this year excepting new seeding which is a fair crop. Some attribute it to the cold weather in May, while others claim the season has been too wet. An old adage is that "a cold wet May will find the barns with grain and hay."

The oat crop, up to the present time, bids fair to be a good one.

The Coudersport Cornet Band passed through here about five o'clock a.m. on the Fourth, enroute for Ulysses, where they were to play on that day. They treated us to some very fine music as they passed through. At about the same hour on the morning of the fifth they passed through on their homeward journey, looking rather careworn and weary. How is it boys, couldn't you get anything in Ulysses to brace up on?

The office seaker is now roaming through the land soliciting your support. You do not have to look for him as he is sure to recognize you now if he never has before. Never mind if your coat is ragged, he will always be pleased to meet you – until after election. Then if he forgets you call it a passing dream and cast your vote for him the next time he is up for office.

Eleven Mile.

The crops are looking finely, notwithstanding too much rain fall of the past month or so.

Hay is now right to cut but they hay weather is wanting.

Potato bugs are lively and very hungry. A very little Paris green in water will check their appetites.

No events more than ordinary are happening hereabouts. Our people are a sober, industrious set, and find enough to do in clearing and improving their lands and in building and repairing buildings.

Births, marriages and deaths are frequent enough to signify to us that there is only truth in this from Knox:

"So the multitude goes like the flower or weed

That withers away to let others succeed

So the multitude comes, even these we behold

To repeat every talc that has often been told."

Last Tuesday, the 10th, Mrs. Joseph Elliott was buried at the Oswayo Centre cemetery. An Adventist improved the opportunity to again expound his wisdom for the enlightenment(?) of the congregation. It must have been tedious for the mothers of the numerous babies and small children present to sit for an hour and a half under such powerful demonstration from both children and speaker. The deceased left a husband and four small children, the youngest a babe of four weeks.

So many such instances have occurred in this section recently as to be remarked upon.

On June 25th, Hiram Goodale was buried in the same cemetery. He left a wife and two small children in quite limited circumstances. He was an industrious, peaceable citizen and neighbor.

Genesee Forks.

G. W. Leach's new store is partly enclosed. It presents a nice appearance, will be a fine store when finished.

A large barn about 40x60 is now being erected on the place occupied by Ansek Kickox, former owned by Wm. Baker.

Brian McGinnis has just finished a horse barn said to be the best in the town of Genesee.

While the Genesee Fork stage, bound for Coudersport on Friday last, was passing through the dugway which terminates below Ellisburg, they met two men with a double buggy driving a pair of mustangs. The mustangs became frightened and unmanageable. The men finding they could do nothing with them, jumped from the buggy and the horses jumped over the embankment carrying everything with them, tumbling and rolling among the briars and logs for a distance of twenty feet. They procured help from the Forks and soon had them on good footing again. As far as I can learn there was nothing materially injured.

Hiram Roberts, of Cory, returned home last Saturday, after a short visit of one week among friends here. Friday night, as he was staying with J. C. Easton, some one was detected trying to get into his room. He noticed first a movement of the curtain, then it was pushed aside and a hand was plainly seen. Roberts jumped up and it being a bright night he saw a man making quick tracks across the lot and over fences.

The Potter Enterprise
Wednesday Evening,
July 25, 1883 –
Vol. X, No. 11

- Burt Rees has bought a dog.

- B. Rennells & Son are shipping a car load of bark each day.

- Ed. Greisel is putting up a fine looking house on the Ross addition.

- Lehman boys have commenced a cellar east of Edward Forster's.

- VanWegen's mill is shipping a large quantity of cherry, ash and maple lumber.

- Dan. Monroe has part of the lumber on the ground for a new house. Ross addition.

- Will Bassett has lumber on the ground for his new house on the Zimmerman square.

- Mrs. P. A. Stebbins is preparing to erect a neat dwelling house, east of Mrs. Mills' new house.

- Ansel Wood cut his hand severely on a scythe while at work for Amos Colcord, last week. He was working at a bur at the heel of the snath and the wrench slipped off, his hand striking the edge of the scythe.

- S. P. Olmsted, J. B. Benson, Jule Hodskin and Ben. Dennis spent last week on the East Fork. They caught lots of trout, shot some woodcock, and S. P. killed a two year old buck (sheep) for a farmer who could not catch the brute.

- New bridge, made out of the old Second street bridge, across the river at Charles Kernan's.

- Timber at the bottom of the old Second street bridge is as sound as the day it was put in, about seventeen years ago.

- Seymour Norton had a collision with the saw at Lyman's mill last week. A badly cut arm was received by Norton as a remembrance of the affair.

West Pike.

Mr. A. H. Haxton has moved into the house formerly occupied by Mrs. Rogers.

C. A. Turck has improved the external appearance of his residence somewhat. He also has the finest cabbage we have seen.

Miss Laura Bennett is no more. She passed from the stage of action as a single lady, a few days since, and has launched her bark on the matrimonial sea. May happiness attend her.

Freeman Run.

A strange thing happened here yesterday. It was pleasant all day not a drop of rain fell.

E. Fournes has bought a new horse rake and H. Bridges a new mowing machine; so you see people are thinking of haying over in this part of the world.

Mr. Pliny Harris is very feeble this summer.

Our day school and Sabbath school are both progressing finely.

Roulet.

Leroy Fessenden, who had the misfortune to cut his foot nearly off a few weeks ago, is out again.

A. V. Lyman lost the end of his little finger in the coggs of a mowing machine, and Miles Marsh, not to be behind the time, dropped a heavy stone on his right hand crushing the thumb badly.

A new bridge has been built over Fishing Creek at this place.

A number of ladies met at the residence of Mrs. R. B. Lane's last Wednesday for the purpose of doing the sewing for the family, as Mrs. Lane has been confined to her bed for nearly one year. We were pleased to hear they accomplished a great deal.

Ellisburg.

There are some improvements in our place worthy of note. Gilliland & Hendryx have their mill running.

Orson Ellis has nearly completed a building which is to be used as a town hall or a wool house, as the case may require. About twenty couple assembled last Friday evening and tried the merits of the new hall and pronounced it a decided success.

S. G. Rouse has built a milk and butter house. Quite a convenience, Prudence says.

We are all rejoiced at having some blacksmiths again who are willing to work.

Our young people are looking anxiously forward to the event of the season, a School Exhibition, which will close our school, Friday evening, July 27th; and, if report speaks aright of the preparations, it will be worth seeing.

It is rumored that Henry Terwilliger has sold his farm to R. L. Nelson. The wound Henry received while wearing the blue makes it impossible for him to work at farming. We shall be sorry to lose Henry.

Pike Mills.

The new school house is about completed and presents a pleasing appearance much to the credit of the contractor, Mr. Davis.

Rev. Crittenden, a missionary, gave an interesting lecture the other evening. He has been trying to establish a Sunday school. It is to be hoped the community will second him and give the new school their support.

Mr. Wallace Mattison is making an addition to his residence.

Mr. Wm. Gale has the foundation for his new residence under way and expects the dwelling to be finished for occupancy this coming winter.

The tannery company is building several tenement houses to accommodate new laborers.

We are anxiously looking for the R.R.

West Homer and South Hill.

Farmers have had one week of good hay weather, which comes very acceptable indeed.

Warren Chesbro has sold his farm to John Taubert, John having sold his farm to a stranger from Sullivan county, N.Y. We think Warren has an idea of going a little nearer the equator to find a home.

We are sorry to hear of the death of Mrs. John Brownlee of North Wharton. She died of Cancer, has had all done for her that kindness or money could do, having visited Rome, N.Y., three times but of no avail. She has been a great but very patient sufferer. She yielded submissively to God's will. We extend our greatest sympathy to the bereaved family.

The ladies of our place were invited to celebrate the birth days of Charles Furgeson and daughter, on the 11th of July. Well we all gathered together with one accord at his house and partook of a delicious supper. Among the rest was Edith Lathrop, and we were all pleased to see her out once more. Mr. Charles Knickerbocker, of Ayers Hill, was also present. We think these little afternoon gatherings a great help to the sociability of the neighborhood.

John Colcord left home last Friday morning with three horses and came back at night with none, but he was drawing a bran new horse-rake. What did he do with his horses?

The few, from our place, that were at the proceedings at Costelloville, the Fourth, pronounced it a success, with the exception of the shower in the evening, but this could not be helped. We think that North Wharton can furl her flag of honor high above the most of her surrounding towns. The whole day was passed with great civility; not one intoxicated person met our observation. We think the people of North Wharton and vicinity have much cause to thank Costello & Sons, as it all came from their skillful management. We do believe that if more of our leading men would make the effort, intemperance would in a great degree be absented from our picnics, camp meetings and pleasure parties in general.

John Klesa is about to occupy his new house.

Arthur Gordenir drives two mules instead of one now-a-days.

The Potter Enterprise
Wednesday Evening,
August 1, 1883 –
Vol. X, No. 12

- L. R. Bliss has his new house up and enclosed.

- The new foot bridge at Main street is completed and proves a great convenience.

- D. C. Larrabee is making arrangements to erect a fine barn in the rear of where his old one now stands.

- Theodore Grabe has commenced the cellar for his new house, on the lot recently purchased of Mrs. Hodskin.

- H. C. Olmsted is making arrangements to erect a fine dwelling house for his own use on the lot he recently purchased of the Cushing estate.

- Wm. Thomas has painted his house, removed some of the shade about it, built a new barn, and is otherwise making things comfortable and homelike about his property.

- The west abutment of the Second street bridge is completed and work is progressing rapidly on the other one. The work will soon be ready for the iron bridge. The entire structure will cost about $1400.

- Miss Jennie White has been engaged to teach the primary department of the Coudersport Graded School. Miss White is a graduate of the Lock Haven Normal, well qualified, and will, doubtless, give the best of satisfaction.

- Main street, from Water to Second, is a mud hole of magnificent proportions.

- Hundreds of tons of hay rotted on the ground last week. Henry Gnau, of Yochum Hill, lost five acres, and the farmer who did not have more or less out, was the exception, not the rule.

Whites Corners.

Farmers are commencing their haying. Grass is good in this section.

H. O. Chapin has moved into F. Farnum's house near the cheese factory; also, his goods from N. M. Brooks' store to the one owned by W. Rutherford.

L. Elliott is filling the store owned by N. M. Brooks and formerly occupied by H. O. Chapin.

Amanzo J. McCutcheon and Miss Lucretia Wallace were married on July 1st. We wish them much joy.

M. Hober sold a large pair of oxen a few days ago for $150.

Our famous horseman, A. V. Elder, has the two best horses in the county.

North Wharton.

The road between here and Keating Summit is in an almost impassable condition. The mud being anywhere from one to four feet deep.

Roulet.

W. S. Burdick, of Alfred, N.Y., has bought a lot near the Roulet depot and intends to erect thereon a planing and shingle mill. Two car loads of machinery are on the ground and work has commenced. Mr. B. comes well recommended not only as a good business man but a good citizen.

There will be a donation at the house of Mike Weimer on Fishing Creek, Friday evening, for Dr. Fisher.

A. V. Lyman is re-shingling his barn.

The party at the Boyington House, Friday evening, for the benefit of R. B. Lane, was a success. Thirty-one dollars being the amount taken in.

A painful accident occured at Burtville Sunday last, by which Mrs. Ole Hanson had her limb broken just below the knee. Mr. and Mrs. Hanson were but driving with their Mexican ponies when they became frightened, throwing Mrs. Hanson out. Dr. Sterns set the broken member.

Colesburg.

Ret. Slade has exchanged his ox team and other property with Calvin Ford for a horse team. Now, Ret, get a wife and your joy will be complete.

James Gross had the misfortune to lose a team horse while drawing a load of merchandise from Wellsville for Mr. Scoville. The loss falls heavily on Mr. Gross as he is a poor man and depended on his team as the main support for his family.

Township Tidings from Potter County, Pennsylvania
Volume I, 1880 - 1884

Mrs. Dunn has leased her farm to E. Beebe and will move to Mansfield in August for the purpose of giving her children better educational advantages.

The Colesburg boys are organizing a base ball club. Their first challenge will be the East Hebrons, and if they succeed in gaining a victory over them, they then will look for larger "Fry."

E. Carr had a sheep killed one day last week by a neighbor's dog, urged in the slaughter by its master, whose brutal proclivities towards his neighbor's stock is becoming intolerable.

**The Potter Enterprise
Wednesday Evening,
August 8, 1883 –
Vol. X, No. 13**

- Blackberries are ripening.

- Mrs. C. S. Jones fell from a step ladder one day last week and was quite severely injured.

- W. I. Lewis lost two hens and a brood of chickens last week. A mink is supposed to have caused the death of the fowls.

- Brine's brick kiln is about ready to open and soon brick laying will commence of M. S. Thompson's extension to Postoffice building and on Rees Brothers double store.

- Nearly all of the arrangements have been completed for the erection of a saw mill at Pomeroy Bridge, Roulet. A. M. Benton, A. G. Olmsted and Mr. Bard are the projectors of this enterprise.

- An Ice Cream Festival will be held in the cheese factory at Genesee Forks, on Friday, August 17th, 1883, afternoon and evening, for the benefit of Rev. Miller. All are cordially invited to attend.

West Branch.

The New York and Northern Pennsylvania Railroad Company's Engineers are here again. They are in camp at or near Walter Thompson's. W. E. Wormelsdoff is in charge of them. They expect to run a railroad line down Kettle Creek.

The wet weather has made it difficult and slow work to gather the hay crop this season, but the crop is a large one.

Potatoes are looking well, so are oats.

Apples are dropping off quite badly.

Clara.

Bark peelers and hay makers vow vengeance on the weather clerk.

James Tyler is peculiarly unfortunate having lost two good horses this spring.

Tim. Glines received, last week, $862, back pension and is to receive $4 per month in the future. Mr. Glines is a great sufferer and deserves all he has got and more.

Lora Allen has closed her school, on Horse Run, this coming week.

West Pike.

West Pike needs a lawyer. John M. Kilbourne must be tired of being consulted almost daily in regard to some point of law.

There was a dance, or a *select* party, at the residence of Daniel Crandal, Friday evening, Aug. 3.

Some of our farmers are struggling on with their haying as best they can, in such weather. We hope there is "a good time coming" when the sun shall shine a whole day.

Hebron.

I am sure if the farmer of this vicinity spoil their disposition meditating on the hay weather this year no one need wonder. Rain, rain, rain, thunder and lightening!

The lightening seems to be fascinated by Mrs. Cone's premises this season, it striking there for the second time the other day, demolishing a fine balsam tree in the yard and making things look blue for a few moments.

Potato tops are beginning to rust badly from the continued wet.

Sol. Lamberton lost a horse not long since.

We have no railroad as yet, but the new covered stage running every day from Oswayo to Ceres and back affords every convenience one could expect from a railroad.

Yesterday a play was enacted in town. It was announced in the morning as a tragedy; perhaps it was, but everybody laughed and I thought it was a comedy. The particulars I can gather are as follows: Jeff. Burdic and wife have been working this summer for Leroy Witter. It seems that Mrs. B. had decided not to live with her husband longer. But Jeff. took it to heart seriously. He announced to all the neighbors as he journeyed toward Oswayo that he wished to bid them a long farewell as he was about to poison himself. Word came, in the afternoon, that he had really taken poison, and some of the neighbors going into Jim Moyer's found him apparently suffering much. About five o'clock Mr. Witter and Mrs. B. went up to view the remains; but it seems Jeff. recovered sufficiently to start off in the buggy with them, and when opposite Henry Lamberton's he was seen (by some who had heard the loud voices in altercation and rushed out) to jump out and run around on the other side of the buggy and strike Witter several times over the head with a stick he had in his hand, upon which "the woman in the case" seized the lines and drove rapidly away. It seems that Jeff. was enraged with jealousy of Mrs. B. and had taken this way to avenge himself. He started for Esq. Estes saying he should give himself up. The finale is yet to come but will, no doubt, be very thrilling. The suicide however miscarried as it appears; at least the subject seemed quite lively last night.

The Potter Enterprise Wednesday Evening, August 15, 1883 – Vol. X, No. 14

- Costello's tannery, at North Wharton, is being enlarged.

- L. C. Kinner, of Shingle House, offers his store and stock of goods for sale.

- A new house is being built on the hill lot above the Keystone mill by John Shafer.

- A partition, with sliding glass doors or windows, is one of the late improvements in the Coudersport Bank.

- Apples will not be a very large crop in Potter this year.

- Oats are about fit to cut. The crop is more than an average one.

- Rattlesnakes are unusually plenty on Pine Creek this year. A few days since one was killed on the West Branch near Mr. Bisbee's. It is rare that they are found so far up the Creek.

- Costello's Tannery, at Camden, N.Y., burned on Saturday night, destroying a large quantity of machinery and leather. This will not interfere with their tanneries at North Wharton and Oswayo, unless it be to increase their production at these points.

Whites Corners.

The farmers are nearly through haying in this section, though the weather has been very unfavorable. There is a good crop of hay.

Mr. Waters has repaired his old house with the intention of using it for a barn. He found it more of an expensive job than he anticipated.

The cheese factory made a sale of cheese last week at 9 ½ c.

There is to be a camp meeting in G. B. Moshier's grove beginning Aug. 16th and lasting four days.

Query: Why is a cigar manufactory for the ruin of young men any more respectable than a whiskey distillery for the same purpose?

Roulet.

Leroy Lyman is building a gambrel roof hay barn, 26x48.

R. Reed has a neat dwelling house nearly ready for occupancy.

A little daughter of Lafe. Knowlton, about three years old, while running on the smooth floor of their porch, fell and broke her limb between the knee and hip in three places.

The Centre school, taught by Miss Bell Baird, of Renova, closed last Friday. Miss B. gave the best satisfaction and her cheerful countenance will be missed by all, especially by the class in Sunday school that she taught so earnestly and faithful.

Raymond.

There seems to be no especial interest just now about here to make out items of news.

Farmers have been very busy the last few days improving the good hay weather.

The cold nights seem to have left us, and corn is taking advantage of hotter weather to reach upwards.

Other crops appear very good, except the apple crop, that is small.

The general health is good, though a few have, or have threatened with, cholera-morbus.

Mr. Daniel Raymond is as nimble as a young man, though nearly ninety years old.

The widow Bonnel, on Cobb Hill, nearly seventy-six, has, during the past year, made five bed quilts, by machine, and worked up, sewing by hand, sixty yards of muslin, besides knitting fifty pair of socks and mittens. And they say too that she has done about as much house work as an ordinary hired girl, excepting washing.

Well, perhaps we may as well tell the rest of the family news. It is reported that Mr. Burton Fassit sleeps good now, has slept good just one week. He was fearful it would be a girl; but it is a boy, a nine pounder. His other children are girls.

The Potter Enterprise
Wednesday Evening,
August 22, 1883 –
Vol. X, No. 15

- Corn is a light crop.

- Streams are getting very low.

- Harvest apples are ripe and fairly plentiful.

- Work is progressing on the Episcopal church.

- Buckwheat looks well. The prospects for "slap jacks" is "more than gorgeous."

- Whortleberries are scarce this year. They are selling at about a shilling a quart in this market.

- Eggs are worth twenty cents per dozen and butter twenty cents per pound in Coudersport.

- The committee expect to let the contract for building the Catholic church, at this place next Monday.

- Water main to be extended north from Second on West street. Work has commenced.

- Hon. A. G. Olmsted is putting in the apparatus for heating his house with steam. First cost about $600.

- John Dorsey has bought the Seifert property at the upper end of Main street paying therefor nine hundred and fifty dollars.

- Ernest Wells, of Oswayo, visited Coudersport Friday, making the trip on his new bicycle in about three hours. His machine is a beauty, costing over $100.

- We understand the Keating lands, east of Main street, are soon to be surveyed into building lots, to the foot of the hill. Those surveyed a year ago have all been sold and many now are very pleasant homes.

Freeman Run.

Haying is nearly done.

Four new fanning mills were left in this neighborhood last week, by a traveling agent.

A pic-nic is talked of bout the time is not yet determined.

A. H. Crosby has been having the mumps by way of variety.

Mr. Pliny Harris is still confined to his bed.

Bingham.

Notwithstanding the wet weather our farmers are well advanced with their work, the good weather of the past two weeks having been well improved.

Four of the five new houses at North Bingham are up, and one of them being built for E. W. Ryan, by Clinton Clark, is rapidly approaching completion.

The railroad iron is now within a little more than two miles of Harrison Valley. The people seem to think that it will be four or five weeks before a train will reach the valley.

West Homer and South Eulalia.

We have not heard many people complain of wet weather during the past two weeks.

Farmers are through haying in this section.

Some have commenced hauling bark to Hammond's tannery.

Truman Quimby has bought or borrowed a new buggy. We *guess* he has bought it. He *rides* in one any way.

Charles Reuning has put up an addition to his house.

Miss Edith Lathrop is confined to her bed again. She has the spinal disease.

Mr. H. Taubert, father of Mrs. John Gordenier, is very sick with lung disease. He is quite an old man and is not expected to recover.

Fruit of all kinds is scarce in this vicinity.

Tis feared there will be a scarcity of potatoes as there is every indication of rot.

**The Potter Enterprise
Wednesday Evening,
August 29, 1883 –
Vol. X, No. 16**

Allegany.

Haying is work of the past, and oats are being harvested.

Winter wheat, that did not winter kill, is good.

The profusion of apple blossoms was like some peoples promises. Apples will not be plenty, in but very few orchards. Plum trees seem to bear well this year.

A frost this morning, but think the fog prevented injury.

One week from next Sunday, on Sept. 9th, a quarterly meeting is to be held at the Judd school house and on Saturday the 8th, the Sunday school pic-nic.

Fannie Matteson and Adrian Gardner are to attend the graded school at Coudersport.

Some of the schools are already supplied with teachers for the winter.

There is talk of a fall term in place of winter at the Judd school house.

Saturday evening last, Libbie Coats, daughter of Chas. Coats, was thrown from a horse and was seriously injured.

- T. J. Gilbert is clearing off his lot, south of Mr. Kiehl's, preparatory to the erection of a dwelling house.

- A large saw mill is to be erected at Pike Mills this Fall. The land has been purchased and other arrangements made.

- The first story of M. S. Thompson's brick addition is nearly up.

- The packing of the water main at Main and First street gave out last Thursday, requiring considerable work and some little time to repair.

- Grant Reed, son of Henry Reed, of Ayer's Hill, fell from a load of oats Monday afternoon and broke both bones of his right forearm. Dr. Buck reduced the fracture.

- Complaints of fruit thieves are again heard. Geo. Boyer has had one apple tree stripped. Dr. French mourns the loss of pears and a number of others are in the same boat. A charge of fine salt from a well loaded shot gun or a few arrests would teach the boys better.

- Mr. Bonawitz, living in Summit township, while at work holding a scraper, by a sudden spring of the team, was struck by one of the handles of the scraper and throw violently to the ground; two ribs were broken and his head and back were severely bruised by the fall.

West Branch.

This is a good time for grumblers. A person does not have to be a chronic grumbler to get in a little work now on the weather. During the haying it has been too dry. Yesterday we had quite a refreshing shower, so let us be thankful for small favors.

Something is the matter with our apples, they are dropping off badly. There will be a light crop here.

Oats are now being harvested and are reported as unusually good, so there is something more to be thankful for.

The Potter Enterprise Wednesday Evening, September 5, 1883 – Vol. X, No. 17

- The building for the Roulet planing mill is up.

- Hard coal is selling at seven dollars and fifty cents a ton.

- Work has commenced for the erection of the saw mill at Pomeroy Bridge.

- Some person's cow destroyed D. B. Neefe's corn patch last Friday morning.

- Last Wednesday afternoon a mink got in the park of the publisher of the Enterprise and killed fourteen large chickens, and also killed one for Henry Nelson and two for Wm. Thomas. Such wholesale slaughter is very disgusting. Since this, Wm. Thomas' coop has had a second visit and nine dead pullets make the score. N. H. Goodsell steps to the front as a mourner with a list of nineteen dead chickens. Mink are unusually plenty and the above would indicate unusually destructive to poultry.

- C. L. Peck has purchased the south half of the Bingham Estate square, on Main street. Consideration $2,800.

- The Second street iron bridge is still one of the things we look for. It was to have been put in place before the first of September.

- D. W. VanWegen has the contract for building the Catholic Church. He completes it, above the foundation, for $1,900; the roof to be of slate.

- The afternoon train on the C. & P. A. Monday consisted of fifteen cars, mostly loaded with bark and lumber. This is the largest train ever hauled over the road.

- Last Saturday morning street commissioner Glassmire moved N. H. Goodsell's fence, in front of Joseph Mann's residence, sixteen feet back from the place it has so long occupied. This move was made by direction of the Town Council upon notice of attorney for W. B. Gordnier.

Bingham.

Burton Henoy, aged about ten years, died so suddenly of typhoid fever that some of the neighbors hardly knew that he was dangerously ill, before he was dead. He had been staying, for a few weeks, at the widow Grovers. He was buried Aug. 26th, at North Bingham, without a funeral. The doctor, when first called to see him, pronounced the case hopeless.

We have had a very heavy storm and it has done much damage by lodging uncut grain. The storm was followed by a frost but the damage was light in most places.

Costelloville.

We are having beautiful weather now, with just enough rain to lay the dust and make every thing grow nicely.

The Hon. Tom Young, of Cincinnati, spent a few days with his mother, Mrs. Brownlee, last week. Mrs. B. is nearly 88 years of age and is now failing quite fast.

We notice an improvement is being made on A. Costello & Co.'s store – a porch, which will be used as a sun bonnet for the boys.

Our school, which has been under the management of L. D. Ripple, has closed for a month's vacation. Mr. R. gave satisfaction throughout the neighborhood, and we are anxious to replace our little ones (which number about sixty) in the school room again with Mr. Riple as their shepherd.

The Brownlee school has opened again. Mr. A. W. Colcord, a State Normal graduate, is conducting the school, and will devote his time, for the next six months, to filling the lads and lassies heads with honey fresh from the Normal.

The young people of Costelloville spent an enjoyable evening at the house of Thomas Moran, on the 29th inst., celebrating Miss Mary's birth-day. There were some forty present, each bringing a token of remembrance, and at twelve p.m., the table, which was spread to receive the presents, became loaded with jewelry, silver ware, dry goods, &c. Ice cream and other refreshments were served at an early hour, and, by the aid of good music, we tripped the light fantastic until two a.m.; then went to our respective homes well pleased with the evening which went so rapidly, and also with Mr. Moran and family's kind hospitality.

Keating.

The fruit crop in this place, this season, is very small. Even black berries are scarce.

Mr. Monroe Dingee is attending school at Coudersport this Fall.

There will be an exhibition and picnic on the 14th of September, in the woods near H. Bridges. Every body and their friends are invited to come and bring their dinner and have a good time.

Raymond.

Really it is too cold to write, but we will try, as wife has a fire below.

No frost just here this morning. In some spots, some time ago, they had their potatoes and corn cut down.

In this immediate neighborhood we have no fears yet of a potato famine.

On the 25th of August, Mr. Levi Moore's 72nd birth day, of which he was reminded the day before by a surprise visit from his family relations, children, grand-children, nephews, nieces and at least one grand-niece, also his family connections. Some forty-five birth-days Mr. Moore has had in this place. His health seems better than it was some years ago. The object of the visit was substantial tokens of regard, and it was a success. May the couple see many more such days.

Eleven Mile.

Frankie Rowlee, a son of the late Wm. Rowlee, aged about ten years, was badly kicked by a colt on the 26th of August. He was driving it, with others, out of the fields and it kicked striking him in the face, cutting his nose open and injuring his right eye so it has been swollen shut, and no doubt he will carry scars hereafter in remembrance of the event.

Preparations are under way to establish a Camp of the Sons of Veterans at Oswayo soon, to be named "Leroy West" Camp – and is to be composed of sons of ex-soldiers sixteen years of age and upwards. Its objects are to perpetuate the Memorial Day duties of the G. A. R. and aid that organization in its other duties and observances. It will be the first camp organized in the county and we hope may prove a success.

The Potter Enterprise
Wednesday Evening,
September 12, 1883 –
Vol. X, No. 18

- Michael Ryan has a new house up south of his father's, on Main street.

- The water company has covered its pipe on West street, and we are happy.

- Nelson Goodsell has put in a new dam, to utilize the water of Mill Creek.

- A sixty foot dance hall will be erected on the fair grounds by James Glase.

Township Tidings from Potter County, Pennsylvania
Volume I, 1880 - 1884

- Edward Forster has commenced work putting up his two stores a second story.

- Will Jackson has erected a store at Borie and will soon stock it with groceries, etc.

- The brick work on the postoffice addition will be completed this week, also that of Griesel's harness shop.

- George Boyer is traveling about on crutches. He had his left foot jammed by a log while working in the woods last week.

- Killing freeze last Monday morning; buckwheat put in late is a failure; corn about the same and garden truck generally killed.

- The finest and largest blue plums we ever saw were left at this office last Friday by Ira Easton, of Genesee Forks. They were of the Weaver variety.

- The frosts of last week damaged buckwheat and corn considerably. Pancakes may be a luxury notwithstanding the favorable appearances early in the season.

- Zimmerman has exchanged four lots on which there are two dwelling houses erected by him, this summer, for Henry Schildberger's farm in Eulalia, containing one hundred and forty six acres.

- Last Tuesday Daniel Wells let his team lose with the harness on while he repaired his wagon. The team picked about the common for a time, but when Mr. Wells went to look for them they could not be found. He searched all day Wednesday without getting any trace of the team. Thursday morning he found his team in Sweden about six miles from Coudersport, where they had been take up, safe and sound.

West Branch.

Some of the hemlock lumber jobs are starting up.

Lon. Mitchell is at work on his job on Wetmore Run. He has about 600,000 to get in.

B. F. Burrous is selling out his Rock Run job to Charles Rexford. Rexford also has the timber on the hill at the head of Rock Run to get in, estimated at one million feet.

Wm. Putnam has commenced his job up Beach Flat Brook.

Parties from Williamsport are looking up the timber on the Russell lands. If that timber is got in this winter in addition to the other jobs it will make lively times here this fall and winter.

Roulet.

Leroy Fessenden and Cale Johnson started a meat wagon – a long felt want – in this place.

Jack Goodal is building a cabinet shop on his lot on Main street.

The little daughter of A. M. Fessenden is very low with scarlet fever.

Work on the sash and blind factory is nearly done, and in about one week it will be in running order.

The steam mill being built by Benton & Co., at Pomeroy Bridge, is progressing finely.

The farmers are complaining of the potato crop, and the frost last night fixed the corn and buckwheat.

C. J. Burt and wife have returned from Kansas.

The camp meeting, held by the U.B. church, on Sartwell creek, was well attended.

Our little town that has been asleep for so many years has at last awakened. The building of the C. & P. A. R. R. through here last summer seemed, at first, a detriment. But upon further development it is far different. The citizens were nearly discouraged, but now the true value of the railroad is showing for itself and they are elated. New buildings are springing up like mushrooms, lands are changing hands, farms are being cut up into village lots, and in short, Roulet is improving, vastly improving and in a few years will be second to none in the county.

Allegany.

We are promised "seed time and harvest," and we had a frost harvester last night that cut everything that a frost will injure that had escaped the frosts heretofore.

Winter wheat is nearly all sown.

Oat harvesting is well under way.

Many pieces of potatoes have been struck with blight and all that was green are frozen.

Miss Nettie Bishop is attending the Normal at Mansfield.

Wm. Cool is attending the graded school at Coudersport.

Wm. Matteson, while driving sheep, lost some of them by their running into the woods, where the road was not fenced. After looking a day or more he found nearly all of them.

The attendance at the pic nic was good, but the weather was not favorable. Owing to the rain it was held in the hall.

Quarterly meeting had a small attendance. Think the cold day must have chilled the religious fever of the people.

The Potter Enterprise Wednesday Evening, September 19, 1883 – Vol. X, No. 19

- M. S. Thompson's store is now the largest in town, 28 feet by 114 feet.

- Orange Hall had five acres of clover in Homer, a sample from which measures five feet in length.

- Roll butter is scarce in Coudersport at 22 cents per pound; potatoes reasonably plenty, at 50 cents per bushel and apples bring fifty cents.

- The stone work of the Episcopal church is nearly up. It is not completed yet and the roof may make quite an improvement in its appearance. At present it is far from handsome.

- The Second street bridge is ready for use.

- Wm. F. Yunge has one house completed and another nearly so on the Lymansville road. Both are rented.

- The railroad is completed to Harrison Valley. An excursion train was run on Monday last. Regular trains will soon be put on.

Freeman Run.

Buckwheat is a light crop here on account of the early frost.

The pic nic on the 14th came together in a hurry in the afternoon and what was there enjoyed themselves pretty well.

Our school closed last Thursday. The school, this summer, seems to have been a success. Thanks to the teacher, Miss Laurie Bridges.

Mr. Pliny Harris is very sick, his recovery seems doubtful.

West Branch.

Our school, in the Crippen Run district, closed Friday. Miss Carrie Ansley, the teacher, gave general satisfaction and is engaged for the winter term.

Miss Nora Metzger's school, in the Burrous district, will close next week.

Stewart &Conable have the job of hauling Gale's bark from the north side of Wettmore Run.

Whites Corners.

Harvesting is nearly through with in this place.

Oats turn out a very good crop.

Mr. A. A. Ross has moved back on the place owned by Mrs. N. M. Brooks.

The people of this place listened to a very able sermon by Rev. Bovier last Sunday evening. We hope he will favor us again soon.

As Mr. John Olney and wife were coming by J. J. Stetson's, Wednesday, their horse became frightened at the milk stand, which is very near the road, and jumped into the ditch, overturning the buggy and throwing them out. They were not injured although the buggy was somewhat demolished.

Allegany.

The house of G. W. James took fire one day last week. When discovered the upper rooms were burning rapidly. Water being near, Mrs. James, with the help of the neighboring women, kept the fire in subjection until the arrival of the men from the fields, when it was considerably damaged and some clothing burned. It was thought to have caught from the chimney.

W. M. Slaughter and F. Smith have bought Mr. Atkins' threshing machine and are now engaged in threshing.

M. A. Veeley has done good business for himself and neighbors with his reaper.

Mr. Byam is building a house on his farm that he bought from Mr. Wells.

A sudden change in the weather, this morning, from warm to cold and wet, which will delay getting grain into the barns.

Hebron.

Corn and beans are frozen and succotache is nowhere.

Ed. Terwillegar, after eight years of terrible suffering, has passed on to the better land, where he no doubt has found the "spiritual body" spoken of by Paul; with no more suffering and sorrow. How blessed must be the change. The remains were taken to Sharon for interment.

Born – To Myron and Belle Howard, Sept. 2d, 1883, a boy, weight 9 ½ pounds.

Lumbering is under way on Whitney Creek this week. The boarding house is to be kept by Will MacDonald.

West Homer.

H. M. Case is attending Court this week as a grand juror.

I hear that we are going to have a new school house. Mr. Rees, of Eulalia, is going to build it.

The pic nic on Freeman Run, last Friday, was not very well attended. I have been told there were only forty present.

Jacob McCann has gone to Pine Creek to work in the lumber woods.

G. M. Baker has got himself a horse team. I hear he bought them of Dan. Hackett; consideration $150.

The dance over at Mrs. David Snyder's last Friday was a decided success. There being about fifteen couple present.

J. B. Colcord goes to Baltimore, the first of October, to attend a course of medical lectures.

O. L. Hall is not quite through harvesting.

Albert Colcord has got his brother Amos' oxen draying bark.

The Potter Enterprise Wednesday Evening, September 19, 1883 – Vol. X, No. 19

- J. M. Bassett has sold out his Coudersport and Germania stage line.

- J. B. Colcord, of Homer, has gone to Baltimore to attend the session of the Medical College, of that city.

- A. G. Olmsted, last week, purchased at administrator's sale, the Cole lot on 2d street, nearly opposite the Enterprise office, size 33x132 feet, price $600.

Freeman Run.

Potatoes are rotting here quite bad and will be rather a light crop.

Mr. John Bundy has a brother, Mr. William Bundy, of Nebraska, and a sister, Mrs. Lucy Covert, of New York State, visiting him.

The new U.B. minister sent on this circuit, is Rev. Mr. Sheets, of Salamanca. He preached his first sermon here last Sabbath.

The fall and winter term of school, near Frank Klein's in this town, will commence the first of October. The school will be in charge of Miss Libbie Crosby, of Homer.

Again death has entered our neighborhood and taken one of our oldest and most respected citizens, Mr. Pliny Harris, who has been sick for a long time, died on the evening of the 21st of September, 1883, aged a little over seventy-one years. His sickness and death was a calm and peaceful one. During his sickness not a murmur or dissatisfied word was heard; he was perfectly satisfied with all that was done for him. He was a good neighbor, a kind husband and father. There is not another in the neighborhood who would be more missed than he will be. Among those who will miss Mr. Harris none will miss him more than the little children of this place as he always had a kind word and pleasant smile for each one of them and even during his sickness he seemed always glad to have them call to see him. Mr. Harris was a strictly temperate man and by his death the cause of temperance has lost a firm friend. On Sunday his burial service was conducted by the Rev. Wm. Marshall, of Coudersport, which was Mr. Harris' request. At the grave, the children and young people of the neighborhood marched around the grave each throwing in a bunch of flowers, thus showing their respect for the dead.

**The Potter Enterprise
Wednesday Evening,
October 3, 1883 –
Vol. X, No. 21**

- Sam'l Thompson has purchased the Burt Rees property on East and Fifth street. Consideration, $1,100.

- Mrs. Rachel Hess, of Cross Fork, had a quilt on exhibition at the Fair, containing 3,686 pieces. At the time she made the quilt her eyesight was so poor that she would thread fifty or sixty needles during the day to use in the evening.

- A few days ago Miss Lucy Hamilton heard the chickens making an unusual cackling in the coop. Investigation showed that a large mink was intent on obtaining a good dinner, and was the cause of the disturbance. Miss Hamilton soon dispatched the animal with a club, thus saving the chickens. On Monday the publisher of the Enterprise shot the mink that killed sixteen chickens for him. "Let the good work go on."

Andrews Settlement.

Threshing machines are busy this week, there being two running here.

Oats are an extra yield.

Early buckwheat it is said is very fine, frost having hurt the later sowing.

Apples are quite plenty and plums were a very good crop which has furnished considerable chance for "cooning" which, by the way, has become downright stealing.

J. C. Curtis has lost a very heavy hive of honey and Reuben Plants two, the hives having been carried some distance before the bees were killed. There is hardly a family here who have not suffered a loss in some way, either in chickens, honey, canned fruit or fruit from their trees. There should be prompt measures taken to stop such proceedings and we think that Mrs. Frank Smith started in the right direction when she shot at a man who was meddling with their bees. Since two fellows were caught at Ellisburg, everybody has been giving the boys from that way the credit of much that does not belong to them. For we heard a man say that he caught some boys attempting to steal chickens (some of the party over sixteen), and he advised them to go and take chickens from their own roosts. We think that was queer advice to give boys. He should have told their parents so that they could have been on their guard and known where their boys were. But hoping some one will make an example of a few so that they may know the consequences of such conduct, I will close.

Ellisburg.

Among the improvements and pleasant things to be mentioned of our place are:

Our school house in undergoing thorough repairs. Wm. Eaton has the job which is sufficient guarantee for good work.

Gilliland & Hendryx have put a planer in their mill which will prove a great convenience to people about here.

We have a select school, with about twenty pupils, under the charge of Miss Hendryx.

Our people gathered together the other night and had a good time besides donating about $25 for Rev. N. North. We shall be very sorry to lose Mr. North, but feel certain that a man of his abilities will rise in the conference.

We are sorry to write that some of our young men and boys are making themselves obnoxious by doing what they please to call "cooning." Honey, chickens, ducks, plums and pears have to suffer. At first, people laughed, but when the "cooning" became a wholesale stealing and the thieves took more than they wanted and left chickens hanging beside the road there was a general inquiry of "who do you suppose it is?" But there is no longer a doubt of who some of the "cooners" are. Two of our young gentlemen went out the other night and when they returned one of them reported they had struck a "pooden" but, when the facts came out, the "pooden," which they struck, was a jar of cream which they got into while trying to escape from a milkhouse in which they were trapped while sampling pears. This has furnished subject for considerable talk. But we should remember that the uncaught are just as bad as the caught.

The Rev. Snead, who held a protracted meeting at the Chapman school house, has gone to Oswayo and is having splendid success. Let the good work go on.

Allegany.

Oats are proving good this year. Mr. Card has the largest yield, per acre, that has been reported.

Buckwheat cakes will be scarce, also full pickle jars.

Two weddings, of late. A. Atkins and N. Cool have each taken companions for life. May they find more sunshine than shadow, and likewise may prosperity attend them.

Township Tidings from Potter County, Pennsylvania
Volume I, 1880 - 1884

**The Potter Enterprise
Wednesday Evening,
October 10, 1883 –
Vol. X, No. 22**

Whites Corners.

Mrs. N. M. Brooks has sold her place to S. J. Stetson, who has rented his farm to Andrew Erway.

N. M. Brooks has sold his farm to H. O. Chapin. Mr. Books intends moving to Troupsburg Centre soon.

Warner & Zimmer have one of the best wagons in town, made by Taggart & Elder.

S. J. Stetson intends leading the life of a gentleman hereafter. He has sold one of his horses to H. O. Chapin and is breaking the other for a carriage horse.

Elder Schoville preached his farewell sermon here last Sunday. He has labored faithfully here and was well liked by many of the people.

Religion and cigar making do not fraternize in this vicinity.

- Ralph Niles has been removed to the Warren Insane Hospital.

- Mr. A. Sandberg is erecting a saw mill on the head of Dingman Run.

- T. J. Gilbert is on the Prouty keeping boarding house for Albert Lyman.

- John Denhoff has moved the house from Mrs. P. A. Stebbins' lot, Allegany avenue, to his own lot, recently purchased of the Keating estate.

- David White has purchased of O. J. Rees fifty feet front on Main street, on which is the house now occupied by Mr. Rees, for $1,100. Rees intends erecting a new house on the corner of his lot remaining unsold.

Sartwell Creek.

Winter has come at last, that is, in this part of the country; but we are in hopes that we will have Indian Summer yet for some are not prepared to house up.

Mr. Frank Jordan is building a new porch on his house on Main street, and he is going to paint it over new. Just look grand, won't it.

**The Potter Enterprise
Wednesday Evening,
October 17, 1883 –
Vol. X, No. 23**

- Z. J. Thompson's chimney burned out on Monday. No damage done.

- The brick work on the Rees building is finished and they are now plastering it.

- The Methodist parsonage is ready for its occupants, it is a neat and tasty building.

- F. B. Nelson has moved into the Rees house recently purchased by Sam'l Thompson.

- Elmer Miller, of Andrews Settlement, left a common radish at this office, which weighed four pounds and measured 21 inches in length and 10 inches around.

- The first snow-storm of the season visited this borough and vicinity on Monday morning last.

Roulet.

Work has commenced on the depot at Pomeroy bridge.

I. J. Raymer has the foundation laid for a house on Main street.

C. C. Johnson and J. Tenbrook are each building dwelling houses on their lots across the river.

Ground was broken last week for the new school house, to be built in place of the old red one which has been occupied some thirty-five years.

Work has begun on the store of the mill company, at the corners.

Leroy Lyman and Fred Yentzer started last Thursday for Michigan, where they will hunt for several weeks.

The infant son of Mr. and Mrs. DuBois was buried last Saturday.

The Potter Enterprise
Wednesday Evening,
October 24, 1883 –
Vol. X, No. 24

- Philander McKinney has purchased the Joseph Butler farm in Sweden.

- The Presbyterian Society are building an addition in the rear of the church – a large parlor, kitchen, woodshed and shed for teams.

- R. L. Clark has moved from Ulysses to Pike Mills.

- Luther Tools has purchased a lot on Hill street, or Prospect avenue, west of R. L. Nichols' property, and commenced the erection of a house.

- Last Sunday afternoon near Ellisburg, a horse driven by Tom. Gorman ran away. Tom, Mrs. Gorman and Mary Clark were thrown from the buggy and all considerably bruised. Miss Clark had her collar bone broken. The buggy is a wreck.

Ellisburg.

It has been pretty cold here the past week.

H. H. Hall went to Oswayo last week to commence his school.

Henry Hurd has sold one of his horses. I was told he got $140 for it.

Mr. Thomas Gilland's house is beginning to look quite like a dwelling now.

The blacksmith shop is going to be moved across the road and a store is to be built where it now stands.

H. H. Hall had a bit and brace stolen the other day, it was not much of a loss, but still it shows which way the wind blows in this country.

West Homer.

Business has been quite lively here for the past week.

Albert Colcord, O. L. Hall, W. A. Crosby and Orson Crosby have been threshing.

A. E. Earle is at work for Albert Colcord skidding logs.

William Lathrop has been to work for Ed Earle, of Cowley Run, but I hear he has quit.

Buckwheat proved to be a pretty poor crop.

We have had a few very cold nights for a while back.

Allegany.

School is in session, with a good attendance. Scholars from adjoining districts are attending, increasing the number of scholars as well as making the school more interesting.

The long talked of change has been made and Judd's school house is to be supplied with preaching by the minister of Oswayo charge.

The new minister, from Oswayo, Rev. Tupper, preached yesterday for the first. All seemed to like the preacher, as well as sermon.

We are having unusual cold weather for October. Some had had their potatoes chilled.

The potato crop seems good although the blight and rot has no doubt injured them considerably.

West Homer and South Eulalia.

The few last mornings make us feel as though we were nearing the Arctic region. Autumn's genial days have nearly gone, and the forests have laid aside their gorgeous plumes. The earth's cold breast is covered with brown leaves. But summer and autumn must pass in their turn, and while grim winter is blowing his trumpet, we can yet have a summer in our hearts. The working class of people can hardly stop to welcome the beauties of summer, 'till they are gone, and then the season seems to them, more like a dream than reality.

We are having some sickness in our neighborhood. Miss Edith Lathrop is still confined to her room.

Fred Crosby has had quite a time with the mumps.

Mrs. Mary Crosby is now very sick. She is being treated by Dr. Mattison. Her fifty-fifth birthday was celebrated the 30th of September by her children and grand children. She knew nothing of it, until they came, bringing in the nicely dressed chickens, with other goodies. After partaking of a bountiful repast they presented her with a beautiful cashimere dress. Would that more mothers could be treated thus.

Mrs. Wm. White was called to attend the funeral of her aged father at Troupsburg, N.Y. She intends to remain a few weeks with her invalid mother.

Warren Chesbro has moved from his farm – now owned by John Taubert – to Lymansville.

Charlie Rees has been giving our neighborhood and vicinity music with his threshing machine. Among the rest he threshed six hundred and fifty bushels of oats for Albert Colcord. We would not be very much astonished to see Mr. Colcord wearing a plug hat. Especially when he gets all his bark hauled.

Our school, on South Hill, has commenced with L. B. Dodd as teacher. Yes, and he boards around. We hope he will not stop with any one that has "sold their bed and sleep on straw." Oh! how he does praise up the doughnuts. I guess he is fishing for the school next term.

Mr. John Palmer, of Ill., is visiting his sister, Mrs. Sallie Foster. He visited his aged mother in Bath, N.Y., and she could not remember of ever having such a child.

The Potter Enterprise
Wednesday Evening,
October 31, 1883 –
Vol. X, No. 25

- Butter is selling for twenty-five cents per pound.

- Leroy Lyman, of Roulet, is enjoying his annual hunt in the wilds of Michigan.

- The first broad gauge car over the narrow gauge came up a few days since loaded with feed for M. L. Gridley and carried back a load of leather from Hammond's tannery.

Freeman Run.

Beautiful autumn weather?

E. Fournes has purchased a fine yoke of oxen.

The little daughter of J. W. Dingee, of Keating Summit, who was badly scalded on the head some time ago is getting better.

W. E. Chesbro, of Lymansville, is in this vicinity this week looking after cherry logs.

West Pike.

We are having some very dark days just now, and rather more storm than is convenient for those engaged in bark hauling.

Mr. C. C. Flynn met with quite a severe accident one day last week. While using a gun, it was by accident, discharged and took one of his fingers off. The wound was attended by Dr. C. S. French, of Coudersport, and Dr. Ritter, of Gaines, and is doing quite well at present.

Mr. C. C. Flynn has sold his place to Mr. A. H. Haxton and will soon vacate the house.

J. M. Kilbourne, we have learned, is soon to open a hotel in this place. We believe he has his sign now.

Our neighborhood was rendered very sad on the 19th inst., by the death of Mrs. Hattie Flynn, who was one of the kindest of wives, mothers, sisters and friends in one. Her illness lasted about five weeks and during the last she was a great sufferer. No one can recall an instance – when as a guest of her house – they failed to receive a hearty welcome. She leaves a large circle of friends and relatives who fully realize their loss. Her husband and child have the heartfelt sympathy of the entire community.

Whites Corners.

Running threshing machines is the chief business at present.

Mr. Tadder has a first class steam machine and is doing good work.

Oats are a good crop in this vicinity.

Buckwheat, especially that which was sowed late, was injured by the frosts.

Potatoes are good, though some are reported to be rotting.

The people of this place turn out better than usual to hear the interesting sermons preached by Rev. Bovier. May he keep coming is the wish of all.

Warner & Zimmer have their store well stocked for the winter trade.

H. O. Chapin will move into his new store in a few days, when he will also be ready to supply the public with first class goods.

Forest House.

The saw mill on Cowley Run is broken down. I hear that the cylinder head was blown off and the driving shaft broken.

There is quite a call for men around here. There has not been a very good supply for sometime back.

W. M. Lathrop, of West Homer, is at work for Ed. Earle, on Cowley Run.

D. P. Reed's teams are hauling lumber over on the river. I should think it was a good ways to haul.

I hear that Jake Reed's John, who has been in the insane asylum, is nearly cured.

Eleven Mile.

This usually quiet valley seems just now to be more so than ever. The crops are all secured, threshing done and now some are plowing and making things secure for the winter, which will soon announce itself. Others are engaging their forces, men and teams, in cutting and skidding the peeled hemlocks and cutting and peeling the few remaining pines, whose century long sway, as forest monarchs, is now nearly ended.

Lockwood Bros. expect to have some two million feet of pine for Weston Bros., cut, peeled and skidded this fall, and if snow comes sufficient for the purpose will have them hauled to the Honeoye Creek and next spring float them, with other millions feet of hemlock, chestnut, &c., to Portville, N.Y., where they will be swiftly converted to boards, plank, scantling and square timber &c. by the mammoth mills of their owners.

Healy & Roche, with their ten horse power thresher, and Kemp Bros., with their new steam thresher, have beat out the grain in this section this fall.

The yield of oats ahs been the best had for years. Other grain yielded very lightly. Corn is a total failure, apples nearly so. Potatoes fair yield but much inclined to rot. Rozell Bros. have about 530 bushels. They also had 175 bushels buckwheat and a large yield of oats.

The postmaster, at Eleven Mile, has moved with the postoffice, about a mile and a half up the valley, thus leaving his former patrons somewhat to the rear and making a quite thickly settled district, of some seven or eight miles in length with various branch roads, without a postoffice at present, only as they go to Millport, Oswayo or Eleven Mile postoffices. It would be only right to have a new office established for their accommodation at some convenient point in this district.

The Potter Enterprise
Wednesday Evening,
November 7, 1883 –
Vol. X, No. 26

- The Coudersport graded school is crowded.

- Bark hauling is playing havoc with the roads.

- Rev. Craw now occupies the new parsonage.

- The dome of the Court House is being re-tinned.

- N. H. Goodsell has made cider of 700 bushels of apples this fall.

- A. F. Hollenbeck is soon to remove to his own house on Water street.

- Mrs. P. A. Stebbins has a neat little house enclosed on Allegany Avenue.

- Wm. Shear is to occupy the house now occupied by A. F. Hollenbeck, Main street.

- The upper floor of N. H. Goodsell's shop fell down last week. Caused by too much load. Nobody hurt.

- The frame of the new Catholic Church is up. The contractor, D. W. VanWegen, has until October next to complete it.

West Homer and South Eulalia.

We have had quite a young winter the past week, disappearing very suddenly last Saturday.

"Lady Moon came down last night" or rather Sunday morning October 28th, and presented Mr. and Mrs. John Gordenier with a young daughter. We do not wonder now that Mr. Gordenier puts on style, why shouldn't he? And now we know why Arthur does not want to go to school this winter, he had rather stay at home and rock little sister.

Alton Earle lost a new $20 watch one day last week while draying bark on Albert Colcord's place. "But don't tell his pa!"

Last fall Glenn Rees took from its nest a young downy yellow bird and put it in a cage with a canary, she adopted it at once as her own, fed and nursed it with great care, and now it is as large as the old bird, sings sweetly and thinks itself a real canary.

Forest House.

The hunters are bewailing the loss of our snow, as they find it quite hard to get any deer without the snow.

Thursday was quite wintry around here.

Wednesday night it snowed here to the depth of seven and a half inches. It has made the roads quite bad.

Having business over towards Costelloville, the other day, I was very much surprised at the condition of the road. I do not see how the teams can draw anything of a load. I think that from here to Costelloville is a good opening for a narrow gauge railroad.

Ed. Earle rolled a log on to one of his oxen last week and hurt it quite bad.

Joe Dingee got one of his horses hurt quite bad one day last week. He was skidding ties with it.

The billiard hall is pretty well patronized I should judge by the appearance of the crowd.

D. Hall is building a small barn.

H. A. Avery has traded off his bay team to Orin Card.

Township Tidings from Potter County, Pennsylvania
Volume I, 1880 - 1884

The Potter Enterprise
Wednesday Evening,
November 14, 1883 –
Vol. X, No. 27

- James Johnson and Mervill Calkins take charge of the American next week.

- Cyrenus Rennells cut his foot instead of the log, which accounts for a slight limp as he walks.

- Heavy wind has blown down considerable of the Fair Ground fence and some of the cattle sheds.

- The narrow gauge from Gaines to Pike Mills is to be constructed in the spring. Some of the grading is being done this Fall at Ainsley's.

- D. F. Glassmire, Sr., has just put in a car load of Chicago oats in his barn. The idea of Potter county sending West for oats is not pleasant to contemplate.

West Branch.

Lewis Campbell is building a house on his farm, he has the frame up and the roof on.

Willis Conable is putting up quite a large building just across the bridge on the Crippin Run road, it is intended for a store and dwelling house.

The lumber jobs about here are progressing finely and are generally in good shape for the setting in of winter.

Railroad work and talk is very quiet here at present.

The Potter Enterprise
Wednesday Evening,
November 21, 1883 –
Vol. X, No. 28

- Bear are reported more numerous than usual this season.

- Burt Rees expects to occupy his new store in about two weeks.

- A. F. Jones Post G. A. R. now uses the Knights of Honor hall.

- I. Griesel has sold out his harness making business to Joseph Griesel.

Clara.

Juna Stevens and family are about to remove to Tioga county.

Our school is in charge of Miss Orisa Hurd.

Miss Laura Tyler is teaching at Sizerville, Cameron county.

A very quiet and well conducted law suit took place yesterday before Squire Allen. The only persons present being the prosecutor, Ashel Christman, the defendent, Rodney Nichols, one witness and the lawyers, W. I. Lewis and A. F. Hollenbeck, of Coudersport.

Hebron.

The lumberman is oiling up his bob sled.

Frank Swimmer does not believe in "root, hog or die" anymore since his pig got out and eat up and spoiled a tub of butter.

Theb. Swift is going to have a nobby residence completed in a short time. We must have a house warming, Theb.

Mr. Keller is building a fine residence on Whitney Creek.

Miss May Stillson has left Hebron for the State of Matrimony. When last heard from she was in company with Mr. A. B. Estes, and Leroy Allen says it is all right and I guess it is.

Our school is to rejoice under the charge of Miss Lillie Doyle again. So "all is well."

The Ceres Stage broken down one day last week and had a tedious drag from Sharon to Oswayo. The driver walking.

Forest House.

There are quite a number of new houses being built here.

Where is our Sunday law? I heard quite a number of guns fired off on last Sunday.

There is to be an oyster supper here Wednesday night, and I believe there is to be dancing too.

A Lyceum was started last Saturday night, there was a pretty good attendance.

There has been quite a good many deer killed here the past week, I know of at least twelve.

I have been told that Mr. Wilfinger is to have a dance when his house is finished.

There is a pretty good turn out to Sunday school and church.

Eleven Mile.

A snowy, blustering week for November this has been; too much so to last long. The cold weather has reminded us of the house unbanked and the potato pits lightly covered, and to perform this necessary labor we have had to face the wintry blasts, or set the boys at it. There is nothing like a young winter in November to even up the work among farmers. They all stop plowing and if prudent and prosperous they will at once store their plows and other implements in shelter, and if of rightful temperament they will then let the weather have its will and take matters cool.

Cattle and sheep seem to enjoy good appetites for their rations, and if this wintry weather hold its own right along the surplus hay may find a market by home consumption.

The schools of Oswayo district are, all but one, in session. Prof. H. H. Hall and Miss Edith Haskell at the village; Prof. J. C. Wilkinson near Kenyon's; Miss Maggie Doyle will teach the upper Eleven Mile school; Miss Marinda Goodal teaches the school at Oswayo Centre and Mrs. Colegrove at the Kemp district. All are teachers of experience and it is hoped their terms may now be a success.

Now let the Assessor plod his weary rounds. Let us hide the dog or send him off to board awhile, for in Oswayo it costs 75 cents to pay his school tax. Dogs are of value there for they pay some $50 towards teachers wages.

Freeman Run.

The hunters are busy.

The annual party of hunters from Scranton are here, putting up with G. C. Lewis. At last accounts the number they had killed was – 0.

Wm. Blarigan, of Roulet, had the luck to kill a fine buck, near C. W. Dingee's, last Tuesday.

Ferris Bundy cut his foot very bad last Monday, while slabing wood.

Frank Klein's logging bee last Wednesday was pretty well attended, though the day was very stormy and cold. Mittens were in good demand.

We believe the average of deer and hunters in this neighborhood is fully five hunters to one deer.

Our school this winter will be taught by Miss Ida Baker of Fishing Creek.

Miss Laura Bridges is teaching school on the Turnpike.

Our Sabbath school is still kept up and is better attended than ever before at this time of the year.

Miles Marsh of Roulet has been threshing for several of the farmers here, this week and last.

**The Potter Enterprise
Wednesday Evening,
November 28, 1883 –
Vol. X, No. 29**

- Mrs. Miles White has purchased of Thompson and Mann the Shear property on East street. Consideration $2,500.

Roulet.

White & Lyman have their Holiday goods in.

Messrs. Benton & Baird are in New York, buying goods for their new store.

C. W. Tauscher has just received several car loads of goods and his store is well filled.

The depot at Pomeroy Bridge is finished and presents a neat appearance.

W. S. Burdick is building a neat dwelling house across the river.

Leroy Lyman arrived home from Michigan, Saturday evening. He and his son Milo killed fifty deer and two otters.

A. V. Lyman has the best piece of winter wheat in this town.

Born to Mr. and Mrs. John Knowlton, a little son and daughter.

Allegany.

The principal topic now is, who favors and who opposes building a new road near Matteson's.

Old Mr. Stryker, while assisting Isaac in some work in the upper part of the barn, accidentally fell and was hurt quite badly.

The many friends of Miss Mary Dwight were glad to welcome her back to Potter. She has been in the West for the last few years, and had been here but a short time, before she was called to take charge of a school. I wish all teachers were as well qualified as she, although I think Allegany may be proud of her teachers, and I wish they might be better paid for their services.

Winter schools commence soon, some next week. J. A. Gardner is to teach at Colesburg, Miss Witter at the Ford school, C. L. Slaughter at Andrews Settlement, Miss Nettie Bishop at Woodville, and Fannie Matteson and Wm. Cool are to teach in Sweden.

Andrews Settlement.

B. F. Bishop has been making quite extensive improvements on his dwelling.

Wm. Currier's new mill is booming.

Smith and Slaughter are nearly through threshing for this year, they report a good Fall business.

C. E. Tucker met with quite a loss a few weeks since, both of his horses dying in one day; but his neighbors turned out in goodly numbers with their teams and nearly finished his plowing.

Edward Tucker is preparing to attend the Commercial school at Elmira.

A new postmaster is to be appointed here soon.

The Potter Enterprise Wednesday Evening, December 5, 1883 – Vol. X, No. 30

- W. B. Rees moves into his new store this week.

- The want of snow is interfering with the lumbering business materially.

- James Johnston is putting up an extensive addition to his livery and hotel barn.

- Miss Bell Haskell has been engaged to assist Miss White in the primary department of the Coudersport Graded School. There were too many scholars for one teacher.

- Hon. Isaac Benson and H. C. Dornan, Esq., have formed a law partnership. They will make a strong team.

Whites Corners.

A. Erway has moved on his farm owned by S. J. Stetson.

S. J. Stetson has moved on the place which he bought of Mrs. N. M. Brooks.

Our school has commenced with Miss Carrie Grover as teacher. She is well liked so far.

D. Hart, of Bingham, and Jennie White, of this place, were married on the eighth inst.

Some sneak broke into the house of J. White, a short time ago, and took a number of valuable household articles also some silverware belonging to his housekeeper.

Sartwell Creek.

Thanksgiving day passed off very pleasantly in this place. There were quite a number of social gatherings and in consequence the turkeys had to suffer the usual penalty.

Winter schools have commenced. First school under the superior management of Sara Cary. Center school taught by Clista Kimm and the third was commenced by Minnie Hammond but on account of illness she has had to return home.

The people of this place collected last Tuesday night at Rev. W. A. Bennett's brining with them their suppers and also leaving nearly twenty-four dollars in the good minister's possession. A good time was also enjoyed.

Mrs. Amanda Fuller left this state a short time ago for the State of Matrimony.

**The Potter Enterprise
Wednesday Evening,
December 12, 1883 –
Vol. X, No. 31**

- Nearly all the cross walks in town need raising. At present they are lower than the road bed.

Forest House.

The mill on Cowley Run has shut down for repairs.

Mr. Ed. Earle of Cowley Run has set out a fine young orchard.

The new school house is not done yet.

Business in the pool room is stopped for the present.

Lumbering is not very brisk for lack of snow.

Briggs' mill has a new planer.

Some of the boys went to Port Allegany Saturday and got pretty well tangled up in Port Allegany whiskey.

Roulet.

C. S. Angood is building a carpenter shop on his lot across the river.

O. E. Marsh, of Yorkshire, N.Y., is clerking in the new store of A. M. Benton & Co.

The tin wedding of Mr. and Mrs. A. V. Lyman was celebrated the evening of the 27th ult., a goodly number of their friends were present, and presented them with several useful presents, among which was a hanging lamp and an arm chair.

The store of A. M. Benton & Co., was opened to the public on the morning of the 3d inst., of course there was a general rush of the fair sex, as there usually is on such an occasion, but whether it was the new goods that attracted them or the new clerk is hard to tell.

The depot has been ceiled, and all that is necessary now to make it a cosy waiting place, is a stove, which we hope the company will furnish at an early day.

Raymond.

We are having many threats of rain, but it does not come. They say the springs and wells are low.

The general health is quite good now, there are a few cases of sickness. Mr. I. Kidney is perhaps the worst off just now, having a severe attack of inflamitory rheumatism.

The schools are going. Mr. F. Woodcock is teaching here, Miss Kochler at the Carr school, Mr. Gardner at Colesburg, Mr. Slaughter at Andrews Settlement, and Mr. Norton on Preston Hill.

There store here is changing hands, Mr. James Moore & Brother succeed Mr. Conable. The latter is fitting up the building opposite for his dwelling. He probably did not know the danger he was exposing to others.

Andrews Settlement.

Yesterday the relatives, friends and neighbors attended the funeral of Mrs. Curtis who died on the eighth, the funeral was held at the residence, and conducted by Rev. Tupper, the Methodist minister in charge here.

C. L. Slaughter commenced teaching the school here last week, he has the reputation of being a first-class teacher.

Township Tidings from Potter County, Pennsylvania
Volume I, 1880 - 1884

We did not hear of many Thanksgiving turkeys being eaten in this place, must be they are all waiting for Christmas.

Nettie Bishop has returned home from Mansfield, and commenced teaching at Woodville to-day.

Those having lumbering to do are waiting anxiously for snow, while the farmer that is a little behindhand with his plowing thinks this open weather a God-send to him.

The Potter Enterprise
Wednesday Evening,
December 19, 1883 –
Vol. X, No. 32

- C. L. Peck had a dozen chickens stolen a few nights since.

- Hops are selling at 21 cents per pound. Last year they brought from 90 cents to $1.00.

- The beautiful snow put in an appearance Tuesday in sufficient quantity to enable ground slide lumbermen to do a good business.

- Ole Snyder and M. J. Colcord have formed a law partnership. Mr. Colcord will have charge of the Coudersport office, over the Corner Store. Give them a call.

- It is said that the Allegany Lumber Company, of which the Bullis Bros. are members, have purchased 400,000,000 feet of timber in the neighborhood of Costelloville, Potter county.

The Potter Enterprise
Wednesday Evening,
December 26, 1883 –
Vol. X, No. 33

- Lumber, bark, log haulers, &c., have had a busy time of it for the past week.

- A. Sidney Lyman, of Eleven Mile, has rented Dr. French's house, Fourth and East street.

Forest House.

The school exhibition here last Friday night was a very pleasant affair, and every one seemed to enjoy it.

Briggs' mill is not running at present.

Mr. Ebenezer Whitney was quite badly hurt a few days ago, a car load of lumber tipped over on him.

The new pool room is completed and in running order.

Lyceum is pretty well attended.

The Potter Enterprise
Wednesday Evening,
January 9, 1884 –
Vol. X, No. 34

- Dr. Wrean is going to North Carolina.

- Wood is selling at $1.50 to $1.75 per cord.

- The cold snap snapped the mercury ten degrees below zero.

- Wm. F. Yunge will soon have a shingle mill in running order, on the Turnpike, cutting out the pine on the Sewards tract.

- The sleighing found most of the lumbermen ready, and anxious to improve it. Those who had from 75,000 to 100,000 to get in have made good time and many of them have finished. Others are well started and a short time will seem out of the woods. Sundays and nights have made no difference with the lumbermen this year. The general impression that this must be a lighter winter has impelled them to use every minute.

Freeman Run.

Mrs. James Bundy has been very sick with pneumonia.

Mr. G. C. Lewis has purchased a portable saw mill. The first location of this mill will be on the farm of Josiah Hackett where Mr. Lewis will saw on a quantity of cherry lumber for W. C. Chesbro, of Lymansville.

Ferris Bundy, who cut his foot several weeks ago, still goes on crutches.

The school, near Frank Klein's, is having a vacation.

West Branch.

Sleighing is now quite good in this valley.

Gale's teams are now hauling bark on sleighs. The largest loads of bark I ever saw are drawn. And very often loads topple over and the language used at that time I think can hardly be found in the English dictionary, nor is it highly edifying.

Mr. Willis Conable's store is now completed. It is 20 x 40 I believe, and presents a very neat appearance.

M. L. Hammond's house is very much improved in appearance by raising the roof and the addition of larger windows.

Hunting for some has been the order of the day. But the luck of many is like the boy who would have caught an enormous trout if it had not fallen from the hook. Enormous deer and bears are seen but they escape just at the wrong moment.

School No. 4 is taught by Carrie Ainesley; No. 3, Hannah Hurd; No. 1, Mary E. Crum.

The health of the people is, generally, good.

Christmas passed very quietly at this place. But at Pike Mills so much spirits were brought in that many were highly exhilarated, but as they are now to have religious services every Sunday we trust the right spirit will ever be felt among them. That which will neither make the hair pull as they complain of nor cause swollen eyes and a bloated visage.

The Potter Enterprise
Wednesday Evening,
January 16, 1884 –
Vol. X, No. 35

- The County Commissioners have appointed George Farnsworth, of Lewisville, Mercantile Appraiser for the year 1884.

- T. J. Gilbert has moved into his new house, on the South side.

Hebron.

Lumbering seems to be the chief interest about here at present, about one hundred thousand feet of logs are being put into the Oswayo Creek daily, between the mouth of the South Branch and the dug-way below.

Miss Lillie Doyle is wielding the birch in our school this winter.

"Grandpa Lewis" whose home is with Mrs. Maurice Clair, has set a worthy example for many a younger man. Although he is seventy years old and has been a humble servant of tobacco since maturity, having satisfied himself that it was injuring his health he, without a word of his purpose to any one, broke off smoking and chewing at once, and is very much pleased with the result; whereas before he could not sleep nights and was suffering terribly from dyspepsia, he can now sleep soundly and eat anything eatable without inconvenience.

Theb. Swift reports their new house a model of comfort and convenience, and those who have seen it agree with him.

Mumm Swift has also a comfortable new house. It beats all how the South Branch is putting on style lately!

Whites Corners.

Mr. John Waters died at his residence on December 30th, 1883, very suddenly. Mr. Waters was very much liked as a neighbor and will be much missed.

Our school is progressing finely under the management of Miss Carrie Grover. She gives general satisfaction.

There is to be a donation, at the house of S. K. Stevens, on Tuesday, January 15th, for the benefit of Rev. Bovier.

Clara.

Our school is doing finely under the supervision of Miss Hurd of Allegany.

Burr Wakely is doing a little lumbering on his own account, this winter.

Asahel Christman is loading logs for Barnes on Whitney Creek.

Harvey Wakely has bought 200 acres of wild land adjoining his father's farm, for lumbering purposes.

Forest House.

Last Friday Mr. Fairbanks, who has been tending lever in Avery's saw mill, had the misfortune to lose a finger.

Charlie Ballou was drawing logs with his horses and got one of them over the banking logs Friday and broke its leg, so he was obliged to kill it.

H. A. Avery has bought a pair of horses.

A. C. Hall lost a good horse last Thursday night. Cause of death unknown.

Harry Otis bought a new organ last week. The agent is reaping a harvest in this place. I believe Harry's was the seventh sold in this place this winter.

Ralph Avery sports a new swell box cutter.

The Potter Enterprise
Wednesday Evening,
January 23, 1884 –
Vol. X, No. 36

- VanWegen's mill has a stock of over a million feet of hemlock already.

- A big black bear was killed on the West Branch, last week, by Jud Burrows. Mr. B. found the bear "holed up" and got within ten feet of bruin before he fired his gun.

- H. C. Olmsted and family have removed to Emporium. Coudersport has lost a good citizen and Emporium makes a gain. Clint will engage in the hardware business at Emporium, and the citizens of that section will find him a very pleasant and reliable man to deal with. We wish him abundant success in his new field.

- Lumbermen report more snow in the woods now than at any one time during last winter.

- David White and family will soon occupy the house bought, by him last Fall, of O. J. Rees.

- Butter is worth 25 cents per pound, and eggs 28 to 30 cents per dozen, in the Coudersport market.

Freeman Run.

H. H. Beebe is putting a porch on his house.

H. Bridges sports a bran new cutter.

G. C. Lewis has his saw mill running and we suppose if one were near enough they could hear the buzz of the mill wheel, noisy and loud.

G. R. Reed and Alfred Reed are having lumber sawed, each intending to put up a new house in the spring.

A. H. Crosby has finished his job of skidding logs on Elm Flat, and moved back home.

John Bundy has returned from his three months trip in Nebraska, looking as natural as old peaches.

Lyceum every Tuesday evening.

Millport.

The chief event of interest in this place seems to be the establishment of a pool table at the corner of Main and Water streets in the second story of a barn owned by Frank Hallet, and rented for the present to Rans. Munger.

Elsie Dickinson reports from the lumber woods of Michigan. Elsie is a live boy, and means, instead of waiting for something to turn up, to turn something up.

Miss Douglas is doing good work in our school this winter.

Oswayo.

There is enough sickness reported to keep the M.D.'s on the go.

The "oil well" is down 1600 feet, or the hole is said to be of that depth, and most of the company wish to sink it to 2000 or find oil. This "wild cat" has had the usual run of ups and downs and fulfilled its duty of getting up an excitement occasionally. A certain clairvoyant has predicted that out of the series of uphill work and mishaps oil should be produced and Oswayo develop as an oil territory. May this prediction be fully realized is the fervent desire of the average Oswayoan.

The G. A. R.'s had a supper of bean soup, coffee and crackers on the occasion of installation of officers of A. W. Estes Post, Saturday evening, the 12th inst.

Commander S. J. White, of G. H. Barnes Post, Sharon, installed the officers elect in public and the attendance was quite large. The new Commander blew the calls. No one seem disposed to attend the Doctor's call, but when the bugle called "cups and platters" all fell to as "one man" and dipped his soup or coffee and drew the ration of "hard tack." The officers for 1884 are Commander L. D. Estes; G. V. Markham, S.V.C.; Geo. Crouch, J.V.C.; J. C. Wilkinson, Adgt.; John Morley, Q.M.; G. R. Wilber, Surg.; N. Hill, Chap.; John Davis, O.D.; V. R. Kenyon, O.G.; J. B. Stewart, S.M.; W. Fessenden, Q.M.S. The Post is in a fair way to prosper under the newly elected officers.

The Sons of Veteran's Camp is to have a public installation of their officers on the evening of the 19th. Commander J. B. Stewart has been detailed to install them. The boys are in earnest to have a live Camp and show themselves true sons of soldiers.

The Potter Enterprise
Wednesday Evening,
January 30, 1884 –
Vol. X, No. 37

- Charley Osmer, of Coudersport, is laid up with a lame foot, the bit of an axe in one foot the cause.

- VanWegen's mill has been idle for a few days, on account of the burning out of two flues in the boiler. It is again running.

- Last Saturday morning was one of the coldest ever experienced in this section. Thermometers in different sections of the borough registered from 22 to 30 degrees below zero.

The Potter Enterprise
Wednesday Evening,
February 6, 1884 –
Vol. X, No. 38

- O. J. Rees has removed to the house recently vacated by Dr. Wrean.

- A. A. Allen, of Lewisville, has rented the house now occupied by Dr. Mattison, and will soon remove to Coudersport.

The Potter Enterprise
Wednesday Evening,
February 13, 1884 –
Vol. X, No. 39

- The Rees shop at the upper end of town, vacant so long that the memory of man runneth not to the contrary, is being remodeled into a hotel by Leonard Davis.

- VanWegen, Quimby & Co., had ten or fifteen thousand feet of hemlock and cherry go estray last week, by the breaking of their boom. The logs will be picked up below, and their loss will be simply the sawing.

- S. P. Olmsted had his dog property increased two hundred dollars worth, a day or two since. His thorough-bred bird dog brought forth nine little thorough-breds.

Freeman Run.
News items are very scarce, exceedingly so here.

Township Tidings from Potter County, Pennsylvania
Volume I, 1880 - 1884

H. H. Beebe is busy putting scroll work around the pillars of his porch.

The donation party last week, at the residence of C. W. Dingee, passed off very pleasantly, about $14 was raised for the Rev. Mr. Sheets.

The recent rains have raised the water and doing much damage to the roads.

West Branch.

We are having quite a flood in the West Branch creek. The road is impassable below here, caused by saw logs that have closed the channel in the creek, causing the water to settle back into the road.

The ice went out on Wednesday, making some ice jams, and taking out two bridges across the West Branch, one at Erastus Crippens and the other at Gale's tannery.

On Wednesday, Mr. Wm. Perry of Lewisville, lost a pair of horses while trying to cross the West Branch at Erastus Crippen's. Mr. Perry's son was driving the team, he attempted to cross the creek above the falls. Mr. Crippen saw that the team was not likely to make the shore, so he went to help them, he reached the horses but instead of his helping them out they pulled him into the water and they all went over the falls together. Mr. Crippen caught on the pier of the bridge and remained there until they got a rope to him and drew him ashore. Young Perry went on down with the team to near an ice jam when he got to the shore and saw the team and sled go under the ice out of sight. The team was found next day some distance below. It is a winder that both men were not drowned, for neither of them can swim.

Hebron.

I regret that I have to report sickness from almost every part of our town. Rosa Clair has been dangerously ill of congestion of the lungs; she is slowly recovering. James Moyer is very sick with typhoid fever. Peter Scutt has a child sick with scarlet fever. Wm. Sprague is not expected to live; has typhoid pneumonia.

Lumbering is lively and long continued. W. J. Brown, of Millport, has twenty teams hauling logs from Crandall Hill, near the old "Cold Spring," to Oswayo; he has a million to get in. Barnes' teams have nearly caught up with the skidders.

Mr. Burdic, of Maine Settlement, has gone home with a horse disabled by a bad calk. Frank Hallet lost a horse from calking a few days since, but about $90 was contributed at once to buy another. Solomon Lamberton has also lost a horse this winter; and Henry Lamberton has lost an ox.

The Potter Enterprise
Wednesday Evening,
February 20, 1884 –
Vol. X, No. 40

- Yunge's shingle mill, at Cherry Springs, is doing a good business.

- A. B. Crowell has purchased the interest of O. J. Rees in the brick block, Main and Second street, erected last Summer.

- The iron and cement for the fire proof vaults in the Commissioner's office has been received. About 30,000 pounds of iron is now at the Court house awaiting the workmen.

- The building boom for next Spring is not very promising.

- W. T. Dike, the Coudersport Baker, has opened a branch establishment at Port Allegany.

- Dr. E. S. Mattison and F. J. Norton now occupy two of A. B. Mann's new houses on Fourth street.

Whites Corners.

The people have been troubled very much for the want of water, but just now have rather too much.

Samuel Robinson, one of the oldest settlers of the town, was buried at this place on the 14th inst.

A. A. Ross has moved from this place to Harrison Valley.

W. B. Jennings has a fine lot of new sap buckets, he is preparing to make sugar.

A few days ago as Alfred Hufteling was hauling bark, he overturned a load, part of it falling on him, injuring him quite badly, but at last accounts he was recovering.

H. Warner has rented his farm to Mr. Ormsby, and has moved into a house near his son's store.

F. Zimmer is having the factory repaired for the summer's cheese-making.

The Potter Enterprise Wednesday Evening, February 27, 1884 – Vol. X, No. 41

- H. J. Olmsted's grocery has changed hands. S. P. Olmsted is now proprietor and all will find him obliging and fair to deal with. Call on S. P.

- Work has commenced on two fire-proof vaults in the Commissioner's office. One will take the place of the old vault with the wooden door, and the other will take the place between the stairs and the office, and opening into the Commissioners' office.

- A very little maple sugar has already been made in this county.

- Wm. Shear and Myres, from Lyman's mill, expect to run the new mill at Pomeroy Bridge.

- John Darcey is making considerable improvement in his property at the upper end of Main Street.

- The VanWegen & Quimby mill is running on full time and disposing of the lumber about as fast as cut.

- S. P. Olmsted is putting up a fine specimen of the wild cat tribe, which weighs 24 ½ pounds. The cat was killed by Leroy Lyman, of Roulet.

Raymond.

Mr. Levi Moore is quite ill. He got a strain while lifting.

Mr. Jno. Bacon is about to move to Westfield. He is now building a house at Gold, for Mr. Frank Raymond.

Mr. Joseph Ayers is setting up housekeeping in Westfield.

**The Potter Enterprise
Wednesday Evening,
March 5, 1884 –
Vol. X, No. 42**

- J. M. Bassett is now running the James Johnston livery.

- James Johnston has purchased the Harrison Valley stage route owned by Mr. Rossman.

- W. W. Grover, of Sweden, will sell at auction on Saturday, March 8th, several horses, farming implements, household goods, &c.

Oswayo.
Everyone in this place is sick with bad colds, or have been, or are gong to be.

There is to be a social dance at the Lee House the evening of March 17th, under the auspices of the G. A. R.; bill $1.50. Hope the "old boys" will have a full house, a good time and no whiskey.

A billiard table in the Lee House parlor is the new attraction. Dell Estes takes the change.

Loaded teams go off the dugroad embankments. Alex. Pilon's team and load of shingles went of some thirty feet down – below the Shingle House, and are all right yet for business.

West Pike.
At present log floating is the business of the day.

Andrew Luce and E. P. Turck have each a new boy, and C. A. Turck is the happy possessor of another girl.

G. H. Flynn has purchased a lot of S. J. Acker and is building a house thereon.

J. M. Kilbourne keeps quite a stock of groceries.

Our place can boast of two groceries within a stone's throw of each other. Opposition is the life of business.

Keating.
We hope it was the March lion that roared so the last of February. We are tired of winter.

G. C. Lewis' saw mill is turning out considerable lumber.

A few Keating folks went to Crandall Hill, on Feb. 29th, to join with the prohibitionists of that place in organizing the prohibition party in Potter. "They do say" we are a trumped up party that must draw its forces from the republican ranks. In that case the Enterprise will probably wish us a limited success? Any one wishing to learn about the platform can do so by writing to Mr. Orson Card, Sec., at Hebron, Pa. We intend to meet in Coudersport, April 1st.

Keating Summit seems to be the boys' purgatory. Some time ago one was nearly killed in jumping from a car. Three weeks ago another had broke his thigh in playing on the hill, and two weeks ago Mr. Borie's little Marty broke his wrist. About time for the next.

Freeman Run.

Folks are beginning to talk of sugaring.

Alfred Rees has gone to Port Allegany to work in the harness shop.

If the old adage, "a fog in February brings a frost in June," comes true this year garden sass will be apt to get nipped a little.

Miss Agnes Bundy burnt her hand quite bad on Monday last.

Jewell Dingee is quite sick with inflammatory rheumatism.

The young people enjoyed a party at John Bundy's Wednesday evening.

The Potter Enterprise
Wednesday Evening,
March 12, 1884 –
Vol. X, No. 43

- A break in the race has stopped business at the Keystone Mill.

- J. O. Edgecomb, formerly of Coudersport, is now keeping a hotel in Tioga, Pa.

- S. P. Olmsted, with the aid of paint, paper, &c., has made his grocery one of the neatest in town.

- The fire-proof vaults in the Court House have been completed. The county records will now be safe.

- A. B. Mann, the coming summer, intends to erect a brick building next to the Bank for a law office, printing office, &c.

- On Tuesday afternoon Frank Monroe, of Coudersport, met with a sad accident while working in the VanWegen & Quimby mill. He was engaged in taking lumber from the saw, and in trying to remove a heavy 3-inch plank it fell, striking him on the left leg, just above the ankle, breaking both bones.

Whites Corners.

Wintry weather at present but no sleighing.

Wm. Jennings has sold his farm to John Riley. Consideration, $40 per acre.

John H. White has let his place and intends moving to Harrison Valley soon.

C. Story intends moving to York's Corners the first of April.

A. P. Elder is the man that steps high at present. It is a boy, weighing eight pounds.

A. J. McCutcheon is building a house on his uncle's farm where he is going to move as soon as the house is finished.

The Potter Enterprise
Wednesday Evening,
March 19, 1884 –
Vol. X, No. 44

- Major Seibert talks of removing from Wharton to Coudersport, and starting a boarding house.

- A. L. Hollenbeck, for the past few months a resident of Colorado, has returned to Potter for a short time. He intends making Colorado his future home.

- Charles and O. A. Nelson have bought the meat market lot on Main street, of Mrs. Haven. Consideration $800. A new building will be erected in the Spring.

- C. J. Marble and family have removed to Potter Brook.

- George Brehmer and family, for the past year residents of Georgetown, South Carolina, have returned to old Potter. Many friends will be glad to welcome them.

- W. C. Yeomans has returned from Columbus, Ohio, where he has been for the past six months learning to hammer saws. He is now prepared to repair saws or furnish new ones.

Millport.

The death of Dillie, wife of James Munger, of this place, has caused a feeling of sadness throughout the neighborhood. She had made many friends and she will be missed by old and young. Her husband has the heartfelt sympathy of all.

The children of Mr. Hyde have had the scarlet fever, but are recovering.

There have also been a few cases of diphtheria. Mrs. Munger is supposed to have died with this disease.

Miss Fannie Brown, of Millport, and Mr. Eugene Drake, of Sunnyside, were recently united in marriage. We wish them all happiness in life.

Albert Graves, of Sharon Centre, lost a valuable cow a few days since. I did not learn the cause of her death.

There is talk of the gas company running the gas to this place.

The people of Sharon Centre have managed to keep up an interesting lyceum through the winter.

Keating.

Mr. B. S. Cowell is about to close his lumber job, having sold his store to Mr. Briggs.

C. W. Dingee was hurt by a falling sapling, last week, but is around now.

J. W. Bundy is quite sick with pneumonia; attended by Dr. Chas. French, of Coudersport.

Jewell Dingee, who has been seriously ill for over a month, with inflammatory rheumatism, is on the gain.

Mr. Arthur Rees returned from Coldwater, Mich., on the 13th inst; his family having come a few weeks in advance. He reached the depot at the Summit so exhausted, with ague, that he could not get to the house of his father-in-law without assistance. A doctor was promptly summoned, but he is still quite sick. We understand he has come back to stay.

Potter county does not make as many flattering promises as some places, but she is a reliable old friend, after all.

The Potter Enterprise
Wednesday Evening,
March 26, 1884 –
Vol. X, No. 45

- New maple sugar sold at twelve cents per pound on Monday.

- M. T. Seibert has rented the Lamberton building, on Third street, and will open a boarding house about the 1st of April.

- Ties and timber are being cut for the extension of the narrow gauge from Gaines to Pike Mills. The road will be built to the latter place early the coming summer.

Forest House.

Mr. Eb. Whitney was very sick Sunday. Also Mrs. Charlie Colwell. Mrs. Colwell has erysipelas in her arms.

Avery's mill is running quite brisk just now.

The dance at the boarding house last week was a pleasant affair, at least all seemed to enjoy themselves.

Mr. Colwell has sold his mercantile business to G. D. Briggs, who took possession immediately. I heard Mr. Bedford, who has been clerking for Colwell, was to leave, but am glad to state he is to remain in his old place.

Quarterly Meeting next Saturday and Sunday, at Liberty, under the auspices of the United Brethren church.

Lots of mud, some rain and not much sugar weather.

Mr. Whitney's son-in-law, Mr. Rees, who has just returned from Kansas, has had a very hard time with fever and ague; but, I am glad to say he is much better and in a fair way to recover from it entirely.

Some of the boys went to Liberty and got full of hard cider and as a consequence some of them got their eyes blacked a little.

The Potter Enterprise
Wednesday Evening,
April 2, 1884 –
Vol. X, No. 46

- E. A. Norton, of Oswayo, is attending the Mansfield business college.

- On Monday last a team belonging to J. M. Bassett became frightened on Main street, and ran away, throwing Mr. Bassett out of the wagon. They jumped the fence south of the livery barn, leaving the wagon on the roadside; damages slight.

Millport.

Daniel Rogers has been quite sick with inflammation of the lungs.

No new cases of diptheria.

People are putting up their fences and getting ready for spring work.

There is also a little business in the way of running logs.

Hon. Wm. Colwell, of Manistique, Mich., has just come to this place and will be welcomed by all.

Hebron.

There is much sickness about here.

Miss Ada Lamberton is very sick. Is thought to have diphtheria.

Henry Lamberton, jr., had the misfortune to get a foot smashed in the lumber woods the other day.

Will Cone has purchased fifty acres of land on the South Branch, of Solomon Lamberton; consideration $800.

Amos Coe and family are at Mrs. Cone's and they are going to move back at once.

Mrs. Terwillegar and daughter Mollie will make their home, for some time at least, in Alfred Center, N.Y., in order that Miss Mollie may have the advantages of the University. Florentine Stevens will occupy Mrs. Terwillegar's house and see to her business in her absence.

Every one almost is suffering from Influenza and neuralgia.

James Mattison has the boss yoke of oxen; coming five years old this spring and weighing thirty-five hundred.

On March 3d the friends of "Aunt Maria" Stillman and husband gave them a joyful surprise. It was their fortieth marriage anniversary. About sixty friends assembled bringing a sumptuous dinner and presents valued at over fifty dollars. "Aunt Maria" as everybody calls her, was overwhelmed with astonishment to think of anybody else doing for her, she having been so much in the habit of doing for others. She has always worked hard, and has raised five children, not her own, beside caring for an invalid husband. Even now she has taken to her heart and home a little motherless babe, and spite of the privations and seeming hardships of life, persists in considering it a blessing. May her days be long upon the earth, and may many, seeing her good works and the beauty and simplicity of her happy life, go and do likewise.

Genesee Forks.

There has been considerable improvement in this place, in some respects, the past winter.

J. Carpenter's store has been remodeled and very much improved. The Postoffice being in the front and the business office in the lower part. It is now so arranged as to present a very attractive appearance.

George Leache's store is completed. It has a large glass front and is nicely finished. A large hall being over the entire store where all the lodges meet. K. of H., G. A. R. and E. A. U.

Childs, proprietor of the hotel, has introduced a pool table, which adds much to the attraction of the bar room, for some. "If you can't pay don't play" is the sentiment adopted, I believe; but read by one, "if you can't play don't pay."

Stephen Hurd has purchased the farm owned by Ansel Hickox.

Athen Allen has rented the Cobb property formerly owned by W. Slawson.

We hear that a meat market is soon to be erected.

The cheese factory is to commence operation May 1st.

Mrs. John B. Leet, who has been visiting her parents (Mr. and Mrs. B. Easton) for the past winter, has now returned to her home in Guyandotte, West Va. While here, news of the flood very much disturbed her, as her family were all there but one child. The first news she had was that Guyandotte's submerged, but on receiving news from them only 8 ½ feet of water was in their house. When they left the house it was by means of a boat, of their own make, stepping into it from the chamber window.

Mr. Jerome Leet, formerly of this vicinity, lost every building, saved nothing but a few household goods. Even his fruit trees were uprooted.

Give me the hills of old Potter.

Mrs. George Hackett has been quite sick, threatened with pneumonia.

Carlos Hackett it is feared will be totally blind. He has suffered much, during the past winter, with severe pain in the head and eyes, thought to be caused by previous injuries received on his head. He can now see but very little.

Religious services at this place once in two weeks, Rev. Congdon pastor.

Roulet.

I. J. Raymer is building a dwelling house on his lot on Main street.

The boarding house for A. M. Benton & Co.'s mill hands is nearly completed.

Will Lewis' house, on Fishing Creek, is nearly ready for occupancy.

Work on the school house has been resumed.

Born – To Mr. and Mrs. John Tenbrock, a little son.

Mrs. R. L. White gave a sugar party at her house last Thursday night. About twenty young people were invited, and all had an enjoyable time.

Keating.

We are informed that the oil derrick on the farm of Giles Allard is completed and ready for operation.

Joe. Wetzel at Keating Summit is very low with inflammitory rheumatism.

C. M. Dingee left his school for the sugar camp.

John Bundy has a large sugar orchard, also G. C. Lewis and E. Fourness. The other neighbors do their work on a modest scale. The cry is for a few car loads of "the beautiful," etc., to bring a plentiful supply of sap, and to haul a few thousand logs to the mill on.

West Pike.

The roads are very bad and business quite dull.

The weather is suggestive of maple sugar, but we haven't heard of their being much made as yet.

Our immediate vicinity was thrown into quite an excitement yesterday by the accident which befell little Virgil Acker. He fell from the store steps striking among the feet of a span of horses that were tied to a tree that stands near the stoop. One of the horses stepped on his head, cutting it severely and mangling one ear very badly. Though seriously injured, we entertain hopes of his recovery ere long.

C. M. Kilbourne has his building up we see. It is rumored that he too is about to engage in the mercantile business.

Harry Flynn, M. P. Flynn's little boy, is reported to be very sick.

Mrs. Jerry Baker is very sick at this writing and fears are entertained that she may not recover.

**The Potter Enterprise
Wednesday Evening,
April 9, 1884 –
Vol. X, No. 47**

- Judge Hammond has sold his house and lot to Lyman and Hall T. Nelson. Consideration $1,700.

- James Wright, a prominent lumberman of Sharon township, has failed. Liabilities about fourteen thousand dollars; assets, very small.

- James Johnston has removed to Dr. French's house recently occupied by Luther Seibert; Seibert has rented rooms in the house occupied by C. W. Hungerford; Ben. Berfield is in the French house with C. W. Welton; Mrs. Irene Berfield has moved to the cottage; Merv Calkins has occupied the house vacated by Benj. Berfield, on Water street; Will Basset is in the house recently occupied by J. M. Bassett and J. M. Basset has moved to the house near his livery stable; M. T. Seibert has moved into the Lamberton building; A. Sidney Lyman moves into the house recently purchased by him of James Johnston, and Fred Devanport takes the house vacated by Mr. Lyman; Dan McConneky has moved into the Butterworth house; the railroad blacksmith has rented Forster's house and Dr. Ashcraft is to occupy Mrs. L. C. Ross' house. There may have been other changes recently, but we do not happen to think of them just now.

- Tuesday was not a good day for the fishing. Not less than fifty pounds were caught within five miles of Coudersport.

- W. A. Butler, of Sweden, has an egg, laid by a golden pheasant hen, which measures 6 x 7 ¾ inches in circumference.

- The Borough Council have appointed M. S. Thompson Street Commissioner and D. C. Larrabee Fire Marshal for the coming year.

- On Tuesday afternoon of last week, L. W. Crawford's dwelling, in Roulet, burned to the ground. The fire is supposed to have caught from a defective stove pipe. Although help was not very plenty nearly all the furniture and clothing was removed. Some heavy articles and the carpets were burned. Mr. Crawford has a very fine library, about half of which burned, and many of the volumes saved were badly damaged. The loss on the library must have been over one thousand dollars, and the entire loss is from three to four thousand dollars. No insurance.

Roulet.
The residence of L. W. Crawford was burned Tuesday afternoon, April 1st. The house, furniture and a valuable library of about one thousand volumes was consumed. No insurance.

South Coudersport.
G. H. Grabe has enclosed his lot.
The Kiehl property has been improved by the setting out of

shade trees, as is also the case in front of the Mark Gillon property.

Edward Forster has rented his house to a Mr. Kennard, an employee of the C. & P. A. R. R.

Will Abson has built a fence on two sides of his lot.

Rev. H. B. Leavenworth has resigned his pastorate of the Baptist church and we understand will preach at Port Allegany.

The sidewalk question has received considerable attention of late in this locality.

An addition is being built to the house of Mrs. Schildberger, recently occupied by Will Bassett.

The lots of J. L. Knox and A. A. Hodskin are being fenced.

Mrs. Vina Baker is building a new porch on her house.

A mud hole at the foot of Dutch Hill needs the care of the street commissioner.

West Branch.

Log driving is nearly over for this season here. We have had a very nice flood.

Wm. Putnam's drive, of about three million feet, went out first.

About a week ago Steel & Co.'s drive, of about one million feet, went out. These all go to Williamsport, and are hemlock.

Since the above drives went out, Lon Mitchell has drove about one hundred thousand feet of hemlock for Mr. Clinton, for his mill that he is building at the mouth of the West Branch. These will be saved at Mr. Gale's saw mill.

White & Metzgar are now filling their boom, at the Mitchell mill, with their cherry, ash and pine logs, they have a stock of about five hundred thousand feet.

Mr. Peter Edgcomb, of Westfield, is here rigging up White & Metzgar's saw mill. He is nearly done and in a few days we will hear the music of the circular saw.

Fishermen, from abroad, have already put in an appearance here.

Some of the men on Steel & Co.'s log drive are just returning and report the drive hung up for want of water at Four Mile Run.

Sharon Centre.

No farming done yet, except a little repairing of fences.

The roads are so bad that not much teaming is being done.

Emigration seems to be at its height just now.

Chas. Cronk, who has been doing Mr. Dodge's chores this winter, has moved out of, and into another, of E. A. Grave's houses, preparatory to moving back on his farm this spring.

Oscar Burdic has emigrated from the house owned by Mrs. Lamb, and taken up his abode in the one vacated by Mr. Cronk.

Mr. Elias Prindle has moved over on Sunny Side, having had to get out of Jerome Dodge's house, on the Wild Cat, in order that Warren Colgrove might have it, as he had taken the farm this year.

There has been considerable sickness here this spring, though at present there is not very much, except a few cases of the measles which I understand are not very serious.

Mr. D. Dodge has lost five or six sheep this spring from some kind of a disease, they don't know what.

Mr. Dana Drake has gone over to Oildom to work, until farming begins anyway, if not longer. He is dressing tools on a well for Mr. Carter.

Business seems to be quite dull here at present, though our young merchant manages to keep up an average trade, and appears to have good spirits, notwithstanding the heartending trials of the past winter.

There is considerable excitement prevailing over the sale of Jim Wright's property on the Honeoye.

**The Potter Enterprise
Wednesday Evening,
April 16, 1884 –
Vol. X, No. 48**

- G. W. Johnston, of Clara, has rented the Ross farm at Lymansville, and will take possession this week.

- A brother of George Green, of Coudersport, was elected a member of the St. Louis Board of Health. This is the first colored man so honored in St. Louis.

- Dr. S. A. Phillips, the dentist, is suffering from a singular accident. In pulling a tooth a piece of the shell was thrown from the forceps striking the ball of his eye. The eye is now badly inflamed.

- Joseph Greisel has purchased twenty five feet front on Main street, from the south side of the old Hotel lot owned by D. F. Glassmire, paying therefor $1,000. Mr. Greisel has commenced the erection of a two story, 24 x 45 feet building for a harness shop and residence.

- Grass is beginning to show up green.

- The snow drifts are about gone from the hills.

- F. B. Nelson is erecting a new barn on Fourth street.

- Frank Stevens started for Southern California on Monday last.

- Luther Tolls has commenced work on his house on the side hill.

- J. L. Knox is building a new side walk on East street, south side.

- A roller skating rink is one of the proposed enterprises liable to strike Coudersport soon.

- John Dorsy is rigging up the foundry building, at the upper end of town, in a substantial manner.

- Laura Boleigh, of Yochum Hill, has recently received a back pension of $2,040, and will receive $8 per month.

Andrews Settlement.

Our winter school has closed a few week's since. It was a success.

Our Summer School is being taught by Miss J. Benzolds. This will be here third term here.

We have had sickness and death in our midst during the winter. A little child of Wm. Dennis died with pneumonia. Mrs. Simmons and old Mrs. Tucker are still sick, but slowly recovering.

Clara Furman has changed her name to Haskell and her residence to Colesburg. May joy, peace and happiness be hers.

New officers have been appointed for the Cemetery, and a movement is being made to build a new fence, and make other improvements. It is to be hoped that the cattle will be kept out at least.

Lyceum has been adjourned until October next.

Dime parties are being held, the proceeds to be used in getting lamps for the school room.

George W. James has been appointed postmaster at this place.

E. J. Kies has moved to the Cavanaugh place.

W. A. Gardner works his father's farm.

Norman Cool has commenced housekeeping at Ellisburg.

Eugene Plants has commenced work for B. F. Bishop.

Freeman Run.

The past week has been a very bush one for sugar makers. Lots of sap to care for which makes plenty of work.

The sick of the neighborhood are on the gain.

G. C. Lewis is running his saw mill night and day now preparatory to moving it to Homer. He is also making sugar, though when he gets time to make that we hardly know. It always did bother people to keep track of G. C. any way.

"Nice weather?" said one of the neighbors to G. R. Reed last Sunday. Riley took off his cap, put it under his arm, scratched his head and replied, "Nice! Well, yes, we think so, it's a girl!"

**The Potter Enterprise
Wednesday Evening,
April 23, 1884 –
Vol. X, No. 49**

- F. A. Nelson has moved back to Colesburg.

- F. B. Nelson has his new barn up on Fifth street.

- A. A. Allen has purchased a lot of W. B. Gordnier, 30 feet front on West street and four rods deep. Consideration, $400.

- The large hotel at Cross Fork, occupied by John D. Merranville, burned to the ground Monday evening. We have not learned the particulars.

- In digging J. Greisel's cellar on Main street, beech logs and brush were found at a depth of about three feet. The logs may have been part of a shanty and the brush, probably, its roof. The logs were as sound as the day they were cut, even the bark remaining. How long they had been in the ground no one knows.

South Coudersport.

The James Johnston house is fast approaching completion, and will be ready for occupancy in about a month. When done it will add very much to the appearance of this section.

L. R. Bliss is preparing to erect an addition to his house.

Mrs. P. A. Stebbins' house will soon be completed.

James L. Knox is building a new sidewalk in front of his East street property.

Born, to Mr. and Mrs. G. H. Grabe, on Thursday, the 17th inst., a son.

Harrison Koon is about to enlarge his grocery store.

Erastus Lewis has moved his barn to the north line of his lot.

H. T. Nelson has moved into the house recently vacated by Judge Hammond.

Patrick Carey has opened a meat market in his building, formerly occupied by Mr. Hanlon.

The Coudersport Cornet Band, having its headquarters in this locality, and feeling desirous of their success, we take this opportunity to suggest that, inasmuch as they are doing all in their power to become an honor to us and willingly furnish the town with music from time to time, we should assist them in their worthy enterprise, either by a donation, festival or something calculated to encourage them. We are informed that the boys are about to uniform themselves. Don't allow them to undergo this expense without doing something substantial by way of assistance.

Dan Neefe and Mrs. Warner have new sidewalks in front of their premises.

Freeman Run.

Once more this little neighborhood has been called upon to mourn and sympathize with those whom death has afflicted. On Monday morning, the 14th, all were grieved to hear of the death of Laurie Bridges, who had been sick with inflammatory rheumatism. Tuesday afternoon came a message, from St. Mary's, telling of the death of her oldest brother, Herman, who had been sick for some time with consumption, the funeral, which had been appointed for Wednesday, was postponed until the next day, to give them time to bring the body of her brother home. The funeral was largely attended on Thursday; the services being conducted by Rev. A. A. Craw. As there was no visable sign of decay, it was concluded only to bury the remains of the son; so strange had been the death of Laurie, so unexpected, that a faint hope was entertained, by some, that life was not extinct. Her remains were kept until Sunday, lacking less than twenty-four hours of being a week from the time she died. Even then the remains looked perfectly natural; that it seemed more like a peaceful sleep than like death. Laurie was one who had many friends, a true christian girl. What more could be said of her.

Herman Bridges was formerly a resident of this place. He leaves a young wife to whom he had been married only about nine months. The family have the sympathy of their many friends in this, their double bereavement.

Clara.

Miss Dora Allen is teaching the school at Millport.

Miss Laura Tyler has just returned after teaching five months at Sizerville, Cameron county.

Monstrosities, of the calf kind, are in order. T. Glines and Peter Bateman have each had a specimen.

The mud is so deep that our telephone don't work, so news is scarce at headquarters.

Whites Corners.

Plenty of mud in this section and the weather very disagreeable.

Very little farming done.

F. Zimmer has sold his interest in the store of Warner & Zimmer to his partner. Will intends to carry on the business alone in the future.

Mr. Zimmer has the management of the cheese factory at this place also the one at the North Fork.

W. B. Jennings has bought a place at Harrison Valley and intends moving there in a short time.

C. Story has moved to Yorks Corners.

C. Slater is repairing his house. He is improving both the looks and convenience of it.

Hebron.

School has not commenced yet. Who is to teach?

Miss Buckbee had twelve teachers in her class, for examination, in this town April 7th.

Henry Press has bought the farm of A. Salomen; consideration, $3,000. Mr. Press has taken possession.

Henry Lamberton has made 400 lbs. of maple sugar.

Delos Lamberton has moved back to Mr. Lamberton's.

Soloman Lamberton is putting in a mill dam.

Quarterly meeting, last Saturday and Sunday, at the Hydorn school house.

Ellisburg.

Sugaring is nearly done and there seems to have been only a few bushes which have come up to their usual record for quantity but the quality is excellent.

We are informed that John Pye and sons, in J. C. Curtis's bush, have made about 2 ¾ pounds to the tree, and that Ira Bishop's bush has scored fully 3 lbs. to the tree.

We are glad to notice the improvements. O. Ellis is digging a cellar for a new house to be built this coming summer.

Wm. Eaton is preparing to add a new porch to his new store, on Brooklyn side.

Mrs. DeRock has a new fence around her lot.

Mrs. Handcock has the lumber on the ground for a house on the road towards Andrew's Settlement.

Many of our farmers are enjoying the luxury of buying hay.

The general health is excellent, though we understand that Mrs. Stillman is quite poorly at present.

Our quarterly meeting passed off much to the satisfaction of all. Presiding Elder Chamberlain gave us two discourses which were real treats.

It is announced that Rev. Leavenworth will deliver his lecture on Thomas Paine, next

Sunday evening, April 27th. Those who heard his lecture some weeks ago will not forget the date.

Sharon Centre.

Our literary society has been adjourned until the coming fall, on account of the bad roads and the long summer days to soon to follow.

Oscar Burdic, since he moved, has reshingled the veranda and repaired the inside of the house which adds much to the comfort of the occupants.

One of E. A. Graves' colts was taken very sick a few days ago, but has now recovered.

The Wild Cat school had to close last week, on account of the measles getting in the neighborhood.

Mr. E. A. Graves has just finished building a good substantial picket fence around his strawberry bed, which looks as though he intends to relish the first shortcake, in preference to letting the average small boy scale the fence and pluck the fruit.

Dana Drake has come home from Rixford, where he has been at work for the past month.

James Donovan has moved back from Rixford, on Mr. D. Dodge's farm, and Dewitt Gustin has moved over in the house vacated by Donovan, where they expect to stay this summer.

Chas. Cronk has again moved. This time he has moved back on his farm.

Mrs. Lamb has rented her house and lot here to Mr. Hawks, who has moved in and taken possession.

T. J. Burdic is quite sick at present though they think he is not dangerous.

The sugar makers, in this vicinity, haven't stopped work yet, though they have made considerable sugar this spring.

The Potter Enterprise
Wednesday Evening,
April 30, 1884 –
Vol. X, No. 50

Roulet.

N. R. Bard has rented rooms of N. French, and removed his family from Port Allegany.

Judge Hammond has rented J. A. Sampson's house and lot, and is now a resident of our little town.

Ed. Strang has bought a farm on Pine Creek, and will move there the last of the week.

Fire in the woods for the past few days has destroyed valuable timber, etc. The mill and dwelling of W. S. Burdick was in danger of being burned on Sunday.

Around Olmsteds.

Mr. Phillip Lehman has removed his garden from the corner above the road to the place vacated by the barn he moved last year. It will add much to the attractiveness of his home.

Jacob Lehman's little babe has been very sick, but is slowly regaining its health.

Mr. Louis Lehman is under treatment for typhoid pneumonia. His friends wish him a speedy recovery.

D. D. Everett's house caught fire about noon, the 26th day of April, from a spark on the roof.

Thanks to Mr. Ingraham, who saw the fire when it first caught, and helped extinguish it. There was no damage except to the roof.

Mr. Chestain, who bought the Fleshutz farm on Nelson Run, is doing a fine job on the old follow. He has made signal improvements in the year he has occupied the place.

**The Potter Enterprise
Wednesday Evening,
May 7, 1884 –
Vol. XI, No. 1**

Raymond.

This neighborhood is going along in its even course, with no excitable interruption, except the fires, which raged terribly Friday last, burning up Mr. George Collins' house and barn, with his best clothes and all of his wife's clothing except what she had on her back at the time.

At the same time it turned Mr. L. D. Swift and family out doors, and laid all he had in ashes, not even saving his Bible.

But fire and wind have not made all the changes. Mr. Burdick has just moved on to the Simon Byam farm.

A. G. Presho's widow has moved into Mr. James Moore's house.

Water does not seem to be scarce, yet the most needed thing, perhaps, is rain.

The prospect now is for a large yield of wheat. We have not seen or heard of a poor piece. But just about here there is not much to be seen.

South Coudersport.

A new fence has been erected on the Gillon property.

L. R. Bliss has made marked improvements on his lot by grading, fencing, etc.

The walk, ordered to be laid on Oak street, from Borie to Main streets, has been built from E. J. Fickler's to A. Jones' corner. What's the matter with the rest of it?

Will Ford is confined to the house by sickness.

The old shop of the late Albert Goodsell has been removed from the street line and now forms part of the dwelling on the rear.

Mrs. John L. Ross has been making some changes in the grounds about her residence, by taking out some of the trees and transplanting others.

On Friday last we were somewhat agitated on account of high winds and the announcement of fires in the woods and log heaps in this locality, one of which, if not detected as soon as it was, would in all probability have destroyed the Catholic church; but by the timely aid of some of our citizens all the fires were extinguished and our village was spared from a calamity the like of which some of us little dreamed.

E. J. Fickler is building a porch on the east side of his dwelling house.

We are informed that Will Bassett has purchased the stock of goods in the store of Abram Jones.

Sharon Centre.

At this writing the meadows begin to look quite green, and the farmers along the valley all seem to be busy, as the last week has been quite favorable for their work.

Our roads are very much improved, judging from the number of persons out riding last Sunday.

Our school began last Monday; Miss Nellie Drake is teaching it.

This time the measles have got in our midst, and Eddie Drake is the unlucky one, though he is getting along nicely.

Ellisburg.

Saving sparkling sap, scalding slimy storage, scrubbing slippery spiles, sugaring sacharine syrup, simultaneously stopped Saturday. Securing sweets to stored sugar, sauce, syrup slapjacks seemed surely secured so satiety said stop.

Farmers are hastening to sow oats and spring wheat so as to have the benefit of the first warm rains.

Smoke of forest fires and fallows are to be seen in almost every direction.

The Union Sunday School at Ellisburg is now fully organized. A cordial invitation is extended to all to attend.

Fishing Creek.

Fires has been the order of the day for the past week, which reached its climax on Friday.

Charles Schoolmaker set a fire in an old bark slashing belonging to Weimer & Johnston, containing about thirty acres, for the purpose of burning off a potato patch. The fire was blown from that into a bark slashing belonging to Orson Corsaw and from thence caught on the roof of an old hog house, belonging to him, and it was soon burned to the ground. The dwelling house of Mr. Corsaw, at times, was in great danger, so the contents were removed and taken to the creek for safety, but while the people were saving the house, these were destroyed.

The fire next caught on the roof of Solon Swreave's house burning it, together with the contents, to the ground. The family saving nothing but what they had on their backs at the time.

The next building to fall a prey to the fire demon was a barn belonging to A. Green. He saving nothing but a buggy and horses and the harness that was on them at the time. The barn contained one mowing machine, one horse rake and other farming tools; about seven tons of hay, 40 bushels of oats, and about 40 bushels of potatoes. His loss is about $1,000.

It also burned most of the fences on the farms of Mr. Morey and Green. It also caught on the roof of Wm. Morey's house several times.

The Potter Enterprise Wednesday Evening, May 14, 1884 – Vol. XI, No. 2

- J. W. Allen's colt, the same one that had a runaway a week or two ago, repeated the performance Monday. Near the tannery he became frightened at a dog, kicked Gail Bebee, the driver, out of the sulkey and ran to the Taggart dugway where he was captured. Alva Taggart undertook to lead the horse back but could not hold him and the horse ran away again. This time he was stopped a mile or two below. Mr. Beebe was considerable bruised about the breast, head and back, but nothing of a serious nature.

Roulet.

Phillips and Richardson, of Port Allegany, are painting the church.

John Abbott has rented the billiard saloon of A. M. Gillett, for five months.

Dr. C. G. Fisher is building a drug store on his lot at the corners. The Dr. expects to have it finished and in running order by the first of next month.

Sharon Centre.

More emigration. This time is it E. A. Graves who has emigrated; he has moved on his farm, up Canada Hollow.

W. H. Rexford has just traded his farm here for L. A. Bunker's farm at Riverside, near Wellsville.

P. Burdic has employed Lewis Sutherland to work for him this summer.

Joe Wiley lost a good horse the other night, and a day or two after a colt.

Ellisburg.

Again we stand in the solemn and mysterious presence of death. Again we ask ourselves the old, but ever recurring question "If a man die; shall he live again?" And as we gaze on the material part of what was Thomas Gilliland, Sr., or as he was affectionately called "Uncle Tommie,"

"Our love does dream, our faith does trust

(Since He who knows our needs is just)

That somehow, somewhere meet we must."

The subject of this sketch was born at Danville, Northumerland county, Pa., in 1796. His father was drowned in the Susquehanna, and his mother, soon marrying again, he was thrown upon the world at a very early age. He lived with his grandfather in Maryland a few years, but joining a family who were going to Ontario county, N.Y., he found himself, at the age of twelve, friendless and alone among strangers. He shared the fate of most orphans, finding, by bitter experience, that "the tender mercies of the wicked are cruel." But having a splendid constitution he grew to manhood. In 1819 he married Jane Carson near Geneva, N.Y., here two children were born to them. But resolving to make Allegany county their home they started in midwinter to make the journey with oxen; but here the saddest event of a long life occurred. Little Emeline, their oldest child, fell from the front of the sleigh and was crushed to death with the runner. After residing a few years at Cuba he removed to this county, in 1848, and has since that time been a useful and respected citizen. Last Sunday morning he passed peacefully away, but he has left us a rich and grand legacy in the example of a useful, industrious life, together with an unspotted social reputation.

**The Potter Enterprise
Wednesday Evening,
May 21, 1884 –
Vol. XI, No. 3**

- F. E. Neefe has greatly improved his house by building an addition, bow window, and porches.

- The machinery for Mr. Scutt's mill at Nelson Station is being delivered. The frame of the mill is partly up.

- R. L. Nichols has purchased of Mrs. M. R. Jones the property on East street occupied by Mr. Case, paying therefor $1,200.

- C. H. Armstrong has purchased one-half of the vacant lot between his grocery and the bank building. Consideration $1,000.

Hebron.

Hail fell here Friday. A frost every night.

School has commenced at the mouth of the Branch, taught by Miss Wilkinson, of Oswayo.

Mrs. Rathbone has moved to Wellsville, where she has purchased a house and lot, and will make her permanent home.

Maurice Clair had the misfortune to lose a young colt last week.

Soloman Lamberton has put in a new mill dam and is sawing to beat all.

Fishing Creek.

Bark peelers have commenced their annual warfare on the forests.

The upper school has been closed on account of the illness of the teacher.

Miss Cora Baker has commenced teaching at the Reed School house, in Roulet.

John Yentzer raised a horse barn the 13th and C. W. Tauscher a grain and hay barn on the 14th. Watson Lyman and A. Green each have the timber out for new barns.

Ed. Carr has purchased the upright part of F. D. Weimer's house and removed it on his lot which he bought of Weimer last Fall.

F. D. Weimer intends to erect a new building in the place of his old house.

Charles Bartholomew has moved on his lot and commenced work.

Fred Yentzer has taken possession of his farm again.

Michael Dehn lost one of his horses recently, smothered by smoke.

Ellisburg.

Let me whisper through your columns, to those wishing hemlock lumber, that there is 2,000,000 feet, seasoned and green, in and around Ellisburg for sale at from $5.00 to $6.50 per thousand.

And now Gran. Hurd can be seen whittling a basswood stick and making mental calculation of how much it will cost to buy "the boy" boots until he is twenty-one.

Sam. Rouse takes the belt for new farm implements this Spring, a wheel barrow and a new roller are on exhibition in front of his barn.

Rev. Leavenworth will preach next Sunday, at three o'clock p.m., and Rev. L. W. Snead will deliver his illustrated lecture, "Common Sense Views on Temperance," Sunday evening. All who are interested in this subject should hear this lecture.

Millport.

Sep. Barnes caught sixty trout on the South Branch last week.

School is in charge of Miss Lora Allen.

Mrs. Libbie Reed had her hands full defending her premises and that of Marion Manly from fire, a short time since; as it happened she was alone and as the wind increased it fanned into a blaze the dying embers in the fallow, and blew them long distances, igniting in many an unlooked for spot.

Mr. Robert Manly is very unfortunate and should have the sympathy of one and all. Eleven weeks ago, when arising in the morning, he fell to the floor; having always been crippled in his feet; and in falling he somehow hurt, as Dr. Turner says, the sciatic nerve; at any rate he has never been able to move one of his limbs since and is in great pain and is perfectly helpless. A short time after he was hurt, the house caught fire in the roof. Mrs. Manly and a daughter-in-law being alone despaired of putting out the fire or getting help so they took everything from the house but the stove and then dragged Mr. Manly out by his arms. He has been worse since then. While they were at work and calling for help, they saw a man passing, which proved to be a Mr. Elliot, familiarly known as "Bugle Eye." It is said they called to him and he stopped, looked at the fire and seeming to think it was none of his business went on leaving them to their fate. Above, in Clara, he met two or three men and talked with them, but did not think it worth while to mention the fire. If there is a hot place in the next world I know he'll find it, and he ought to here. George Hay was at work on the hill in the woods, and hearing cries of distress, ran to their assistance and saved most of the house although the roof was burned off one part, and much damage done.

South Coudersport.

Will Ford, who has been seriously ill for some time past, and about whom doubt of recovery were expressed, is now convalescing, thanks to good nursing and skillful treatment.

James L. Knox has been very ill at his home for nearly a week, but is now thought to be recovering.

Dan Vanwegen is confined to the house with an attack of influenza.

O. E. Armstrong has rented the house of Mrs. P. A. Stebbins and will move in a very short time.

M. L. Gridley has fenced in a pasture lot on the Ross lands.

James Johnston has moved into his new house, and added much to the appearance of the inside by painting and papering.

Mrs. Schildberger has made considerable improvement around her lot by grading, fencing, etc.

John Denhoff has a cellar dug, and we suppose by that that he intends soon to build a house thereon.

Township Tidings from Potter County, Pennsylvania
Volume I, 1880 - 1884

Whites Corners.

Farmers are nearly through with their seeding for which, however, the weather has been very unfavorable for the last few days.

The Summer term of school has opened with Miss Hattie Horton as teacher.

Mr. Jones, of West Union, has moved into the house formerly occupied by Amanzo McCutcheon and owned by H. O. Chapin.

Quarterly meeting was held at this place on Sunday last.

Wm. Warner's store was burglarized a few weeks ago. A quantity of jewelry and other property was taken. There is no trace of the burglars yet.

The Potter Enterprise Wednesday Evening, May 28, 1884 – Vol. XI, No. 4

- Roscoe Stearns has sold his mule team to Joseph Lent of Costelloville.

- County Commissioner Spencer has sold his farm in Genesee to S. C. Hurd and Son – 128 acres at $30 per acre.

- Strawberries sold in Coudersport last week at 25 cents per basket. Lettuce, beans, peas and onions are selling at very reasonable prices.

- Uncle Sam gave Eugene Bishop, of Raymond, a comfortable lift, financially, a few days since, in the way of a back pension.

Ellisburg.

June 8th will be "children's day" at Ellisburg Sunday School. All are cordially invited.

Bark peeling is the order of the day. Wages being high and help scarce.

Adelbert Pye has his new house well under way.

C. C. Allen does not recover as fast as his many friends would wish.

And now Charles Pye is whitling the stick and wondering about the boots, "It's a boy."

Keating.

"All the talk," is the coming post office. Homer talks of adding an office on the route. Seems to us she is rather late about it.

Sonrise occurred at the house of A. H. Crosby, some time since, though not recorded in your valuable journal. "How old is he?" asks the admiring visitor. "O, he'll be a year old next April." reply the proud and happy parents.

Folks do hate to plant their gardens. Before June the frosts may destroy all, and after June the bugs of various sorts and sizes most surely will.

The school began in school house No. one, on the 20th inst., a Miss Allen, of Lewisville, as teacher.

The sickness, that struck down the inhabitants here last winter, has left many too feeble for labor, and a feeling of sadness pervades the community, as they look on their new made graves.

Let us hope summer will bring many blessings.

The Potter Enterprise
Wednesday Evening,
June 4, 1884 –
Vol. XI, No. 5

- Joseph Hull lost a good work horse last week. A falling tree killed it.

- D. F. Glassmire's new Skating Rink will be opened Monday evening next.

- S. P. Olmsted has opened up his soda fountain and now supplies the thirsty.

- Snow fell to the depth of four inches on the hills, last Friday forenoon. It melted before night.

Roulet.

John Weimer has reshingled his house, built a porch, and is now painting it.

A. Marshner is building a cabinet shop on his lot on Main street.

The funeral of H. T. Barr, who died the 13th ult., was largely attended. He was buried under the auspices of the G. A. R., members of the A. F. Jones Post, officiated.

R. L. White, A. V. Lyman and A. W. Johnson have bought all the land of J. G. Saunders on the north side of his farm, and are fitting it up in lots.

South Coudersport.

The old dwelling house of Mark Gillon has been torn down to make room for an addition to the new house.

Will Ford is having a cellar wall laid under his new house.

E. J. Fickler is giving his house a couple coats of paint, which adds very much to its appearance.

There is talk of a new sidewalk at the lower end of Main street, to terminate in front of the Ryan property.

The festival for the benefit of the band given at the Court House by the ladies of Coudersport on Friday afternoon and evening, although arranged for in a hurry, was a very successful affair, the band realizing $42.55 therefrom.

West Branch.

There was a hard frost and some ice here Thursday and Friday mornings and now it snows.

It looks now as though the apple crop would be injured very much. The apple trees were in full bloom and some of them look now as though they had been scorched by fire.

Our schools are now open for the summer term, the upper school is taught by Mrs. Mary E. Crum, of Genesee Fork. The school here by Miss Bowen, of Cameron county.

The Potter Enterprise
Wednesday Evening,
June 11, 1884 –
Vol. XI, No. 6

Freeman Run.

School for the summer has commenced under the care of Miss Ella Allen, of Lewisville.

We are going to have a postoffice, we are; and not only an office but the mail will come to it twice a week. Three cheers for all and thanks to H. Bridges who has done much in getting it established.

Henry Harris sold two cows last week for forty-three dollars apiece.

But very little bark is being peeled here so far.

Oswayo.

We received a report of the Decoration Day services at Oswayo too late for publication last week. Our correspondent says:

After the soldiers graves were decorated, the grave of a soldier's son was decorated by the sons of veterans. As this is a "new departure," I will give you the exact words of the Post Commander as they passed from the soldiers graves to that of the son:

"We will now pass to the grave of a soldier's son. Here lies the remains of one of our comrades sons. The father died while in the service of his country and the son was a member of a 'Camp' of the son's of veterans, which was named in honor of his father. The object of the Camp is to continue the observance of Decoration Day. As the soldiers of the war of '61 pass away from earth, it is for the sons of veterans and all the rising generation to watch with jealous care the future welfare of this glorious Land of Liberty which they have inherited from their fathers at such a cost of blood. Yes, the price was the lives of fathers, husbands, sons and brothers. Young men, young ladies and children, let the one principle be firmly imbeded in your minds, that as you find these United States, free and independent, so you will leave them to future generations, that the Star Spangled Banner may ever wave

'O'er the land of the free
And the home of the brave.'

"We think it fitting that the sons of veterans should decorate the grave of their comrade on this occasion. Therefore, we ask them to proceed with such ceremony as they think proper."

The grave was beautifully decorated when the benediction was pronounced and we marched away, feeling that we had, once more, paid our tribute of respect to those departed heroes who so manfully risked their lives in defense of their country at the time of its "great peril."

Hebron.

The freeze of last week did less damage than was feared at first, though the grass is injured considerably, the beech trees are spoiled for the present. The snow that fell Friday morning was our only salvation. It is feared that fruit will be a failure.

Henry Lamberton found over one hundred wire worms in one hill of corn; they are doing fearful work almost everywhere this year.

Last Thursday was "house cleaning" at the school house.

S. Keller has his residence nearly completed; it is a pity so fine a one should not be out where it can be seen more.

Positively no news.

The Potter Enterprise
Wednesday Evening, June 18, 1884 – Vol. XI, No. 7

- C. L. Peck is having water carried into his house.

- Greisel's new harness shop is progressing finely. It will add to the appearance of Main street.

- Dan Dolway, one of Albert Lyman's teamsters, was sun struck yesterday while unloading lumber at the depot. Dolway had not been feeling well for a day or two, and did not eat his dinner, this may have had something to do with the matter. Dr. Charles French was called and by prompt and efficient work brought him out all right. It was a close call.

Freeman Run.

The Quarterly Meeting of the United Brethren church will be held here in the grove near the Harris school house, the 21st and 22d of this month. Presiding Elder Gage will be here. All are invited to attend.

The funeral of Fritz Hammel who died Monday was held Wednesday at the Klien house. Fritz was a bright promising lad, besides being an only son. The services were conducted by the Rev. Mr. Marshall, of Coudersport.

The friends of Mr. and Mrs. A. H. Crosby gave them a surprise party last week, on the 10th anniversary of their marriage, bringing them many nice and useful presents of tin.

F. N. Bridges has gone to Coudersport to learn photography of L. R. Bliss.

The Potter Enterprise
Wednesday Evening, June 25, 1884 – Vol. XI, No. 8

- The church at Sweden Valley was dedicated with suitable ceremony on Friday last. A large number of people were present. The church is a very handsome one, well finished and cost about $2,000. Albert Lyman contributed one-half the funds necessary and the rest was pledged by others before the church was dedicated. A few men like Mr. Lyman in any town would prove a great blessing, and too much praise cannot be given him.

The Potter Enterprise
Wednesday Evening, July 2, 1884 – Vol. XI, No. 9

- Wm. Brine is putting up a kiln of very fine brick, two miles up the river.

West Branch.

We had a shower last Wednesday afternoon that raised the water in the streams up to full banks, it swept off the creek fences and a part of White & Metzger's mill dam. White & Metzger had got their stock of logs sawed out, so their damage will not be very severe.

Township Tidings from Potter County, Pennsylvania
Volume I, 1880 - 1884

The Potter Enterprise
Wednesday Evening,
July 16, 1884 –
Vol. XI, No. 10

- Westley Rees, of Coudersport, has received a back pension of $1,800 with an allowance of $14 per month hereafter.

- Rev. H. B. Leavenworth has sold his house and lot, on Water street, to Mrs. Charles Nelson. Consideration, $900.

- The school directors, of Coudersport, have located a new school house, at the mouth of Stone Run, in the East Fork district.

- A. A. Allen has commenced work on his West street lot, above Second. He has a portion of the lumber for a fine new house on the ground.

- Westley Rees has purchased, of Mrs. George Boyer, a lot on the west side of East street, above Fourth, paying therefor five hundred dollars. He intends putting up a dwelling house on the lot.

- Corn is looking well.

- Blackberries promise a big crop.

- Grass will be a very light crop this year.

- Raspberries are quite plenty, but the price is a little steep.

- Huckleberries will be scarce. Fires last spring burned over many of the patches.

- W. C. Rennells wore his foot in a sling last week. A horse stepped on the aforesaid foot.

South Coudersport.

Items of interest from this locality have been exceedingly scarce for some time past, and there is not much improvement in that line at present.

Mrs. Rees' private school is well patronized, between 25 and 30 pupils being in attendance. Those who patronize the above institution will be amply repaid, as Mrs. Rees is a teacher of fine qualifications.

W. B. Gordnier has the contract for furnishing patent desks for the new school house in Sylvania.

Boyer & Yeomans have opened a new meat and produce market in the Carey building, which will be quite a convenience to dwellers in this neighborhood.

Mrs. A. B. Goodsell has had her house re-plastered.

The addition of blinds to the tenant house of Mrs. P. A. Stebbins makes a marked improvement in the appearance of the house.

Rev. Chas. Dodd is drawing good audiences at the Baptist Chapel Sabbath mornings and evenings. A Sabbath school was organized on Sunday last, with the following officers: Supt. J. W. Allen; assistant sup't F. J. Norton; secretary and treasurer, T. J. Gilbert.

Lumber is on the ground for a new dwelling house on the Schildberger lot.

Amos Colcord, who has a farm just below town, has placed on the fences surrounding his berry patch, signs which read "no trespassing."

Berry pickers please take notice. Maybe Colcord will let you pick 'em for halves.

Whites Corners.

With the exception of potatoes, which are injured some by the bugs, crops are looking well.

The Fourth passed off about as usual with the exception of a cyclone on that day and one the next which did great damage destroying buildings and killing stock in this vicinity.

The cheese factory works up about 10,000 pounds of milk per day.

There has been a Sabbath school organized here. Another stranger has moved into the place whom they have for superintendent.

Freeman Run.

Mrs. J. W. Dingee, of Keating Summit, who has been very sick, is gaining slowly.

G. C. Lewis lost a fine hog last week.

The tornado on the Fourth passed through a portion of this place, taking down a large amount of timber near Joe Codington's.

Our school is progressing finely under the care of Miss Ella Allen, of Lewisville.

A large meteor was seen here on the evening of the third.

Fishing Creek.

Surely, this has been a progressive year in this place. There are five new buildings under construction at present.

F. D. Weimer has the frame of his new house up.

E. M. Baker has fully recovered from his injuries received by his fall in the sack race at Coudersport. He says it will take more than one Fourth to kill him.

Mr. James Phenix and Miss Lydia Yentzer went to Oswayo the Fourth as two, and returned as one. May they enjoy a long and happy life is the wishes of their many friends.

Several of our young people took in the ball at Oswayo, July 4th, and report a pleasant and enjoyable time.

Forest House.

Mr. King, of Smethport, was over last week to look after the damage to the timber on the Keating lands, by the wind storm of the Fourth. He has disposed of a part at least, and Mr. Bima and three other men commenced peeling Monday morning.

Earl Crane, of Coudersport, is doing a good job on Mr. Hall's house and the family will move in soon.

Our school is in session. The one near Younglove's closed after a session of one month.

Joseph Dingee lost ten dollars out of his vest pocket Saturday while piling bark on the dock. Thinks he pulled it out with a piece of bark.

Same day a jobber lost his pocket book containing some money and valuable papers. He had his crew out looking for it Sunday, but has not found it yet.

Wheat, oats and potatoes are looking good.

There is room for men that want land for farming purposes.

Township Tidings from Potter County, Pennsylvania
Volume I, 1880 - 1884

The Potter Enterprise
Wednesday Evening,
July 23, 1884 –
Vol. XI, No. 11

Raymond.

We seem very fortunate here in one respect, cool nights, making sleep come easy, and many mornings sharp enough for frosts, and yet none appears excepting a little in some localities.

The health is usually good.

Mr. Valorous Byam, whose death was daily expected, is up and working some.

Mrs. J. L. Swain, long an invalid, is worse lately.

Mr. V. Byam lost a horse some time ago and now his other one has a broken leg.

Allie Presho waits on the customers in the store with one arm hanging by his side. Was thrown from a horse some time ago.

Grass is light. Coloradoes and wire worms are plenty. Crops generally look well.

Mrs. Hudson Hendryx, of Ellisburg, fell from a scaffolding some time ago and hurt her back badly. She was after eggs.

The Potter Enterprise
Wednesday Evening,
July 30, 1884 –
Vol. XI, No. 12

Odin.

Haying is in full blast.

Born – July 20th, to Mr. and Mrs. James Mitcheltree, a daughter.

Elmer Bundy has a bad swelling on his foot.

West Branch.

White & Metzgar are shipping their cherry lumber. They have sold to parties in Buffalo. A Mr. Munday, of Buffalo, and A. G. Lyman, of Lymansville, are doing the counting. The lumber has to be hauled to Gaines for shipment as our railroad extension to Pike Mills failed to put in an appearance on the Fourth as expected.

Wm. Trask has gone to New Bergen to build a saw mill and cut out some lumber for Mr. E. Peltz.

Bark peeling is nearly done here.

Haying is pretty well along. It is thought that the freeze the last of May injured the crop.

South Coudersport.

The borough council have been looking at the streets on our side of the river, and we hope soon to see street commissioner Thompson doing something in that line.

The South Hill road is in a very bad condition. The rains of the summer having washed out deep gullies in the road rendering it almost impassible for heavily loaded teams.

A. Keihl is laying a flag stone walk from his front door to the gate.

The American hotel fence is covered with Barnum's show bills.

Merv. Calkins and family started back to their former home, Lake Benton, Minn., on Tuesday.

J. M. Bassett has been improving the interior of his livery barn.

We are informed that A. C. Millard will open a wagon ship in a short time.

The cross has been placed on the steeple of the Catholic Church.

The Potter Enterprise
Wednesday Evening,
August 13, 1884 –
Vol. XI, No. 14

- Wm. Shear has purchased two lots of Luther Seibert, west of Daniel Monroe's lot, south side.

Whites Corners.

A great many marriages are taking place in and near this place. Charles Smith, of this place, was married to Miss May Cummings, of Harrison Valley; Elmer Downley, of West Union to Lucinda Harrington, and Miss Myra Harris to Thomas Quick, of Dennis Hill.

Mrs. J. J. Smith, an old resident of this town, died at her home on Sunday July 27th. She was an obliging neighbor and was universally liked and respected. She leaves a large circle of friends to mourn their loss.

Ellisburg.

A meeting was called to organize a circulating library for Ellisburg and vicinity. A constitution was adopted and the necessary officers were duly elected consisting of a president, secretary, treasurer, librarian and seven directors. One hundred and fifty volumes were purchased and paid for at a cost of $1.00 per volume and a provision for additional volumes as funds accrue. All was done cheerfully and is a step in advance to supercede the cheap truck of worse than useless books with which the community is flooded.

Ellisburg and Genesee Forks are supplied with regular religious services every Sunday, and the time, we trust, is not distant when houses of worship will be erected for the better accommodation of meetings and the promotion of more enlarged ideas.

Fishing Creek.

A few days ago Will Yentzer was quite badly hurt by the falling of a tree caused by the wind blow. He is recovering as fast as could be expected, but will be laid up for some time to come.

The young people enjoyed a social hop at C. W. Tauscher's on Friday evening, August 1st.

Most of the farmers have commenced haying while a few of them are holding off for a more definite settlement of the weather.

Eugene Phenix has sold his three-year-old steers to Dan. Yentzer; consideration $100.

F. D. Weimer has purchased another horse of Leroy Lyman.

South Coudersport.

Henry Schidberger has let the contract for building his new house to Birney Rees, who has commenced work on the frame.

Benj. Rennells is repairing the South Hill road. That, of course, means good roads in that locality for some time to come.

Clarence Keihl leaves here in a few days to erect a dwelling house for Rev. Leavenworth, at Burtville.

The platform, tables, etc., for the Catholic picnic are completed, and no pains seem to have been spared to make ample accommodations for those who attend.

W. W. Moore, formerly of this place, has rented the store of Abram Jones, where he will engage in the manufacture of monuments, tombstones, etc.

The cellar wall is being laid on John Denhoff's lot prior to the erection of a new house.

A new building is being erected on the Keihle lot. The second story of which will be used by Clarence Keihle as a carpenter shop, and the lower part as a woodshed.

West Homer.

Not having any correspondence from this place in a long time, I have seized my pen, with a firm grasp, to let you know of some of the doings of this out of the way place.

In the first place we will talk about the weather, which has been very gloomy for those that were trying to make hay, but the prospect is better.

Everybody and Jack have been to Costello blackberrying, with more or less success, one or two with less.

Albert Colcord and the boys went got 42 quarts. They report them as scarce.

O. H. Crosby is nearly done haying.

H. M. Case is building a new house.

I notice that Charles Reauing has the frame of a granery up.

Richard Parsons has erected a fine barn this season and contemplates building a new house this fall, besides the many other improvements on his place.

Oh, by the way, our school closed with an entertainment and picnic in the Hall grove on the 2d (and if the school work is to be judged by the efficient management shown there, our teacher, Miss Libbie Crosby, has been doing thorough work). Everybody partook of a bountiful repast and there was enough for more.

G. M. Baker has been drawing bark for his folks, for a few days.

G. C. Lewis' mill is shut down through haying.

Albert Colcord sports a new mowing machine.

Albert Klesa is building a new house.

After living for years without either a stage or postoffice, we now have two stages and expect soon to have a postoffice which will be a great convenience to the citizens of the lower end of town. What our town needs at present more than anything else is considerable right down earnest temperance work, for which we stand in great need.

**The Potter Enterprise
Wednesday Evening,
August 20, 1884 –
Vol. XI, No. 15**

Around Olmsted's.

The bark jobs are nearly all finished for the season, leaving a dismal tangle of brush and logs in lieu of the "Forest Primeval."

Still, as poets have used that subject as threadbare as Beautiful Snow and poetry is getting quite out of style unless it be some old fashioned bit to match the parlor furnishings, we'll not mourn if blackberry vines take the place of hemlocks.

Mr. Skutt's boiler is cracked, and that may be the reason for his absence this week.

It is reported that Mr. Fox has found a bee tree. Hope he'll make a honey party this Fall.

Hay was a light crop, and grasshoppers are devouring gardens.

Henry Lehman and family will camp out on Bachelor Hall on Nelson Run, while he prepares a building site on his place in Elm Flats. Great flats, by the way, just about large enough for a picnic grove. Maybe there's some great Indian legend, like the one of Rose Lake, to support the name.

All the would-be berry pickers wear mourning this year, the last Spring's fires have destroyed their fruit.

West Homer.

Mrs. Charlotte Quimby has a new picket fence around her dooryard.

Joseph Coddington is laying up the cellar wall for Richard Parsons' new house.

W. H. Crosby has commenced his harvesting.

E. A. Earle peeled the most bark of any one in this section this season, while Charlie Head takes second place.

O. L. Hall sports a thirty tone haystack.

We notice that the street commissioner has been having some good work done on the South Hill road; but if he will look he will find that the drains of those cellars above the road at the foot of the hill empty right into the road, and last Spring made mud that was little less than infernal; all of which is respectfully submitted.

The Potter Enterprise
Wednesday Evening,
August 27, 1884 –
Vol. XI, No. 16

- Blackberries sold as low as three cents per quart in Coudersport last Saturday. The crop is immense.

- The Coudersport School Board let the contract for building a school house on the East Fork to William McFall. The contract price is $480. The bids ranged from $480 to $600.

Forest House.

Bark jobbers have, most of them, got the logs cut ready to be skidded.

Briggs' mill shuts down in a few days as the stock is nearly all sawed out.

There is some talk that Goodyear is going to build a big saw mill down at the big fill.

Pretty good turnout to attend church here Sunday evenings.

West Branch.

We are now getting good corn and hay weather. It comes rather late in the season but it may do some good.

There are a few cutting hay yet.

Corn is making a large growth and if the season holds out long enough will make a good crop.

Those that cut their hay in the early part of haying will have a splendid after growth for fall feed.

Oat harvest has commenced and the crop is looking well.

Apples will be very scarce.

Blackberries are in their prime and are said to be plenty.

White & Metzgar are nearly through shipping their lumber.

Odin.

George Reed has sold his farm to J. M. Barrows.

James Bundy expects to build a new house this Fall.

Some of the neighbors turned out and gave E. Z. Dingee a lift in his haying recently. Mr. Dingee's health is very poor.

A large bear is prowling around in this vicinity and has taken two sheep for Mr. E. Z. Dingee.

Mr. Coon Chestain is very sick with rheumatism.

Genesee Fork.

H. L. Jones has a large and well filled store, doing a thriving business. Mr. Martin Briggs is also engaged in the mercantile business; also J. Carpenter, who are said to be doing a good business. Genesee Fork is getting much of the trade which formerly went to Wellsville.

The Misses Monroe are engaged in Millinery.

Mrs. Diffin is engaged in dressmaking.

With all the other lodges a temperance lodge is now talked of.

Mr. Childs is yet doing a thriving business in the hotel.

Mr. Lilly is running a meat market.

Mr. G. Slawson has a new house nearly completed.

We also notice that Mr. Harris has a new barn completed.

Hebron.

Everything is getting pretty dry over here, yet the prohibitionists are as active as ever.

Henry Lamberton has a cow missing about two weeks ago. A few days ago he found her in the woods with a broken leg and some bruises; she had evidently been dead for some time. He also lost a yearling last week.

Miss Laura Tyler closed her school at the Hydorn school house last Thursday. She has been tendered the school at the Greenman school house the coming session but has not decided as yet to take it.

The picnic in the grove by Mr. Frink's on Tuesday was a very pleasant affair, and a very large number of people seemed cognisant of the fact. The exercises were all good; consisting of several fine recitations, lots of nice singing and instrumental music, a temperance drama entitled, "Don't Marry a man to Reform him," and a grand essay on temperance read by Mrs. Groves of Coudersport. Mrs. Groves is a charming speaker and her words of appeal must have touched many hearts. She showed that as a question of finance as well as a question of morality and right living, the temperance question was assuming mammoth proportions. In-as-much as three-fourths of the pauperism and crime in the world was traceable to intemperance it behooved us as voters and tax payers to not shirk the responsibility resting upon our shoulders of meeting this question firmly and intelligently.

We were glad to see that Mr. Ayers had not grown old yet as regards his voice. He sang a solo in a manner that put the younger men quite in the shade.

The only unpleasant incident of the day was the severe illness of Mrs. Mary Kenyon, who was obliged to go home early in the day. She was attended by Dr. Chas. French, who was on the ground, just returning from visiting Mrs. Amy Madison who is quite sick.

The literary exercises were followed by a fine dinner. A barrel of ice water was a delightful accessory to the latter.

The speaker's stand was tastefully draped and decorated with beautiful flowers and the whole affair did much credit to those who got up the entertainment; many of whom must have worked very hard.

For a year, previous to this Summer, Mrs. Stephen Reynolds has been in poor health. When they commenced haying she commenced raking with the sulky rake. After the lameness of the first day or so she commenced to feel better. She has raked eighty tons of hay this Summer and considers herself a perfectly healthy woman. Ladies, try it! Patent medicines and family physicians are nowhere beside healthy exercise in the open air where you get plenty of oxygen not "compound" or patented.

Fishing Creek.

Most of the farmers have finished haying and a few have commenced to cut their oats.

The hay crop has turned out better than it was expected it would and the other crops look good.

Bark peeling is nearly closed up for this year.

H. Baker sports a new mowing machine and A. Yentzer a new wagon.

The Potter Enterprise
Wednesday Evening,
September 3, 1884 –
Vol. XI, No. 17

- Seymour Norton, of Coudersport, has been granted a back pension of $944.

- Work has been commenced on A. B. Mann's brick building, to be West of the Bank.

West Branch.

It is reported that the Addison & Northern Pennsylvania railroad has gone into the hands of the Erie, and that it will be made a standard gauge, and completed to Pike Mills this season.

Willis Conable is digging a cellar, preparatory to erecting an addition to his store and dwelling. In digging the cellar he has struck a nice vein of water.

Odin.

On Thursday last the men and boys of the neighborhood turned out to either drive out or kill the bear which has been prowling around here. It is supposed that he has left as nothing more has been seen of him.

Frank Klein has a hand full of oats which measure six feet and nine inches, which goes to show that a man may be a good blacksmith and a good farmer too.

"Be sure to get our mail when you go to town," is a saying of the past. We get it regular twice a week now, rain or shine.

Clara.

School began one week ago Monday in charge of A. J. Evans. We consider ourselves fortunate in securing his services again, his being so successful in his teaching previous to his graduating at Mansfield guarantees us nothing inferior in grade since.

T. Glines is repairing his house extensively, is to have a verandah on the south and east with a bow window and lots of nice things.

Mr. and Mrs. Gillian, who live on Mr. Fosmer's place, had the misfortune to lose a babe two months old, last week.

About a week ago Mr. Brooks had a horse and bridle stolen; after several days the horse came home alone, but the bridle was among the missing.

Zanonia Reed has moved up on Whitney Creek to do a job of lumbering.

West Homer.

Miss Nora Quimby returned Saturday from Scranton, where she has been learning dressmaking.

Alton Earle has had six teams hauling bark for him the past week. I hear that Alton is going West the last of this week, and rumor says that when he returns he will bring Mrs. Alton.

Parsons has got his cellar done and the sills on for a new house.

Albert Colcord has got his fallow nearly all logged up.

John Taylor, who recently came from Nebraska, has bought fifty acres of land of John Airhart and is going to build a house on it as soon as possible.

Raymond.

Allegany is improving. The Conable boys have a reaper; they fetch down a field of grain in short metre time. As Potter improves the reaper will crowd out cradles. The roller, too, is getting to be used much more than formerly.

The hay crop is not a failure. Farther east it is a good crop. The grain crops all seem good. The hot suns threatened the buckwheat, perhaps hurt it some, but there is a vast amount of it from here to Harrison Valley, all down the Cowanesque to Lawrenceville, and on to Painted Post, Monterey, Lake Lamoke and Wannettie, farms have their full share of this grain, and everywhere it looks well.

Many apple orchards about here promise well, but apples seem very scarce farther east; so are berries. As for Walnuts, butternuts and chestnuts there does not appear to be any from here to Painted Post. Hickory nuts, however, abound.

On the Magee road they are taking up good iron rails and putting down steel rails. That, said a railroad official, looks as though they were about to extend the road beyond Harrison Valley.

Township Tidings from Potter County, Pennsylvania
Volume I, 1880 - 1884

The health of this region seems very good for this time of the year.

Around Olmsted's.

Mr. Schutt's new boiler is larger than the old one, and he is expecting a mason to set it in the arch, soon. Mr. W. Schutt is making road up Brehmer hollow to the job there. John English is to haul bark to Hammond's, and Albert Reed and Martin Watson agree to skid the logs and deliver to the river.

Two drunken fellows went over the hill howling and firing pistols the other day. But Potter is a temperance place!

Your correspondent was on Crandall Hill, Aug. 14th and visited Mr. Robert Peet's new barn, not finished, but being boarded up. It is 38 x 42 with deep basement for carriage room and stable. Made of thoroughly seasoned timbers, solid clear plank and inch battens, braced and stayed at corners in the most substantial manner with seasoned hard wood plank and scantling. All but six bunches of shingles are extras. Over 600 pounds of nails are to be used, and Mr. Cy Clone can take it for a foot ball; it will hold together to roll a number of miles. Mr. Peet will let the young folks *hop* on the floor, when it is laid; guess they'll wish him and his barn good luck! 'Tis an honor to Potter county and its owner will not need to "tear it down and build it bigger," unless he outlasts Methusalah.

The Potter Enterprise Wednesday Evening, September 10, 1884 – Vol. XI, No. 18

- The Water Company is extending a main up East street from Third.

Fishing Creek.

Harvesting oats and buckwheat is the order of the day. They are both excellent crops.

Richard Morey has sold his ox team to A. M. Benton & Co. Consideration, $150.

A. Yentzer has started his threshing machine. J. Teuscher will accompany him this fall.

John Teuscher had his finger bruised quite badly Saturday last. He was holding up a horse's foot while A. Yentzer cut the toe caulk off and received the full blow of the hammer on his finger.

F. D. Weimer has his new house shingled.

Solon Shieaver says his clothes are all too small and that he will have to get No. 14 boots for it is a boy.

C. W. Teuscher has purchased land of D. Yentzer on which he intends to erect a saw mill soon.

Jack Frost has paid this place two unwelcome visits of late doing slight damage to the vines and beans.

West Homer.

J. B. Colcord is to work for his uncle Amos.

Wm. Cobb took a small drove of cattle from this neighborhood last week.

Alton Earle started for Iowa Monday morning.

Richard Parsons raised his new house Friday.

Mrs. Curtis Baker and Mrs. Maria White have each a new sewing machine.

Charley Head and wife are about to move to Virginia.

Now the farmer looketh long and anxiously for the threshing machine.

Albert Colcord has concluded that he will no longer be an insurance agent but return to his anvil and fallow once more.

J. E. Quimby has placed a new wheel in his mill.

South Coudersport.

The lot surrounding the Baptist Chapel is being graded.

Ed. Griesel's house, on the Gordnier lands, is enclosed.

Dan. Vanwegen has moved into part of the old Carey house.

Work has commenced on the new house of L. D. Horton.

T. J. Gilbert is painting his house.

John Denhoff has commenced his new house.

We are informed that Mrs. Rees will open her school in a few weeks.

J. M. Bassett has erected an office next to his livery barn.

The Potter Enterprise
Wednesday Evening,
September 17, 1884 –
Vol. XI, No. 19

- Water in the streams and springs is getting very low.

- The race track at Lewisville has been completed.

- D. W. Butterworth has purchased the James Johnston property.

- Dan McConneky, conductor on the C. & P. A. railroad, has purchased the Edward Forster property, south side.

- Sunday and Monday mornings the ground was covered with frost; ice formed an eighth of an inch thick Sunday morning. It has caused some damage to late corn and cut short the crop of tender vegetables in the garden.

West Branch.

Lon Mitchell has taken the job of getting in the West Branch Creek all of Canfield's hemlock timber that will come into the creek by away of the Wetmore Run, supposed to be about two million feet. He commenced work on the job last Monday.

Messrs. Brown, Conable & Co. are building a skating rink at Pike Mills. The building will be 100 x 35 feet.

John Helfrecht is doing the threshing here with his steam power.

S. M. Conable has returned from Wisconsin where he has been spending the Summer.

Whites Corners.

Farmers are nearly through harvesting and crops are very good. Potatoes are excellent but show some signs of rotting. Apples will be a small crop.

Threshing is the order of the day and the whistles of the steamers can be heard on every side. E. Tadder has a fine machine

Township Tidings from Potter County, Pennsylvania
Volume I, 1880 - 1884

which is doing good business as are also a number of others.

C. Slater is improving his house very much. Charley will hardly know himself when he gets it finished.

Query: What sort of regulation is a cheese factory run on where some of the patrons are allowed to water their milk, others to skim their cans while some must send the pure milk and still others are not even allowed to dip whey?

Hammonds.

Not much news this week.

The dance at Mr. Hall's was well attended, about thirty couple being present.

There were two deer seen here on Monday morning in a potato field, by the road side, and Mr. Davis went after them but they were gone. It was a good thing they had for some team or person might have been shot. As we think here he is a better shot with his mouth than with the gun.

Bark is coming in at a great rate by wagon and car.

Forest House.

We have had two very hard frosts here, but the farmers had most of their crops out of the way. There was some corn hurt but the most of it was cut.

Rev. W. S. Holland, after a years labor in this place, has returned to Costelloville. He is going to preach there the coming year.

Ed. Earle's team returned from West Homer last Friday where it had been working this Fall. I hear Ed has got a large bark job here now.

Will Barnes has been working for Al Williams this Fall, and last Thursday he had the misfortune to cut his foot very bad.

Very hard rain here last Thursday night.

The woods are full of hunters now.

Mr. Raymond, of Gold, passed through this place last Friday with a large drove of beef cattle.

Roulet.

Most of our farmers have been improving the fair weather by harvesting their grain.

A. V. Lyman has harvested and threshed out his crop of winter wheat, which has yielded 150 bushels; an average of 21 bushels to the acre on his hillside land.

The select school is being taught here by Miss Amy White, of Coudersport.

White & Lyman have improved the looks of their store by laying a new floor.

L. W. Crawford's new house is nearly complete.

The Misses Mary and Dora Boyington have returned to Olean, to resume teaching, after spending ten weeks vacation at their home.

There will be an ice cream festival held at the Union Church, on Thursday evening the 18th. A cordial invitation is extended to all.

South Coudersport.

While John Denhoff and Earl Crane were at work one day last week, on the house of L. D. Horton, the scaffold on which they were standing fell. John Denhoff received a slight cut on the head and a sprained ankle, while Crane escaped with a slight sprain of the wrist.

The infant child of John Golding died at the house of H. Schildberger last week. It was buried in the Coudersport cemetery.

We are informed that Tim Kanealey has purchased the James Turner property, at the foot of South Hill.

Mrs. Rees was called to the bedside of her father, Jacob Peet, on Freeman Run, last week, who has been seriously ill, but it is though some better at this writing. Owing to the above circumstance, Mrs. Rees has postponed opening her school for the present.

Hebron.

Quarterly meeting at Hebron Center next Saturday and Sunday.

A crew of men have been at work making a new channel, about thirty rods from the head of the dugway near J. S. Barnes, for the Oswayo Creek. The bank is to be cleared and the Creek straightened to run close to it. Frank Hallet is doing the stumping with his machine.

The first day at work on the creek, Byron Howard cut his foot very bad. He had to be carried home where he will doubtless stay for the present.

James Strait has sold his farm, stock and farming utensils to Mr. Densmore for $900. Mr. Densmore takes possession the first of next month. Mr. Strait intends going to Kansas.

Henry Lamberton had the misfortune to lose another cow the other day. This is the second in a few weeks.

The Potter Enterprise Wednesday Evening, September 24, 1884 – Vol. XI, No. 20

- Henry Ruscher, of Ayers Hill, has just been awarded a little over $800 back pension, and an increase that brings his monthly pension up to $30.

- We are glad to announce that a fine hearse will be added to Grabe's furniture and undertaking establishment, in a week or ten days. It is a necessity Coudersport has long felt the want of and Mr. Grabe deserves thanks for supplying it.

Odin.

Will Barnes cut his foot quite bad last week.

The infant child of George Wetsel, of Keating Summit, was buried here last Sunday.

Rev. N. C. Sheets has been returned to preach another year.

J. H. Barrows had a logging bee a few days ago and a good job was done.

Potatoes are rotting badly.

Hammond's.

They have lots of trouble with the drag chains breaking in the tannery of late. I do not know what it is, but it carries the bark somewhere after it is ground. We don't believe they know enough to run it.

Dance down at Palmatier's on Friday night last. How thick dances are about here.

The water runs very slow at the spring.

The Potter Enterprise
Wednesday Evening,
October 1, 1884 –
Vol. XI, No. 21

- W. K. Jones and Edward Forster have put up street lamps in front of their business places.

- In returning from the fair, last week, D. D. Colcord's buggy was run into by a reckless driver and Mr. Colcord was thrown down the bank a number of feet. He was severely bruised. A lady and child, in the buggy with him, were thrown out, but beyond a severe fright were not hurt. Mr. Colcord's horse ran away smashing up the buggy and harness considerably. If damages are not paid a law suit will probably result.

- Buckwheat cakes are on deck again.

- Coudersport and Wellsboro are now connected by Telephone.

- James Johnston has purchased, of W. I. Lewis, a house and lot in Duke Centre.

- J. A. Quimby is building a ten-pin alley, opposite the American House, south side.

Fishing Creek.

Times are lively getting through the large quantity of hemlock bark peeled this summer, a part goes to Hammond and the rest goes to Port Allegany.

The infant daughter of George Stillwell died on the 12th inst., aged four months and twelve days.

H. Baker has let his log cutting to the Koon Bros.

West Homer.

Mr. Jerome Hopkins, of Ulysses, is doing the threshing in this place.

H. M. Case raised his new house last Saturday.

Mrs. Charlotte Quimby had the misfortune to lose a fine two-year-old steer last Sunday.

Miss Winnie Glaspy, Miss Susay Colcord, Miss Anna Reaning, Miss Rosa Quimby and Mr. John Colcord are attending school at Coudersport from this neighborhood.

Albert Klesa has his new house nearly completed.

Elder Sheets has been returned to this circuit for another year.

Costello.

William Putman is remodeling his dwelling by putting on a new roof and adding a kitchen to it.

The Supervisors of Sylvania and Portage townships have done themselves an honor by building a new bridge across the Sinnemahoning at this place. Seth Briggs, of Wharton, had the job.

John Brownlee and Sons are building themselves a new house.

L. D. Ripple is teaching in the Brownlee school house.

The new school house, at Costello, is finished and it is one of the best in the county.

Dr. Geo. Rees starts for Cincinnati soon, to resume his study of medicine.

John Sullivan has built himself a new house this past summer.

The tannery is running as usual.

This place supports two pool tables at present.

Forest House.

There was a rather hasty wedding here the other day. The happy couple made arrangements with the Preacher to meet them at the station and perform the ceremony just before train time. The Rev. was a little behind time, and the train whistled when he arrived, but he was equal to the occasion and made them one and sent them on life's journey rejoicing. Mr. John Rycraft of this place and Miss Cora Wales of Freeman Run were the happy parties.

Quite a number complain of rheumatism.

We had a very hard rain here Sunday night. It was accompanied by a very hard wind, which blew down a good deal of timber.

Joe Dingee has sold out his interest in his lumber job to Charlie Rycraft.

This place is getting to be quite a tony place, it sports a barber shop now. All we want to be a city is a skating rink.

G. D. Briggs' mill is running again.

J. B. Colcord, of West Homer, passed through here to-day on his way to Baltimore to attend a medical school.

The Potter Enterprise Wednesday Evening, October 8, 1884 – Vol. XI, No. 22

- The Catholic church is nearly completed.

- There is some talk of organizing a Lutheran church in Coudersport.

- Zacharias, the barber, talks of fitting up bath rooms in connection with his barber shop.

- Major Seibert has rented the American Hotel. Mr. Rogers has sold the house to L. H. Cobb and expects to go West.

- The telephone office has been removed from the Nichols House to Rees' drug store. Covey had become tired of the jingle of the bell.

- The railroad from Gaines to Pike Mills is being rapidly pushed to completion. In a very short time Pike Mills will be connected with the outer world.

- Before the mud gets any deeper the Main street cross walks should be raised.

Forest House.

H. A. Avery has sold one of his horse teams to Charlie Rycraft. Consideration I hear was $325.

Miss Vina Dingee, of Coudersport, commences school here to-day.

Miss Carpenter, of Angelica, N.Y., is teaching the Younglove school.

West Homer.

Charlie Head has changed his mind about going to Virginia and now intends to go to Nebraska.

John Taylor has raised a house and Joseph Baker a barn lately.

Mr. Parsons has his house nearly ready to move into.

J. E. Quimby is still repairing his mill.

Born, on Sept. 26th, to Mr. and Mrs. O. L. Hall, a girl.

On Oct. 5th, to Mr. and Mrs. Adam Hartwick, a boy.

Hebron.

The late rains and warm weather are threatening all crops out of doors with decay.

A terrible thunderstorm visited us recently, accompanied by severe wind which tore down lots of fence, but have heard of no other damage.

Mr. Densmore has commenced a cellar for his new house. They move into the old one and take possession of their farm to-morrow. Mr. Strait, who moves out, goes to Millport for a while but has not bought yet.

Miss Alice Perkins, of Bingham, has a class in music on Crandall Hill and would like a class in an adjoining section. She is highly spoken of as a teacher.

Wallace Dwight has moved to Oswayo. George Hulbert occupies his house and is to work the farm the coming year.

If logs are banked on the dugway this winter the road should be widened for some distance. This need has been felt for some time.

Around Olmsteds.

What has become of all the wild bees? Potter used to be a famous hunting ground for honey in the days the oldest inhabitant loves to recall. Autumn, and no wild honey nor venison? "Why is this thus?"

Winter grain was thankful for the rain – what was in the ground at least. Rye fields are most unsown.

Henry Lehman is busy on his road up Elm Hollow. Had a bee last week and intends making another.

Mr. Schutt's mill seems to be in good working order now.

A very sickly time.

Mrs. Everett has been quite sick with congestive fever.

James Bundy was taken violently with cholera morbus and had to go home.

The Harris settlement is afflicted again, E. Fourness and his son both being sick.

The lumbermen here are so fearful of contracting the disease they pour something into their water to keep off the chills.

Clara.

Tim Glines has almost made a new house out of his old one. Joe Fessenden and Marion Manley do the carpenter work.

Mrs. Lydia Brooks has a fine lot of cabbage for sale.

Our school has several students from Millport. They can not afford a good school down there.

Chas. Johnson writes that he reached Eau Clair just in time for the flood.

South Coudersport.

Mr. Holland has taken considerable interest in raising

some blooded poultry this year, and was just commencing to receive reward for his labor, when some fiend fed the young chickens Paris green which resulted in the death of twenty of Mr. Holland's young chickens. Now, if the party who did this dirty work knows when he is well off he will refrain from any devillishness of this sort in the future.

The new house of ex-Sheriff Monroe is being painted, inside and out.

Mr. Horton's new house is about ready for occupancy.

Tim Kaneally moved into the Turner house (recently purchased by him) on Thursday.

L. R. Bliss has erected a small green house on the south side of his house.

Wilber Quimby will occupy the house where Conductor McConaky now lives, as soon as vacated.

A. C. Perkins has improved the appearance of his house with a coat of paint.

G. W. Rogers commenced moving his goods to Ulysses on Monday.

Hammonds.

Mr. Amel Karnickle was married to a lady, just over from Germany, on Saturday of last week, and after the wedding they had a nice little dance. Those that attended enjoyed it very much.

There was a concert at this place on Sunday afternoon. Oh! my, what nice music.

One side of the ovens at the tannery are shut down for repairs.

Oats are worth 50 cents per bushel at the tannery store.

Very muddy here at present.

The beam hands have to lay off for a few days.

**The Potter Enterprise
Wednesday Evening,
October 15, 1884 –
Vol. XI, No. 23**

Fishing Creek.

A. Yentzer has found his tread power too slow and has purchased a steam power.

Geo. Stillwell has sold his interest in his lot and tools to Julius Tauscher. Consideration $400.

Watson Lyman is making improvements around his barn, by grading off the knoll and logging.

On Monday last John Tauscher had the misfortune to slip and fall on a sharp limb, lacerating the palm of his right hand in the worst shape imaginable. It will be some time before he will be able to use it, if he does at all this fall.

**The Potter Enterprise
Wednesday Evening,
October 22, 1884 –
Vol. XI, No. 24**

- Mrs. Isabella Ross is building an addition to her house.

- A. B. Mann is building an addition to his house.

- Mrs. P. A. Stebbins has purchased the unsold Keating lands in this borough, known as the Eulalia Farm. We understand it will be put in market just as fast as purchasers want it. If cut up into lots at reasonable prices, Coudersport will grow very fast. Rents are very high now, and many renters will buy and build. A few years ago the Keatings put several squares on the market and it resulted in many new houses on the south side. A large portion of the tract will be fenced in the spring for pasturage until wanted for building purposes.

- D. W. VanWegen has rented the house vacated by John Ormerod.

- Daniel Monroe is adding a porch to his house, south side of the river.

White's Corners.

G. K. Erway has bought the farm formerly owned by Erastus Outman, paying $1575.

James Smith has bought a farm near Mills, of J. W. Stevens.

The cheese factory sold over 20,000 lbs. of cheese this week.

Mr. John Riley and Miss Fannie Statham were married a short time ago. John has a housekeeper now.

Odin.

Splendid Autumn weather and the farmers are busy harvesting their potatoes. Some complain of the rot and some that the wire worm are eating their potatoes badly.

C. H. Barnes is putting up a new house.

G. R. Reed has moved his family to Summit.

Much sickness prevails here at present. Mr. James Bundy is just recovering from a severe attack of cholera morbus.

Edward Fournes is very sick with billous fever and his son Meredith is just recovering from an attack of typhoid fever.

Miss Eva Lewis is very sick with inflamation of the liver.

The Potter Enterprise Wednesday Evening, October 29, 1884 – Vol. XI, No. 25

- W. K. Jones is building the finest chicken house in town.

- Ed. Lyon had a foot badly jammed by a wagon wheel, a few days since.

- E. N. Stebbins is getting timber on the ground for a new barn on West street.

- A chimney in John M. Hamilton's house burned out last Sunday. In some way the fire spread from the chimney, catching in the woodwork between the brick walls, and for a time smoke came out around the window frames at a rate that was decidedly uncomfortable. Small hose was attached to the water works, portions of brick were removed and the fire extinguished. The plastering and carpets were considerably damaged by water.

Raymond.

Whopping Cough is prevailing in this region.

Mrs. Clark Green is failing – is going very much as her husband did.

Charles Green has sold his farm to Mr. Semil Baker and has moved to his mother's (Mrs. Clark Green) farm, but Mr. Baker remains another year on the Amos Raymond farm.

Township Tidings from Potter County, Pennsylvania
Volume I, 1880 - 1884

Ellisburg.

Time flies, snow flies, wild geese fly, stumps and dirt fly, for dynamite gets under a few of them near this place – election lies fly, and boys don't feel encouraged about trying to be presidents.

R. L. Nelson's house gets repaired from cellar to garret.

Elijah Estes' house gets a plastering, as well as Henry Hurd's chambers.

W. H. Lewis comes and marries Mary Plants Kelley and takes her to North Carolina and leaves one less chance for the young men.

West Homer.

Charley Head and wife started West last Monday.

Alton Earle returned from Iowa on Monday with his bride.

The light snows of the past week have had the effect to start out our Nimrods, with blood in their eye. Two of them stayed in the woods and watched one lone coon all night, recently; said coon being all the game that I have heard of any of them killing this fall.

Mr. Gibson is teaching the school on More's Run.

Miss Libbie Crosby is teaching on Ayers Hill.

Miss Orissa Hurd of Genesee is to have charge of the West Homer school this winter. It does not begin until December.

The Potter Enterprise Wednesday Evening, November 5, 1884 – Vol. XI, No. 26

- They have a skating rink at Pike Mills, and Julius Zimmerman of Coudersport is manager and instructor. Julius is one of the best of skaters.

White's Corners.

S. J. Stetson has let his farm to L. Stone to work the coming year.

A. J. Erway intends to move back on his place next week.

R. H. Taggart is painting his house.

C. Slater has a very nice coal stove to put in the house he has been repairing.

West Homer.

H. M. Case expects to move into his new house the first of next week.

Eli Glaspy is building an addition to his barn.

Cattle buyers come around and enquire the price of stock and drive off without looking at it.

Tin wedding at the house of O. H. Crosby, the 29th inst., but on account of the rain but few were present.

John Gordnier has a new hard wood floor laid in his kitchen.

John Taylor moved into his new house last Wednesday.

Coon meat is plenty, but deer meat very scarce with our hunters.

Ed. Tyler is building an addition to his barn.

Albert Colcord has a long string of new board fences.

Levi M'Cann is repairing C. L. Vergason's old house for a dwelling.

Charles Reuning had the best potato crop in this neighborhood. He had 208 bushels.

**The Potter Enterprise
Wednesday Evening,
November 12, 1884 –
Vol. XI, No. 27**

- Carpenters, laborers and the like find plenty of work in Coudersport.

- Charles Zacharias is building an addition to his Main street property. We understand the addition is for bath rooms, in connection with his barber shop.

- The new Episcopal church was occupied by the congregation for the first time on Sunday last. It is finished in good style and presents a very handsome appearance.

- The railroad is slowly creeping along from Gaines to Pike Mills, but in a few weeks the construction train will reach the latter place. The depot at Pike Mills has been located west of the tannery buildings in the valley of the West Branch.

- L. D. Horton has moved into his new house. Dr. Mattison moves into the house vacated by Rev. A. Cone. Fred Allen moves into the house vacated by Dr. Mattison. John Ward has moved into B. Rennells' house, south of the blacksmith shop.

South Coudersport.

H. T. Nelson has built a two-story woodshed to the rear of his house.

The Keystone Mills has started up again. Mr. Dwight has added some new buckwheat machinery and otherwise improved the working facilities of his mill.

Dan McConneghy has built a new barn in the rear of his lot.

N. H. Goodsell has added a new moulding and matching machine to his mill.

Dell Shay shot a fine buck, down the river, one day last week.

L. H. Cobb is putting a new hardwood floor in the bar room of the American House.

W. A. Crosby has been surveying some village lots on the land recently purchased by Mrs. P. A. Stebbins.

Around Olmsted.

Mr. John Lehman is busy with one of his numerous brothers, getting the lumber off where he had it peeled last year.

Mr. Schutt is having a long log road built on the hill.

Those who envy lumbermen the wealth they coin, ought to view the expense of teams, roads and slides.

Lots of whiskey unloaded here, but it is winked at. When apples are too scarce to make cider, suppose the poor boys will have to drink firewater.

Work is getting scarce in the lumber woods.

Forest House.

Jim Williams is building a kitchen addition to his house.

Township Tidings from Potter County, Pennsylvania
Volume I, 1880 - 1884

H. A. Avery has got several teams drawing wood.

Singing school gets along finely.

Lots of hunters in the woods now, and not many deer.

Tom Glover killed two the other day and that is all I have heard of being killed.

The Potter Enterprise Wednesday Evening, November 19, 1884 – Vol. XI, No. 28

- K. Zimmerman has sold his shoe store and stock to a Tioga county gentleman. For one-half the building and one-half the lot he is to receive $1,250. Mr. Zimmerman is going to be a farmer.

West Homer.

Mrs. Charlotte Quimby had the misfortune to lose another steer with the black leg or murrain.

Steam thresher at Albert Klesa's on Saturday.

John Gordinier has torn down one of his old log houses.

G. C. Lewis now intends to leave his mill here this winter which will be a great accommodation to the people of this place.

Clara.

Leon Tyler had a birthday party last week. Don't remember the date, anyway they played a play that Mr. Keller don't want to play any more.

We think we've got the best school in the county.

The literary society meets Saturday evenings. S. Barnes thinks they are very interesting.

Hebron.

Mrs. Julia Hill died this week of cancer, at the home of her son, Nathan Hill. She was a great sufferer and at an advanced age, and must have considered it a joyful thing to lay down her worn out mortal body and put on that new one "not made with hands, eternal, and in the heavens."

Mr. Robert Densmore has his new barn nearly completed and is getting out pump logs, which Nathan Hill is to bore and lay down, for him, next week.

School commenced last Monday, at the mouth of the South Branch, with Miss Clara Emerson as teacher. They have cleaned the school house and everything seems favorable for an excellent term of school.

Mr. Solomen Lamberton is putting up an addition to his mill.

I am sorry I did not get around to tell you about the silver wedding at Sylvester Greenman's. It was several weeks ago but it is talked about yet as one of *the* events of the year. About 150 guests were present and as they all came laden with some gift, their presence will be gratefully remembered. An elegant dinner was provided all went merry as a marriage bell.

Miss Laura Tyler is teaching again at the Hydorn school.

Miss Alice Perkins has a music class on the hill.

Township Tidings from Potter County, Pennsylvania
Volume I, 1880 - 1884

The Potter Enterprise
Wednesday Evening,
November 26, 1884 –
Vol. XI, No. 29

Ellisburg.

Ellisburg is on the move, or has been.

Thomas Gilliland has moved into his new house.

Richard Ellis has bought the house and lot belonging to the Wm. Ellis estate and moved also.

Mr. Nickerson has moved into the rooms vacated by said Ellis.

Wm. Eaton has dressed up his rooms with coats of mortar.

Ira Bishop raised 298 bushels of oats on five acres of ground and 110 bushels of corn on one acre. He thinks that is better than he did last year, for instance.

Charles Pye and Sherman DeRock have trapped about 25 mink, coons and muskrats. This is no fish story.

The school, under the direction of Mr. Hall, has a good attendance. If we wish to know more about progress, behavior and so on, there is a way to find out.

This weather reminds us of the first two lines of

"Man was made to mourn."

Turkeys begin to wish there weren't any proclamations.

Forest House.

Al Williams has built a new house at the Summit, just below Avery's Hotel, and moved into it.

Briggs' mill is running now.

Goodyear has commenced to send his logs down to Shippen, from his job at the Trestle or Big Fill, they go by rail road.

Rev. Holland preaches here every Sunday evening.

The woods are full of hunters now. I believe there is three men to every deer in these woods.

Mrs. Dennis Hall fell down stairs recently and hurt her collar bone and came near breaking her left arm. She is doing as well as can be expected.

There has been quite a good many sick here this Fall.

There has been quite a large number of deer killed here during the past week.

Tom. Glover killed a nice deer last Thursday.

Jim Howard, of Farmers Valley, killed two deer Friday afternoon.

Rained here some Sunday.

Raymond.

Crops are gathered, threshing is about done, and quite an amount of ploughing has been done; and now the fat fowls may tremble under the Thanksgiving Proclamation. What a deal of death is mixed up with the Thanksgiving! But never mind the turkey will be so good. If abundant crops ever call forth thanks, surely now is the time to swell the great son of national praise.

The public health, this way, seems good.

The school here is taught by Mr. F. Woodcock.

Mr. A. Gardiner will teach the Preston Hill school.

Miss Satie Gilliland will have charge of the school at Andrews Settlement.

Fishing Creek.

C. W. Tauscher has his dam done and his timber out ready for his mill which he intends to get in running order on short notice.

Geo. Stillwell has moved into one of Mike Dehn's houses.

Wm. Weimer has his cellar dug, and nearly walled up, for his new house.

School commenced at the Clara school house, No. 2, with Miss Clistia Kimm as teacher.

Miss Ida Baker is teaching in the Greenman district, Hebron.

Solomon Shriever has his house up and has moved into it.

Quite a number of our nimrods were out in the woods to try the hunting while the light snow we had lasted. But had poor success.

C. W. Taucher and Will Yentzer killed a fine large buck Saturday last.

The Potter Enterprise
Wednesday Evening,
December 3, 1884 –
Vol. XI, No. 30

- Last Saturday afternoon O. E. Harris, of Sweden, left his team in front of Thompson's grocery while he lifted a barrel into the wagon. As the barrel struck the wagon the team jumped and Mr. Harris was unable to reach the lines. In front of the Enterprise office the rear part of the wagon was left. The team then ran around the two squares, down West street to Water and up Main Street, bringing up short against Wm. Thomas' dray, on the South side of the Corner Store, and within six rods of the spot where the started. Two bolts repaired all the damages.

Odin.

Hunters are plenty.

Mrs. Mary Fourness, who has been sick for nearly six weeks with typhoid fever, is now gaining slowly.

G. C. Lewis killed two nice deer Thursday.

Forest House.

There was a wedding here the 27th. Mr. Mel. Hall and Miss Mary White were married, at the residence of the bride's parents, by Joseph Dingee, Esq.

Mr. Avery has left his mill for this season to Mr. Dibble to run by the thousand. Mr. Dibble intends to start up this week.

Lumbermen have been improving what little snow we have had.

Lots of deer have been killed around here during the past week.

There was a dance at the boarding house Thanksgiving evening.

The Potter Enterprise
Wednesday Evening,
December 10, 1884 –
Vol. XI, No. 31

- Dr. O. T. Ellison is building an addition to his saw mill.

- The East Fork school house has been completed.

- Our lumbermen are looking very anxiously for snow.

- Geo. Scott and family, of Lewisville, have removed to Coudersport.

Shingle House.

Shingle House is soon to be connected with the outside world by a telephone line. The men are now engaged in setting the poles.

Our school closes Dec. 10th for a two weeks vacation.

Our enterprising merchant G. Dodge is in Buffalo buying a supply of winter goods.

Pike Mills.

Undoubtedly your correspondence from other sections of the county would be of more interest to the many readers of your worthy paper than from this small but rapidly growing town, Pike Mills. Like many of the old settled places in this county, it has taken a step in advancement that will continue so long as business in the way of tanning and lumbering exists. There is, already at this place, in running order, two large establishments, viz.:

W. & L. R. Gale, tannery, capacity six hundred sides per day.

R. W. Clinton & Sons' steam saw mill, capable of cutting forty thousand feet of lumber per day. These alone would be quite sufficient of supporting and giving employment to a large number of men.

The A. & N. P. R. R. have, at this writing, their track laid within two miles of this place and expect to be running cars into Pike Mills very soon and this will add very much to the business of this place. It looks as though this would be the terminus for some time.

But very few are sick. Mr. Henry Tice is confined to the house part of the time.

Hunting has not been very good, only a few bear and not many deer have been killed.

Lumbermen have their cutting and skidding about done and are anxiously waiting for snow.

There is some talk of a Christmas tree, at the Rink, Christmas Eve.

The Rink is open every afternoon and evening, but is not well patronized as in the past.

On account of the rain Saturday evening the dance was postponed.

The latest enterprise is a ten pin alley now under construction.

Odin.

H. H. Beebe is at home, also his new accordian, just step in and hear him play.

Mrs. May Fourness is gaining, but her eldest daughter is quite sick, the fourth one who has been taken down in that family.

H. Harris killed his hog, weight 350, being an old bachelor he thinks the weight of domestic animals at butchering time more important than that of babies.

The Potter Enterprise
Wednesday Evening,
December 17, 1884 –
Vol. XI, No. 32

- About 3,000,000 feet of Hemlock will be put in the Allegany above town this winter – if the weather permits.

- Fred Devanport has opened a meat market in the D. F. Glassmire building, and we understand K. Zimmerman will soon open another market. With five meat markets in town meat ought to be cheap.

Whites Corners.

There is good sleighing here at present and the prospect is good for more. People are improving it to the best advantage.

J. F. Erway is very busy clearing a piece of land and cutting the timber into wood. This seems to be an improvement upon the old way of burning it on the land.

G. B. Moshier has bought a new organ.

**The Potter Enterprise
Wednesday Evening,
December 24, 1884 –
Vol. XI, No. 33**

- The Bell telephone line connecting Shingle House with the main line at Ceres is completed and in active operation.

- Albert Lyman is hauling a large quantity of hard wood lumber from his Sweden mill, for shipment at this place.

- Merrick Jackson has built a very neat house and recently moved in.

- Almond Hall, of Forest House, has been suffering from malarial fever. Tuesday but little hopes were entertained of his recovery.

Pike Mills.

W. W. Madison has purchased a new lot of buggies and cutters and will soon have a first class livery in running order.

Last Saturday morning Mr. Ensign, an employee at R. W. Clinton & Son's saw mill, met with quite a serious accident. He was in the act of stepping from the tressel to a pile of lumber, when his foot slipped and he fell to the ground, a distance of eighteen feet, hurting his hip very bad and bruising him otherwise.

The railroad moves very slowly for want of ties.

On account of Miss Bell Locey resigning, the lower school house has been closed for a short time it was opened again on Monday by Mrs. C. L. Merrick.

Mr. Kohler has opened a new harness shop.

**The Potter Enterprise
Wednesday Evening,
December 31, 1884 –
Vol. XI, No. 34**

- Wm. F. Yunge and George Ross have rented the Keystone Mill.

- Oats are from 32 to 35 cents per bushel in this section.

- Handsome monuments have recently been placed in the cemetery at the graves of S. Ross, J. S. Ross and Joseph Mann.

- James Morley has purchased the Cole lot, on the hillside, west of town, eleven acres, at $100 per acre. He intends erecting several tenant houses on his new purchase.

- Mark Gillon has returned from Port Allegany and opened a tailor shop in the Forster block on Main street.

To be continued...

Surname Index

Abbott 94 116 176 256
Absom 102
Abson 121 145 190 198
    199 248
Acker 70 75 176 241 246
Adams 5 116 158 169
Ainesley 235
Airhart 271
Allard 118 246
Allen 27 33 105 144 192
    209 229 230 238 245
    250 252 255 258 259
    260 263 264 282
Allison 101
Ames 123
Andrews 3 36 38 56 91
    101 144 159
Angood 191 233
Annis 38
Ansley 26 219
Anson 34
Armstrong 13 35 56 130
    132 147 173 257 258
Arnold 38
Ashcraft 67 101 115 157
    247
Atherton 40 42 67 157
    187 191
Atkins 219 222
Austin 25 68 137 146
Avery 6 228 236 244 277
    283 284 285
Ayers 47 64 241 270
Aylesworth 108 143
Aylsworth 141 150
Bachus 12
Backus 44 52
Bacon 82 241
Badger 25
Bailey 6 16 19 29 72 90
    131
Baird 191 211 231
Baker 30 35 37 51 55 59
    63 67 78 86 101 108
    109 128 149 154 156
    160 161 191 204 220
    231 246 248 257 264
    267 270 273 280 285
Ballou 236
Banks 4
Bard 209 253
Bardon 121
Barlow 20 63
Barnes 52 72 76 105 112
    117 131 159 161 165
    173 174 184 192 196
    236 238 258 274 275
    280 283
Barr 25 87 101 112 116
    260
Barrows 269 275
Bartholomew 257
Bartoo 51
Basset 97 134 247
Bassett 7 34 75 110 139
    205 220 241 244 248
    254 265 273
Bateman 252
Beckwith 5 86
Beebe 17 31 61 96 98 104
    114 136 141 158 171
    190 195 198 209 237
    239 255 286
Beeby 107
Beers 169
Begell
Bendel 14
Bendell 71
Bennehof 60
Bennehoff 91
Bennet 162 179
Bennett 205 232
Bennette 176
Benson 19 26 33 46 60 67
    83 111 113 139 151
    155 164 168 190 205
    232
Benton 2 13 39 168 209
    218 231 233 246 272
Benzolds 249
Berfield 135 170 247
Berger 101
Berhands 19
Bernhour 46 55
Bice 69
Billings 191
Bima 264
Bird 2 22 32 101 154
Bisbee 211
Bishop 2 22 33 40 48 85
    94 123 127 139 142
    148 152 168 179 218
    231 234 250 259 284
Blackman 62 75 176
Blakeslee 128
Blanchard 90 192
Blarigan 230
Bliss 14 24 99 207 251
    254 262 279
Boleigh 249
Bonawitz 214
Bonnel 212
Booth 107 113
Borie 241
Bovier 219 226 236
Bowen 260
Boyer 101 144 214 217
    263
Boyington 10 11 22 23 31
    32 69 83 99 127 145
    150 155 158 198 208
    274
Boyle 148 161
Bradford 49
Bradley 161
Brahmer 11 89
Braitling 16 114 154
Brehmer 58 149 190 243
Breisnic 58
Breisnick 56 99 134 177
Breunle 189
Bridges 10 46 98 106 124
    129 154 158 171 190
    193 205 219 231 237
    251 260 262
Briesnick 161
Briggs 105 115 119 233
    234 243 244 268 269
    276 277 284
Brigham 80
Brine 1 11 14 15 209 262
Brisboides 155
Bristol 10
Brizze 43
Brizzee 27 107 117 121
Brockway 121
Bronson 72
Brooks 6 82 92 122 128
    152 169 174 175 180
    184 191 193 198 208
    219 223 232 271 278
Brown 1 2 13 46 50 55 61
    62 69 70 75 81 101
    123 131 139 159 167
    173 174 239 243 273
Brownlee 57 146 156 185
    206 215 276
Buck 9 24 30 70 119 120
    133 134 157 214
Buckbee 184
Buckley 40
Budd 79
Bull 116
Bullis 139 234
Bundy 6 10 123 158 183
    190 193 195 197 198
    202 220 231 235 237
    242 243 246 265 269
    278 280
Bunker 256
Burdic 72 95 210 239 248

Surname Index

253 256
Burdick 42 59 79 85 169 172 208 231 253 254
Burleson 53 78 83 166
Burrous 217
Burrows 36 73 126 185 237
Burt 10 11 16 21 29 31 40 43 46 60 86 87 88 142 149 158 159 191 196 218
Burtis 2 7 13
Burton 32 152 212
Butler 78 224 247
Butterfield 100
Butterworth 1 22 75 78 92 105 111 112 116 173 247 273
Byam 194 219 254 265
Calkins 102 229 247 265
Cameron 189 197
Campbell 33 183 195 198 229
Canfield 6 273
Capel 42
Capple 67
Card 11 25 29 64 79 86 92 121 122 134 150 155 162 166 168 171 176 179 222 228 241
Carey 108 124 143 145 146 183 190 251 263 273
Carmer 185
Carpenter 3 4 20 33 38 45 51 63 65 67 72 103 104 106 122 130 157 162 186 191 245 269 277
Carr 109 130 209 257
Carriel 75
Carson 256
Carsten 155
Carter 249
Cary 69 232
Case 220 257 267 276 281
Cavanaugh 165
Cavenaugh 25
Chaffee 151
Chamberlain 55 252
Chapell 185
Chapin 28 132 158 161 192 208 223 227 259
Chaplain 135
Chapman 42 44 176 182
Chappel 33

Chase 83 110 172 193 198
Chastain 69
Chasten 193
Chesbro 5 6 41 151 163 168 170 206 225 226 235
Chestain 254 269
Childs 125 245 269
Chiles 157
Christman 203 229 236
Church 30 37 41 90
Clair 236 239 257
Clancy 127 157 161 192
Clark 11 21 44 49 63 65 102 104 109 115 125 148 165 213 224
Clear 84
Clinton 248 286 287
Close 197
Coats 213
Cobb 21 27 28 33 65 70 149 180 272 277 282
Codington 135 190 264
Coddington 31 189 268
Coe 192 245
Colcord 100 134 144 170 197 205 207 215 220 224 225 234 263 267 271 272 273 276 277 281
Cole 1 6 17 32 75 83 93 110 220 287
Coleman 136 171
Colgrove 53 80 101 144 154 230 248
Collins 85 129 133 152 182 254
Colston 153
Colvin 200
Colwell 109 167 244
Conable 104 151 167 219 229 233 235 270 271 273
Cone 110 174 184 190 192 199 210 244 245 282
Congdon 246
Conroy 222
Conley 29 122
Conly 136
Cook 197
Cool 22 23 26 30 39 45 66 115 134 145 157 171 182 188 218 222 231 250
Coon 10

Cornell 139 157 160 163 164
Corsaw 1 4 255
Costello 39 55 57 61 63 68 71 76 84 89 134 135 143 146 154 182 207 210 211 215
Cott 185
Coulston 81 82 95
Covert 220
Covey 11 15 24 29 60 75 112 151 170 190 277
Cowburn 144
Cowell 243
Crandal 210
Crandall 75
Crane 141 143 162 264 274
Craw 228 251
Crawford 10 45 78 108 173 247 274
Crippen 239
Crittenden 100 101 135 175 194 206
Cronk 248 253
Crosby 31 89 93 94 100 106 154 166 168 171 190 212 220 224 225 237 259 262 267 268 281 282
Crouch 238
Crowell 43 52 53 120 239
Crum 19 31 38 40 50 54 56 60 70 77 192 235 260
Crumm 51
Culiver 173
Cummings 2 7 159 266
Cunningham 78
Currier 152 231
Curtis 42 49 221 233 252
Cushing 207
Cutler 27
Daggett 50
Dale 177
Dalrymple 93 100 194
Daniels 32 54 56 81 87
Darcey 240
Davenport 154 159
Davidson 7
Davis 15 112 117 206 238 274
Davison 111
Dawley 20
Day 10 76 119 173 180 184
Dehn 74 85 90 128 141

Surname Index

186 257
Delemater 164
Dell 189
Deming 5 66 79
Demings 74
Demming 88
Demmings 111
Denhoff 39 144 153 183
   190 223 258 267 273
   274
Dennis 152 159 197 205
   250
Densmore 275 278 283
Dent 149
DeRock 252 284
Devanport 247 286
Dibble 285
Dickinson 79 83 90 141
   203 237
Diffin 269
Dike 155 182 240
Dillenbeck 106 134
Dimon 20 37 41 42 91
   125
Dingee 6 17 23 31 41 58
   83 98 99 115 125
   127 129 136 141 147
   158 162 166 179 188
   195 216 226 228 230
   239 242 243 246 264
   269 277 285
Dingman 51 120 170 182
Disbrow 143
Doane 16
Dodd 225 263
Dodge 6 7 65 144 172
   248 253 286
Doerner 96 101 160
Dolway 262
Donovan 253
Dornan 232
Dorsey 212
Dorsy 249
Douglas 38 103 237
Douglass 199
Downley 266
Doyle 64 160 168 194\
   230 236
Drake 123 243 249 253
   255
DuBois 224
Duel 66
Dunbar 42 184
Dunham 34 74 83
Dunn 209
Dwight 35 60 66 75 119
   125 143 179 181 231

278 282
Dyke 14 187
Earle 45 119 224 227 228
   233 268 271 272 281
Eastman 55
Easton 38 42 65 125 204
   217 245
Eaton 2 25 142 149 152
   222 252 284
Eckert 53
Edgcomb 248
Edgecomb 29 242
Edwards 129 161 189
Eimer 191
Elder 153 208 223 242
Elliot 42 198 258
Elliott 105 204 208
Ellis 9 38 48 62 63 84
   106 175 206 252 284
Ellison 4 11 15 18 30 35
   36 102 170 173 202
   285
Emerson 283
English 272
Ensign 287
Ensworth 71 122
Erway 2 7 191 223 232
   280 281 287
Este 123
Estes 54 96 117 118 176
   194 210 230 237 241
   281
Evans 2 46 152 165 175
   181 271
Everett 87 123 148 253
   278
Everette 188
Fairbanks 127 236
Farnam 115
Farnsworth 55 235
Farnum 50 174 208
Fergason 24
Ferris 21
Fessenden 5 10 19 52 83
   88 108 112 122 138
   142 145 186 205 217
   238 278
Fickler 184 195 254 260
Fish 49
Fisher 53 137 158 168
   176 191 256
Fleshutz 191 254
Flynn 75 102 176 226
   241 246
Folmer 154
Ford 20 22 34 107 127
   142 177 186 208 254

258 260
Forster 12 15 29 43 56 67
   113 130 132 204 217
   247 248 273 276 287
Forsyth 19 22 32
Fosmer 271
Foster 46 225
Fournes 31 41 123 154
   171 179 190 205 226
   280
Fourness 115 136 190
   246 278 285 286
Fox 20 268
Franke 111
Frantz 105
Freeman 20 38 125 132
   166
French 8 12 23 26 72 82
   99 115 152 160 193
   214 226 234 243 247
   253 262 270
Frink 64 269
Fuller 14 17 20 63 65 232
Furgeson 206
Furman 250
Gage 262
Gale 9 50 55 70 113 124
   143 154 166 169 180
   181 206 219 235 239
   248 286
Gallagher 163
Gardiner 284
Gardner 2 17 30 45 67 82
   107 121 157 158 186
   213 231 233 250
Gates 155
Gear 83 93
Gee 126
Gibson 37 281
Gifford 189
Gilbert 17 24 149 213
   223 235 263 273
Gillian 271
Gilliland 48 52 61 62 67
   106 109 121 206 222
   224 256 284
Gillmore 126
Gillon 190 198 248 254
   260 287
Glace 60 83 133
Glase 97 216
Glaspy 63 103 276 281
Glassmire 1 8 12 15 19
   24 47 52 67 69 78 86
   104 111 113 116 122
   126 138 140 144 153
   178 191 201 215 229

Surname Index

249 260 286
Glines 175 180 209 252 271 278
Glover 37 104 120 283 284
Gnau 208
Golding 275
Goodal 217 230
Goodale 73 204
Goodall 116 193
Goodsell 4 18 22 23 32 52 109 155 214 215 216 228 254 263 282
Goodyear 268 284
Gordenier 213 228
Gordenir 207
Gordinier 283
Gordnier 15 30 60 116 138 170 189 215 250 263 281
Gorman 224
Grabe 78 88 98 113 156 185 207 247 251 275
Granes 126
Grant 49 54 61
Grave 248
Graves 2 39 79 243 253 256
Green 14 47 86 91 101 117 121 151 179 189 200 249 255 257 280
Greene 74
Greenman 21 26 99 138 283
Greisel 3 83 89 114 117 119 155 156 170 204 249 250 262
Griesel 16 190 229 273
Gridley 30 39 80 86 113 127 157 160 170 191 226 258
Grimes 87 186
Grocebeck 4
Grom 143
Gross 208
Grover 51 71 232 236 241
Groves 133 269
Guernsey 4 47 100 104
Gustin 253
Hacket 33
Hackett 38 42 96 154 158 178 182 183 187 191 220 235 246
Haight 140
Hall 17 48 89 104 149 151 156 157 160 163

168 189 194 218 220 224 228 230 236 268 274 278 284 285 287
Hallauer 71
Hallet 33 237 239
Hallett 76
Hallock 56 81 163
Halock 154
Hamilton 32 42 178 221 280
Hammand 175
Hammel 262
Hammond 19 79 88 111 120 147 183 213 232 235 247 251 253
Handcock 252
Hanlon 251
Hannas 82
Hanson 108 145 201 208
Harrington 266
Harris 20 38 56 67 99 136 158 162 171 175 205 212 219 220 221 261 266 269 278 285 286
Harrison 2
Hart 23 232
Hartwick 278
Harvey 133 157 165
Haskel 127
Haskell 22 28 30 46 60 61 67 70 74 85 107 121 156 163 177 230 232 250
Haskins 49 63 144 163 177
Hauber 65 146
Haven 13 14 242
Havens 13 63
Hawks 253
Hawley 9 70 114 123
Haxton 199 200 205 226
Hay 152 258
Hazen 86
Head 35 64 101 268 273 278 281
Healy 97 100 194 227
Heggie 100 128
Helfrecht 273
Helwigg 176
Hemple 70
Hendryx 42 44 52 63 67 130 152 206 222 265
Henly 173 174 184 196
Henoy 215
Henry 32 34 40 56
Henyan 90
Henman 6

Herring 152
Herrington 144
Hess 221
Heysham 94
Hickox 38 40 63 67 245
Hill 79 179 238 283
Hillegas 179
Hirch 166
Hirsch 175 178
Hoard 67
Hober 208
Hodskin 205 207 248
Hoffman 180
Hogarth 58 151
Holcomb 7
Holland 53 57 61 71 76 114 129 135 161 166 167 168 170 177 179 278 279 284
Hollenbeck 13 22 29 33 39 113 168 228 229 242
Holly 13
Holt 189
Hone 169
Hood 12
Hopkins 3 276
Hopson 151
Hornsby 63 67 76
Horton 259 273 274 279 282
Hosley 21 27 33 50 55 133 156
Hotchkiss 130
Howard 220 275 284
Howe 2 35 40 43 47 163
Howland 66 80 117 164
Hubbard 7
Hufteling 240
Hulbert 278
Hull 201 260
Hungerford 247
Hunt 100
Hunter 7 129
Hurd 37 38 40 42 67 91 96 103 125 152 162 177 182 187 224 229 235 236 245 257 259 281
Hurlburt 142 146 192 198
Hyde 49 128 243
Impson 31
Ingraham 14 59 84 254
Ives 36 50 70 121
Jacklin 34 45 49
Jackson 18 21 47 56 81 197 217 287

Surname Index

James 30 48 124 182 219 250
Jeffers 7
Jennings 122 240 242 252
Jeorg 58
Jewell 10
Johnson 39 54 69 78 107 113 120 169 170 217 224 229 260 278
Johnston 48 58 80 83 98 109 120 128 139 145 179 185 194 232 241 247 249 250 255 258 273 276
Jones 2 6 11 13 24 29 34 36 47 56 58 62 66 106 115 133 143 144 147 148 156 183 209 229 254 257 259 260 267 269 276 280
Jordan 74 75 82 85 171 223
Joseph 88
Judd 10 22 26 30 55 60 66 100 101 105 106 146 182
Kane 41 161
Kanealey 275
Kaneally 279
Kaple 63
Karnickle 279
Keating 212 223 264 279 280
Keeler 44
Keihl 265 266
Keihle 58 60 151 190 267
Keller 49 192 230 261 283
Kelley 85 102 116 281
Kelly 100
Kemp 65 180 181
Kempt 79
Kennard 248
Kenyon 64 168 169 238 270
Kernan 7 16 71 205
Kibbe 42 65 90 118 148 172 202
Kibbie 133
Kickox 204
Kidney 233
Kiehl 213
Kiehle 176 247
Kies 20 85 115 142 155 250
Kiester 135
Kilbourne 61 62 70 75 93 209 226 241 246
Kimm 69 83 134 145 168 188 232 285
King 72 78 113 264
Kinner 6 144 210
Kinney 131 140 196
Klein 105 220 231 235 271
Klesa 5 154 178 207 267 276 283
Klien 195 262
Kline 101
Knickerbocker 207
Knight 2 7
Knowlton 191 211 231
Knox 15 16 99 144 145 149 173 185 248 249 251 258
Kochler 233
Kohler 200 287
Koon 66 251 276
Krusen 133
Lamb 248 253
Lamberton 98 173 175 192 199 210 239 243 244 247 252 257 261 269 275 283
LaMont 68
LaMonte 182 185
Lane 25 53 153 169 170 205 208
Larkin 19 87 104 137
Larkins 118
Larrabee 4 7 8 10 13 15 16 19 22 25 32 44 69 96 124 139 179 188 196 207 247
Lathrop 163 166 207 213 224 225 227
Lawrence 32 60
Leach 20 67 93 177 204
Leache 67 245
Leavenworth 114 248 252 257 263 266
Lee 1 9 39 48 49 84 112 114 241
Leech 38 157
Leet 109 245 246
Lehman 75 92 111 141 204 253 268 278 282
Lent 47 63 64 92 94 259
Leonard 7
Lewis 9 16 18 21 23 31 33 42 56 61 67 72 75 79 80 91 98 103 110 121 125 129 139 141 158 166 169 171 174 177 183 195 198 209 229 230 235 236 237 241 246 250 251 264 267 276 280 281 283 285
Lilly 269
Lindsey 188
Litchell 166
Locey 287
Lockwood 227
Logue 141
Long 71
Lord 44 144 166
Louge 126
Lougee 157
Lovell 181 194
Luce 241
Ludington 59
Lunn 49
Lyman 3 4 18 19 27 29 32 44 45 64 83 86 87 90 93 96 100 108 109 112 114 118 119 120 122 132 136 138 139 142 150 151 154 155 162 173 179 191 193 194 198 201 205 208 211 223 224 226 231 233 234 240 247 257 260 262 265 266 274 279 287
Lyon 24 29 36 47 280
MacDonald 220
Mack 189
Macmurray 203
Madison 270 287
Maher 117
Maltby 30 59 74 78
Manley 278
Manly 175 258
Mann 36 75 111 112 139 185 196 215 231 240 242 270 279 287
Manning 30 74 86 94 137 149 191 196
Marble 243
Marion 72
Markham 238
Marsh 165 205 231 233
Marshall 34 221 262
Marshner 260
Martin 46 50 61 70 75 80 93 147
Matteson 20 22 28 30 34 35 39 46 60 62 92 107 119 148 157 181 182 213 218 231

Surname Index

Mattison 9 14 16 21 30 58 67 92 101 133 138 147 178 206 225 238 240 245 282
Mayer 33
Maynard 201
McAdam 9
McCann 220
McCarn 122 282
McConaky 279
McConneghy 282
McConneky 247 273
McCormick 58 116
McCutcheon 208 242 259
McDermott 96
McDonald 157
McDorman 45
McDougal 130 147
McDowell 5 74 88 92 113 171 179 188 202
McFall 268
McGinnis 194 204
McGonegal 8
McGonigal 12 90 117
McIntosh 171
McKewen 50
McKinney 224
McMahon 198
McMullin 73
McNamara 12 33
McNulty 201 202
Mehring 119
Meine 166 195
Merranville 250
Merrick 47 287
Merrill 39 78 89 92 116 144 156
Merrit 54
Merritt 43
Metzgar 9 10 28 248 265
Metzger 4 30 39 114 150 167 171 175 219 262 269
Miles 101
Millard 201 265
Miller 17 29 38 44 55 67 69 70 78 81 95 106 140 158 176 177 182 194 209 223
Mills 205
Mitchell 71 153 161 217 248 273
Mitcheltree 17 154 179 265
Moffit 181
Monroe 31 34 40 43 54 59 77 93 95 155 182 190 205 266 269 279 280
Moody 106 110
Moore 68 104 127 145 202 216 233 240 254 267
Moran 215 216
Morey 4 191 255 272
Morgan 118
Morley 114 116 182 185 238 287
Morris 68
Morrison 186
Moses 40
Moshier 211 287
Moyer 35 90 98 101 112 165 210 239
Mulhollon 141
Munday 265
Munger 33 72 180 237 243
Munson 112
Mustoe 69
Myres 240
Neefe 21 34 35 66 88 169 199 214 251 257
Nelson 20 22 32 36 39 41 42 43 55 60 85 92 128 129 130 155 170 176 178 191 194 197 198 199 200 201 206 214 223 242 247 249 250 251 263 281 282
Neother 53 166
Newton 83 93 174
Nichols 14 76 92 93 102 112 124 132 143 151 168 195 203 224 229 257 277
Nickerson 284
Nieman 25
Niles 9 151 223
North 44 87 121 130 181 194 222
Norton 16 205 233 240 244 263 270
Nye 1 132
O'Donald 201 202
O'Harra 132
Oleson 108
Olmsted 3 8 19 29 30 38 51 56 66 86 110 151 159 177 205 207 209 212 220 237 238 240 242 260
Olney 219
Omerod 126
Ormerod 139 280
Ormsby 26 240
Osmer 238
Otis 236
Outman 280
Owens 79 88
Palmatier 276
Palmatire 55
Palmer 16 39 109 152 197 225
Palmeter
Palmetier 142
Pangburn 179
Parsons 267 271 273 278
Pauson 65
Pawson 6 73
Pearsall 33 120
Peck 4 22 26 34 41 96 97 100 110 164 186 195 214 234 262
Peet 5 20 22 24 28 30 53 57 76 103 117 134 135 146 154 160 170 182 197 272 275
Pellum 2
Peltz 132 265
Perkins 128 177 278 279 283
Perry 13 42 67 90 239
Persing 158
Phenix 188 264 266
Phillips 1 3 7 16 144 174 180 186 249 256
Pickett 52
Pierce 13 24 102
Pike 5
Pilon 241
Pinney 71 114
Place 49
Plagueman 3
Plants 17 221 250
Pomeroy 35 108 150 162 198
Porter 121
Post 87 100
Potter 156
Presho 48 76 77 101 109 114 148 163 254 265
Press 252
Prindle 49 248
Prouty 37 71 151
Pursley 53 68
Putman 276
Putnam 217 248
Putt 158 185
Pye 130 252 259 284
Quick 266

Surname Index

Quimby 17 54 102 103 155 156 160 163 166 168 189 213 238 240 242 268 271 273 276 278 279 283
Race 38 42 96 162 187 191
Randall 67 68
Ransome 51
Rathbone 173 257
Rathbun 100 103
Rawson 7
Raymer 224 246
Raymond 3 19 33 50 98 100 101 102 109 110 114 116 148 188 193 197 200 211 241 274 280
Razy 64
Read 92
Reaning 276
Reauing 267
Reed 16 35 74 79 111 147 149 152 169 192 198 211 214 227 237 250 258 269 271 272 280
Rees 4 12 15 16 43 45 63 66 76 83 89 103 118 120 122 139 154 155 178 179 185 199 204 220 221 223 225 228 229 232 237 238 239 242 243 244 263 266 273 275 277
Reese 106 135 161 183
Reeves 40
Regan 23
Reves 60
Reissman 14 16 35 114 133 139 171 183 192
Remington 165 180
Rennells 16 41 50 66 80 89 136 140 154 159 163 169 178 204 229 263 266 282
Rennels 106
Reuning 15 133 213 282
Rexford 25 217 256
Reynolds 39 72 90 117 121 152 158 195 270
Rheinhault 196
Rice 123 196
Richardson 256
Rigney 117
Riley 242 280
Riman 125

Ripple 25 57 68 89 103 177 215 276
Ritter 73 226
Robbins 18 21 28 98 112 121 123 177 182 187
Roberts 204
Robins 182
Robinson 240
Roche 227
Rodgers 25
Roe 65
Rogers 2 28 48 134 161 163 199 205 244 277 279
Rooks 81 90
Ross 8 80 88 95 121 142 170 184 190 198 205 219 240 247 249 254 258 279 287
Rossman 241
Rounsevill 1
Rounseville 7 19 21 24 35
Rounsvill 111
Rounsville 110
Rouse 206 257
Rowlee 100 112 118 216
Rozell 97 227
Rukgaber 190
Ruscher 275
Russel 95
Rutherford 189 208
Ryan 74 89 96 178 186 213 216
Rycraft 277
Ryon 90
Salomen 252
Sampson 253
Sanbourn 22
Sandbach 25
Sandberg 223
Sands
Saunders 69 260
Schaudenberger 185
Schautenberger 100
Schidberger 266
Schildberger 217 248 258 263 275
Schilderberger 22 105
Schoolmaker 255
Schoonover 20
Schutt 272 278 282
Scott 285
Scovill 197
Schoville 164 178 223
Schweitzer 2
Scott 194

Scovel 38 40
Scoville 17 20 181 208
Scutt 239 257
Searles 7
Seibert 182 242 243 247 266 277
Shafer 211
Shannon 97 113
Sharpe 98 105 138
Shattuck 112 173 194
Shay 282
Shear 33 44 164 228 231 240 266
Sheets 220 239 275 276
Sheldon 27
Sherman 38 125
Sherwood 42 48 124 199
Shieaver 272
Shriever 285
Shuts 41
Sikes 117
Simmons 250
Sinette 176
Skutt 268
Slade 67 208
Slater 252 274 281
Slaughter 35 61 67 88 115 158 171 182 219 231 232 233
Slawson 20 37 38 40 63 67 157 245 269
Sloat 79 107 173
Slocum 67 137
Smith 28 33 35 40 42 50 52 62 64 65 67 81 100 109 110 112 116 123 124 126 133 138 140 153 165 168 182 189 197 219 221 232 266 280
Smock 39 49
Snead 222 258
Snow 113
Snyder 148 159 184 220 234
Solomon 192
Spafford 91
Spencer 40 94 96 97 259
Sprague 239
Stannard 32 42
Starkey 82
Statham 172 174 280
Staysa 4 90 121 160 203
Stearns 29 259
Stebbins 8 15 16 19 24 27 29 32 36 43 74 80 178 192 205 223 228

Surname Index

251 258 263 279 280
282
Steel 248
Stephens 102 125 177
Sterns 191 208
Stetson 129 153 219 223
232 281
Stevens 1 6 7 8 47 75 80
95 116 124 125 173
175 180 196 198 199
229 236 245 249 280
Stewart 27 53 112 219
238
Stillman 44 64 67 106
130 163 167 192 245
Stillson 9 199 230
Stilson 184
Stillwell 276 279 285
Stocum 141 183 195
Stone 281
Story 242 252
Stout 81
Stowell 175 183
Strait 275 278
Strang 253
Stratton 2 11 20 28 30 74
Striker 26
Strong 70 143
Stryker 55 57 73 88 117
145 148 182 231
Sullivan 145 277
Sutherland 256
Swain 100 265
Sweet 182
Sweeves 101
Swetland 2 9 25 102 111
168
Swift 192 199 229 236
254
Swimmer 161 192 229
Swreave 255
Tadder 226 273
Taggart 132 133 142 153
183 198 223 255 281
Tassel 23 28 31 151 176
Tassell 22 39 46 80 93 99
Taubert 184 189 206 213
225
Taucher 285
Tauscher 19 23 24 32 35
37 51 145 158 231
257 266 279 284
Taylor 107 271 278 281
Tenbrock 246
Tenbrook 99 162 224
Terwilligar 219 245
Terwilliger 117 206

Teuscher 272
Theis 25
Thomas 14 103 107 160
207 214
Thome 148
Thompson 10 12 16 24
27 29 32 43 46 56 86
96 105 111 126 136
155 182 186 193 209
214 218 221 223 231
247 265
Tice 286
Tillburgh 50
Tolls 249
Tomkle 158
Tooke 63
Tools 224
Tracey 39 50 168
Tracy 58
Trask 200 265
Trumans 81
Tubbs 123 138
Tucker 48 232 250
Tupper 225 233
Turck 70 176 199 205
241
Turner 16 26 33 36 48 63
86 138 165 174 175
184 190 258 275 279
Tyler 4 24 26 48 84 110
197 198 209 229 252
269 281 283
Vanderburg 116
Van Kuren 90
Vannater 68
VanVorhees 115
VanWegen 34 39 183 190
204 215 228 236 238
240 242 258 273 280
VanWinkle 114 119 120
201
Varney 140
Veelie 128
Veley 8 92
Velie 69
Velley 28 45 46 98 107
115 117 134 153 171
186 219
Vellie 20 174
Vergason 282
Vincent 70
Voss 44 83 136
Wagoner 3
Wakely 88 236
Wales 277
Walker 97 119
Wall 215

Wallace 208
Walley 22
Wallis 8
Ward 128 282
Warner 35 105 108 164
179 184 223 226 240
251 252 259
Washburn 186
Waters 184 189 211 236
Watson 272
Weaver 59 104 109
Webb 145 198
Webster 42 127 130 152
192
Weidrich 120
Weimer 4 5 16 22 37 111
116 120 142 208 255
257 260 264 266 272
285
Wells 48 63 78 100 157
164 172 181 194 212
217 219
Weltch 9
Welton 45 72 114 247
Wentworth 132
West 28 167 178 215
Westcott 94
Westfall 148
Westley 263
Wetmore 55
Wetsel 275
Wetzel 246
Wheaton 35 50 71
Wheeler 69 71 117 123
Whipple 163
Whitaker 38
White 2 7 10 22 23 32 65
69 93 108 109 114
115 122 124 126 127
129 131 136 138 139
142 147 150 153 155
158 160 167 174 175
178 189 192 197 207
223 225 231 232 237
238 242 246 248 260
262 265 269 273 274
285
Whitford 117
Whitman 178
Whitney 6 41 98 129 136
147 234 244
Wilber 112 238
Wildman 92
Wiley 256
Wilfinger 230
Wilkinson 112 168 230
238 257

Surname Index

Williams 115 135 157
    163 187 274 282 284
Willoughby 23 44 45
Wilson 11 67 130
Wimer 30
Wimmer 120
Windsor 10
Winegar 152
Witter 14 95 111 150 157
    179 186 196 199 202
    210 231
Wormelsdoff 209
Womelsdorf 15 101 199
    200
Wood 9 102 151 205
Woodard 155 169
Woodcock 70 129 233
    284
Woolfinger 148
Worden 95
Wormelsdorff 80
Wrean 186 234 238
Wrench 76 102 103
Wright 51 82 109 130
    188 247 249
Yager 50
Yale 100
Yentzer 4 11 37 52 69 83
    90 91 124 134 136
    138 224 257 264 266
    270 272 279 285
Yeomans 243 263
Young 53 63 133 156 215
Younglove 264
Youngs 154
Yunge 58 159 218 234
    239 287
Zacharias 277 282
Zimmer 122 127 137 146
    159 164 184 223 226
    240 252
Zimmerman 29 89 93 105
    109 190 198 205 217
    281 283 286

www.ingramcontent.com/pod-product-compliance
Lightning Source LLC
Chambersburg PA
CBHW050129170426
43197CB00011B/1774